**One of the Top 20 Amazon Nonfiction Books of the Year**

★★★

**Shortlisted for the Nach Waxman Prize for Food and Beverage**

"[*Endangered Eating*] is as much a fascinating study of heirloom cider apples and Buckeye chickens as it is a commentary on the way politics, money and convenience have conspired against America's culinary history." —Kim Severson, *New York Times Book Review*

"From Coachella Valley's date gardens to heirloom cider apples in New York's Hudson Valley to Choctaw filé powder in Louisiana, each stop [Sarah] Lohman makes is more interesting than the last. . . . But *Endangered Eating* isn't just a foodie travelogue (with recipes sprinkled throughout). Lohman encourages people to follow her lead and learn more about their food's origins. We can start by reading her intrepid book." —Alexis Burling, *Washington Post*

"Lohman deftly combines history and people-forward accounts of her travels across the country to learn from food producers. The result is a thoughtful, compelling read about why these food traditions matter and are worth preserving. —Bettina Makalintal, *Eater*

"*Endangered Eating* is culinary historian Sarah Lohman's surprising journey across the United States, visiting the vanishing futures of native peanuts, apples, Ojibwe wild rice, Hawaiian sugar cane." —Christopher Borrelli, *Chicago Tribune*

"[Sarah Lohman's] enthusiastic charm and what you sense is genuine Midwestern niceness shine through. She's also impressively plucky . . . [and] is assiduous in tracking down early recipes and describing cooking techniques. She also gets to show off her scientific fluency (she comes from a family of scientists)." —Corby Kummer, *New York Times*

"When Sarah Lohman describes herself as a 'historic gastronomist,' she is being too modest. She is, in addition, an accomplished writer, an intrepid traveler, dogged researcher and pundit. She knows what Americans eat, what our ancestors ate, and why."
—David Holahan, *USA Today*

"Lohman is serious, but lighthearted, about her work; she's a skilled cook, but she seems to most enjoy the treasure hunts that certain recipes require."
—Jessica Weisberg, *The New Yorker*

"Through eight first-person essays, Loman tracks down the farms, restaurants, growers, and fisherman that are part of the life cycle of ingredients like heirloom cider apples from the Hudson Valley, dates from California's Coachella Valley, and even Navajo Churro sheep in the southwestern United States. In doing so, she illuminates how the delicate balance of agriculture, demand and production impact what is available and how we can protect heritage ingredients from being lost forever."
—Korsha Wilson, *Food & Wine*

"Lohman wanders the nation armed with a notebook and a fork in search of disappearing foodstuffs. . . . [*Endangered Eating*] is about not just the foods but also the cultures that produced them, and Lohman does all of them justice."
—Paul Rauber, *Sierra* magazine

"Sarah Lohman sheds light on the urgency of safeguarding Indigenous culinary customs through her tales of traversing America in search of endangered foods. In *Endangered Eating* she highlights the influence of colonization upon foodways, and also advocates for the localization of food systems and greater support for food producers and community organizations."
—Liza Greene, *Food Tank*

"In *Endangered Eating* Sarah Lohman gives readers a new and powerful lens through which to view the past, present and future of food in America."
—Dan Saladino, author of *Eating to Extinction*

"From sheep to wild rice, the foods we eat for both hedonistic exploits and sustenance have been going extinct; every time we breed a food to survive the rigors of worldwide transport, we lose all its delicious attributes. Sarah Lohman shares compassionate stories about the importance of these foods and outlines what you can personally do to ensure their continued and delicious survival. Lohman carries Twain's torch with her passion, love, and want to preserve these amazing foods for future generations." —Jeremy Umanksy, chef and co-owner of Larder Delicatessen and Bakery

"The prose [of *Endangered Eating*] reminds me of *The Omnivore's Dilemma*. I am finding the writing to be extremely clear with palpably effervescent enthusiasm." —Chef Jonathan Wu

"[*Endangered Eating*] is enjoyable, entertaining, and meaningful. . . . A tasty sojourn through the landscape of America's endangered foods, served with a scoop of energy and a dash of hope." —*Kirkus Reviews*

"[Lohman's] descriptions of unprecedented textures, tangs, and mouthwatering subtleties are masterful. Not just for foodies, this is an entertaining and enlightening account." —*Booklist*

ALSO BY
SARAH LOHMAN

———

*Eight Flavors:*
*The Untold Story of American Cuisine*

America's Vanishing Foods

# ENDANGERED EATING

Sarah Lohman

**W. W. NORTON & COMPANY**
*Independent Publishers Since 1923*

For information about permission to reproduce selections from this book, write to
Permissions, W. W. Norton & Company, Inc., 500 Fifth Avenue, New York, NY 10110

For information about special discounts for bulk purchases, please contact
W. W. Norton Special Sales at specialsales@wwnorton.com or 800-233-4830

Manufacturing by Lakeside Book Company
Book design by Marysarah Quinn
Production manager: Julia Druskin

ISBN 978-1-324-08633-8 pbk.

W. W. Norton & Company, Inc., 500 Fifth Avenue, New York, N.Y. 10110
www.wwnorton.com

W. W. Norton & Company Ltd., 15 Carlisle Street, London W1D 3BS

10 9 8 7 6 5 4 3 2 1

This book is dedicated to my mom, Karen Lohman. She's my first reader, my copyeditor, and my formatter of thousands of footnotes—as well as my champion, my supporter, and my advocate. She's an incredible woman and I wouldn't be half the person I am today without her.

I love you, Mom.

SXWO'LE
STRAITS SALISH
REEFNET FISHING

C A N

Washington

Montana

Oregon

Idaho

Wyoming

Nevada

California

U N I T E D

| Utah | Colorado |
|------|----------|
| Arizona | New Mexico |

DIBÉ
NAVAJO-CHURRO
SHEEP

KUPUNA KŌ
HAWAIIAN LEGACY
SUGARCANE

"COACHELLA
VALLEY DATES

Hawaii

M E X I C O

D A

N

MANOOMIN
ANISHINAABE
WILD RICE

Wisconsin

HEIRLOOM
CIDER APPLES

New
Hampshire

Iowa

Illinois    Indiana

Pennsylvania

BUCKEYE
CHICKENS

Maryland

TATES

Kansas    Missouri

Virginia

Oklahoma

Tennessee

North
Carolina

Arkansas

South
Carolina

Texas

Georgia

CAROLINA AFRICAN
RUNNER PEANUTS

EXAS
GHORN
TTLE

KOMBO HAKSHISH
CHOCTAW FILÉ POWDER

Florida

# CONTENTS

# INTRODUCTION

## What Is Endangered Eating?

While many organizations advocate for the preservation of endangered animals, Slow Food International fights for the conservation of endangered *edibles*. As a part of their mission, Slow Food curates an ever-growing, online catalog of ingredients that it has determined are both in danger of extinction and worthy of being preserved. This list is called the Ark of Taste.

The Ark of Taste contains over 5,000 "delicious and distinctive" foods from 150 countries, ingredients like Bay of Fundy dulse seaweed from Canada, Catamarca llama meat from Argentina, traditional Lambic beer from Belgium, and *su filindeu*, the "threads of God," a Sardinian pasta known as the rarest on the planet. The current United States Ark includes more than 350 entries from all over the country.

I had always thought of American cuisine as ever expanding to include new foods. But after scrolling through the entries on the United States Ark of Taste, I realized there are hundreds of plants, animals, and food traditions that are *disappearing* from my country's food repertoire.

Over the course of a year, I traced a selection of Ark of Taste entries to their homes, following the seasons of their harvest. I met the farmers, shepherds, fishers, and makers who produce these rare foods and who have invested their lives—and finances—into these products' growth. Frequently, these ingredients are key to the identity of the cultures they come from, representing a deep, spiritual connection between humanity and the Earth.

But often on my journey, I discovered that the path to saving these ingredients wasn't clear-cut. Nor was the question of who should have access to these ingredients—and at what price.

* * *

SLOW FOOD INTERNATIONAL was founded in Italy in 1986 in reaction to the opening of a McDonald's near the Spanish Steps, a famous Roman landmark. In the organization's own words, they "prevent the disappearance of local food cultures and traditions, counteract the rise of fast life and combat people's dwindling interest in the food they eat." The Ark of Taste was launched in 1996 and is now the core of the organization's work.

To add a food item to the Ark, the process begins with regional Ark of Taste committees who work with local Slow Food chapters, as well as individual advocates to identify and nominate food items. The list includes plants, foraged and farmed; animals, wild and domesticated; processed products like preserves, baked goods, cheeses, and spirits; and even traditional techniques. When an item is submitted, the nominators must answer a list of questions and include context about the item's cultural and agricultural significance. Once a nomination is approved by a regional or state chapter, it is submitted to the international Slow Food office in Italy. There, the information about the nomination is verified by a team of experts that includes veterinarians, historians, agroecologists, and agronomists. They consider four factors when selecting new Ark of Taste ingredients:

### Endangered
Produced in limited quantities, the food will not be

around in another generation or two without immediate action. Risk factors may be biological, commercial, or cultural.

### Good
Whether an animal breed, baked treat, fruit, spice, grain, or beverage, the food is prized by those who eat it for its special taste and its cultural or historical significance.

### Clean
Everything on the Ark of Taste has the potential to be grown, raised, or produced without harm to the environment.

### Fair
No commercial or trademarked items are allowed onto the Ark of Taste, only foods that anyone may champion, produce, share, or sell.

When a new food is "on-boarded" to the Ark, Slow Food takes a multi-pronged approach to increasing the rare ingredient's visibility. The organization may begin by working directly with producers to identify solvable issues that would increase or sustain production of that food, as well as offering aid through the support of veterinarians and agronomists. Slow Food creates events to generate press for the food, encourages chefs to incorporate the ingredient into their menus, and facilitates access to seeds for farmers and gardeners through companies like the Seed Savers Exchange and Baker Creek Heirloom Seeds. In general, the organization facilitates ways for the public to seek out these foods, learn their stories, and purchase and consume them, except when it comes to endangered wild species, which initially may need conservation.

The "ark" references Noah's Ark, the Old Testament story in which God commanded Noah to build an ark and save two of every land animal from the earth-cleansing flood. But it's not a perfect foodie metaphor; the duos that have made it on board are more like the Angus beef and beefsteak tomatoes of the world—foods that are already well-known and successful. In the case of foodways in America, a rising tide has not lifted all boats: modernization and colonization have allowed cherished, delicious foods to get washed away in the "flood."

\* \* \*

I HAD BEEN SORTING THROUGH Ark entries on their website for weeks when I serendipitously met a rare food face to face. On a beautiful September day in 2018, my mom and I were driving back roads in rural Ohio, heading to a remote farm to pick late-season blackberries. I planned to turn the fruit into blackberry brandy using a recipe I had found in an 1890s' manuscript. My mom made a left turn onto Route 511 near Kipton—an abandoned gas station on one corner of the intersection and pastures stretching out on all sides—and my eyes landed on the animals grazing to the left of the road.

"That's a Texas Longhorn!!" I yelped. The animal was unmistakable: two horns branched out horizontally from either side of its head, about eight feet tip to tip.

Always willing to humor me, my mother turned the car around and pulled over at the pasture. I leapt out. The enormous buff-colored animal gazed at me placidly from the other side of the fence, his preposterously huge horns curving gently toward the sky.

I had never seen a Longhorn in the flesh before, and never imagined I would stumble across my first one in Ohio. They are the iconic animal of Texas, after all. Because of the Texan tradition of eating their meat, the Longhorn is listed on the Ark of Taste. When the Mexican province of Coahuila y Tejas was being colonized, Christian missionaries brought cattle with them. But the missions these men founded were often abandoned due to conflict with the locals or disease. The cattle left behind went feral, eventually developing into Texas's first naturalized cattle breed, the Texas Longhorn. Recaptured, they were a favorite of ranchers for their heartiness and were kept primarily for their meat, but also for leather, tallow, and labor. At the end of the nineteenth century, instead of being slaughtered locally, cattle began to be shipped to Midwest slaughterhouses. Longhorns fell out of favor because not only did they not put on weight as quickly as other breeds, but their wide horns did not fit into narrow railcars and crowded feedlots. The Texas Longhorn is currently listed as critically endangered, meaning only a few thousand registered animals exist worldwide.

I left the Longhorn's pasture fence and trudged up a steep driveway, hoping to find someone who could answer my many questions. One of the owners happened to be riding down the drive on a motorbike. He looked confused when he spotted me—a tattooed, blue-haired young woman—trudging up his driveway. I flashed my big, toothy smile, introduced myself, and told him I wanted to know more about the Longhorns.

"Oh, they're so docile!" CJ, the rancher, told me with a grin. "They'll eat an apple out of your hand if you have one. We have twelve—all bulls."

"Why?" I asked, stunned.

"Why keep them? Well, they're really fun to look at! And they're so gentle. And they're really inexpensive lawn mowers." And that was enough for CJ. And good for him—his twelve bulls are twelve more in the battle to fight extinction.

I made Mom stop to see the Longhorn cattle again on our way back home, our buckets filled to the brim with nine pounds of overripe berries. There were three bulls in the pasture this time: the beige one I had seen earlier, a chocolate-brown friend, and a white bull with brown flecks. They navigated deftly around one another, occasionally using their horns to dislodge flies from their backs. As I watched the animals graze, listening to their rhythmic chomp-chomp as they ate, I realized the Ark of Taste had already made me more aware of my world. In the past, I would have just driven by this field. Instead, I stopped and felt a genuine sense of awe at the chance to witness these animals. I wanted more opportunities to experience rare foods of America.

For every item on the Ark, I knew there must be a story behind its fading away, as well as—hopefully—its redemption. After communing with the Longhorns, I planned to pursue an Ark of Taste entry from eight different regions of the United States: the Mojave, in particular the Coachella Valley of Southern California; Hawaii; the Southwest, primarily the Four Corners region of the Navajo Nation; the Salish Sea in northern Washington state; the upper Midwest; New Amsterdam, including upstate New York, Queens, and parts of New Jersey; Acadiana on the Gulf Coast; and the Lowcountry of South Carolina. I traveled roughly west to east between February and November of 2019.

In California, I visited Date Gardens and chewed the sweet flesh of dates found nowhere else in the world. In Hawaii, I climbed mountains to understand the complex system of agriculture historic Hawaiians used to cultivate brilliantly colored heirloom sugarcane. In the Navajo Nation, I assisted a shepherd in slaughtering and butchering a Navajo-Churro lamb, an animal long prized by the Diné for its fleece and meat. In the Pacific Northwest, I hauled in nets of pink salmon on a reefnet fishing gear, a complex, ancient, and highly effective indigenous technique. In the Midwest, I slid through wild rice beds in a canoe, learning how to "knock" the precious *manoomin* into the boat. In New York, I hunted in centuries-old orchards for rare cider apples that hung on trees so geriatric they were held up by crutches. In Louisiana, I experienced traditional Cajun cuisine cooked with filé powder, a flavoring and thickener made from sassafras, now rarely processed in the traditional manner. And in South Carolina, I stood in a field of the first peanut cultivated in North America, the Carolina African Runner peanut, believed to have been extinct since the 1930s.

These foods led me to the stories of people, both historical and contemporary, who shepherd, farm, fish, and forage these precious ingredients. There's David Fairchild and Walter Swingle, the "agricultural explorers" of the turn of the twentieth century, who sent dates from the markets of Baghdad to be grown in California; and growers like Sam Cobb who continue the tradition of small, family-owned date farms today. And Lili'uokalani, the last Queen of Hawaii, who ruled while American sugar moguls tried to depose her; and farmers like Anthony DeLuze, who grows traditional sugarcane in an urban Honolulu plot. There's Manuelito, the Diné hero who worked to protect his people's independence and flocks of sheep; and Ron Garnanez and Aretta Begay, advocates who care for their own flocks and promote the Navajo-Churro breed today. There are the Lummi, who historically caught salmon in the Puget Sound before colonists pushed them from their claims; and Kyle Kinley, who captains the first Indigenous-owned, commercial reefnet gear on the water in over a century. There's Nanaboozhoo, the historical hero of the Anishinaabe people, who discovered *manoomin*; and Roger Labine and Tracy Goodwin, who work to preserve this sacred food in their communities today. There were the skilled, enslaved orchardists and cider makers like George and Ursula Granger, and contemporary cider makers like Charles Rosen, who hope to preserve endangered apples by reviving historical ciders. There are the Choctaw people, who were the first to introduce sassafras powder to the Creoles of New Orleans hundreds of years ago; and Lionel Key, of Uncle Bill's Spices, who was the last person producing sassafras filé in the traditional manner. There were the free Black women, like Celia Hall, who sold groundnut cakes on the streets of Charleston in the nineteenth century; and farmers like Nat Bradford, who seek to revive heirloom crops like the Carolina Runner peanut. These custodians of America's culinary heritage often fight against legislature, financial burden, and the effects of climate change to keep their food traditions from disappearing.

Although the reasons these foods may be on the brink of extinction are various, the Ark of Taste offers a simple solution for how to prevent them from vanishing: "Eat it to save it." Slow Food believes that if we create awareness and demand, these foods won't disappear. But is the solution to saving these ingredients so simple? There's only one way to find out: let's eat.

# ENDANGERED EATING

# Coachella Valley Dates

It was a sunny, but chilly, day in February 2019 when I visited the Sky Valley date farm of Sam Cobb. Sky Valley is part of the Coachella Valley in Southern California, nestled between two nature preserves, Joshua Tree National Park and the San Bernardino National Forest. The Coachella Valley stretches south from Palm Springs through the towns of Indio and Mecca and ends in the man-made Salton Sea, less than a hundred miles from the Mexican border. Sometimes called the American Sahara, it's not uncommon to have more than one hundred days a year over 100 degrees. But aquifers run deep underground, filling springs and oases. The hot temperatures, and access to plentiful water, make the area ideal for growing dates.

Dates have been grown in the Coachella Valley for over 120 years, originally from imported seeds and suckers—baby trees that grow off the trunks of established trees—from Baghdad and Algiers, Pakistan and Egypt. The plants arrived as part of a government program to bring profitable agriculture to what was perceived as empty desert.

In the 1910s, the secretary of the USDA visited the valley to address the new date growers. He commented afterward that it had been so hot he nearly perished, and he "wondered whether the government could find any justification for encouraging people to make their homes in such an insufferably hot part of the country."

Of course, Coachella wasn't the vacant, unsettled desert that the American government made it out to be. It had been occupied for at least 5,000 years by the Cahuilla Indians. The Cahuilla were expert well-diggers, built irrigation systems to grow crops, foraged for plants, and hunted game. They were doing just fine without the American government, and, in fact, had been left alone through most of the nineteenth century because of the valley's extreme climate. At the turn of the twentieth century, the valley was thought of as one of the US final frontiers. When the Southern Pacific Railroad came through in 1872, building a depot in Indio (then named Indian Wells), it was a herald of the changing times. In 1876, the Cahuilla were pushed to the Agua Caliente Reservation, which ironically makes the tribe the largest landowners in the Palm Springs area today. Removed from much of their traditional lands, the Cahuilla began to work on the farms and ranches of white settlers or sold them hand-made items. Many of the early settlers acquired their farms through the Desert Land Act, a federal law allowing men to apply for land in the Southwest as long they planned to "irrigate" and "reclaim" the land. In the case of Indio, this was land that had previously belonged to the Cahuilla.

Today, it's estimated that over 90 percent of the dates grown in the US come from the Coachella Valley, about 35,000 tons annually. Although the Coachella Valley primarily grows commercial date varieties like Medjools and Deglet Noors, several small farmers still carry on the tradition of growing unique date varieties that were developed in the area a century ago. It's these rare American dates, grown nowhere else on the planet, that have been onboarded to the Ark of Taste: Empress, Abada, Blonde Beauties, Brunette Beauties, Honey, McGill's, Tarbazal, and Triumph.

I had come to Sam Cobb Farms with Dr. Sarah Seekatz, the world's foremost expert on Coachella Valley dates. She wrote her dissertation on the subject and also grew up in the area. Sam had promised to show us a rare date palm, an Empress. Sam's Empress trees were given to him by another date garden owner, Ben Laflin, Jr. Laflin, who passed away in 2015, was born in the Valley. His parents had founded the Oasis Date Gardens. Laflin eventually took over from his parents and ran the Gardens with his wife for most of his life, even traveling to Morocco to visit the country of origin of his family's palms.

Sam led us between the rows of date palms to the foot of an Empress tree. Sam doesn't harvest his Empress dates—because he only has a few, he feels he doesn't produce enough to sell—so the bundles of mahogany-red fruit hung without a cover to protect them from rain and pests. Sam grabbed his ladder, pushed it between the palm fronds, and confidently ascended.

"You've been doing this long enough, you know where to put it between the fronds, when it's going to shift and settle as you move farther up, when the wind is going to shake it," he told Sarah and me as the wind buffeted the ladder. It didn't bother Sam, and he picked a few handfuls of Empress dates, and climbed back down to deliver them.

The Empress dates had a distinctive coloration: red-brown but opaque at the top. We split them open first to check for pests—then Sarah and I popped them in our mouths.

The flesh melted on my tongue, releasing sweet spice and caramel, with fresh fruitiness at the end. Sarah's eyes widened.

"Oh, Sam, you should sell these," Sarah gasped.

"You think so?" Sam said, scrunching up his face.

"Yes!" we both shouted before devouring another date.

After a few more bites, I headed up the ladder for a closer look. As large as a basketball at the top, the date bunch hung from the tree like a chandelier. A thick central stem jutted out from between the palm fronds, bending toward the earth from the weight of the fruit. Many smaller stems grew off it with a dozen or so dates attached to each, like the chandelier's crystals. And at that moment, the sun was at just the correct angle to illuminate the fruit from behind, and the Empress's extraordinary color came to life—a chandelier made of dark red rubies.

* * *

DATES ARE THE EDIBLE FRUIT of a palm tree: wrinkled, generally brown, and about 1.5 to 2 inches long. They belong to a category of fleshy fruits known as drupes, which have a single seed or pit. Drupes include coconuts, olives, black pepper, various nuts, and stone fruits like peaches. Dates are very sweet, usually about 60–70 percent sugars, including sucrose and fructose, but they also contain about 1.5 grams of fiber, a decent amount of potassium, and a little bit of protein. Additionally, a date contains small amounts of B vitamins, manganese, calcium, and magnesium.

The date palm originated in the area that encompasses the Arabian peninsula as well as what is today Iran, Afghanistan, and Pakistan. They grow specifically in places where there is very little rain but access to water in rivers or underground aquifers. They have an ancient connection to humans: dates were a part of the human diet thousands of years before agriculture. Dental calculus—that's plaque—recovered from Neanderthal skeletons in Shanidar Cave, Iraq, revealed minute fossilized plant particles from dates. But dates are also some of the world's oldest cultivated fruit. In fact, no wild varieties exist today; dates *only* exist within cultivation.

The date palm has symbolism in three major religions: in the spring, Christians carry date palm fronds into church on Palm Sunday to represent Jesus's arrival in Jerusalem; in the fall, date palm fronds are one of the Four Species of plants used to celebrate Sukkot, a Jewish harvest festival; and for Muslims, dates are the traditional food to break the daily fast at sunset during Ramadan and also feature prominently in Eid al-Fitr, the feast that ends the month-long holiday.

To propagate dates, you can't plant a date seed. Well, you can, but like many tree fruits, what grows out of that seed is genetically different from the parent. This is one way a plant ensures survival; genetically diverse offspring have a better chance of continuing to grow, adapt, and propagate. Most of the trees grown in this way do not produce edible, or at least desirable, fruit. So if you like attributes of one date palm—say, the dates are particularly plump and sweet—you want to plant a sucker instead. Suckers are tiny palm trees that grow out of the base of the parent tree in the first ten to fifteen years of its life. They are chiseled off the base of the palm and planted, and will begin to produce dates in about ten to fifteen years.

Unlike other palms, male and female flowers grow on separate trees. The male plants produce a tight pod that cracks open in the early spring to reveal a broom-like appendage covered with thousands of tiny blossoms. Without human intervention, the date palm relies on pollinators to carry the pollen to female flowers on female trees. One of the first Americans to witness date palm pollination in Egypt in 1901 reported:

> In the first orchard which I visited, the owner was hand-pollinating his trees. One of the men was sitting on the ground tearing apart the long, slender stems of a male flower-cluster. The plume-like cluster, resembling carved ivory, has side branches or stems zigzagging at short, regular intervals from the main stem. In each angle rests a flower which drops its yellow pollen in a tiny cloud. The Arab was deftly tying two or three together. High up in one of the nearby palms, held to the trunk by a strap around his body, another Arab was fastening their male clusters securely in the center of the young flower-clusters of a female palm. . . . I was witnessing an agricultural practice dating back far beyond the dawn of recorded history.

The strap referred to was saddle-like, woven from palm fronds. The worker used his own body weight to create tension to hold him to the tree, scooting up the trunk a leap at a time.

The techniques of palm pollination have changed little over the centuries, although in Coachella today specialized cherry-pickers with hydraulic platforms lift workers up the tree trunks. Pollen is collected in little green sprayers that look like plastic mustard bottles and are squeezed by workers over the female flowers. The trees are pollinated in the early spring, and the fruit harvested in the fall.

Some dates need to have their bunches thinned early in the season, which allows the remaining dates to grow larger—a common practice with Medjools. Additionally, the center is cut out of a bunch to keep the tree from overproducing, thus guaranteeing a consistent crop from year to year. In the fall, the same tree must be harvested several times, as dates don't ripen all at once. After the harvest, dead fronds are cut off, and new fronds are trimmed of their long, dangerous thorns.

The date farms that sprang up in Coachella in the early twentieth century were founded and owned by white migrants, and labor was a family affair. During the Second World War and the following years, when the Bracero Program brought guest workers from Mexico, the most difficult farm labor was passed to male Mexican workers. By 1964, when the program ended, over 90 percent of the labor on date farms was done by these workers, now called *palmeros*. As they settled in Coachella and started families, the culture of the valley changed. Currently, the area is over 90 percent Latine.*

Being a palmero is a dangerous and highly skilled job: palmeros fall from the trees and high equipment, and are prone to spider bites, cuts from sharp tools, pesticides exposure, and extraordinarily high temperatures—up to 123 degrees in Palm Springs, and 126 degrees farther east in Thermal. For comparison, the hottest temperature ever recorded in America was 134 degrees in Death Valley.

There are hundreds, potentially thousands of varieties of dates worldwide. Some dates, like the Medjool, are particularly plump, sweet, and fruity. Other dates are very fleshy, like the Barhi; some, like Halawi dates, are chewy. Still others are dry, like the Thoory date. A major selling point of these dry dates in the early twentieth century was that they could be carried loose in a pocket without making a sticky mess. Oddly, the ability of dates to be stored in one's pockets remains a selling point; I heard that countless times until I finally asked Sarah

---

\* A note about this term: recently, there has been a movement in the Spanish-speaking Americas to reject "Latino," the default, masculine term for a mixed-gender group. In the United States, the term Latinx is popular, but that word is unpronounceable in Spanish. So, I have chosen the word being used in other Spanish-speaking countries, Latine, as the gender-inclusive word for this community.

Seekatz if she had ever put a date in her pocket. Her answer was no. In fact, I asked every date enthusiast I could think of, and none of them carried unpackaged dates in their pockets. I later hosted a date-tasting party, and several participants decided to put Thoory dates in their pockets. One volunteer, Ashley, complained that it popped out of her pocket when she went to use the toilet—but I would say that's a side effect of how women's jeans are tailored. Another guest, Jeff, texted me, "I found that date in my pocket a week later—it was still good!"

The United States has been importing dates since its existence; in 1824, 44,425 pounds of dates were imported into the US. Dates were historically associated with the winter holidays. After the dates ripened in areas around the Persian Gulf, they were packed and shipped from Muscat, a port city in present-day Oman on the Arabian Sea, arriving in America in November. They came fused into a solid block, and a grocer would use an ice pick to tear off chunks of pressed dates and weigh them out by the pound. One nineteenth-century observer noted, "They were probably the stickiest thing that a housewife could buy at the grocery store."

\* \* \*

TO CONCEIVE OF BRINGING the date industry to America required imagination, scientific knowledge, money, and the gumption to go get the plants. At the turn of the twentieth century, David Fairchild and Walter Swingle were two USDA botanists inspired by historical botanical explorer–collectors, such as the botanists Captain Cook took with him on his voyages around the globe at the end of the eighteenth century. Fairchild and Swingle assembled a team of botanists, headed by themselves, that traveled the world identifying and collecting cultivated plants that were either entirely new or a better variety of a familiar crop. This team would bring dates to America, to the Coachella Valley.

David Fairchild was born in Michigan in 1869. A decade later, his literature professor father took a job at Kansas College and the family moved to Manhattan, Kansas. Two thousand people lived in the town at the time of their arrival, and the area was stricken by a plague of locusts.

Fairchild enrolled in Kansas College at fifteen to study botany and horticulture, and there he befriended Walter Tennyson Swingle, after Swingle delivered a "scholarly address on the fungi which cause such diseases as wheat rust" at a natural history club meeting. The passion with which Swingle was able to hold forth on fungus amazed his colleagues, because in other contexts he was "easily embarrassed and inclined to stammer." Fairchild would write later: "we sat spellbound while he presented his discourse. Entranced, we watched Swingle's long arms wave about and his piercing gray eyes dart from one to the other of us."

Swingle never fully lost his stammer. Despite his speech impediment—or perhaps because of it—he had a lifelong fascination with languages, which served him well as a budding botanist. Few seminal botanical or agricultural texts had been written in America by the late nineteenth century, let alone in English. To learn, Swingle needed to be fluent in French, German, and eventually Arabic. While Swingle spoke in a focused and measured manner to overcome his stammer, Fairchild wrote of himself, "I am often criticized for my habit of talking too much."

In 1887, Kansas College hosted a celebrated English naturalist who, among other accomplishments, had traveled over 14,000 miles around Malaysia and the South Pacific. As one of Fairchild's biographers wrote, "[Fairchild] suddenly realized that botany didn't have to be about familiar brown farm crops. Studying plants could lead to romantic adventures and exciting glimpses of life in exotic lands." By the end of that year, Fairchild had sailed a lap around the Indian Ocean with a rich benefactor, collecting plants.

In 1889, Fairchild was hired by the Department of Agriculture in the Section of Plant Pathology and moved to Washington, DC. Within two years of his arrival at the USDA, he asked Swingle to join him. They worked together on a team devoted to rapidly expanding the country's understanding of crop-plaguing diseases and how to defeat them. An official photo of the "Personnel of the Section of Plant Pathology" from 1891 shows a young Fairchild and Swingle with five colleagues, all of them white men. Fairchild and Swingle are clearly the youngest, and the only ones with clean-shaven faces. Fairchild was well defined by his prominent ears, deep-set eyes, and long, angular face. He slouched in his formal Victorian, high-collared suit. Swingle's face was more boyish, his gaze less intense. He sported a hard part in a mop of light, curly hair.

Unsurprisingly, Fairchild and Swingle were housemates in Washington, DC, and traded stories nightly about their travels to study botany—Swingle has spent a year in Europe while Fairchild was in Asia. Both had come away from their experiences with the idea that America needed new crops, to diversify the foods Americans were eating and to increase revenue for farmers. They envisioned a team of government scientists that would travel the world to collect new crops to send back to the United States and gather information about their cultivation abroad. The new department would also provide support to launch new agricultural industries. The name they came up with for this position sounded just as adventurous as the job itself: Agricultural Explorer.

After petitioning their boss at the USDA, they set up the Office of Seed and Plant Introduction and established a "plant introduction garden" in south Florida. They spent their evenings scouring books to create lists of plants they wanted to introduce to the US. Fairchild wrote years later, "Plant introduction has two distinct phases. First, the securing of plant material in foreign countries and landing it alive in America; and second, the dissemination and establishment of the plants in the fields, gardens, dooryards and parks of this country." The two scientists would eventually collect and introduce Egyptian cotton, various melons, citrons, blood oranges, pistachios, Smyrna figs, and the cherry trees that bloom each spring in Washington, DC, among many others.

Early on, they wondered if there were plants that could be introduced to the deserts of the American Southwest, areas they felt were largely unsettled and in need of economic improvement. They sought crops that were not only tolerant but desirous of extreme heat and salty or alkaline soils.

"It was Swingle that first thought of dates," Fairchild wrote later. "He brought home every book he could find in the library that bore on the subject of dates. I can hear his tone of dismay as he called out to me after what had been an evening of happy excitement, 'The Date-palms take fifteen years to fruit!' . . . as I look back now I wonder why we cared whether it took fifteen years or fifty, the fun came in getting the palms in to America, watching them grow, and helping the industry develop."

If it's not already apparent, Fairchild was the documentarian of the two. While Swingle did write, his output was largely technical bulletins for farmers. Fairchild was more poetic. His extensive archives reside at the Fairchild Tropical Botanic Garden in Coral Gables, Florida, about ten miles south of Miami. Fairchild founded this botanic garden near the home he retired to in 1935; the garden opened in 1938 with the help of friends and investors. Fairchild collected many of the plants that still grow in the garden, including a giant African baobab tree by the front entrance.

I arrived in Miami in early March 2019, just a few weeks after I saw date palms in Coachella that descended from trees Swingle and Fairchild had collected on their travels. The Florida heat was blissful, and later in the trip I would sit on a sunny lawn at Fairchild's home, now a museum, near palms he collected from all over the world, gazing at Miami across the bay.

At the offices of the Botanic Garden, I was led to a windowless room that housed Fairchild's papers. Boxes of thin paper notebooks contained his field notes, or "explorers' notes" as he called them, "which we kept always with us when we browsed in libraries, museums, or herbaries." The tiny pages were filled with even tinier handwriting. There were metal file cabinets full of letters, and drafts of all of Fairchild's manuscripts—he wrote several books. In one file cabinet, I found what I had come for: an unpublished manuscript on the origins of the date industry in America. It's unclear what book these pages were intended for when they were composed in 1931. Parts of the text would appear later in Fairchild's autobiography, *The World Was My Garden: Travels of a Plant Explorer.*

Fairchild wrote, "The idea of planting the Southwestern deserts with date palms appealed to the American imagination," and the government was eager to invest. A new railroad had been constructed between New Orleans and Los Angeles, and Indio—a small settlement in the Coachella Valley—was a significant stop. The railroad access and the increased development it brought helped to convince the government that investing in desert farms would be profitable.

"A new world was literally out before us, the world of oases and camels and palms," Fairchild wrote of the trips he and Swingle took. Of Swingle's first date-retrieving trip, we have only a few specifics from the letters he wrote home to Fairchild. In the spring of 1899, he wrote from Algeria: "Have made dust fly for the last two weeks. Spent 4 days in Sahara and bought 20 palms off Arabs. . . . The Sahara is wonderfully interesting. . . . I have in my note book 50 names of dates grown in Sahara near Biskra; many good." He shipped twenty suckers home, none of which survived the long trip. Swingle selected suckers based on dates he sampled in the markets and date gardens. "It was necessary for Swingle to make judgments about flavor, texture, desirable size, keeping qualities, sweetness, susceptibility to insects, diseases, rain, yield ability, evenness of ripening, adaptability to the Southwest—a myriad of factors to weigh in choosing the best varieties with which to start," Fairchild wrote. Swingle continued his travels through Morocco, and in the spring of 1900 sent back "eight tons of palms, comprising 447 offshoots and representing 27 varieties . . . to everyone's delight 95% of the suckers lived." Swingle and Fairchild had developed a method of packing the small date suckers: "I mixed a liquid mud and puddled them. When this dried they were encased in a thick coating of clay. I then sewed each one up in sacking." They would ship them with identifying tags, which weren't always attached—or legible—by the time the suckers made it to the United States.

When Swingle returned to the United States in 1900, Fairchild was the next to go out, in 1901. But when he arrived in Alexandria, he received "a cablegram announcing the sudden death of my father. It was a tremendous shock and I was crushed with grief and loneliness . . . Anyhow, I had no alternative but to push on. Life is nothing but pushing on, after all. . . . Mounting a donkey, I started for the date-growing region of the Nile delta."

Unlike Swingle, Fairchild spoke no Arabic, and was often exasperated when trying to communicate. He worked with embassies and landowners, tracking down date suckers to be sent home. Fairchild's responsibility was not just to collect dates, but to collect information on how the dates were grown. Many of the practices in the Middle East had not changed in thousands of years, but were entirely new to Fairchild. He wrote of his experiences in Egypt: "It is interesting to work out the horticultural practices of antiquity as they are depicted on drawings and seals in a museum, but it is far more so to see them still being carried out by a generation perhaps 3,000 years removed from the men who carved the seals." Fairchild worked eight months in Egypt before heading to Baghdad.

During his trip, Fairchild collected many date varieties that are grown in the Coachella Valley to this day: golden-brown "Saidy" (Saidi) dates from Egypt; chewy Halawi (Halway) dates from Karachi; and "Zehedi" (Zahidi) dates from Baghdad, "a so-called 'dry' date, the individual fruits of which do not stick together," and which could, obviously, be carried in your pocket.

While Fairchild traveled abroad and continued to send home suckers, Swingle was put in charge of establishing the American date industry. By this point, Swingle knew more about date palms than any other living American.

The USDA established a Date Experimentation Station near the Salton Basin in 1904, but in 1905, the Colorado River broke through a canal diversion point and flooded the low-lying basin. This event created the Salton Sea. When the inland sea's rising waters threatened to flood the Date Station in 1907, it was moved to Indio in the Coachella Valley on 20 acres of donated land. Swingle was its superintendent until 1934, although much of his supervising happened from DC while an on-site agriculturalist did the hands-on work. Swingle would spend much of this time traveling between his home and office in DC, the plant introduction station in Florida, and the field station in Indio.

The new location was ideal for date growing. The Coachella Valley and surrounding area resembles the climate and terrain of the Middle East so much that the town where I rented an Airbnb is the site of the Twentynine Palms Marine Corps Air Ground Combat Center, a setup of mock villages designed to train soldiers for deployment in the Middle East. A friend of mine who trained there called it "a damn near carbon copy of Iraq and most parts of Afghanistan."

But there were issues with the early date introductions to Indio. Aside from imported suckers dying in transit after the multi-week journey from Africa or the Middle East to the Coachella Valley, there were also issues with locals selling inferior shoots that had come from ornamental date plantings. There were insect infestations, as well as fields full of Deglet Noor dates that did not ripen. And Swingle, in a management position for the first time, was floundering. One of his biographers noted: "Under his management the office budget was always spent before the year was out. He would cancel employees' vacations at the last minute, take spur-of-the-moment trips to California, Arizona, Florida, wherever, not knowing how long he would be gone; he would leave the staff to pick up and carry on his instructions, and then rage when he got back if they had not known what he had in mind. At the same time, his superiors were storming at him for undertaking unscheduled projects, for not documenting methods and objectives, for running out of funds mid-year."

Swingle had been commissioned to write a USDA bulletin called *The Date Palm and Its Utilization in the Southwestern States*, a helpful guide to farmers wanting to invest in dates. Swingle believed that date farming would be a financially successful endeavor, and he believed that once the government released his bulletin, the demand for date palm suckers would skyrocket as agricultural entrepreneurs invested in their own date gardens. So his plan was to use his insider information to get ahead of the game: he would establish the first for-profit date palm plantation in the United States before his bulletin was released, and would position himself to provide all the date palm suckers the first wave of entrepreneurs needed.

Swingle wrote to his father in 1898, "There would be a fortune in it and, once started, a princely revenue from the sale of suckers alone." He anticipated a profit of $150 (about $4,000 in today's money) per acre per year. Swingle partnered with his father to import 156 date suckers from his contacts in Algeria and have them planted in 160 acres in the California desert. He even considered importing camels to work on the farm, but in the end decided against it. By Swingle's calculations, the plant sales would net him $24,000 ($640,000) within a few short years after his bulletin came out.

But, at almost the same time his report came out, his scheme collapsed. The USDA was "roiled by scandals about scientists in other divisions who allegedly profited from their research." It was considered a conflict of interest for government employees to enrich themselves with information that was supposed to be made available for free. Swingle decided to sell his share in the business to avoid a scandal. He profited only about $600 (or $16,000 today), far less than what he had anticipated.

By 1910, the date industry was finally coming to literal fruition. Toward the end of his date manuscript, Fairchild wrote: "Of course this is just the government's part in the story. It does not touch the heroic struggles made by individuals who have spent their lives and their money trying to make fortunes out of dates. That is another chapter, which someone else who knows it better than I must write."

In the same file with Fairchild's unpublished date manuscript, there was a small stack of original photographs, organized for their placement in the final book or article. Fairchild was an avid photographer and documented his trips to Egypt and Baghdad. But there were also a few images from the early date industry in Coachella: the shacks of the first Date Station in Mecca; a muddy field planted with rows of baby date palms; and bunches of plump dates grown from suckers Swingle collected in the Sahara. But the image I found the most captivating was of a blond-haired child, about six years old, standing in a cultivated field of date palms. He is dressed only in a white shirt that comes to his knees, his skinny, tanned legs sticking out the bottom and his bare feet in the dirt. He's standing under a young date palm, perhaps twice his height, inspecting a bunch of dates, about to harvest the ripe ones. He is clearly "child labor," a member of one of the early white families that settled the area. These farmers seldom had employees. The whole family worked toward making their agricultural venture profitable.

Many of the valley's earliest farms—called "date gardens" to evoke the biblical Garden of Eden—wouldn't last more than a decade or two. These failures were at least in part due to how the USDA's Date Experiment Station distributed plants early on: as seedlings grown from date pits. The purpose of the Date Station was to get the industry started, and part of that was giving away free plants. But at first, there was a limited number of imported suckers; the imported trees had to be grown to a point where they could produce their own suckers. Dates themselves were far easier to import, so the scientists pitted them and planted them. This system was difficult for the growers in multiple ways: they were caring for younger plants and had to wait longer for the trees to produce fruit. Additionally, it took four years to determine the sex of the tree, and half of the seedlings would be male. Not only do male palms not produce fruit, but one male tree can pollinate up to fifty female trees. And perhaps most important, a date grown from a seed is genetically different from the parent plant. So, while the mother palm bore delicious fruit, its seedling might produce dates that were unappealing in texture, flavor, or appearance—or all three.

Early settler Ben Laflin, Sr., got his 160 acres through the Desert Land Act in 1911. A long-time sufferer from malaria, he moved from Berkeley to the desert because the warm, arid climate was often recommended for treating maladies at that time. He believed the date industry would provide an income while he reclaimed his health. He planted thousands of date seeds but ended up tearing out all these plants over the next fifty years, replacing them with suckers. By the 1950s, he was the valley's largest planter of Medjool dates and his farm was famous for quality. It's from Ben Laflin, Jr., that Sam Cobb received his Empress date palms years later.

An early farmer who had success with his seedlings was Everett Davall. He came to the Coachella Valley in 1912. Like Laflin, he planted USDA seedlings and got wildly different results from tree to tree. But he identified three trees that he thought produced excellent fruit. These would become three new American varieties, to this day unique to the Coachella Valley: Honey, TR (originally Third Row, later officially changed to Teddy Roosevelt, and now known as Triumph), and Empress. Davall propagated his new varieties by suckers and made these unique dates the focus of his business. His unusual, tasty dates won mail-order fans across the country.

Although the Davall family still grows dates, the dates are exceedingly hard to come by. You can purchase dates from them online, but certain varieties sell out quickly. I had to wait a full year after my visit to Coachella to order Empress from the next crop. Their Empress have the texture of dulce de leche and the flavor of movie theater popcorn. Honey dates, another of their original dates, were available at several vendors in the Valley; the Ark describes them as similar to a Deglet Noor, "the flesh is soft and melting with a mild and pleasing flavor."

Other farmers came in the early 1920s, buying up farms that had failed and making successes out of them. Floyd and Bess Shields arrived in the Coachella Valley in 1923 and took over a seedling date garden. Floyd was impressed by two different seedling dates the former owner hadn't had much luck selling, and named them Blonde Beauty and Brunette Beauty, evoking appealing women. He advertised that his date garden was the only place in the world where these unique dates could be purchased—and limited each customer to one box in order to emphasize their value and rarity.

The farmers sold dates directly to customers, and by the 1950s had created a tourist destination for Americans who wanted to visit Palm Springs and see the desert. California Highway 111 cut through the valley from Palm Springs to the Salton Sea and was lined with date shops. Each shop had its own gimmick to attract customers: The Pyramid date shop was in the shape of a pyramid, and Sniff's Exotic Date Garden had set up a tent like the ones used by nomadic tribes in the Sahara. Other shops sprang up with architectural elements borrowed from India, Egypt, and the Arabian peninsula. The proprietors felt the visual aesthetic should play off the desert surroundings and the date palm's history to create an exotic destination a tourist could reach without leaving the United States.

As Dr. Seekatz explained to me, California has always had a unique way of selling itself as somewhere else. Hollywood does it; Disneyland does it; and if you've spent any time in the state, you've probably come across a historical site related to "mission history." The interpretation of the latter is often referred to as the "Spanish fantasy past," a made-up world where Spanish colonialism benefited the Native Americans; new white migrants could connect their history back to these European settlers. Through these mission sites, California sold time travel back to a romanticized Mexico and a nostalgic "old Southwest" so effectively that there were Americans in the 1890s writing to different tourist bureaus asking, "Do I need a passport to come to California?" So, too, the Coachella Valley began to manufacture its own creative history, based not on Spanish missions but on the valley's connection to the Middle East via the date palms. As Dr. Seekatz put it, Californians had a habit of "stealing the history, remaking the history in their own way, and then using it to profit."

The Middle Eastern fantasy brought people to the valley and into the date shops. The travelers would then taste date varieties from the Middle East that had never been available in America before, and special dates that could only be found in the Coachella Valley. Customers would buy a few boxes of dates, and get on the mailing lists for their favorite shops. Every November, after the date harvest, a catalog would arrive at their home address, and it would become a tradition to order dates from Coachella annually for Christmas.

\* \* \*

WHEN I FIRST ARRIVED IN COACHELLA in February of 2019, I had expected sunny days and blazing hot temperatures. I got an overcast sky, pouring rain, and the thermometer barely touching 50 degrees Farenheit. But friends who grew up in the desert assured me that this rainy day was a special gift, and by the end of the week, the landscape would explode in wildflowers. So, after my first chilly day bundled up in my rented bungalow in Twentynine Palms, I was able to strike out the second morning in better weather. I set my Maps destination for Shields Date Gardens, still in operation in Indio, and took the highway through the Morongo Valley, the mountaintops of the pass peaked in snow. Before the Shields family settled in Coachella, this road was unpaved, and the trip from Twentynine Palms to my destination in Indio would have taken two days. But by the 1950s, the roads had been improved. The creation of these highways, and the mid-century obsession with driving, were imperative to the formation of the date industry.

Mr. Shields was perhaps the most innovative of the date shop owners in terms of gimmicks. Approaching the storefront, a passerby can't miss the knight: a cutout at least 25 feet high, painted in full armor, his shield decorated with shields and the name "Shields," points from the road to the storefront. The roadside knight was built in 1954; the store he gestures to, in 1950.

Historically, another eye-catcher would have enticed tourists: roadside signs boasting of Shields's educational slideshow, "The Romance and Sex Life of the Date." Originally a live talk given by Floyd Shields himself, it's not as lascivious as it sounds. The presentation explained date propagation and farming, to impress upon Shields's visitors how difficult and costly it was to produce a high-quality date. The talk was given a dedicated theater when the new store was built with an automated slideshow and pre-recorded audio. The store no longer shows Floyd Shields's original slideshow, but instead a modern video documentary of the same name that incorporates the history of dates with Floyd's original audio explanation of production.

When I pulled into the Shields parking lot, there were towering date palms everywhere. As a Midwestern gal, it was unlike anything I'd seen before, and there was definitely a biblical feel about it. And the current owners of Shields have decided to push the biblical connection. Behind the store is a garden made up of rosebushes and date trees too old and tall to be good fruit producers; for a few dollars' admission, you can stroll through this garden and see silver, fiberglass Jesus statues portraying moments from the Bible. The sculptures include depictions of Jesus's birth, an enormous crucifixion scene and his empty tomb on Easter morning after resurrection. At first, the presence of the statues struck me as strangely evangelical. But I began to realize there were two sides to creating this tourist mirage of visiting fantastical Arabia. One aspect is religion, Christianity specifically, even though Jerusalem is attached to many faiths. When these date palms were planted, many Americans believed that those living in the Holy Land were still living the lives of those in the Bible, virtually unchanged in the last 2,000 years. The date industry has long played off that imagery; in fact, the advertisement for the very first Date Festival in 1921 was a Nativity scene. A bright star over a desert landscape leads the way for a caravan of camels and men in traditional head coverings. The catch-phrase below the image is "All 'The Wise Men' Are Going."

Shields's religious statues might seem a strange juxtaposition to the "Sex Life of the Date" signs in the gift shop. But the other way that Americans have largely understood the culture of the Middle East is through the stories of *The Thousand and One Nights*, or the *Arabian Nights*. It's a collection of medieval, or perhaps even ancient, stories told by the main character, Scheherazade, to a king. The king, who has decided he hates women after his wife cheated on him, assaults a different new virgin every night and then has her executed. Until he gets to Scheherazade, who tells him a story every night, leaving the ending until the beginning of the next evening. In this way, she preserves her own life, and eventually the king falls in love with her and stops murdering virgins. The first translated version of this work was available in English in the early eighteenth century. These stories include the famous tale of Aladdin, but feature many other thrilling adventures with ghosts, monsters, and sex. So, Shields's embraces both aspects of the traditional American understanding of the Middle East: Jesus is out back, but come learn about (date) sex in the front.

Back at the visitor center, the Shields's date showroom awaited me, featuring free samples of all their date varieties. I beelined to their specialty dates. I tasted the Blonde Beauty date first, and after that, nothing could compare. I was in love. Blonde Beauties are a butter-scotch color with a heavenly texture; drier than many commercial dates, with a papery skin, chewy flesh, and a satisfying bit of crunch from crystallized sugar. And the flavor? Every bite is buttery brown sugar caramel.

Shields makes date milkshakes from the Blonde Beauties. The showroom has a milkshake counter, decorated in retro pastels, where they serve the Coachella Valley's most famous confection. The Shieldses didn't invent date shakes; that honor has been credited to Russ Nicoll, the owner of the now-closed Valerie Jean Date Shop. The story goes that he heard "that some Middle Easterners existed solely on goat milk and dates." Dates and goat or camel milk are a popular breakfast, dinner, or snack throughout the Middle East, and a staple of nomadic peoples. There is a popular recipe online attributed to the greater Middle East, where dates are soaked over-night in goat's milk and then blended with honey and ground car-damom. It not only sounds delicious, but allegedly it will improve one's sexual vitality.

Nicoll was first credited for the invention in print in 1938, but the date shakes were already nationally known by then. At any rate, when Nicoll created the date shake, milkshakes were having a moment, as soda fountains boomed in the wake of Prohibition. The "drink mixer" and "liquefier blender" were both released in 1922. So, with the equipment available, and the idea that dates and milk might taste good together, the date shake was born. The shakes became broadly popular in the Coachella Valley, and to this day are still considered an important part of the tourist experience in the area. Sarah Seekatz told me, "There was a time when date shakes were very easy to find in local restaurants. In fact, I remember the Del Taco in Indio selling date shakes too."

Shields blends vanilla ice milk with their Date Crystals—dried, shattered Blonde Beauties that Mr. Shields, ever the innovator, cre-ated to use up dates that didn't make the grade to sell whole. When my number was called and I picked up my shake, my first slurp was cooling, necessary after a walk in the sunny date garden. Then the texture hit me: creamy, with a little crunch from the ice. Then the flavor: caramel. Pure liquid caramel with a little fruitiness at the end. In addition to the Blonde Beauties and their famous milkshakes, Shields sells several other rare dates that occupy a space on the Ark of Taste: deep brown Brunette Beauties, the other Shields original date; Honey dates, one of the Davall seedlings; and Abada dates, a deep black, very sweet date originally found growing feral by date farmer D. G. Sniff in 1936. They're so dark and shiny, they reminded me of scarab beetles.

I asked the operations manager of Shields, Jessica Duenow, why they bothered to grow these rare, niche dates. She answered immediately: "For the history and the legacy. Mr. Shields produced them, so if we have the trees, it only makes sense to continue growing them. And for someone that might think there are only Medjool dates out there, we want to show them something different."

For customers who prefer a classic date, they also sell many of the varieties originally imported from the Middle East: Barhi, Deglet Noor, Halwai, Khadrawi, Medjool, Thoory, and Zahidi dates, as well as a variety of date confections, date sugar, and date syrup. I tried them all. As I climbed back into my car, still sipping my enormous date shake, I was reminded of a Fairchild quote about his explorations in the markets of Baghdad:

"Tasting the quality of anything as sweet as dates may sound like a pleasant job. However, although eating a dozen dates may be a pleasure, tasting two dozen is less enjoyable, and eating three dozen at once will ruin any stomach as surely as a rough sea voyage."

\* \* \*

BY 1930, AMERICA WAS PRODUCING two and a half million pounds of dates annually. Previously, dates had been so rare and expensive that they were only eaten whole on special occasions. But now there were lots of dates, some not large or attractive enough to be packaged whole. Both date growers and date importers wanted Americans to consume more dates. The easiest solution was to create recipes.

The earliest date cookbook was released by the Hills Brothers, date importers who launched a massive marketing and branding campaign in the 1910s. Their *Dromedary Cook Book*, named after their brand of packaged dates, was published in 1912. It included recipes that are still familiar today, like date muffins and date bars (made with lard!), but also more adventurous fare, like a date-based chili sauce and date sandwiches, featuring a filling of chopped dates and cream cheese. The first Coachella Date Festival in 1921 also released a cooking pamphlet; one recipe in it is simply called "a good laxative." The pamphlet included a section called "Dates as Used in Cookery by the Arabs," and contained a few simple recipes, like dates cooked with flour and oil, several methods of candying dates, and "Salad: Young flowers of male palm are used for salad. Mix with French Dressing." Mrs. Shields was known for issuing recipes for their special products; a "Hungry Children's Sandwich" was simply Date Crystals soaked in milk and spread on bread. Her brown sugar and chopped nut date-drop cookies sound better.

I have two tall bookshelves in my bedroom filled with historical cookbooks, so I can lie in bed and think about culinary history. I'd always been puzzled by the preponderance of date recipes in the first half of the twentieth century, and now I had my answer: that's when dates came to America. The earliest recipe I found for dates in my collection comes from the 1902 *Encyclopedia for the Home*: a "date loaf cake" that layers chopped dates with lemon batter. The "date cake" in the 1907 *Woman's Favorite Cook Book* includes nuts. Date nut cake or quick bread was the most common date recipe from this point forward. However, the 1929 book *Anyone Can Bake,* released by the Royal Baking Powder Company, included recipes for "date dainties," date bread, date loaf cake, date muffins, and date sticks. And the 1947 edition of *The Settlement Cookbook,* given to my maternal grandmother on her wedding day, contains over twenty recipes for dates, from candy to sausages.

The Greatest Generation was assaulted with date recipes and dates were appearing more regularly in the grocery store, beautifully branded in their own packaging. Both my mom and dad, seventy-four and seventy-eight respectively, remember the package of Hills

Brothers Dromedary dates appearing in their family's refrigerators in December. My mom even remembers what my grandma made from them: Cherry Winks, a Christmas cookie filled with chopped dates and maraschino cherries, the only Christmas cookie my grandpa liked. Other Baby Boomers I interviewed remembered Date Pinwheel Cookies from the *Betty Crocker's Cooky Book,* and of course, date nut bread, often slathered with cream cheese. In fact, the coffee brand Chock Full o'Nuts had a chain of diners in New York City in the mid-twentieth century that was famous for its date nut bread and cream cheese sandwiches.

# Date Nut Bread

This recipe withstands the test of time; it's moist without being wet, beautifully spiced, and the dates and walnuts add an appealing textural contrast. It reminds me of zucchini bread, one of my favorite summer treats, baked to use up an overabundance of vegetables. Toasted and spread with a smear of cream cheese, the bread makes a hearty breakfast any time of year. Adapted from Chock Full o'Nuts.

MAKES ONE LOAF

### INGREDIENTS
1 cup pitted, chopped dried dates
¾ cup boiling water
1½ cups all-purpose flour (feel free to substitute up to ½ cup whole-grain flour)
1½ teaspoons baking powder
½ teaspoon salt
1 teaspoon cinnamon and ¼ teaspoon nutmeg (or 1¼ teaspoon pumpkin pie spice)
1 cup walnuts, coarsely chopped
3 tablespoons butter, softened
¾ cup lightly packed brown sugar
2 eggs
1 teaspoon vanilla
For serving: 8 ounces of cream cheese, slightly softened

*recipe continues* >>

1. Preheat the oven to 350°F. Lightly grease a 8.5" × 4.5" loaf pan.
2. Pour boiling water over the dates, stir, and let stand for 15 minutes.
3. Whisk the flour, baking powder, salt, and spices in a medium bowl. Stir in walnuts and set aside.
4. In a stand mixer, cream the butter and sugar on medium speed until crumbly. Add eggs one at a time, then vanilla, mixing after each addition. Scrape down the sides of the bowl with a spatula.
5. With the mixer on low, alternate adding batches of the flour mixture and the date mixture (including remaining water), half of each at a time, until combined.
6. Pour batter into loaf pan and bake 45–55 minutes, until bread is almost completely firm (a few crumbs should still stick to a toothpick inserted into the loaf).
7. Let bread stand for 10–15 minutes, then remove from pan and cool fully on a rack. To serve, slice bread and spread with a tablespoon or two of cream cheese.

\* \* \*

IN 1947, THE SAME YEAR my grandmother got married and got her date-recipe-filled *Settlement Cookbook*, the Riverside County Fair and National Date Festival was officially launched. Although there was a Date Festival in 1921, it was a one-time event; the annual festival started after the Second World War. It adapted the valley's Middle Eastern theme, with the fairgrounds surrounded by a wall that is a mishmash of Islamic architecture: domes and cupolas, stripes of light and dark brick, and scalloped arches. The fair architecture was designed by Harry Oliver, a Hollywood production designer known for his whimsical sets. In 1949, two years after the festival started, Oliver completed the Old Baghdad Stage. Designed to look like a "caliph's palace in medieval Baghdad," with a minaret, keyhole arches, and windows with carved wood latticework, it evokes the movie magic of Rudolph Valentino's *The Sheik* and Douglas Fairbanks in *The Thief of Baghdad* more than it does an actual street in Baghdad. The stage became home to the Annual Arabian Nights Pageant, a spectacle based on the stories of *The Thousand and One Nights*. Mr. Shields wrote in 1957, "The presentation of the Arabian Nights Pageant has a cast of more than 150 people taking part either in the cast or the production staff of this civic endeavor. . . . Nowhere else will visitors be able to witness such a spectacle as this—a pageant that will thrill young and old alike with its drama and beauty."

Each year of the pageant boasts a new script based on one of the *Arabian Nights* stories—a story wasn't repeated until 1984—as well as original music. "They always had a genie, elephants and camels," a witness remembered of the early years. "Lots of chiffon, sequins, and the costumes showed quite a bit of flesh."

The costumes were also original, created every year by wardrobe head Zenda Elliot. Not just for the pageant, but also for Scheherazade's court, a beauty contest featuring ten or more teenage girls. The pageant winners donned feathered headpieces, sequined bras, sheer harem pants, and showed bare midriffs—like the costumes in the television show *I Dream of Jeannie*. The high school girls in Scheherazade's courts appeared at events and in press photos locally and nationally to entice tourists to the festival; in images, they are often posed adoringly around a single man, alluding to a shah and his harem. As Sarah Seekatz put it, "They were literally selling dates with the bodies of women."

In photos from the first decade of the festival in the 1950s, the bare skin seems particularly shocking. But there is also a hint of sexual liberation. The images of laughing, gorgeous women in harem costumes feel to me a bit like modern Halloween—or perhaps the festival scene at Coachella—events when women can wear whatever sexy outfit they want without affecting the perception of who they are the rest of the year. These women of Coachella's past wore a fantasy costume that invoked ideas of sexual availability that would be socially unacceptable at any other time. And with a communal nod and wink, it's understood that they're just playing, that this is a "good girl." Seen in this light, I can understand how putting on the fantasy of a lavish, hedonistic, sexual—yet biblical—Middle East would have felt particularly freeing in mid-twentieth-century

America. But it also put forward a version of the Middle East that was stuck in the past.

The Riverside County Fair and National Date Festival, as well as the Annual Arabian Nights Pageant, continue to this day. I attended the festival on day three of my trip, a Saturday; it was sunny and the temperatures would hit the mid-60s during the day. My dear friend Kim joined me; she had driven down from her hometown of Las Vegas. Kim has maroon hair, horn-rimmed glasses, and unbridled enthusiasm. Sarah Seekatz met us at the festival to act as our guide. Sarah's grandmother had danced in a harem girl outfit in the Arabian Nights Pageant long ago, and Sarah herself went on her first date to the festival as a teen.

During our day at the fair, I rode a camel (slowly, in a circle). We toured a large building featuring prizewinning produce and a single date vendor, as well as displays of date memorabilia and a pavilion put together by Shields explaining the date-growing process. We watched a date-cooking contest with about a dozen participants and prize money funded by the California Date Board. A single, adorable family swept most of the awards. But for the most part, the event was a normal county fair for an agricultural community: a 4-H barn was filled with sheep awaiting judgment, Quonset huts housed prizewinning baked goods and a gem show, and, in the stadium, there would be drag races and a Salt-N-Pepa concert the following weekend.

As the sun set and the carnival rides began to glow with multicolored lights, it was time to take our seats for the Annual Arabian Nights Pageant. The stage was illuminated in fuchsia and indigo as over forty performers, ranging from children not more than ten to seasoned community theater legends, marched out on stage. They were dressed in classically fantastical Middle Eastern costumes in a rainbow of colored polyesters and sequins. The pageant was two hours long and featured an extraordinary amount of musical numbers and a dedicated dance troupe of local teens. The music was appropriated from other sources: my favorite moment of the show was a rendition of "True Colors" by Cyndi Lauper, rearranged over a rapid drumbeat. Later, after versions of "The Gummy Bear Song" and "It's Raining Tacos"—vintage YouTube hits—a pack of live llamas were led across the stage. When the show was over, Kim pronounced it "the most Vegas thing I've seen outside of Vegas."

By the end, most of the audience seats were empty. The show's length and the falling temperatures had driven people away. When I asked Sarah Seekatz what she thought, she looked out over the empty seats and said, "It all seems very fragile."

I admired the efforts of the costumed performers but struggled with the idea of appropriating historical Islamic culture to celebrate the American date industry. When I visited the fair, the US was enforcing a travel ban against citizens of many of the countries the pageant allegedly celebrated.

The festival went through big changes when a version of the Middle East different from *I Dream of Jeannie* began to appear on the news in the 1970s: the kidnapping and murder of Israeli athletes at the 1972 Munich Olympics by Palestinians, the 1973 oil crisis, and the 1979 Iranian hostage crisis. While Americans had previously viewed the Middle East through the stereotypes of harem girls and wealthy sheiks, in the 1970s, different Muslim stereotypes took over: oil barons and religious extremists. Then we entered the first Gulf War in 1990, and our country was changed forever on September 11, 2001. "And then in the larger popular culture," Sarah Seekatz told me, "it was not OK to celebrate the Middle East."

As demographics changed and fewer residents were directly involved in date farming, the fair became less of a tourist destination and more a local county fair. French fries and a Monster Truck show fit the needs of the Coachella Valley population in the twenty-first century more than dates and camel races.

For many, the remaining Orientalist elements are "less about creating this idea of Arabia," Sarah clarified, "and more about carrying on this nostalgia and the legacy of what this area was in the sixties."

"But they could celebrate dates without a pageant," Kim offered. "It could be about the food and the agriculture." She had lamented earlier that she wanted more date-themed eats and activities at the fair, a food festival on par with Gilroy, California's garlic festival. Gilroy is famous for its rows of food vendors selling garlic-laden treats, and one of its most popular attractions is the garlic topping contest, where local ag workers compete to process garlic at lightning speed. Gilroy's festival draws 100,000 people over a single weekend. It turned out that Kim's comment was prophetic. The fall after my visit, a new date festival was founded.

\* \* \*

AFTER DECADES OF US MILITARY engagement in the Middle East and North Africa, many new Americans have emigrated from that part of the world. Immigration from these countries was virtually nonexistent before 1980 and peaked in the last decade. As more people come from the Middle East, Middle Eastern foodways have become a part of American food. For example, I don't leave the grocery store without buying hummus. And many popular cookbooks reflect this shift, including *The Bread and Salt between Us: Recipes and Stories from a Syrian Refugee's Kitchen* by Mayada Anjari, *Zaitoun: Recipes from the Palestinian Kitchen* by Yasmin Khan, *Arabiyya: Recipes from the Life of an Arab in Diaspora* by Reem Assil and *The Arabesque Table: Contemporary Recipes from the Arab World* by Reem Kassis.

The growing Middle Eastern population has brought more variations of fresh dates and date products to markets across the country. Ramadan now represents a spike in sales second only to the traditional Christmas season. When I first interviewed Sarah Seekatz during my trip, sitting beside her parents' pool at their house in Indio, she mentioned seeing fresh Barhi dates for sale for the first time—a treat only available in date-growing regions, well known by people from the Arabian peninsula. Most dates are harvested after they've dried on the tree and become fully sweet; but Barhis can be harvested at several stages of ripeness. When they're yellow and underripe, they have the texture of a raw potato and the astringency of a dry wine. A little riper, and they have the soft juiciness of a plum. Shields sells fresh Barhis in season, and the summer following my Coachella trip, I tried some from a local grocery store in Portland, Oregon. Additionally, date syrup and date sugar have become increasingly common, thanks in part to the Paleo and Whole 30 diets, where they are approved foods.

In November 2019, Mark Tadros launched the Date Harvest Festival. Mark is the president of Aziz Farms, a small date garden his father, an Egyptian immigrant, founded in the 1980s. The single-day festival attracted almost 5,000 attendees and sold over $10,000 worth of dates.

It was the senior Tadros who first began buying fresh Barhi dates from farmers and driving into LA to sell them to the Egyptian community—literally out of the trunk of his car. Today, the Tadros farm specializes in Barhis. Mark returned to help manage the family farm nine years ago after a career as a chef. Aziz Farms was the only vendor selling dates at the Riverside County Fair in 2019, and Mark participated out of an interest in preserving the festival's connection to small date farms. But while he was there, he had a revelation: the National Date Festival was not supporting the date industry in the same way it had in the mid-twentieth century. It was originally held in February to sustain an interest in dates outside of the traditional Christmas season. But over the twentieth century, many date growers began selling their dates to packing houses at harvest time, in the fall; by February, there was no economic incentive for date growers to participate in the event. Mark thought that a refocused festival, scheduled in the fall, might shine a fresh light on Coachella's date industry.

A classic food festival, the Date Harvest Festival took place in a beautiful park on a sunny day, and featured "dates that you've never heard of," including his own family farm's Red Barhis, incredibly rare in America; food vendors selling date-focused foods like date cotton candy and date–chicken sausage; samples of date-based products like date syrup and date vodka; cooking demos; live bands; a Ferris wheel; and a "family zone with tractors to climb on."

Mark says Gilroy's garlic festival, in his mind, is the "perfect marriage of food and agriculture." But he wants to go beyond a festival; he "wants consumers to associate dates with the Coachella Valley, the same way they know Idaho's russet potato and Napa Valley's wine." He wants the Coachella Valley to be known as the place that grows the best dates money can buy.

Tadros says he's a proponent of a rising-tide-lifts-all-ships mentality. "I believe that we raised awareness. I believe that people really enjoyed it," Tadros told me of the festival. He's already thinking about the festival in year two, and how agro-tourism can be brought back to the Valley.

A big part of that is education. The American public would need to not just ask for "a date," but to seek out a California-grown Medjool or, even better, a Blonde Beauty. Or perhaps even the new varieties being developed by farmers like Sam Cobb. There's nothing a small farm wants more than to plant a crop they know will sell out. And that kind of demand means unique dates will continue to be propagated in Coachella.

---

# Crispy Sautéed Dates on a Cloud of Whipped Saffron Ricotta and Focaccia

"This dish is a messy pleasure," Rawaan Alkhatib told me. A writer and multidisciplinary artist of Palestinian and Indian descent, she is currently working on a cookbook dedicated to dates. Her recipes are pulled from all the cultures connected to dates, from the Gulf States of the Arabian Peninsula to Coachella Valley, and include some of her own innovative creations. Here dates are fried in ghee (clarified butter), a method I remember from the 1921 *Date Cook Book* from the International Festival of Dates. Ghee-soaked dates, a common Ayurvedic combination, are eaten in India. Rawaan's version pulls inspiration from Italian cuisine, presenting the fried dates on a bed of fluffy ricotta and crunchy focaccia. If you can't obtain focaccia, try toasting up a flatbread like naan or even pizza dough, liberally drizzled with olive oil.

SERVES 4 AS AN APPETIZER

INGREDIENTS
**A generous pinch of saffron threads**
**2 tablespoons warm water**

1 teaspoon lemon zest (about half a lemon)
1½ cups fresh whole-milk ricotta cheese, at room temperature
¼ cup ghee or olive oil
16 medium dates, pitted and halved (I used a combination of
    Blonde Beauty and Empress dates)
A slab of fresh, crunchy, oily focaccia
Flaky finishing salt and freshly ground black pepper

OPTIONAL:
A healthy pinch of red chili flakes
A drizzle of honey (I used gallberry honey, another Ark of Taste
    item from Florida, which was perfect—but feel free to use what-
    ever you have on hand)

1. Steep the saffron threads in the warm water for 15–20 minutes until the liquid turns the color of the sun.
2. Whisk or blend the saffron threads and their water with the
   lemon zest and ricotta until you have a smooth, fluffy mixture, about 30 seconds.
3. Heat ghee or oil in a sauté pan over medium-low heat. Place
   the dates in the pan carefully (oil can pop and splash) cut side
   down, and cook until they start to caramelize and are just
   heated through, no longer than 30 seconds. Be careful—they
   burn easily.
4. When you're ready to serve, put the focaccia on a serving platter and spread with a thick layer of the ricotta, as though you
   are frosting a cake with generous abandon—an offset spatula
   can help here. Then, tumble the dates and their infused oil
   over the ricotta cloud, and sprinkle with enough flaky salt that
   it is unmistakably salty. Top with coarsely ground black pepper, and, if using, red pepper flakes and honey. Place within
   easy reach of your guests and let them tear in.

\* \* \*

MY LAST MORNING in the Coachella Valley was clear and chilly. It
was Sunday, the morning after we had attended the Arabian Nights
Pageant, and I hugged Kim goodbye. She left to drive back to Las

Vegas, and I climbed into my own rental car to meet Sarah Seekatz at Sam Cobb Farms.

Instead of continuing straight toward Palm Springs, I took a left at an enormous wind farm into the Sky Valley area. The land was flat, but occasionally orderly rows of date trees would obscure the view. I turned down a short driveway that led into a few acres of palms and the Cobb family's weekend farm stand. Dates for sale were displayed on a long table shaded by white canopies. Set up in a parking lot, surrounded by the palms, it was as simple a store as it comes.

Maxine—an elementary school teacher, Sam's wife and Sarah's family friend—runs the farm stand on the weekends. At that moment, she was taking care of the steady stream of patrons who pulled into the gravel parking lot and left with two or three—or five or six— boxes of dates.

Maxine greeted us warmly, then went around a trailer to fetch Sam; Sarah and I gazed at family photos hanging on the wall and in a book on the table: Sam as a young farmer in the 1970s; Sam and Maxine's large family posed in the date grove; Sam and his four-year-old grandson seated on a green John Deere tractor, both smiling ear to ear. Sam told me later he hopes his grandson will take over the farm one day.

Sam was smiling his big smile as he came out to greet us. The first thing Sam will tell you about himself is that he loves farming. His website, designed like the label of Dr. Bronner's Soap, mentions it several times. His enthusiasm leaks through even in his site's use of exclamation points: "Dates are a fascinating crop to grow!"

Originally from the San Joaquin Valley near Fresno, he remembers being three or four when he saw his first tractor in the fields across from his parents' house. The farm machinery was magnetic for little Sam, and all he knew was that he wanted to drive a tractor one day. And being in that farming community, he realized later, exposed him to over two hundred different crops. "I'm familiar with almonds. Grapes and peaches . . . and cotton and corn and wheat and barley." Sam always knew he was going to be a farmer. But, as he told me, his family had a different perspective. "They thought I was nuts. 'You don't want to be a farmer. We just got out of the fields, why do you want to go back in?'"

Sam is Black. If your community carries the legacy of enslavement, they might not appreciate—or might full-out reject—the notion of going back to the farm. But part of what drew Sam to farming was pride in his family's legacy: his grandfather had farmed 240 acres with mules in Mississippi in the 1920s, his father farmed the same land, and his brother raises cattle on part of that original homestead.

Sam went to Fresno State University and got two degrees in agriculture. His first venture in the 1980s, a vegetable farm, didn't go well. "I wound up going bankrupt," Sam told me. He went back to school, and was sought out by the USDA for a job in soil conservation. He was eventually assigned to the Coachella Valley, where he discovered the date gardens.

In 2002, Sam bought these five acres in Sky Valley with the idea that he was going to grow date palms to sell for use in landscaping— the Zahidi date palm in particular is a popular and profitable variety because of its full foliage and beautiful shape. To start his stock, he put out an APB to his community, asking if anyone had date trees growing suckers and if he could come take a few. It was a smart way to start a business: he didn't have to invest money in inventory. On the other hand, he was never quite sure what type of date palm he was getting— maybe it's a Zahidi, but maybe it's a Medjool, or maybe it's a seedling that grew up from a discarded date pit. And that's how he ended up growing some of the rarest dates on the planet and starting a few new varieties of his own.

As Sam's trees fruited, he realized he was growing some good dates. So he began boxing them up and selling them, and that's what people told him: "You grow good dates!"

"So I made that my slogan: 'I grow good dates!' It's on my box and my website and everything," Sam declared with pride. With his success, he's built the farm up to 120 acres, with most of the land about 100 miles away in Blythe, near the Colorado River.

One date that he's known for he calls Candy, for its "chew like a Snickers bar." He developed it from an old American variety called

Calipatria that he got from his friend Ben Laflin. Another of Sam's dates, a dark black date he calls Black Gold, he found on the side of the road. "The tree had come up from a seed," Sam said, "and we went and collected all the suckers from it and brought it home. And we had no idea what it was." Within a few years, the tree bloomed and produced dates. He thought it was such a good-tasting date that the world needed to know about it. "I said, 'That's gonna be my black gold!'" Another date he calls Safari is blonde and surprisingly savory. Sarah bought three boxes because she had never tasted a date like it. Much like the date farmers that settled the valley at the turn of the twentieth century, Sam keeps his signature dates unavailable anywhere else.

We tasted dates as we walked. Sam untied the white weatherproof bags wrapped around the bunches to protect them from rain, birds, and insects, and selected choice dates for us to munch. On my way out, I bought a sampler of Sam's dates, and a year later I would email him to ask if he would custom-pick me a few pounds of Empress, which he generously did. Since my visit, Sam has decided he will harvest his Empress for retail sale.

On my way back to my Twentynine Palms bungalow that day, I took the long way through Joshua Tree National Park. The Joshua trees—tall yuccas "caught in the act of unworldly gesticulation," as Floyd Shields once wrote—were surrounded by fields of yellow flowers that had exploded after the torrential desert rains. As I drove through the park's vistas, I wondered what Fairchild and Swingle would think of the date industry today. Fairchild wrote at the end of his date manuscript: "Again the scene of 1898 . . . comes to my mind, and I hear once more Swingle's voice 'It takes fifteen years to fruit a date palm.' Double these years have gone, and what Swingle then set out to do he has done."

Swingle worked for the USDA until 1940, when he reached mandatory retirement at the age of seventy. By that time, he was still actively involved in the development of the date industry, among many other projects. He had met and married Maude Kellerman, a gifted botanist and ecologist, in 1915, and they had four children together. His life had involved research journeys around the world, and he authored

230 publications. One colleague said of him, "I've never heard anyone come up with so many ideas on the spur of the moment in my life! Some of them were way out, but he gave us a lot to choose from!" He died in Washington, DC, on January 19, 1952. By the time of his death, the profits from the date industry had far surpassed the government's financial investment.

Even so, the date industry in the US today is still niche. In California, the domestic industry is made up of fewer than 100 growers who employ about 1,400 people, and produces about 35,000 tons – equivalent to the same amount of dates as we import. Although a few of the old date farms remain—like Shields in Indio and Oasis Date Gardens in Thermal—most of the date farms aren't the small, family-run businesses that existed when the Date Festival started. When the first generations of Coachella farmers began to pass away, their children didn't want to take on the difficult labor and financial risk of date growing, especially specialty strains like the now nearly lost TR and McGill dates. Only a dozen producing palms are left of the TR date, and only three McGill date palms are known to exist. I was not able to locate dates of either variety on my trip.

The date industry has shifted to wholesale, with massive farms producing one or two standardized varieties for companies like Dole. As consumers, what we expect from food is consistency. We have an expectation that every package of dates (or craisins, or red seedless grapes, or whatever) we buy from the grocery store will taste the same.

In 1955, Roy Nixon of the USDA published a report of thirty-nine different unique American varieties of dates. Current Ark of Taste dates are included on his list, but there are also lost dates like the rich, sweet Desert Dew and the foggy-skinned Smoky. Where are these dates now? Were they not worth propagating, or are they treasures waiting to be rediscovered?

The bigger question remains: how do we ensure the survival of the rare dates that are still being produced in the Coachella Valley? This is where Slow Food comes in. Slow Food encourages a deeper relationship with what we eat, even asking us to go to the effort of physically traveling to the place where, in this case, a special date is grown. I'd like you to do that. Or maybe, if you're already vacationing in Palm Springs, you could take the time to go to Sam Cobb and get some good dates. Or, if you can't travel, maybe just order some special dates online as a treat.

For most of Coachella Valley's history, tourists were lured to the area by the promise of an exotic Arabian fantasy. Today, many tourists are foodies, and can be drawn by the allure of good food, the promise of learning something new, and the chance to support a small farmer. This kind of tourism would mean the best part of Coachella's past would be preserved: delicious, American dates.

TWO

# *Kupuna Kō*

## HAWAIIAN LEGACY SUGARCANE

I hopped off the bus in front of the Pearlridge Mall in Waimalu, O'ahu, a suburb west of Honolulu on the Kamehameha Highway. The six-lane highway was behind me, roaring with late afternoon rush hour traffic, and the new Hawaiian Rail Project—light rail public transit—was being constructed above it. It was May 2019, and a "hot one" even by local standards. I dripped sweat as I walked a block past the Sears parking lot and took a right onto the gravel road that led past a watercress farm. The farther I walked, the traffic sounds faded and were replaced by the chirruping of birds. Then came Anthony DeLuze's farm. Anthony's three-acre farm is a riot of tropical plants fed by natural springs, an oasis surrounded by concrete and cars. Some might look at Anthony's plot and call it disorganized, especially compared to the orderly rows of corn and soy I know well in the Midwest. But his personal motto is "to work with the land, not to work the land." An organic farmer, he makes a point of allowing the land to rest, feeds it with compost, and accepts there will always be weeds.

As I walked farther, I saw rectangular pools of water sprouting the distinctive heart-shaped leaves of taro; banana trees with green, egg-shaped fruit; and tall stands of grassy *kō*—sugarcane. Some kō resembled bamboo in color and appearance, but other stands had stalks thicker than my arm that were striped with painterly pinks and yellows.

I had come to Hawaii, and to Anthony's farm, to understand the story of *kupuna kō*—Hawaiian legacy sugarcane. When Anthony first extended his invitation to me to visit, he wrote: "Ma ka hana ka ike. Learning is in the work . . . or the doing." It was a sentiment that resonated with me; so I got on a plane and was ready to get my hands dirty.

Hawaii's story of sugar is intertwined with the history of the indigenous Hawaiian people. In fact, this plant arrived with the first humans to settle the Islands. Sugarcane would later fuel the colonization of the Islands by white foreigners, and the sugar industry was a major impetus for the illegal overthrow of the Hawaiian monarchy and the kingdom's annexation to the United States. But today, commercial sugar production no longer exists on the island; the last sugar mill closed in December 2016.

The Ark of Taste has five entries for Hawaiian sugarcane, chosen to represent the over forty varieties of legacy kō that have been identified as unique to the Hawaiian Islands. For example, Halāli'i is a bright green and yellow cane, named for an area of the island of Ni'ihau where it originated. Laukona is a light yellow cane with vertical green stripes, named after the winter storms that blow up from the south. The word *laukōnā* also means "many dislikes" or "hardhearted, merciless, or implacable." True to its grumpy name, it's known as the only ritual cane that can be used to break love magic, a spell cast to infatuate a target. Māikoiko is a deep black cane with white, waxy lateral rings. Pua'ole is a unique, exceptionally sweet cane that doesn't flower—its name translates to "flowerless." Uahiapele means "smoke of Pele," the Hawaii volcano goddess, and is a striking dark purple or olive green covered in smoky gray wax.

Kupuna kō has many threats to its existence. The feral pig population on the Islands is out of control, and the pigs have a taste for sugarcane. Additionally, with housing and hotel developments exploding, old family properties get sold and bulldozed, and the family cane patch with it. The largest commercial sugarcane growers on the island today are distilleries, who are using kupuna kō to produce rhum agricole. It's a spirit distilled from pressed cane juice, as opposed to molasses like most rums, and highlights the unique flavor of the legacy cane.

I met Anthony at the end of the dirt road; he was in his late thirties, and was wearing a practical outfit of knee-high wellies, blue patterned swim trunks, and a gray sleeveless T-shirt. His light, curly hair was tied back in a ponytail, his left forearm patterned in traditional Hawaiian tattoos.

Anthony comes from the north side of Oʻahu and "was raised in the ocean, raised in the mountains." He grew up in a house on a lane where all of his Mexican–Hawaiian family lived. There was always food growing in his backyard and in the yards of his relations: chickens, bananas, taro, "a massive old ʻulu tree: breadfruit. Two big, massive mango trees"—and sugarcane. A couple of times a year, especially on brutally hot days when everyone needed a little refreshment, a family member would hack down a stalk of sugarcane and split it into pieces for the kids to chew on. Anthony grows cane on his farm now for his kids, to teach them some of the old Hawaiian ways.

As a young man, Anthony battled depression and alcoholism. "You have to make a change," he said about the time in his life when the cycle of drinking and depression was at its worst. "I just wanted my life back and my kids . . . I just was so far away from my roots."

And then, in 2010, the landowners of a plot that had been abandoned for thirteen years were looking for a farmer to recover it. That's when Anthony met his farm. He began growing traditional plants, like taro and kō. But there were also practical reasons to grow kō on his farm. New research shows that cane helps to fix nitrogen in the soil when it's used as mulch. It's effective at smothering weeds, it can be a windbreak for other crops, and it holds soil in place around streams and taro patches. And, of course, you can eat it.

Anthony took me on a sugarcane tasting tour, moving between stands of his cane that were wildly different colors. He chopped down a cane from a towering stand at least 16 feet tall. The cane was wine-grape red, and the color gave it its name: Honuaʻula. "Honua is the earth and ʻula is red," Anthony explained. Literally, "red earth."

I held out the shaft of sugarcane, as thick as my wrist, so Anthony could chop it into a manageable length with his machete.

"Trust me?" he asked, readying the blade. "Shouldn't," he laughed, with a mischievous smile.

With a solid whack, Anthony cut the long cane into two equal lengths, and my hands remained intact. From there, he peeled the cane with deft downward sweeps of the machete, then coaxed off thick, pithy splinters of juicy cane. He handed me a piece and I clamped it between my molars and chewed. My mouth was flooded with the flavor of demerara sugar and molasses. I felt as refreshed as if I had just chugged coconut water.

We came to Anthony's stand of Uahiapele cane: at least 15 feet high, colored olive green and smoky gray, and so thick it would dislodge the gears of a sugarcane handmill. Another thunk of Anthomy's machete and the cut end of the soft Uahiapele cane dripped with juice, like a ripe fruit. It tasted fruity, too, and like a vanilla shave ice.

The next stand was Pakaweli, a stunning cane with bright pink and yellow vertical stripes. The pulp on the inside glowed gold, like a sunset. The juice tasted like toasted marshmallows.

The last stand on our tour was Moano, its skin mottled with rust reds, oranges, and yellows. It tasted like caramel.

"This is kinda inspiring me," Anthony said, looking back over our progress through his cane varieties. "I don't know exactly what it's going to inspire yet, but you know, I grow all these canes and we eat all these canes once in a while, but I think this might be the first time that I've gone down the line and just sampled one after another."

* * *

SUGARCANE IS ONE OF THE LARGEST members of the grass family, second only to bamboo. There are two wild sugarcane species: thin-stalked, grassy *Saccharum spontaneum*, which is believed to have originated in India and grows wild from northern Africa to New Guinea, and *Saccharum robustum*, which comes from New Guinea and potentially a few surrounding islands and whose thick stalks resemble domesticated sugarcane. These two wild plants were crossed and selectively bred by humans over thousands of years, resulting in at least four species of domesticated sugarcane.

S. *officinarum*—Hawaii's legacy cane—originated in New Guinea around 8000 BC. The cane was chewed by the people there both for its caloric content and for its nutrients: iron, calcium, magnesium, and potassium. It's since been bred into countless hybrids and cultivars for commercial use around the world. These canes can grow up to 25 feet high; their stalks are large, thick and colorful; and they have a higher sugar content than other wild or domestic species.

Sugarcane juice is heavier than water. It weighs almost 9 pounds per gallon, compared to water's 8.3, and its mouthfeel is more viscous. The first time I sat down to a cup of pressed cane juice was at the Kō Hana distillery, a rhum agricole producer on O'ahu not far from Anthony's farm. The color of the juice ranges from brown to bright green, and the cup I was given was light yellow-green, cloudy and a little foamy. Its flavor brought up an unexpected memory: it tasted like corn smells. It took me immediately to summers in Ohio, sitting outside, shucking fresh corn for dinner. Which makes sense—sugarcane and corn are closely related.

It's sugarcane juice that is processed into crystallized sugar. When sugarcane spread around the planet, it traveled in two directions from its origin point in New Guinea: west to mainland Asia and east to Hawaii. A single variety, commonly called Creole, was carried west. The earliest definite record of sugar-making comes from a Hindu religious document written about AD 500. The sugarcane juice was evaporated and clarified in wide, shallow pans until it crystallized. This sugar would have been the dark brown, slightly moist sugar that is known today as jaggery. Evaporated cane juice contains both sucrose crystals and molasses—liqud sucrose with other trace sugars and minerals like iron and calcium. While in modern processes the molasses is removed to create white sugar, the jaggery-making process retains the molasses. By the seventh century, Creole was being grown in Persia and processed into confections. By the eighth century, cane cultivation had spread around the Arab Empire surrounding the Mediterranean, and by the end of the tenth century, crystallized white sugar, known as rock sugar, made its way into Europe. By the end of the sixteenth century, colonizers established sugar plantations in the Caribbean.

While a single variety made the westward journey around the globe to the Caribbean, sugarcane's expansion east was far more diverse. The Polynesian people brought cane with them on their voyages and planted it in new settlements. They were extraordinary ocean navigators; from about 1200 BC to AD 1200, they settled the Pacific islands from Tahiti to Easter Island, New Zealand to Hawaii—and it's believed they also made landfall in the Americas. They were capable of traveling thousands of miles over open ocean thanks to *te puke*, double-hulled koa-wood canoes with sails woven from hala tree leaves with coconut-fiber lashings.

Polynesian navigators, or "wayfinders," used astronomy to deftly travel the open water. Hōkūle'a was the most important, the star known as Arcturus in Latin. It rises and sets over the latitude of Hawaii. Once the navigators discovered Hawaii—using other indicators like clouds, waves, and birds—they could easily return by following Hōkūle'a. By AD 1000, the first human settlements were established on O'ahu and Kaua'i.

One boat could carry about two dozen emigrants, as well as chickens, pigs, dogs, and agricultural plants. When the settlers packed their canoes to establish a colony on a new island, they brought not only the food they needed to survive the voyage, but plants to propagate once they arrived. They brought plant tubers, root suckers, and cuttings. The early settlers traveled back and forth to more established settlements in the Pacific, bringing more plant species back with them, until about AD 1300. Twenty-three different plants were eventually established in Hawaii and became the basis of their agriculture. These are the *kupuna*, or elder, crops.

Sugarcane is propagated by planting cuttings from the stalk that take root. There is anthropological and genetic evidence that sugarcane, as well as taro and bananas, were brought to Hawaii one thousand years ago on the initial voyage of Polynesian settlers, and were bred and propagated by Hawaiians. Because of the diverse climates and growing conditions, dozens of varieties of sugarcane were developed on all of the islands.

Early Hawaiians used sugarcane for a variety of purposes: the leaves were woven into decorative thatching in homes and the flowers were harvested to make sweet-smelling pillows and leis. The flowers were also used in funerary practices, as well as spread on grass sledding tracks to make the trails suitably slippery for *hōlua*, or mountain surfing.

Cane also had important religious and ritual significance. It appears early in the Hawaiian creation chant, the Kumulipo; Kō'ele'ele sugarcane is mentioned by name in the early verses listing important plants and animals born in the sea and on the land. Another cane, Halāli'i, was a favorite offering to gods, particularly Kāne and Kū. The cane Manulele was famous for *hana aloha*, love magic, rituals performed to make a person fall in love with you or to strengthen the bonds of love. *Manulele* means "flying bird," and a ritual done with the cane would carry your love to a distant person like a flying bird. Other canes were used for love magic: Pāpa'a to strengthen an existing relationship, Pilimai for flings, and Laukona to break things off.

Cane juice, particularly from a variety called Nānahu, was blended with charcoal to create ink for traditional Hawaiian tattoos. Medicinally, the juice was applied to cuts and was blended into oral medicines. It was also used in diagnostic and healing rituals.

Hawaiians also ate sugarcane, chewing on it to consume the juice or pounding the pith with rocks, then squeezing the juice out of the softened fibers. The collected juice was drunk as is, boiled down and condensed as a food for infants, or used to sweeten traditional desserts like *haupia*, a coconut pudding, and *kūlolo*, a fudge-textured sweet made from taro and coconut, wrapped in *ti* leaves, and baked in an underground oven. In Hawaiian culture, sugarcane was never refined and commodified the way it was in Europe and Asia.

After Hawaiians stopped commuting to other Polynesian settlements around 1300, they became isolated from outside cultures, and remained that way until the end of the eighteenth century. First contact with European cultures would change their community, and the future of their kupuna kō, forever.

\* \* \*

ON JANUARY 18, 1778, Captain James Cook and his crew spotted O'ahu. Cook had already spent a good deal of time on other Pacific islands. He had learned some of the Tahitian language and was the first white person to note that the Polynesian islands were one extended culture, defying the Western conception that only Europeans had the knowledge for long-distance sea voyages.

As Cook navigated the ocean around O'ahu and Kaua'i, looking for a place to drop anchor, he noted villages and crops he recognized: "several plantations of plantains and sugarcane, and spots that seemed cultivated for roots," probably taro. Cook came ashore during a time of feasting and celebration for the god Lono, and was treated with traditional Hawaiian hospitality. He and his crew were given gifts and fed; some Hawaiians may have believed Cook and his crew were gods. The crew traded metal and nails to Hawaiians to resupply their ship with food and to Hawaiian women for sex.

About a year after his arrival in the area, while anchored near the Big Island, a dispute arose about a boat stolen from Cook's ships. One of Cook's men shot and killed a high-ranking chief named Kalimu. Cook himself tried to grab the highest-ranking chief as a hostage and then slashed the face of one of the chief's sons with his sword. This son, Ka-lani-mano-o-ka-ho'owaha, "with a powerful blow of his club knocked Captain Cook down against a heap of lava rock," wrote Hawaiian historian Samuel Kamakau. "Captain Cook groaned with pain. Then the chief knew that he was a man not a god, and, the mistake ended, he struck him dead . . ."

When Cook arrived, the Hawaiian population was estimated to be between 300,000 and one million people—a wide range because Europeans have historically underestimated indigenous populations all over the Americas. Forty years later, in 1819, the population was 145,000. European diseases were to blame: a measles epidemic in 1848 killed 10,000 people; a smallpox outbreak in 1853 killed 15,000. By the time Kamakua was writing his history in the 1860s, Native Hawaiians numbered about 70,000 individuals. Kamakua wrote, "Today in some

places the ground is white with their bones, and land goes unculti-
vated because there are none who need it."

After Cook's first contact, Hawaii became a regular stop for whal-
ing ships crossing the Pacific. Hawaiians started vegetable farms to
provide food to sell to the crews, growing native crops like sweet
potatoes and also introduced produce like white potatoes, watermelons, pumpkins, oranges, lemons, figs, and tamarinds. Cattle and poultry were also raised and sold. Small farms of sugarcane popped up to
produce semi-refined sugar for ships' supplies. Port towns like Honolulu and Hilo changed to accommodate the desires of the sailors: bars,
gambling halls, and a sex trade. Hawaii also began to export luxury
products, like sandalwood, which was sold to Western trading expedi-
tions, who then traded it with China.

Hawaiian men would often join the crews of these whalers and
trading ships. A young man named ʻŌpūkahaʻia joined a crew bound
for New York City; after arriving in the United States, he traveled to
New Haven in 1809. An unusual visitor in Connecticut, he was taken
on as a student by the president of Yale, and was educated in Christianity and English literacy. ʻŌpūkahaʻia trained to be a minister with
the intent of returning to Hawaii as a missionary. But before he could
return home he contracted typhoid fever, and died on February 17,
1818, at the age of twenty-six.

One of his teachers collected his diaries, letters, and interviews into
a book, *Memoirs of Henry Obookiah*. The book inspired an urgent call
among American missionaries to fulfill ʻŌpūkahaʻia's dream to bring
Christianity to Hawaii. A little over a year after his death, missionaries
embarked from Boston: four native Hawaiians trained as missionaries
and twenty-nine white New Englanders: the Binghams, Thurstons,
Ruggles, Whitneys, Loomises, and Chamberlains. Their descendants
would become some of the richest and most influential people in
Hawaii. It was they who would view sugar as a profitable commodity crop, and took the risk to sell this Hawaiian product on the world
market. Some of the sugar mills they founded still stand.

The first sugar mill in Hawaii was established on Kauaʻi in 1835 by
three missionaries' sons. But the partners had no experience in sugar

growing and their product was terrible. The plantation quickly went under and was sold to Dr. R. W. Wood, an immigrant from New England. He too struggled to make the mill profitable, but by the 1850s, it was in the black.

In these early plantations, the cane grown was all native Hawaiian varieties. Laborers harvested cane by hand and cut it with a cane knife, a short machete with a hook on the end. Fresh-cut cane was carried to oxcarts and transported to the mill, which was a small machine, about a foot square, mounted outdoors on a pillar. Cane was fed into the side of the mill and passed back and forth through the rollers by two workers, while a third man led a mule or ox in a circle attached to a long wooden arm that powered the rollers' movement. The juice flowed out a tap in the side and was collected for processing.

The sugarcane juice was boiled in a series of open iron kettles, arranged largest to smallest, their undersides set into a brick furnace. A wood fire was built under the kettles, and as the juice boiled, impurities were skimmed off the top. As the cane juice evaporated water and thickened, it was transferred to smaller and smaller kettles until it had transformed into a thick sludge. This molten sugar was then transferred to a cooling vat, then finally to a barrel or conical mold. Molasses gradually drained from the barrel, leaving crystallized sugar behind. If a conical mold was used, the mold was flipped tip side down into a clay vessel. The sugar crystallized in the cone while the molasses dripped into the container below.

To supply human labor for the difficult, dangerous, and low-paying plantation jobs, planters recruited workers from China. In 1852, two hundred Chinese laborers arrived in Hawaii under a labor contract and were distributed among the plantations. Skilled workers like blacksmiths, masons, coopers (barrelmakers), and engineers were usually Hawaiian or white. The plantation manager and sugar boiler—the worker who oversaw the delicate operation of sugar crystallization—were considered the highest-ranking positions and were usually white. Laborers lived in traditional thatched homes if they were Hawaiian or wood-framed barracks if they were Chinese, while skilled workers and managers lived in wood-framed cottages with gardens.

Food for workers was a major plantation expense. Enormous quantities of rice had to be purchased and imported for the new Chinese workers. Hawaiian workers were supplied *poi* (traditionally fermented taro) and fish, frequently in the form of salted salmon from the Pacific Northwest. It may seem odd that, in an area as plentiful in fish as the Hawaiian Islands, this staple was imported from the American mainland. Before first contact with the West, food production was the main "job" of a Hawaiian, and there was ample time to fish. But now in a Western economy, Hawaiians had to work at their jobs on the sugar plantations throughout the week and no longer had time to catch their own food. The introduction of Pacific Northwest salmon led to the creation of a dish now considered classic Hawaiian cuisine, lomi lomi salmon, a salad made from salted salmon, tomatoes, and onions.

Meanwhile, thousands of miles away and in another country, the American Civil War broke out. It would have been difficult to imagine that the conflict could have any effect on Hawaii. But with the North's supply of Southern sugar cut off, they turned to Hawaiian sugar imported via San Francisco. In 1860, there were twelve plantations on the Islands, and by the next year, there were twenty-two.

To meet increased demand, the plantations had to update their technology, from animal power to steam. Trains hauled the cut cane in from the fields on portable railroad tracks, while steam-powered rollers pressed the juice from the cane. Instead of human labor skimming boiling juice in open kettles, the juice was processed in vacuum pans that allowed it to boil at a low temperature. And instead of allowing the molasses to slowly drip from conical molds for weeks, centrifuges spun crystallized sugar and separated the molasses in a few hours. Because this new technology made the processing of sugar more efficient, planters began to buy more land to grow more cane. These expansions were costly, and agencies evolved to both loan money and arrange for the sale and shipping of sugar. These agencies were primarily established by the children of the original missionary families. Their family names would hold economic power in the Islands well into the twentieth century: Castle & Cooke, C. Brewer & Co., and Alexander & Baldwin. They held political power as well, as these first-generation white Hawaiians began to take positions in the government.

The gradual success of the plantations created major changes in Hawaii's government. Kamehameha, the ruler of the Big Island, conquered the Hawaiian Islands in 1795 and united them under his rule. In 1840, Kamehameha's son, King Kauikeaouli, made Hawaii a constitutional monarchy, as opposed to his father's absolute monarchy. Then, in 1848, King Kamehameha III radically reformed the system of land ownership. In what became known as the Great Mahele, he did away with the *ahupua'a* system—a way of communal landownership and caretaking—and split the land between "the king, the government, the chiefs and the commoners," putting tracts of land into individual, rather than communal, ownership. Deeds were set aside for the allotted land for each group; but the native Hawaiians, unfamiliar with the concept of individually owned property—and not educated about the legal process—were not able to claim their land. Of the 1.5 million acres set aside by the king for ownership by the commoners, only 28,658 acres—less than one percent—actually went into the commoners' hands. Haoles, or non-Hawaiians, living in Hawaii could declare their allegiance to the king and then legally buy land. When the Kuleana Act of 1850 allowed the government to sell unclaimed land deeds, two-thirds of them went to haoles. By 1890, foreign investors controlled 90 percent of Hawaii's land.

\* \* \*

MY AIRBNB WAS ON THE WESTERN EDGE of Honolulu, the second floor of a family home. I awoke the day after meeting Anthony to the neighbors speaking in Hawaiian underneath my window. A radio played across the street, blasting a conservative talk show that proclaimed it was "the only news you can trust."

After showering and putting on a new black and beige flowered muumuu, I walked the mile slog to the bus stop, past the Navy Exchange gas station, Navy Federal Credit Union, and Pearl Harbor Navy Exchange Mall. The bus took me eastward and down into the city, eventually letting me off near the park that surrounds the former royal residence, 'Iolani Palace. Finished in 1882, it's known as the only "American Florentine"-style building in existence. The architecture blends Italian Renaissance style—Corinthian columns and towers topped with square, concave "campaniles"—with Hawaiian elements; in particular, both its two stories are surrounded by a lanai, an expansive porch. Glasswork throughout the palace depicts Hawaiian plants like ferns and taro.

I joined a tour group assembled on a lanai, and we were asked to put on blue cloth footies—like shower caps for our shoes—to preserve the historical structure. After an introduction in the grand foyer, we were directed up a sweeping staircase made from glowing native kōa wood, and invited to run our hands along the banister. The sensation took me immediately back to another house museum, the Lower East Side Tenement Museum in New York City, where I gave tours for eight years. We began our tours of that 1860s' apartment building the same way, inviting visitors to touch the banister as they ascended the stairs. I asked visitors to imagine all the thousands of residents of this space who used that same banister every day. But it wasn't new immigrants who had used this banister in Hawaii; it was royalty.

Upstairs, my tour group was invited to view the toilets. The palace had running water when it was completed in 1882, and electricity by 1886—five years before the White House. The table in the dining room was set with pink Bohemian crystal coupes, porcelain from Paris bearing the Hawaiian coat of arms, and a solid silver epergne gifted by Napoleon III in 1858. A dinner in this room on Wednesday, February 14, 1883, was served à la russe, or in courses. The six courses featured a blend of Hawaiian ingredients and popular English and French cuisine: curried mulligatawny soup; seafood dishes of Hawaiian fishes uhu, ulua, oio, and moi; pheasant and wild duck with mushrooms; and stuffed and braised beef à la mode. The desserts were undoubtedly made with local sugar: wine jelly, sponge cake, strawberries and ice cream, as well as "Papaia" (papaya) and fruit cake, and a dish called Iolani Pudding. Finally, there were liqueurs, more fruits, "pompoms," tea, and coffee.

This stunning royal palace was built by profits from sugar. Money flooded into Hawaii's economy after King Kalākaua signed the reciprocity treaty of 1875, an agreement with the United States that sugar could be imported by the mainland tax-free. But the royal palace would become a royal prison when Queen Liliʻuokalani, the last reigning monarch of Hawaii, was arrested during the overthrow of the Hawaiian government.

The queen's birth name was Lydia Liliʻu Loloku Walania Wewehi Kamakaʻeha. She was born on September 2, 1838, near the Punchbowl Crater, the remains of an extinct volcano in Honolulu. At four years old, the future queen was sent to the Chiefs' Children's School, a boarding school established by missionaries at the request of Hawaii's chiefs. The school focused on her instruction in English. But what the queen remembered most was being hungry: "It seems to me that they failed to remember we were growing children. A thick slice of bread covered with molasses was usually the sole article of our supper, and we were sometimes ingenious, it not over honest, in our search for food: if we could beg something of the cook it was the easier way; but if not, anything eatable left within our reach was surely confiscated. As a last resort, we were not above searching the gardens for any esculent root or leaf, which (having inherited the art of igniting a fire from the friction of sticks), we could cook and consume without the knowledge of our preceptors."

In photos of Liliʻuokalani, both before and after she became queen, she was always dressed in the latest Western fashions. In one image from the 1860s, she is corseted and in a hoop skirt wearing a plaid dress with a fitted bodice and off-the-shoulder sleeves. A cameo is clipped at the center of her lace collar and her hair is parted in the center and pulled back in a style that covers her ears. She looks every bit an American Civil War-era belle, except for her gaze: locked on the camera, cool and powerful.

It was Lydia's brother, King Kalākaua, who sat on the throne starting in 1874. Nicknamed the Merrie Monarch, he was elected to his position by the Hawaiian legislature; the last of Kamehameha's bloodline had died, and Kalākaua ran for the position.

King Kalākaua revived aspects of Hawaiian culture that had been oppressed in the years after the missionaries' arrival, in particular the hula, which had been banned in 1830 as it was deemed too sexy by the missionaries and recent Christian converts. The largest annual hula competition in Hawaii today is named for him. It was he who commissioned the unique and stunning 'Iolani Palace, but also he who negotiated the Reciprocity Treaty with the American government and issued water licenses to the white sugar planters—so his legacy is complicated.

When the Civil War ended and sugar prices slumped, plantation owners pressed the Hawaiian government to work out the Reciprocity Treaty. Untaxed sugar could be sold at prices that were competitive with sugar produced in the American South or the Caribbean. Within these negotiations, the sugar planters also pushed for Hawaii to become part of the US. In the long run, they saw it as more profitable; they would never have to worry about import taxes. But there was another aspect to the push. At this point, the planters were the grandchildren of the missionaries who came in the 1820s, but they retained much of their grandparents' worldview. Their mindset focused on acquisition of property and wealth as the tenets of a healthy society, ideals that aligned with the American way of life more than that of the Hawaiians.

But King Kalākaua wasn't interested in giving up Hawaii's status as an independent nation, and the US, at the time, was not interested in acquiring the Islands. When the Reciprocity Treaty of 1875 was finally signed, the sugar industry boomed once again. Within less than a decade, there were ninety sugar plantations and mills on Hawaii. The Islands produced 14,010 tons of sugar in 1866 and 38,647 in 1880, a 250 percent increase. The boom began to attract foreign investors in addition to the missionaries' sons who traditionally ran the sugar industry.

Planters looked to the dry, sunny sides of the islands to increase their sugarcane acreage, but they needed to move massive amounts of water from the wet sides of the islands to grow their monocrop. It takes 500 gallons of water to produce one pound of refined sugar. Water, like land, was communally owned in Hawaii until the Great Mahele. Native Hawaiians dug, built, and managed 'auwai, irrigation ditches that brought water down from the mountains to irrigate taro fields on the ahupua'a. The Hawaiian government started granting licenses to private individuals to divert water in the 1870s. The first sugar irrigation ditch was built on Maui; it transported water from a distant watershed to Samuel Alexander and Henry Baldwin's plantation. Although these irrigation systems are referred to by the diminutive term "ditches," they consisted of miles of tunnels through mountains, wooden flumes that spanned deep valleys, wide canals, and massive reservoirs. Planned by wealthy plantation owners, the ditch infrastructure was built by the same cheap immigrant labor, mainly from China, that did the tough work on the farms.

Lydia became King Kalākaua's heir apparent in 1877, after the death of their younger brother. By this time, she was a well-known composer; she wrote her most famous song, "Aloha 'Oe," in 1878. When leaving the country ranch of her friend Colonel James Harbottle Boyd, she witnessed Boyd kiss his girlfriend goodbye, and that tender moment inspired her verses. The Royal Hawaiian Band played the song at an 1883 celebration in San Francisco, and it became a huge hit with an American public increasingly obsessed with Hawaii. It was also played 125 years later at the inauguration of Hawaiian-born President Barack Obama. Lydia would write over two hundred pieces of music in her lifetime, including the Hawaiian national anthem, "He Mele Lāhui Hawai'i."

In 1887, while she was attending Queen Victoria's Jubilee celebration in London, she got word from her brother of an uprising in Hawaii. The second-generation missionary cohort, whose financial interests were actively tied to sugar, had taken over the government.

"Having matured their plans in secret," wrote Lydia in her autobiography, "the men of foreign birth rose one day en masse, called a public meeting, and forced the king . . . to sign a constitution of their own preparation, a document which deprived the sovereign of all power, made him a mere tool in their hand." This new constitution, which through "violence had procured the King's signature," became known as the Bayonet Constitution.

The document limited voting rights and elected government positions to property owners with "property valued at no less than three thousand dollars, or [who] received an income of no less than 600 dollars." Voters had to be white or Hawaiian, but two-thirds of Hawaiians did not meet the land and income requirement. Additionally, the king was no longer allowed to appoint his own cabinet. It would be appointed by the elected governing body, the House of Nobles, and the cabinet had to approve the king's decisions. The control Hawaiians had over their own island and government had been whittled down to nearly nothing.

After Lydia received news of the Bayonet Constitution, she rushed home to Honolulu from London, a journey of a month in 1887. She noted that when her brother the king greeted her, he seemed in bright spirits, but "we could see on his countenance traces of the terrible strain through which he had passed." A few months after Lydia's homecoming, the new cabinet re-signed the reciprocity agreement with the United States. The US had asked for a natural harbor called Wai Momi, or "pearl waters," and the new Hawaiian government signed it over. It would come to be known as Pearl Harbor.

By 1890, the king's health was failing, and he made the decision to go to San Francisco for a vacation from the tensions at home. He sailed to San Francisco in November 1890. Before long, he suffered what appeared to be a stroke and was confined to his hotel. His health quickly declined and on January 20, 1891, he died.

On January 29, the ship that had borne the king away returned to port in Honolulu, bringing both the tragic news of his death and his remains. Cabinet ministers insisted that Lydia become queen on the spot. "I was compelled to take the oath to the constitution, the adoption of which had led to my brother's death," she wrote. At fifty-two years old, Lydia became Queen Liliʻuokalani.

She came out swinging. "Petitions poured in from every part of the Islands for a new constitution," she wrote, one that would restore the powers of the monarchy as well as expand voting rights to more Hawaiian citizens. The petitions carried 6,500 signatures—two-thirds of Hawaii's registered voters. She did what her people asked, which she was allowed to do even under the current constitution: she wrote a new constitution and presented it to her cabinet for approval on January 14, 1893.

Queen Lili'uokalani's actions threatened the rich minority whose wealth depended on annexation. About one hundred of this cohort wrote an open letter declaring the queen "to be in attempted revolution against the constitution and government." Three days after she presented the new constitution, the missionary cohort occupied the government building, declared a new provisional government, and appointed Sanford Dole (yes, of the Dole pineapple company) Hawaii's first president. The USS *Boston* was dispatched by the American government to Honolulu, ready to deploy troops to support the new government. With the Hawaiian royalty deposed, the US could swallow up the new territory with very little effort.

Queen Lili'uokalani was arrested on January 16, 1895. There is an image of her, stony-faced and strong, being escorted by three uniformed officers into the palace, now her prison. She was confined to two rooms on the second floor. She later wrote, "That first night of my imprisonment was the longest night I have ever passed in my life."

On January 22, she was presented with a paper from the Dole government. It was an act of abdication. She was told that if she didn't sign it, she and six other revolutionaries—her friends and associates— would be executed. "For myself, I would have chosen death rather than to have signed it," she wrote soon afterward. But for the safety of her friends, she abdicated the throne.

The queen was charged with treason. "The only charge against me really was that of being a queen," she commented. After a public trial, she was convicted and sentenced to a fine of $5,000 and imprisonment at hard labor for five years. Her sentence was never carried out and likely was never intended to be. "Its sole present purpose was to terrorize the native people and to humiliate me," Queen Lili'uokalani wrote. She spent about eight months as a prisoner before she was paroled and pardoned. Ever resourceful, the queen made the best of her time locked in the palace. She composed music, translated important Hawaiian histories, and sewed an enormous quilt.

Shortly after her release, Queen Lili'uokalani decided to travel to America. She informed President Dole that her intentions were simply for a change of scenery to forget the sorrow of the last few years; she said she planned to visit family in San Francisco and friends in Boston. And although she would do those things, her true purpose was to travel to Washington, DC, to advocate for Hawaiian independence.

She traveled by train across the continent on the *Sunset Limited*, a route that is still operated by Amtrak between Los Angeles and New Orleans. With the meditative comfort of scenery rolling by, the queen later wrote of the journey:

> Miles after miles of rich country went by as we gazed from the windows of the moving train, and all this vast extent of territory which we traversed belonged to the United States. . . . I thought what splendid sugar plantations might here be established, how easily and profitably rice might be grown, and in some other spots with what good returns coffee could be planted . . .
>
> And yet this great and powerful nation must go across two thousand miles of sea, and take from the poor Hawaiians their little spots in the broad Pacific.

When Queen Lili'uokalani arrived in Boston, she began work on her memoir. Her book was published in January 1898, just a month before she and four Hawaiian delegates presented a petition to Congress with 20,000 signatures from native Hawaiians opposing annexation. But the queen's advocacy was ultimately in vain. President William McKinley valued the Islands as a military outpost. Hawaii was officially annexed to the United States on August 12, 1898, though it would not become a state for over sixty years.

Lili'uokalani's book resonated with Hawaiians. The foreword of the 2013 annotated edition notes that early copies of the book "in Island collections have been literally read to pieces." The queen remained an inspiration to her people for the rest of her life, continuing to speak out against annexation, as well committing her life to charitable work, musical composition, and the documentation and translation of important Hawaiian histories. She died in 1917. There is a sovereignty movement in Hawaii to this day.

\* \* \*

NOT ALL THE SUGAR PLANTERS supported annexation to the United States. Annexation meant that the plantations now had to abide by federal immigration policy and labor laws. Immigration by means of contract labor was illegal in the United States, so, upon annexation, 32,000 workers were immediately released from the labor contracts they had signed to come to Hawaii. Now these workers could push for competitive wages or even migrate to the American mainland.

The Chinese Exclusion Act of 1882, a racist law forbidding the immigration of most Chinese people, now applied to Hawaii and cut off its supply of Chinese laborers. So planters began to recruit from Japan; by 1900, more than half of Hawaii's population was Japanese.

When the US limited Japanese immigration at the turn of the twentieth century, plantations turned to Filipino workers. The Philippines was an American territory and its citizens were American nationals who could freely migrate. A small percentage of workers from Puerto Rico also came for the same reason. Filipinos made up nearly 20 percent of Hawaii's total population by 1930.

Labor was recruited by the Hawaiian Sugar Planters Association (HSPA), founded in 1895, which set up offices internationally. Blas Eugenio was a retired plantation worker interviewed in 1987 by the Center for Oral History at the University of Hawai'i at Mānoa. Eugenio was born on February 1, 1909, in Laoag, Ilocos Norte, Philippines, and emigrated in 1928 to work at the Koloa Sugar Plantation on Kaua'i. When his recruitment went through, he told his parents he was going to try his luck in America, and that he would send money home. His parents told him, "Okay, go, but be careful. Be a good boy over there."

Eugenio started work at 5 a.m. and worked ten hours; he was paid one dollar per day. His first job was a *kālai*, hoeing the cane fields, then a *hapai kō*, a worker who carried stacks of cut cane on his back and piled it to be loaded into train or mule carts. Then he became a cane cutter. "You work just like a mule," Eugenio said of this work. "In the morning you come sweat from top to bottom, you know. All your clothes wet already." Cutting and carrying cane was still done by hand in Hawaii through the 1950s.

Eugenio lived in a "bachelor's barracks." Housing was free, but he felt it was just as bad as the housing he had experienced in the Philippines. The plantation provided kerosene and water and took care of hospital bills for the workers. But if an employee was injured and could no longer work, "they no pay you nothing," Eugenio said. "For example, you happen to hurt in the working place, or you die over there, get accident over there, they no pay you nothing. . . . You just died just like chicken, you know. You no more nothing. They treat you just like more worse than animals."

Japanese and Filipino laborers often arrived with their families, and women became a more common sight on the plantations. They often worked the same strenuous jobs as men but were paid far less—or nothing at all. On a Wailuku plantation, female workers went on strike for 50-cent wages because they received only three meals a day as their pay. The laborers and managers compromised on 25 cents per day. And women are always subjected to the "second shift." After working up to ten hours a day on the plantation, they then had to care for the household, preparing food and cleaning.

Eventually, laborers pushed back against the low wages and poor working conditions. There were twenty workers' strikes in 1900 alone, and wages rose from $18 a month to $22 a month by 1918. However, $22 was less than the average *weekly* wage in the rest of America.

Barrack housing also gave way to duplex or fourplex bungalows, or housing with separate rooms for single male workers. The government began to regulate health and safety, and required "adequate cooking facilities, waste removal, and clean water" after several outbreaks of disease in the plantation camps, including bubonic plague.

The immigrant and migrant groups were kept separate in the camps, both for the comfort of being in a familiar culture and also because the plantation managers felt it would discourage labor organizing. Different amenities began to appear, such as tofu stores and bathhouses in the Japanese camps. A 1942 map labels sections of cottages by group: "Hawaiin, Moaula Japanese, Moaula Filipino, Hagasi Camp, Chong Camp, Spanish, Korean, Skilled Employee, and Portuguese Camp," giving a sense of the tremendous immigration that powered the plantations and created the diversity of Hawaii today.

By 1915, Hawaii was the third largest sugar producer in the world, after Cuba and Java. The irrigation infrastructure was largely completed by 1920, and the acreage of the plantations peaked at 236,000, up from 10,000 acres in 1867. After this point, sugar production continued to increase, but relied on increased production per acre.

The HSPA launched a breeding program with the intention of producing heartier, more productive cane. They started by crossing Hawaiian *officinarum* sugarcane varieties, kupuna kō, with wild *spontaneum* and *robustum* from India, adding hardness and disease-resistance to the soft heirloom canes. Legacy sugarcane varieties were discarded in favor of these new hybrids designed for mass agriculture.

In the 1950s, cane hybrid H50–7209 was developed. It grew tall and straight, was drought-resistant, had a hard shell that was resistant to insects, and had high juice and sucrose content. It was ideal for the massive twentieth-century sugar refineries, and by 1960 it made up 40 percent of cane plantings in the state. Sugar production doubled between 1920 and 1960, from 41 tons per acre to 83 tons, sometimes reaching 93 tons per acre—the highest per-acre yield on the planet.

By the mid-twentieth century, work at a Hawaiian sugar plantation meant a stable, well-paying job with union protection. But a workplace that respects its workers is too expensive for capitalism; sugar production was moved to countries without unions and worker protections, where the bottom line was as low as possible. Hawaii could not compete with growers in India, Brazil, and the Dominican Republic. In those countries, land costs as well as labor costs are lower, and sugar production is often subsidized by the government. American consumers expect a low price on a bag of white cane sugar, and one of the results of this expectation was the end of sugar cultivation in Hawaii.

When the plantations were shuttered, it was often crushing to their staff. Cynthia Juan, interviewed by oral historians in 1997, grew up in a family where everyone worked on a plantation, and married into another one. She was interviewed three years after the closing of the Hāmākua Sugar Company on the Big Island, where her husband, son, and father-in-law were employed.

"I think that's what my husband misses a lot, is what they call the *kaukau* time," she said of the community at the plantation. "They would sit down, and they would eat lunch and everybody would share whatever they had. They all bust 'em open and they'd all eat." With workers having heritage from all over the world, lunchboxes were a diverse treat. "So really, plantation life is a sharing of almost your entire life, you share with each other. And you get the good from everybody. It's hard sometimes to describe."

During Hāmākua's final season, in December 1994, Juan's family decided they were going to go watch the last harvest of the fields. They saw the fields burn, a technique some plantations employed to remove the sharp cane leaves before the stalks were cut.

"And there was my father-in-law, there was my husband, and there was my son, and they were all standing together. I was farther in the back with the two girls. And something just struck me as three generations here, and we're seeing this. It's as if they were burning up our lives."

Juan and her family kept a stalk of sugarcane growing in their backyard, which her husband, Norman, cut and replanted every New Year's Eve. "So this is something that he's told the girls, 'You know, if Mommy and Daddy are not around, we want you to do it.' So he's keeping a little part of his tradition, the lifestyle of the plantation alive."

HC&S (formerly Alexander & Baldwin) on Maui was the last sugar plantation to shut down, at the end of the harvest in December 2016. This closure was so recent that when I visited in May 2019, thousands of acres formerly dedicated to growing cane were still sending up feral shoots. Although cane is replanted after harvest for the heartiest crop, if it's left in the field it can continue to grow up from the roots. This second growth is called ratoon cane. I drove past miles and miles of it, the dominant plant of the landscape stretching on either side of the road from the mountains to the sea. It is a former monoculture, waiting for its next phase—which will likely be housing development.

The legacy of the plantations still affects the people and the landscape of Hawaii. Even after HC&S's closure, the water rights remained in their hands. It was only in November 2019 that a landmark water rights negotiation returned the majority of the water to small farmers. The demand for land by the navy and the tourism industry has made millions for former sugar planters. Castle & Cook was one of the largest sugar investors of the nineteenth century. The sale and development of their land on Oʻahu and Lanai grossed billions of dollars, and Castle & Cook's CEO, David Murdock, is one of the richest men in the United States, with a fortune of about $2.2 billion.

Currently, no one is growing sugarcane to produce sugar commercially in Hawaii. With the exodus of Hawaii's other major agricultural industries, such as pineapples, farmers have to rethink how to turn a profit. Some are turning to "value added products"—agricultural products that require an extra level of processing, such as vanilla, chocolate, coffee, and distilled spirits.

Distilleries have popped up across the Islands in the last decade. Currently there are thirteen distilleries in Hawaii, producing rum, vodka, shōchū (a Japanese spirit made from sweet potatoes, barley, or rice), okolehao (a spirit distilled from ti roots), whiskey, gin, and hand sanitizer (during the Covid-19 crisis). Two distilleries, Kō Hana on Oʻahu and Kuleana Rum Works on the Big Island, are producing rhum agricole, a grassy, vegetal spirit that was originally developed on Martinique in the nineteenth century. The white or dark rum is made by distilling fresh-pressed, fermented cane juice. It takes four tons of cane to produce 500 gallons of pressed juice, which is fermented and distilled into 55 gallons of rhum agricole. Because of the quantity of cane required, Kō Hana and Kuleana Rum Works have become the largest commercial cane producers on the Islands.

Because this rum is made from pure cane juice, it captures the true essence and flavor of the sugarcane. Both distilleries have opted to grow kupuna kō. Kō Hana currently grows 35 acres of legacy cane on Oʻahu—not too far from Anthony's farm—and plans to have 100 acres by 2024. Kō Hana makes their Hawaiian Agricole Rum from individual varieties of hand-cut legacy sugarcane. They mark each bottle with the variety of cane pressed and the season the cane was harvested. When distilled, each cane variety tastes distinctly different, the flavor notes ranging from briny, peppery green olive to sweet banana–papaya. Kō Hana embraces the variability—to them, that's the thrill of a small-batch product featuring a unique ingredient. And putting the name of each legacy cane variety on the bottle creates a direct association for the consumer. When I sampled the rum in their tasting room, my favorite was a rum distilled in October 2018 from Mahaiʻula, a bright red legacy cane. Whenever I pop the glass stopper out of its clear, square bottle, the rum smells of mowed grass and demerara sugar. It is the smell of fresh-cut sugarcane.

## The Bright and Sunny

Rhum agricole is often sipped straight, or with a twist of lime, to let its flavors come through. But this light cocktail is another great way to enjoy it. Don't skip the bitters; it ties together the grassy notes of the rum with the spicy ginger beer. The overall effect is like drinking a handcrafted cane-sweetened cola. Thanks to Robert Dawson of Kō Hana for the suggestion. For a nonalcoholic version of this drink, substitute sugarcane juice for the rhum agricole and use nonalcoholic bitters.

MAKES ONE DRINK

INGREDIENTS
6 ounces ginger beer
1 lime wedge
2 ounces rhum agricole
2 dashes aromatic bitters

Pour ginger beer into a Collins glass filled with ice. Squeeze the lime over the drink, twist the peel, then toss in the wedge. Add rhum agricole and stir, then finish with the bitters.

\* \* \*

KULEANA RUM WORKS' CANE FARM is down a long country lane in Hawi, an area on the northernmost tip of the Big Island. I drove past fields full of cattle and a wind farm, and the road ended in a foot-path down to a fishing spot by the ocean. I parked outside a tall electric gate, and after a few minutes Kuleana's founder, Steve Jefferson, pulled up. He burst out of his car, talking a mile a minute. Tall and lanky, he gesticulated wildly with his hands and moved with a determined, kinetic energy.

As he unlocked the gate to the cane field, Steve explained that Kuleana grows 20 acres but also purchases legacy cane from anyone they can. Their business creates a market for farmers practicing diversified agriculture, who are growing legacy cane as one of many local crops, a system that more closely resembles traditional indigenous agriculture.

A former developer, Steve and his wife were building houses in the early 2000s. Around 2006, just before the economic crash, his business began to stagnate. "You could tell that people were kind of done spending more and more money for things," Steve said. So he and his wife decided they were going to buy a sailboat and "go sailing around," with their one- and three-year-old kids. On an expedition to the Caribbean, they visited Martinique, and stopped by one of the island's many rhum agricole distilleries. On the way, they passed through a large sugarcane plantation and thought, "Oh, cool. It's totally like Hawaii." And when they tried the rum, Steve was blown away. He looked at his wife and said, "We've got to move back to Hawaii and start our own distillery."

The family weathered the recession in Colorado before returning to Hawaii in 2012 to open a distillery. The first task was finding the right sugarcane to make his rhum agricole. Steve got connected with Dr. Noa Kekuewa Lincoln, Associate Professor of Indigenous Crops and Cropping Systems at the University of Hawai'i at Mānoa, an authority on Hawaiian sugarcane. Lincoln had been working with living collections of kupuna kō since undergrad, and in his view distributing kupuna kō to diverse, living collections reduces the risk of losing any varieties. The more people who grow it, the better. In fact, it was Lincoln who submitted the kupuna kō varieties to the Ark of Taste. Lincoln invited Steve to visit the collection at Amy B. H. Greenwell Ethnobotanical Garden on the Big Island, about an hour's drive south. Steve got cuttings of all forty legacy varieties that Lincoln had identified. He started by growing two acres of cane, and after a few years he had enough cane to plant 20 acres.

We walked through the cane field, the bright red stalks and purple foliage of the colorful legacy cane plainly visible in the rows. Pua'ole, the flowerless cane; Laukōna, Halāli'i, Māikoiko. As Steve looked at his land, he told me why he chose the name Kuleana for his distillery. The word in Hawaiian means both responsibility and privilege.

"We've accepted it as our kuleana to establish maybe the world's largest native Hawaiian sugarcane farm with the most complete collection."

Steve opens the farm to anyone who wants to take cuttings to plant, whether for commercial or private use. "Some people feel like Westerners shouldn't have this," Steve said about the cane. "Great! You don't even have to talk to me. If you want, I'll just give you the code for the gate and you can take cuttings and take it back to wherever and we don't even have to talk. Because it's not our cane. How could we possibly sell it? To pretend like it's ours, it's beyond foolish."

The cane in Steve's field is cut and pressed with small, motorized presses, more akin in size and design to the mule-driven mills of the early nineteenth century. As soon as the juice is pressed, it begins to ferment, and the temperature in the fermentation tanks is carefully controlled. "Certain temperature ranges create certain esters," Steve told me. Esters are flavor compounds which yeast produce during fermentation. "We like a certain ester profile that makes these really fruity, tropical, luscious, just really good flavors."

We left the field for Kuleana Rum Shack, the distillery's nearby restaurant and tasting room, twenty minutes south along the coast in Waimea. The interior was designed with the no-fuss concrete utilitarianism of a garage. It's not something a mainlander might find welcoming, but in Hawaii, hanging out in your garage is what you do. A garage provides shade and protection from rain while allowing in the cool breeze. Steve wanted some of this vibe in Kuleana's space. The tasting room opened on January 20, 2019, just four months before we sat down at the bar. The menu featured fresh fish that had been swimming at 2 a.m., as well as a take on Hawaii's famous *musubi*, a sushi roll made with Spam. Their cocktail menu is also a book, with a full history of the cane written by Dr. Lincoln. There are centerfold pages on different heirloom canes with glossy color photos—including images of grassy-green, fresh-pressed juice. We ordered a flight of Kuleana's rums, a daiquiri, and a Mai Tai.

## Sugarcane Mai Tai

This Mai Tai is inspired by the drink served at Gaylord's, a former sugar plantation turned tourist destination on Kaua'i. A chilled, restorative drink for a hot day, it's lightly sweet and sour, and highlights the flavors of molasses and almond. Gaylord's features Koloa rum distilled on Kaua'i—another distillery that has started planting heirloom sugarcane. But it works equally well with a rhum agricole.

There are a few other ingredients that can be hard to find but make a huge difference in the quality of the drink. You can make orgeat, a sweet almond syrup, but I like the brand Liber & Co., which you can order online. Depending on where you live, you may be able to find fresh-pressed sugarcane juice, which is the best; bottled, pasteurized juice can be ordered online or you can find cane juice in cans in the grocery store, shelved with products from the Caribbean. It's worth sourcing: the rich, caramelized nose it adds to this classic cocktail is a game-changer.

You can make a nonalcoholic version of this drink by subbing in strong, cold green tea for the gold rum, orange juice for the Curaçao, and sugarcane juice for the dark rum (using 1.5 ounces of sugarcane juice for the whole drink).

TO MAKE THE VANILLA SIMPLE SYRUP

1 cup granulated white or demerara sugar
1 cup water
1 vanilla bean, split and scraped

Combine sugar and water in a mason jar or sealable plastic storage container with a tight lid. Shake until sugar is dissolved. Add the vanilla bean and allow it to infuse in the refrigerator for at least 24 hours and up to one month.

TO MAKE THE COCKTAIL

IN A COCKTAIL SHAKER, COMBINE:
¾ ounce fresh squeezed lime juice (about ½ lime, then toss the rind into your glass)
¼ ounce vanilla simple syrup
½ ounce orgeat
1 ounce rhum agricole
½ ounce Curaçao (NOT the blue stuff. You can substitute triple sec or Cointreau)

Shake with several ice cubes until cold. Strain into a rocks glass filled with lots of crushed ice.

THEN ADD:
½ oz fresh cane juice
1 ounce dark rum, "float" by pouring over the back of a spoon.

OPTIONAL:
garnish with a sugarcane swizzle stick

\* \* \*

WHILE WE CHATTED AT THE BAR, Steve pointed out that rum is a colonial by-product. While sugarcane is native to the Pacific, Western colonizers brought the technology to process sugar into molasses, and then to process molasses into rum. So, is it appropriate to take kupuna kō and use it to make a product that came from Hawaii's colonizers? I put the question to Steve.

Steve seemed flustered. "Yeah, so we're not trying to get into the politics of colonialism or whatever. Because we're actually, everybody who lives in Hawaii is actually a by-product of colonialism except for the native Hawaiians. Everyone who is here has some sort of tie because of that. And that's kind of what's made Hawaii Hawaii. And you know, none of us can speak for actions that others of us did in the past, nor we can in the future. But what we can do is sort of learn about what was done and why it was done."

I sipped through my flight and tried to process what Steve had said. Before we left, he turned one of his rhum agricole bottles around so I could see the label. The bottle itself looked like the type you write a message in and throw into the ocean, wooden stopper included.

"This is designed to be a delivery device for the story of Polynesians, of the Wayfinders, right? The double-hulled canoe. The celestial navigation story," he explained, referring to Kuleana's logo, a line drawing of a traditional Polynesian vessel on the ocean, stars in the sky behind it. The back of the bottle gave a brief history of sugarcane's voyage to Hawaii, and the definition of *kuleana*.

"By having a strong Hawaiian value as our name, it's daring, but it's more important for us that people learn the story. And it's just good business, because people like a good story."

* * *

BEFORE I CAME TO HAWAII, I had loved the idea of preserving a traditional crop through a craft spirit. But now, the idea wasn't sitting as pleasantly. When white Americans came to Hawaii, they forced Hawaiians to reject their own culture. The missionaries replaced the Hawaiians' religion, encouraged them to cover their bodies with Western clothes, and prevented them from dancing the hula. The plantation owners replaced diverse Hawaiian agriculture with monocrops and eventually replaced the Hawaiian queen with their own government.

But colonizers will allow a part of a culture to exist as long as it is prettily packaged for white, Western consumption. Docile, smiling hula girls are acceptable; so is Hawaiian music when it's sung by white Americans like Elvis Presley or Annette Funicello. The distilleries on Hawaii use the images and stories of Hawaiian culture in their branding. How long before single-varietal-pressed legacy sugarcane juice appears in organic markets next to the coconut water? And when it does, will it be a blessing that preserves kupuna kō, or cultural appropriation that steals identity—and profits—from native Hawaiians?

Weeks earlier, on Anthony's farm next to the highway and the Sears in O'ahu, I had asked him how he felt about the distilleries.

"If they support the indigenous culture, I'm on board," he responded immediately. "But . . . I don't think it's a *kānaka maoli* that's making that rum?" I confirmed it was not; neither of the rhum agricole distilleries I had visited had an indigenous Hawaiian in charge. "So it's an appropriation. I mean, they can probably go to sleep at night because they're saying, 'Hey, well, I'm keeping these native varieties alive!' But you're not giving back. You're giving back to yourself. The only way I think I would feel good about something like that rum kine ting is if they were actively giving back to the community. More than just the money.

"I think it's even worse because it's an alcohol, because alcohol has systematically destroyed indigenous cultures. . . . You only have to open your eyes and see Native America gets frickin' all this shit for being drunk and all of this crap. But who brought them the frickin' alcohol?"  •

Hawaiian legacy sugarcane collections, like Anthony's or Kuleana Rum Works', mean that an endangered plant is being preserved. But many Hawaiians feel kupuna kō should never be commercialized. There are already Hawaiians out there individually preserving their traditions in a rapidly changing world, as their ancestors did before them. An outsider like me can't know how many stands of kupuna kō grow in backyards and how many varieties have continued to grow for generations, passed down in the same family. There's a part of me that feels that these backyard stands of kupuna kō, harvested and sliced into chunks for thirsty kids, are the best kind of preservation. Not everything is for everyone, and Hawaiians have had enough taken from them.

# Dibé

## NAVAJO-CHURRO SHEEP

Navajo oral history says Talking God—who helped to form First Man and First Woman from ears of corn—also formed the Navajo-Churro sheep. He shaped their bodies from the clouds, their legs from willow branches, and their hooves and horns from a rainbow. Tobacco leaves became the sheep's ears and dawn became their faces, with rock crystals for their eyes. Then, Talking God blew the breath of life into the sheep and gave them to the Navajo.

I was thinking about Talking God and his gift as I tentatively approached a pickup truck with a Navajo-Churro ram tied up in the bed. It was June of 2019, and I was in Shiprock, New Mexico—less than 40 miles from Four Corners—at Diné Be'Iiná, "Sheep Is Life," an annual festival celebrating the Navajo-Churro. I had come aboard as a volunteer to assist the traditional foods demo, where we would butcher a ram. Until I spotted the ram in the pickup truck, I wasn't certain that "butchering" also included slaughtering. This would be my first time butchering a whole animal, and my first time being present at the death of anything larger than a fish.

When I approached, the ram shifted his head so he could peer at me over the tailgate. His horns were tied to the truck bed so he could only get one eye up, a golden iris with a horizontal pupil in the center. The ram had the typical look of a Navajo-Churro: he weighed about 150 pounds, 100 pounds lighter than a modern commercial ram of the same age. His light brown wool had been sheared, and he had a splotch of white on his forehead and down his nose. His horns were thick at the base and spiraled out from his head like those of a bighorn sheep. But unlike their wild cousins, it is not uncommon for a Navajo-Churro to sport four horns, and in rare cases, even six or eight horns.

When I'd worked with sheep before, they were easy to startle, happy to run you over, and entirely fixated on food. Not Navajo-Churro. They look you in the eye and size you up. You get a sense of individuality and personality. That's their wildness, preserved feral instincts that give them the capability to survive in the difficult climate and terrain of the Southwest.

This ram was raised for food and would be killed respectfully. Over the course of two days, he would be butchered and eaten from nose to tail, leaving behind only a handful of bones and a few internal organs. I'd help to cut away his skin and turn his guts into sausage. I'd eat his grilled meat and would learn to love Navajo-Churro skirt steak sliced and wrapped in a fresh whole wheat tortilla with a little flaked salt on top. This animal that was once a separate being, looking at me over the truck gate, would be transformed into a part of me.

Butchering this Navajo-Churro ram was Slow Food's mantra, "Eat it to save it," in the truest sense. A demand for the Navajo-Churro's meat is part of ensuring both the breed's survival and the survival of the traditional pastoral way of life for the Navajo.

The Navajo-Churro is one of the earliest domesticated animal breeds in America, the result of centuries of skilled husbandry. It has been called "the pride, food, clothing and money of the Navajos." The Navajo—or Diné, in their own language—are known worldwide for the quality of the warm, waterproof weavings made from Navajo-Churro wool. Diné associate the taste of mutton with the cuisine of home, and Navajo-Churro meat is considered medicinal by the Diné people. The sheep graze on plants that are respected as important medicine, so the meat is thought to embrace the healing qualities of the forage on which the sheep feeds. Navajo-Churro have very little lanolin—the oil that makes the fleece of other sheep feel greasy—and very little body fat. It's this fat and oil that gives the meat of other sheep breeds a musky funk. But Navajo-Churro meat is uniquely sweet and herbal. And while it's rare to eat an animal older than a lamb in other breeds, with the Navajo-Churro, you can eat animals up to five years old and the meat still tastes sweet—but you have to slow-cook it, I was advised.

On two separate occasions, the United States government nearly eradicated the Navajo-Churro sheep and the Diné way of life. In the 1860s, the Diné were forced into a concentration camp called Bosque Redondo, their animals seized or slaughtered by federal troops. After the Diné were allowed to return to their homeland, the federal government decided that overgrazing by sheep created soil erosion, and in the 1930s ordered that the sheep be slaughtered in a program called "stock reduction." Before stock reduction, the Diné owned almost 1 million sheep; by the 1970s, there were fewer than 400 Navajo-Churro left.

The breed remains threatened, but stable. According to the Livestock Conservancy, about 5,000 Navajo-Churro are registered nationally. To continue the work of preserving the breed, Navajo-Churros were boarded onto the Ark of Taste in 2006 to bring awareness to the sheep's culinary uses. Because Navajo-Churro sheep are particularly culturally significant, a "presidium" was formed. The Navajo-Churro Sheep Presidium is a loose collective of individuals and organizations that specifically supports Diné shepherds in finding a market for their meat. The presidium has focused locally in the Southwest, aiming to get Navajo-Churro meat added to restaurant menus and CSAs and sold at farmer's markets. They maintain a list of Navajo-Churro producers as well as a team of advisors who provide education for shepherds who want to improve their flock. And they create recipes, host cooking demos, and generally promote consumption of Navajo-Churro meat.

\* \* \*

WHEN I FIRST ARRIVED IN THE SOUTHWEST, I drove north out of Albuquerque, New Mexico, and emerged into a landscape I had only been familiar with from the television series *Breaking Bad*. But the desert was surprisingly green after a wet spring that had been desperately needed. After several years of crippling drought, many shepherds had sold their Navajo-Churro flocks, unable to feed their animals without wild forage and water. Other ranchers had relied on donations of hay to keep their sheep alive. Now, the luscious grasses and abundant flowers lined the washes and climbed the cliffs, heralding what would hopefully be easier times.

Just as the sun was setting, I rolled into my Airbnb in Aztec, New Mexico, just outside the Navajo Nation. "Aztec," historically, was a word used for any ancient Indigenous structures, and the town is named for the Puebloan Ancestor ruins within the city limits. This area is known for its ancient Puebloan ruins, including Chaco Canyon, and Mesa Verde in Colorado. The people that had once lived in these settlements migrated away about 600–700 years ago, during a time of sudden, deep erosion called "gullying" that had caused the water table to drop dramatically. It's their movement out of this area that allowed the Diné ancestors to move in.

The Diné are Athabaskans, a group that crossed the land bridge from Asia around 14,000 years ago. Most of the Diné's relatives populate Alaska and Canada, but the Diné themselves didn't stop migrating south, over thousands of years, until they reached the San Juan River.

The Diné creation story—*Diné Behane'*—is the telling of a journey. The narrative describes the travels of First Man and First Woman as they make their way through different worlds populated by different animals. A point of conflict forces the characters to climb up into each new world. Finally, they emerge into the Glittering World, Dinétah. Dinétah exists in the physical world as the land bordered by four sacred mountains: Sisnaajiní (Blanca Peak), Tsoodził (Mount Taylor), Dook'o'oosłííd (San Francisco Peak), and Dibé Nitsaa (Hesperus Mountain), which literally means "Big Sheep." Arriving in this area both spiritually and physically is what made the Diné themselves. In many versions of this story, sheep make an appearance.

Among the Diné, this story is understood to be as old as time itself. But domestic sheep arrived much more recently, with European colonists in the sixteenth century. Some believe that the presence of sheep in the creation story was to make the Diné ready to acquire the Navajo-Churro when they arrived. The sheep described could have also been wild bighorn sheep, which were hunted by the Diné ancestors, or even a type of native dog, whose pelt was used by other Indigenous groups for weaving. Others think the sheep were added to *Diné Behane'* as the oral history was retold over time, incorporating new events, when the sheep became an integral part of Diné culture.

Zefren Anderson, a Diné weaver, multimedia artist, and historian, has one more interpretation of the animal described in the creation story. I met Zefren briefly at Sheep Is Life. Tall and impeccably styled, with long, straight hair and round-framed glasses, he spent most of his time at the festival giving demos on how to process Navajo-Churro wool and weave with it. I watched him and his eager students wash wool in a little water before wringing it out and stretching it in the sun to dry. We spoke further by phone a few months later.

Zefren was inspired to learn more about the Navajo-Churro's origins after an apprenticeship with master weaver Roy Kady. Since then, Zefren has probably done more research on the arrival of the Navajo-Churro in Dinétah than any other person.

"The origin of the sheep is something that is very personal to most Navajo weavers and families," Zefren emphasized. "And that's why I always tell them this is my family and my origin, and I'm not necessarily saying it works for every Navajo family or individual or with their beliefs." He has come to a place where the historical record can coexist with the Navajo creation story.

Zefren has scoured historical documents and analyzed the specific texture of Navajo-Churro wool to track the history of the Navajo-Churro. "If you ever look at really good chief blankets," Zefren told me, speaking of the oldest examples of weaving from Navajo-Churro fleece, "they're not only lightweight, they're water-resistant, and they have a very high luster and sheen to them."

Navajo-Churro have an inner coat of lustrous wool and a shaggy outer coat that can reach up to 14 inches in length. The low lanolin content of the wool means that very little water is required to wash it, which is ideal in desert conditions. The wool is perfect for hand weaving because it is remarkably straight, strong, and durable. And it comes in over a dozen different natural colors, ranging from dark black to pure white as well as heather gray, tan, peach, and a light reddish-brown. Navajo-Churro wool is so recognizable and connected to Diné weaving that in the Art of Native America gallery at the Metropolitan Museum of Art in New York City, a Diné chief's blanket dating to 1840 is labeled "handspun undyed and indigo-dyed Churro fleece." The sheen of the wool in the blanket is unmistakable.

So, where did this unique wool and this unique sheep come from? Zefren believes that at least three different breeds of sheep were crossed to create the Navajo-Churro. One is the Spanish Churra sheep, an ancient breed from the hot and arid region of Castila y León, Spain. The Churra have white wool and black markings on their faces and legs, tasty meat, and survive well in extreme conditions. Conquistador Francisco Coronado brought a flock of Churra with him to North America in the 1540s.

After the Spanish Churra sheep were introduced, a French Huguenot named René Goulaine de Laudonnière arrived in Florida in 1564. In his "self-published epic," as Zefren described it, "he's accused of impropriety by one of his subordinates because he hires a woman to take care of his 'diverse amount of sheep and poultry.'" De Laudonnière likely brought a French breed of sheep to North America. In 1565, the Spanish expelled all the French living in Florida (after a deadly battle at de Laudonnière's settlement, Fort Caroline), and, as Zefren said, "vast amounts of livestock are put in control of the Franciscan order as they established their missions in Florida."

Spanish settlement began expanding into the Rio Grande valley, the eastern border of Dinétah, at first "illegally" and, starting in 1588, "legally" with the King of Spain's permission. As early as 1581, the Franciscans had begun sending missionaries into the area. In this era, the Franciscans wore a gray or brown habit of lustrous twill wool. The gray was created from black and white wool woven together. The raw material was sometimes sent from Spain, but the Franciscans also brought sheep with them to their missions.

In 1629, the Franciscans established a mission at Awatovi, a Hopi town, which they called San Bernardo de Aguatubi. At first, they made few converts to Christianity among the Hopi. But after a friar performed a miracle by allegedly curing a blind boy, many Awatovi Hopi converted. The town and mission remained until 1680, when it was destroyed by other Hopi resisting Spanish colonization and Christian conversion.

Archeological digs at Awatovi reveal that, before European contact, discarded bones were most commonly those of deer and pronghorn sheep. Domestic sheep and goat bones replaced them after the town became a mission. Awatovi was a huge contact point between the Europeans and the Navajo, with the Hopi as the intermediaries. Some Navajo traded with and some raided the Hopi to build up flocks of sheep. By 1630, a friar named Alonso de Benavides noted that the Navajo had large flocks of sheep.

The Spanish Churra, de Laudonnière's flock, and the Franciscans' sheep—some combination of these three genetics, and a few hundred years of isolated breeding by the Diné, created the Navajo-Churro. The Diné allowed ewes and rams to mate throughout the year, meaning that many lambs were born in winter, when forage was hardest to find. Only the toughest lambs survived, creating a breed built for the difficult conditions of Dinétah. The Diné also bred for wool color, trading rams between families to create diverse flocks. And, somewhere along the way, breeding created the most unique attribute of the Navajo-Churro: four horns. There are only five other breeds of sheep in the world that have the polycerate, or multi-horned, genetic mutation: four in the UK and one in Iceland.

By the early eighteenth century, the Diné had become known as shepherds and weavers. The weavings were utilitarian, warm and waterproof, woven from the raw colors of the Navajo-Churro wool, and their symmetry and unique, lustrous wool made them stunning. By the early nineteenth century, these blankets were coveted by neighboring Indigenous groups, as well as the Spanish and even Americans.

It was typically women who did the wool processing and weaving, and who owned and tended to the flocks. They took the sheep out of the corral in the morning and again in the late afternoon, and spun wool or weaved while they watched over the animals. Because they owned the livestock, women were considered wealthy, and had power and autonomy in making decisions for themselves and their families. Men and women had different but equally valued roles in Dinétah.

During the spring and summer, part of the family—again, usually the women—would move with the sheep in search of water and good grazing, while most of the family—often the men—would stay on their land and tend to the crops. In the winter, the entire family moved with their flocks to their winter hogans, which were close to wooded areas that supplied fuel, hunting grounds, and winter forage for the sheep. This pattern of seasonal movement is known as transhumance, and the Diné's transhumance was connected to the needs of their sheep.

\* \* \*

WHEN I ARRIVED FOR THE SHEEP IS LIFE FESTIVAL in Shiprock, I followed handmade signs that Zefren had spray-painted with a fuzzy, leaping Churro into the gravel parking lot. The festival was held at the local Diné College campus, and the lot was filling up with trailers and pens that housed bleating lambs. The festival was a chance for often far-flung shepherds, Diné and non-, to get together and expand their breeding stock by buying new rams. Others were there to buy their first sheep for a starter flock.

Shiprock gets its name in English from the jutting rock remnant of an ancient volcano that resembles a sailing ship, the desert playing the part of the rolling ocean. The Diné call it *Tse' Bit' A'í*, "Winged Rock." The town falls between the Four Sacred Mountains in Dinétah and is the second largest community in the Navajo Nation, which is the sovereign country of the Diné people. It covers much of the Four Corners region of New Mexico, Arizona, and Utah, approximately 17.3 million acres—roughly the size of West Virginia. It's home to more than 176,600 Diné—although there are at least 399,494 people who self-identify as Diné nationwide. It's the largest Indigenous tribe in the United States.

On their sovereign land, the Diné can make and enforce their own laws. Although the land of the reservation is owned by the federal government and its infrastructure is federally funded, the Diné have their own tribal government and maintain their cultural beliefs and language. Diné is the third most commonly spoken language in Arizona and New Mexico, after English and Spanish.

At the festival, the sheep would be judged for breed certification as well as for competitive awards. Shepherds hauled in freshly shorn wool to sell to national buyers, and there were several meetings of the various Navajo-Churro advocacy groups and breeders' associations. The festival was also open to the general public, and included curious outsiders who were perhaps familiar with Navajo weavings but nothing else. The educational part of the festival took place in the college's courtyard, surrounded by low, tan brick buildings: lectures, weaving, and spinning demos for both kids and adults, and booths for the Navajo-Churro Lamb Presidium and a shop with Sheep Is Life swag.

Between the ranchers and their lambs for sale, and the weavers and their wool, was the traditional foods demonstration area. A big grill fashioned from an old propane tank sat next to a pile of chopped cedar wood, and a pickup truck was parked under the shade of a tree. Two men, one in his sixties and the other in his twenties, unloaded cooking supplies from a truck. I approached and said I was a volunteer looking for Aretta Begay, head of the Navajo-Churro Sheep Presidium and the event organizer, for my assignment.

The older of the two men replied, "Well, I don't know where she is, but I need help." I accepted with enthusiasm. By the meat and the fire is exactly where I had hoped to be.

The man who had asked for my help was Ron Garnanez, shepherd, weaver, and president of Sheep Is Life. He had done the cooking and butchering demo here for ten years. Ron had tied his gray-white hair in a traditional knot and wore a yellow Slow Food T-shirt. His voice was always gentle, whether he spoke in English or Diné. His helper was Leron, tall in cowboy boots, a gray baseball cap over shoulder-length black hair, a wispy goatee on his chin. Leron had last volunteered at the festival a decade ago, when he was still a teen, before moving away to another part of the reservation. He had returned to the area with his family and radiated happiness that he could be at the demo that morning.

I started work: rinsing dishes with a hose and setting up tables with equipment while Leron chopped wood for the fire. We chatted while we worked.

"Oh, I love the sheep," Leron told me. He owns a small herd of Navajo-Churro, thirteen adults plus some lambs. He butchers and cooks the animals the same way that Ron would demonstrate that day.

"The Churros are stunning. They're so beautiful," I remarked, having seen them for the first time in person in their parking lot pens.

"You know, that's what I always say! I always say that." He glowed like a proud parent. "They're like the mustangs of the reservation. Very, very hardy. They can give birth in the snow and those lambs will survive. They're just amazing. They're just magical."

Ron handed me a blue corn cake for breakfast, a dry and fluffy flapjack, and asked me to peel potatoes for the blood sausage we would make that afternoon. Leron cut sharp cedar sticks that would be used to hold together the organ casing, stuffed with a blood filling.

Then it was time to butcher. Visitors gathered and elders set up camp chairs. A kindergarten and first-grade class arrived with their teachers, who carefully arranged the little students on the dusty ground. The school comes every year, one teacher told me. Some of the kids who lived on farms had perhaps seen butchering before; others hadn't. Throughout the demo, I heard the teachers patiently repeating, "They're butchering. That's meat. This is where meat comes from." This was a lesson that I wished more people who choose to eat meat got the opportunity to learn.

Leron lifted the ram out of the back of the pickup, laid him on the ground on his side, and tied his legs together.

"Good morning, everybody," Ron announced. "Is it still morning? Yá'át'ééh, yá'át'ééh." The audience chuckled and greeted him in return. It was about 11 a.m.

Ron used an old Diné word that I didn't catch. "Do you have any idea what I just said?" he asked the children.

"You're butchering!" a few called out.

"Yes. It's kinda more of an ancient word than ná'á'ah. So, I think it's a more friendlier way of saying it than ná'á'ah. You're harvesting, not butchering."

"This is a Navajo-Churro, almost two-year-old ram," Ron explained. "The reason why I choose a ram is I want you to experience the taste of the meat. Because the commercial breed of ram, they don't taste good." Another knowing chuckle from the audience.

The ram was lying quietly on the ground. I realized my hands were trembling with adrenaline.

"The very first thing you do is you pick them, you say, 'I want that one.'" Ron pointed to the air, reenacting selecting a sheep from his flock. "So you're chasing it around, chasing it, chasing it, chasing it. And after a while, you get that feeling that maybe this is not the one." The audience again chuckled. "Then, lo and behold, the One steps in right there. That's how they kinda pick me. So that's how it's easier to deal with the butchering process." Because, the belief is, one of the animals chooses to go.

"And then you take a tuft of hair from the back of their head right back here." Ron grabbed a pinch of fluff from just behind the ram's skull. "We leave it in the corral." He mimicked dropping the wool in the dirt. Through this process, the spirit of the animal remains in the corral. "You're taking the shell."

Ron signaled to Leron that he was ready. Leron grabbed the animal's horns, pulling its head back to expose the neck. "You see this jawbone right here?" Ron showed the audience. "That's where it should be, right where this jawbone is"—and with that, he cut the animal under the jawbone, across its throat, through the muscle and through half of the trachea. The ram audibly gasped; the crowd was mostly silent. A bowl was placed underneath the neck to catch the blood, and it splattered against aluminum, bright red and frothy.

It wasn't until the ram relieved its bowels that the children reacted with a unified "Ewwwww!" The ram gasped its last breaths in tiny trumpet-like bleats. "It's dying," another child commented, not in horror or sadness, but in understanding.

The ram's scrotum was cut off first, because, Ron explained, it can cause a poor flavor in the meat if left on too long. Then, Ron showed me two special cuts he makes in the sheep's underside, specific to butchering Navajo-Churro. The cuts show the Holy People that this is a sheep, man's food, not a wild food stolen from the Holy People. The high cut is to thank Father Sky for the rain, and the low cut is to thank Mother Earth for the food.

"So that's your prayer," Ron said. "Butchering is also like a little religious practice."

Ron asked me to hold one of the ram's legs. I held its little wrist, still warm, in my hand. I turned the leg and created the tension that allowed the hide to be cut off. Ron handed a knife to me, and Leron showed me how to cut the thin layer of fat under the skin while pulling the pelt back.

"Cut white," Leron said, slicing about a half-inch above the meat, the pelt separating a knife stroke at a time. "Cut white right here. Cut white."

It was a long process, and we had been working more than forty minutes before the animal was hung from a tree, and Ron removed the hide with a final pull.

"Ok, who wants a blanket?" Ron asked the assembled crowd, and some of the kids shouted "Me! Me!" in response. The pelt was set aside to dry.

By this time, the schoolkids had lost interest and were poking at ants on the ground and chattering. The teachers took them away to another part of the festival, and about a half dozen people pulled their chairs in, close enough to peer into the animal's carcass. What had been a large lecture became an intimate class. One of the participants was an advisor to the Miss Navajo Nation pageant, a four-day competition of "Navajo knowledge and skills" that includes butchering a lamb. A white husband and wife, ranchers from Colorado, were also there. They had a flock of Navajo-Churro and liked that the breed was smaller than commercial breeds, which made it much easier for a single person to butcher. A few Diné elders, men and women, also sat spectating.

The ram was broken down into its parts, each praised for its many uses and delicious flavor. The front legs were cut off; Ron showed me how to feel for the joints, much like carving a Thanksgiving turkey. The head was removed, singed on the fire, and set aside for roasting later. The brisket came off, a chest cut sometimes called skirt steak, the butcher's cut, or the shepherd's cut. Unlike a cow's brisket, it's quick-cooking and can be thrown directly on hot coals, so the shepherds have something to eat as they head back out to care for the flock.

Ron cut open the belly. I held a bowl to catch the animal's warm guts, which slid into the vessel with a watery plop. The empty inside of the ram smelled clean, due to its free-range, forage-fed diet. Ron pulled the caul fat off the organs, a web of white, which he handed to me to be laid in the sun to dry. When it's dry, it becomes brittle, and it is often broken into pieces and eaten with the liver or mixed into sausages. Finally, the rack of ribs was removed with a hatchet.

A pit was dug into the dirt, and Ron poured water through the large and small intestines, squeezing it out with any feces into the pit. Very little water was used with remarkable efficiency, and the waste that ended up in the pit would be safely buried. Some of the sheep's four stomachs were cleaned out in a similar way and set aside for blood sausage. The green grass in one stomach was cleared out and thrown into the pit—but, as one woman pointed out, this partially digested forage was traditionally eaten. It was like a probiotic, she told me, but was also valuable because there weren't many greens in a historical Diné diet.

Another stomach is considered powerful medicine when eaten raw. When offered a piece, I thought to myself, "Are you really going to eat that raw stomach?" On these trips, when someone asks if I want to do/ try/experience something/go somewhere, my policy is to always say yes. I popped a slice of raw stomach in my mouth. It was surprisingly crunchy and tasted like a barnyard.

The gall bladder also merited praise. Ron said that sometimes you'd drink the contents of the gallbladder, or dip cooked meat into its juices, like a sauce.

An older man added, "We used to save it for the elders. They got first dibs on it." He went on to reminisce: "In 1971, I spent three days with a traditional family out by Window Rock," the Navajo Nation capital in Arizona, "and that's all they fed me, morning noon and night. Mutton. When I finally left, I was thinking to myself, 'By golly, if I don't ever eat another piece of mutton, it would be all right with me.' About a week later, I started getting those cravings." The Diné listening laughed knowingly. "And I was working there in Farmington and there was a real nice café there. At least once a week, I'd go to the café and I'd walk in, those ladies they got to know me and they'd come over and they'd hand me a menu. Just as I reached out for the menu, they'd snatch it back and say, 'Ah, we know what you want! Mutton!'"

As Ron and I worked, men and women, Diné and white, sat under the shady tree, trading stories and peals of laughter. The conversation flowed back and forth in English and Diné.

When the carcass was broken down and the organs cleaned, it was time to make 'ach'íí'. Sometimes called twisters, these are sections of the small intestine wrapped around strips of fat pulled from the organs. When grilled, they cook crispy on the outside while the fat melts in the middle, gushing out when you take your first steamy bite. I stood around a table with three elder Diné women who showed me how wrap the intestine tightly, and without gaps, around the fat. When I displayed my efforts, they cooed in Diné, and I laughed, flattered and shy. In English they added, "Very good!" I have never felt more proud.

"OK, time to grill!" Ron announced when the 'ach'íí' were finished. An elder named Sarah—who had traveled around the world with her daughter, most recently to China, and who wore a conical *dóulì* hat to keep the sun out of her eyes—worked on whole wheat tortillas, taking balls of dough from a bowl and tossing it back and forth between her skillful hands as the dough stretched and widened. Then she slapped them on the grill.

For the first round, all the quick-cooking—and quick-spoiling—bits went on the fire. So, on went the organ meats: the heart, the liver, the spleen stuffed with fat and green chilies, the 'ach'íí'. Then some of the cuts of meat: the ribs and the skirt steak.

"No seasoning?" I asked as the meat was loaded onto the grill.

"No season," Sarah told me. "We never put season on anything. The sheep already has it."

The meal was free for all the festival visitors, to give them a taste of the sweet Navajo-Churro meat. We lined up, grabbed a tortilla, and filled our plates with slices of spleen, 'ach'ii', ribs, and my favorite, skirt steak. Food—especially meat—tastes different when you have spent the day with it. The smell of the animal in its life is in the taste of the meat, but perhaps only the butcher knows it's there.

About 4 p.m., we got started on the blood sausage. All the Diné were the most excited for this dish. It's something you can only make when you butcher and the blood is fresh.

## Navajo-Churro Blood Sausage

Ron began by taking a very large pot and filling it three-quarters of the way full with water. He set it over the fire to boil. He asked me to slice jalapeños thin, while he took the bowl of the ram's fresh blood and mixed in the potatoes I had chopped that morning. Sliced fat from around the intestines was added as well, and he broke the caul fat into pieces—now waxy and dry—and added it to the mixture.

"The more fat in it, the better it is," Ron instructed. He added my sliced chilies, perhaps 1 cup, to the bowl, then blue cornmeal.

*recipe continues >>*

"Blood, chilies, potatoes, cornmeal," I repeated, writing my mental recipe.

"Salt," Ron added.

To get some sense of proportions, I later checked a Diné recipe from a 1970s book called *Cook Book: The Navajo Homemaker*, released by the Office of Navajo Economic Opportunity. The recipe suggested 4 cups of sheep blood, 1½ cups sheep fat, 1½ cups cornmeal, 1 tablespoon salt, and 3 cups chopped potatoes.

"Whatever you want to put in," elder Sarah instructed. "If you have cabbage, you put cabbage."

"You get creative!" added another elder woman nearby.

A foraged herb that Ron called wild parsley went in. For a stronger flavor, he recommended roasting it before you add it to the sausage. Ron mixed all the ingredients together with his hands.

Ron cautioned me to wait for the water to boil before starting to fill the organs with the sausage mixture. If the sausage sits too long, the cornmeal settles and the texture is uneven. So when the water boiled, that was our cue to fill the organs with the sausage mix. We tied one end of the large intestine and stuffed in the filling. If the intestine rips, that's OK, you tie it off and start again. Ron instructed me to squeeze out any air bubbles but give it some room at the ends, because the filling will expand when it cooks and you don't want it to burst. We turned the sheep's multiple stomachs inside out and filled them three-quarters full, then secured them at the top with the sharp sticks Leron had made that morning.

Leron came over to inspect our progress. "I can taste it already!"

"You mouth is watering, huh?" Sarah teased.

The sausages went into the pot of boiling water and cooked for about an hour, until they were firm and dark. We sliced them while they were still hot and served them immediately.

Those who remained at the festival—the weavers, the shepherds, and a few late-coming visitors—gathered around quickly, not wanting to miss out on this rare treat. The sun was low on the horizon, sending long red streaks of light into our space under the tree. And as always happened when the Diné gathered, folks started telling stories. Leron was chatting with a festival visitor as he sliced into the blood sausage. I caught the conversation just as Leron asked the visitor if he had ever heard of Manuelito.

"No, who's Manuelito?" the man, an Anglo rancher, asked.

"He's one of our great heroes."

* * *

MANUELITO WAS BORN ABOUT 1818 near Bear Ears, Utah. He was given many names over his life: Askii Diyinii (Holy Boy), Naabaahi Jóta' (Warrior Grabbed Enemy), Naabáána Badaaní (son-in-law of Late Texan), and Hastiin Ch'il Hajin (Man of Black Weeds, referring to the place of his birth). The name Manuelito was given to him by the Mexicans, and became the name he was most widely known by.

His son, Naaltsoos Neiyéhí or Bob Manuelito, was interviewed by anthropologists in the 1960s. Naaltsoos was in his nineties at the time.

"Manuelito was born after his mother endured three days of hard labor," Naaltsoos recounted. "When his father learned of his son's birth, he took the newborn outside and presented him to the east, to the Holy People, and prophesied that his son would be a great leader."

In the most famous photo of Manuelito taken as an adult, by an Anglo photographer, he is pictured shirtless, with a woven Diné rug over his lap, cradling a rifle in his right arm. You can see a scar, from a bullet wound allegedly inflicted by his enemy and captor, Kit Carson. He has high, prominent cheekbones, and looks into the distance with a hardness around his eyes.

Manuelito had four wives, but his favorite was Asdzáá Tł'ógi, or Juanita. She was born around 1845, and oral histories say she was perhaps from Zia Pueblo, brought to Dinétah enslaved as a child. But she was considered Diné and free by the time she was in her twenties. She is stunning in photos, holding the camera in a bold gaze. She is always dressed in layers of traditional Diné clothing: moccasins and wrapped leggings, intricately woven *biils*—two woven rugs, stitched together into a dress and cinched at the waist—and silver and turquoise necklaces, bracelets, and rings.

The United States conquered New Mexico in 1846, absorbing the former Mexican territory into what is now the Southwest. The first peace treaty between the American government and the Diné was signed shortly after. In 1850, a second treaty was ratified, and a concession of this agreement allowed for the establishment of military bases and trading posts on Diné land. This treaty led to the building of Fort Defiance in 1851, a US Army outpost that still exists as a town northwest of Gallup, New Mexico. Conflicts arose around the new American forts, particularly because the tenants claimed prime Navajo-Churro grazing ground for their own livestock. In 1857, a new commander took over Fort Defiance, Major William Thomas Harbaugh Brooks. Manuelito, by this time viewed as the leader of the local Diné clans, didn't welcome the new commander right away, a snub which made Brooks nervous. When Manuelito did visit, he and Major Brooks had an angry exchange over the grazing lands.

On May 29, 1857, US troops tried to drive flocks of Diné sheep, most of which belonged to Manuelito, off of land where they wanted their own flocks to graze. Manuelito stood his ground, telling Major Brooks that he claimed the "water, grass and grounds . . . that he was born and raised there, and he would not give it up." Brooks responded that he would use force to access the grazing lands, and that night, his troops slaughtered all Diné sheep in the fields.

"Our duty remains to chastise them into obedience to our laws," Brooks wrote. "After tomorrow morning war is proclaimed against them."

Although the conflict was between Fort Defiance and local Diné clans, war was declared against the whole Navajo people. Over the next two months, at least two hundred Diné men were killed in battles around Fort Defiance, while the Americans suffered few casualties. After a brief peace, Manuelito stormed Fort Defiance with a thousand

Diné warriors on April 30, 1860. The Diné lost, but only narrowly. This near win prompted the federal government to instigate a forced removal of the Diné people from their homeland, to a place far east of Dinétah called Bosque Redondo, about 1,000 acres surrounding Fort Sumner in modern-day New Mexico.

The governor of the New Mexican territory wrote of this plan, "To gather them together little by little onto a Reservation away from the haunts and hiding places of their country, and there be kind to them. . . . Soon they will acquire new habits, new ideas, new modes of life: the old Indians will die off and carry with them all latent longings for murdering and robbing; the young ones will take their places without these longings; and thus, little by little, they will become a happy and contented people."

The governor enlisted Kit Carson to enact his plan. Carson was born in Kentucky in 1809, and as an adult he followed the frontier westward. He gained renown as a murderer for hire, killing Native Americans. In 1863, Carson sent a message to the Diné: "Go to the Bosque Redondo, or we will pursue and destroy you. We will not make peace with you on any other terms."

Carson marched into Dinétah with over five hundred soldiers. His troops destroyed crops, cut down orchards, and slaughtered the sheep. He made pacts with other tribes who had been warring with the Diné, and enlisted them to burn homesteads and capture Diné. Women and children were enslaved; men who surrendered were humiliated and murdered. Some families escaped capture and hid in the mountains. Carson waited for starvation to force them out.

Oral histories passed down through families remember the horror of Carson's campaign. Jane Begay, one of several Diné elders interviewed in the 1970s about their families' memories of the period, recounted a story passed down by her great-grandmother:

> My mother gave birth to several girls, but only one son. They
> were fleeing from the enemy when the son was born, and
> they had very little food. The baby was fed plant seeds, but
> he did not survive. He died from lack of mutton . . . They

never had enough mutton to eat because they were always
on the move, fleeing from the enemies. . . . The soldiers
had already taken away the sheep. . . . A Navajo woman and
a man on horseback told them that the People were taking
shelter at Fort Defiance. They were told that it was becoming impossible to find a safe place to hide. Many of the
People had been killed. . . . The People all moved toward
Fort Defiance.

By the end of 1863, thousands of desperate and starving Diné had
turned themselves in at American forts. Six thousand Diné were in cap-
tivity by March 1864 and began the Long Walk to Bosque Redondo.
The Long Walk was no single event, but many separate treks endured
by groups of Diné. The Walk took two weeks at least, stretching over
242 miles.

"Some of the old people fell behind and they wouldn't let us go
back and help them," Luci Tapahonso wrote in her poem "In 1864."
"Some babies, children and some of the older men and women were
swept away by the river current. We must not ever forget their screams
and the last we saw of them—hands, a leg, strands of hair floating."
Mary Juan was told by her grandmother, "Some of the People's feet
were frozen or frostbitten while on the Long Walk. They would hud-
dle along the side of the road covered up with rocks or cedar trees to
keep them warm. They were left behind."

For many years, Manuelito evaded capture and was among the
Diné in hiding. His resistance became a symbol of hope and courage to those who were interned. Recognizing this, Carson targeted
Manuelito. A Santa Fe newspaper wrote, "With his [Manuelito's] capture the last vestige of Navajo power in the Navajo country will be
broken up."

Manuelito had about fifty followers with him, and a few horses
and sheep. He told a fellow Diné, "Here is all I have in the world. See
what a trifling amount. You see how poor they are. My children are
eating roots." But he would not surrender. He said, "his God and his
mother lived in the west and he would not leave them; that there was

a tradition that his people should never cross the Rio Grande. . . . He had nothing to lose but his life; and they could come and take that whenever they pleased, but he would not move."

His wife, Juanita, was still by his side. Bighorse, a Diné warrior, said of her, "She is a very tough lady. She is brave and uses guns and bows and arrows. She is always by Manuelito."

In 1866, Manuelito and his followers finally turned themselves in. Manuelito was "wounded and ill," and chose the uncertainty of internment at Bosque Redondo over the certain death of remaining on the run. But what he found at Bosque Redondo was a nightmare: a barren, treeless landscape. An American soldier described the only water source as "a little stream winding through an immense plain, and the water is terrible, and it is all that can be had within 50 miles. It is full of alkali and operates on a person like castor oil."

A military outpost, Bosque Redondo had adequate housing for the US officers and soldiers, but no housing was built for the interned Native Americans. The Diné dug shallow holes in the ground and covered them with branches and brush. Firewood was not provided; families walked for miles to collect enough fuel to stay warm and cook their food. There was no sanitation system, so the already alkaline drinking water quickly became contaminated with human waste.

The presence of thousands of Native Americans at the internment camp stressed the resources of the entire New Mexican territory. With much of the locally produced food going to feed those interned, prices for commodities like meat skyrocketed. The Diné were expected to start farming to feed themselves, but the soil in the area was too poor to grow crops. The stunted corn that did grow was consumed by a plague of insects. The government-provided rations were "scanty and often spoiled," and consisted of foods entirely unfamiliar to the Diné. The government gave out coffee, bacon, and rations of flour that were documented to contain "bits of stale broken bread, and something that resembled plaster of Paris."

Only a handful of Navajo-Churro sheep survived to make the walk with their shepherds to Bosque Redondo. They were too precious to eat, but there was too little wool to weave the Diné's traditional warm, dry clothing. It was at this time that many Diné began dressing in the Spanish style that is considered traditional in the culture today: calico or sateen skirts and velveteen blouses. They began to weave with commercial yarn, producing blankets to try to stay warm.

The Diné died in incredible numbers of exposure, starvation, and disease. Mary Juan recounted her grandmother's story of being enslaved by one of the American troops that manned the internment camp. "I usually chopped wood for them," she told her granddaughter. "The . . . men were very mean. 'You work for me. You are my slave,' they told me. I never made any of them my husband, not for one night."

The Bosque Redondo prison camp operated for five years, from 1863 to 1868. In those years, 11,000 Diné were interned there, and more than 2,500 died. The cost to the federal government was 10 million dollars. Finally, the government realized that the camp was a humanitarian and economic failure and decided that it had to end.

Civil War hero General William Tecumseh Sherman led the US delegation at the negotiating table to decide the fate of the Diné. Sherman initially pushed for the Diné to be removed to "Indian country," Oklahoma, where the Cherokee and Choctaw had been marched and resettled. Barboncito, a Navajo leader of renown, famously replied, "I hope to God you will not ask me to go to any other country except my own."

On June 1, 1868, Manuelito and other Diné leaders marked an "X" on the treaty, the document that would allow them to return to Dinétah. It is rare in American history that Indigenous people sign a treaty with the US government that is cause for celebration; the 1868 treaty is one of these exceptions. June 1 is still celebrated as Treaty Day among the Diné people.

The Diné were restricted to a smaller slice of land than their traditional homeland, but it was, at least, between the four sacred mountains. There were conditions, including American education for the children and adherence to Christianity. But the United States agreed to recognize the Diné as a sovereign people, who would set up their own self-governing nation.

By the end of the month, the more than 8,000 survivors of Bosque Redondo began the journey home, a line of humans ten miles long. Manuelito said, "The days and nights were long before it came time for us to go to our homes. . . . When we saw the top of the mountain from Albuquerque we wondered if it was our mountain, and we felt like talking to the ground, we loved it so, and some of the old men and women cried with joy when they reached their homes."

The trauma of the years at Bosque Redondo stayed with the Diné people. Tribal elder Mary Pioche told Diné historians in the 1970s, "When men and women talk about Hweeldi [Bosque Redondo], they say it is something you cannot really talk about, or they say they would rather not talk about it. Every time their thoughts go back to Hweeldi, they remember their relatives, families, and friends who were killed by the enemies. They watched them die, and they suffered with them, so they break into tears and start crying. That is why we only know segments of stories, pieces here and there. Nobody really knows the whole story about Hweeldi."

When the Diné returned home, Manuelito was appointed head of the Navajo police, the Diné-directed law enforcement that still exists to this day. Determined to keep the Navajo Nation as a sovereign people, he made several trips to Washington, DC, to meet with the president. His first journey was his most famous, an 1874 trip to meet with President Ulysses S. Grant. Juanita accompanied him on this journey, the only woman in the delegation. Several famous portraits of her were taken on this trip. Although many Diné women had begun to wear skirts and blouses by this time, Juanita was always in her traditional, woven biil, buckskin leggings, and moccasins.

Juanita's granddaughter remembered, "When the men became homesick and hungry, she brought forth Navajo food: jerked meat, parched corn, and a paste made from ground piñons mixed with parched corn. . . . Her husband Manuelito wanted his wife Juanita to go on the trip because she spoke well and maybe she could persuade the president to let the Navajos keep their lands. Manuelito said the president's back was 'stiff' and perhaps Juanita's words could soften him."

Manuelito became a role model in his support of American education for Diné children. He believed education was both a tool and a weapon that could be used to ensure the survival of the Diné in Anglo America. He is quoted as saying that it was as though the Diné were at the bottom of a canyon, and education was the ladder that would let them climb out. To this day, the Diné value education—Sheep Is Life, for example, took place on the campus of the Diné-founded Diné College, the same institution that documented oral histories of the Bosque Redondo in the 1970s.

But Manuelito's words were also exploited by Americans. The Bureau of Indian Affairs used his "ladder" as fodder to force Diné children into boarding schools, where they were treated as prisoners and frequently beaten and starved. The schools forbade the Diné language and traditions, and even forced changes in physical appearance. Many Indian schools across the country would take "before and after" photos, showing the contrast between long hair and traditional garb and a dramatic "civilizing" of the same student, with short hair and an Anglo suit.

Manuelito bore his own personal trauma when it came to American education. To set a good example, in 1882 he sent two of his sons to boarding school in Carlisle, Pennsylvania. In less than a year, both contracted a deadly disease. One died in Carlisle, the other shortly after returning home. This tragedy may have been Manuelito's undoing. In 1894, he died "from a combination of alcoholism and pneumonia." He is remembered by the Diné people as "a warrior who resisted foreign domination."

Juanita moved in with daughters near Tohatchi and dedicated the rest of her life to caring for her family. She raised her grandchildren, herded her sheep, and wove. Her grandchildren remembered clearly the events of the day of her death, sometime around 1910. She rode her donkey to Tohatchi, herding the family's sheep to be dipped—a chemical bath that prevented parasites like ticks and lice, required by the federal government. That evening, staying with extended family, she complained of a stomachache and went to bed early. She never woke up.

\* \* \*

ON THE SECOND MORNING of the Sheep Is Life festival, I woke up still smelling of cedar fire and sheep even after a shower. I was on-site early to catch the Navajo-Churro judging. But when I arrived at 8am, the show tent was empty and most of the ranchers were still having their coffee. It wasn't uncommon for schedules to run at a leisurely pace out here.

In the parking lot, some of the Navajo-Churro lambs gamboled outside of their pens. Their bright, black eyes, nubby horns and natural smiles were a joy. Their long tails still dangled between their legs. Most sheep—including the Navajo-Churro—get their tails docked, or shortened, for sanitary purposes. I walked around and chatted with a few white ranchers, down from Colorado, about the competition and what the judges would look for. I was told the four horns the breed is prized for can also cause problems in the animal's appearance; sometimes the horns can corkscrew and grow into the face and they must be carefully filed down. Wide, curling horns are the most desirable. Multiple pairs of horns can also lead to a genetic condition called a cleft eye. The shape of the eye socket looks like a triangle, not an almond. It doesn't hurt the sheep but counts against them in terms of the breed standard.

Starting in the early twentieth century, the Navajo-Churro were forcibly interbred by the Federal Government with other varieties of sheep like Rambouillet. The Government felt these crossbred sheep would be more profitable: they hoped they would mature faster and produce more meat, as well as wool that could be sold at a higher price. But the short, fibrous wool of these hybrids were not good for hand-spinning and weaving, and the Rambouillet-bred sheep weren't as skillful foragers and survivors as the pure Navajo-Churro.

Since the 1970s, breeding programs have worked to recover the traditional Navajo-Churro characteristics based on historical depictions, descriptions and wool samples. Each animal a breeder wants to be registered must be inspected in person, and as one rancher told me: "You can have two registered parents, but there's no guarantee the offspring would be registered."

The sheep are most celebrated for their wild and capable spirit, something that isn't considered in the physical judging, but seems to come along with the selected physical characteristics. One rancher told me a story about how he lost his sheep for ten days at a past Sheep Is Life festival:

"Somebody came down from Salt Lake, and they wanted to demonstrate to everyone at Sheep Is Life how wonderful border collies could be for moving your sheep around." The shepherd asked the rancher if he could borrow a few of this sheep for the demo. "And I had brought four sheep to sell and I said, sure, I'm going to sell them anyway. I said, you want me to drive over there? 'Oh no, we'll herd them over.' So I let the sheep out . . . and then the sheep said, screw this, jumped over the dog and disappeared into the woods of Canyon de Chelly, like a million square miles of wilderness." He laughed, remembering his exasperation.

"These sheep, they'd been born at our place. They'd been fed every day and watered. And they survived for like ten days. We tracked them, and finally found them. I have respect for them, the fact that this domestic animal could survive. We'd be out tracking, we saw bear tracks, we'd hear coyotes. They had basically no water. They survived. . . . I don't want to breed that out of them."

In the Traditional Food Demo area, our task of the day was to make a dinner to feed all the festival workers and volunteers, as well as anyone from the breeder's meetings that wanted to stick around. We heated water for sumac tea: two handfuls of dried staghorn sumac berries added to a large, tin coffee pot of hot water, and then a spoonful of sugar for each cup of liquid. It would be cooled, then iced, until it was a light red color, tart and fruity, and as sweet as Kool-Aid.

Ron gave Sarah the legs from the ram to de-bone and slice for soup. A few other women worked as well, and we sat around a big table. The air was cool, our corner of the festival was quiet, and the smell of cedar smoke and brewing coffee wafted over us. I peeled and sliced pounds of potatoes and carrots and listened to the elder women talk to each other in Diné. After one woman hiccupped, and all the others cracked up, Rose, another elder, turned to me and translated:

"When you're hiccupping, it means you want mutton. That's why they're laughing."

We filled a big pot with the sliced mutton, carrots and potatoes, celery, wild parsley, salt, and pepper. We made blue corn mush and fry bread, deep-fried flatbreads made from white flour.

I helped to serve dinner to those who worked so hard to make the festival possible. I cleaned up, washed the dishes, and as the sun's rays were getting long and golden, I shook Ron's hand in the Diné way and thanked him for all his time and patience. I said goodbye to Leron too, and thanked him for all the time he took to talk with me.

\* \* \*

AFTER BOSQUE REDONDO, the federal government wanted the Diné to return to self-sufficiency, so they were given 14,000 sheep and 1,000 goats, and another 10,000 sheep three years later. The Diné also collected the feral survivors of their pre-Bosque Redondo flocks out of the mountains. The government forbade the sale of sheep outside of the Diné, so that flocks would reach maximum productivity in the short-est amount of time. By the mid-1880s, just twenty years after Bosque Redondo, the Diné herded nearly one million sheep and goats. To feed their growing number of sheep, Diné shepherds moved freely across the lands between the four sacred mountains, often off the reservation that had been assigned to them, to the fresh forage of public-domain lands. The federal government accommodated the Diné by adding to the initial reservation, and it reached nearly its current size by 1901.

Several large environmental and political shifts occurred at the beginning of the twentieth century that would deeply affect the Navajo Nation. Americans discovered springs in an area known as "the check-erboard," a patchwork of reservation land, public domain, and property belonging to the Atchison, Topeka and Sante Fe Railway. The presence of water meant that it was possible to graze cattle there, which brought Anglo ranchers into areas traditionally used for grazing Navajo-Churro sheep. While Diné shepherds had used these springs communally, Anglo ranchers laid claim to the land and fenced it off. While some ranchers allowed Diné access through their privatized land, or to Diné allotments contained within their fences, many other Anglo ranchers "tore down hogans, shot Navajo livestock, and threatened shepherds, even children, with guns." Since the 1880s, nearly half of the Diné population and their livestock had lived off the official reservation. By the 1920s, these families and animals were pushed into a much smaller area.

Diné families got rid of horses, which took more forage than sheep, and improved shearing methods to maximize profitable wool from fewer animals. But the growing human population meant that the land needed to support more animals. By the 1930s, the vegetation around watering holes on the Navajo Reservation was permanently destroyed by grazing livestock.

In 1936, the Hoover Dam was completed on the Colorado River just south of Las Vegas. There were immediate concerns about silt building up behind the dam, which soil scientists attributed to the San Juan and Little Colorado rivers, which flow through the Navajo Reservation. It was believed that overgrazing paired with drought was causing topsoil to be washed away as rainwater rushed over it instead of percolating down into the earth, forming streams which gullied and carried away the valuable topsoil. However, ungrazed areas, rich with grasses, exhibited the same gullying in this era. Today, environmentalists know that the gullying in the 1930s was just one instance in a cycle of erosion caused by larger geological and meteorological patterns. But the federal government blamed the increased erosion on the Diné and their livestock.

The Bureau of Indian Affairs and government soil scientists approached the problem with a formula: one acre of range could support a specific number of sheep. To fix erosion, they estimated that the herds would have to be reduced from 1.3 million animals to 560,000.

T. John Collier, the head of the Bureau of Indian Affairs during this time, is remembered as a cultural pluralist, who believed in allowing Native people to be economically independent of the United States and to maintain their traditions. But when he brought stock reduction proposals to the Diné council, he didn't solicit their input or ask their thoughts on the most effective way to heal the range. Bosque

Redondo was still alive in the Diné's memory, and opposition to government plans carried with it an implied fate. Women felt particularly powerless; although they owned most of the sheep, many did not speak English so could not express their protest to the federal government.

Collier's plan for stock reduction was implemented in two phases, one put forth as voluntary, the second mandatory. The first phase, in 1933, set a goal of reducing 100,000 sheep. The government would buy these animals from the Diné shepherds, but at shamefully low prices: one to two dollars a head, when the market rate was three dollars or more. This meant that only old, unproductive animals were sold, worth the offered price or less. Because healthy, productive sheep were still in the flocks, the cull was rapidly replaced by new lambs the next year. In total, 86,500 sheep were collected, falling short of the BIA's goal.

The second phase started in 1934. It called for the removal of 150,000 goats and 50,000 sheep, for which the government would pay $1 a head. The BIA felt the goats had no market value and that they were even more destructive to the range than sheep, whereas to the Diné, the goats were priceless. A slaughtered goat "would feed a family of five for a week, plus provide a pelt for bedding or sale," while the one dollar the government paid would buy four cans of tomatoes [or] eight cans of milk, or less than one sack of flour at the trading post." Goats provided milk for orphaned lambs—and children—and the poorest families kept goats for their meat so that the sheep could be saved for wool.

Some Diné protested and refused to sell their flocks. Oral histories frequently cite individuals jailed for refusing to reduce their stock. One man described how jail barbers cut off his traditional knot of long hair to shame him; while he was in jail, over 600 of his sheep were seized. Others talk about the authorities—often Diné policemen—simply seizing animals without asking. Many shepherds fled to the mountains to hide with their sheep, just like in the time of the Long Walk.

Although the BIA was successful in acquiring nearly 200,000 animals, the effort was a poorly planned disaster. The intention was to send the sheep and goats to canneries to be butchered, and to redistribute the canned meat on the reservation. But many of the Diné flocks were in remote locations, far from railroads, requiring government agents to drive animals over hundreds of miles of difficult terrain. Getting the animals to canneries was more expensive than their market value, and furthermore, the stockyards and butchers reached capacity early in the roundup. The BIA ordered 70 percent of the goats and sheep the government bought "condemned and slaughtered on the spot." While some BIA agents allowed Diné families to slaughter their own culled animals and preserve the meat, at least 7,500 goats and 3,500 sheep—40 percent of all purchased animals—were driven into canyons, shot, and left to rot. In 1939, Collier ordered the slaughter of horses. For the most impoverished Diné families, these were the only stock they had left; they were dependent on horses for travel, farm labor, and meat when necessary. Fourteen thousand horses—one quarter of all the horses on the reservation—were slaughtered or sold.

Howard Gorman, a Navajo tribal council member during and after the stock reduction, remembered the pain of the wasteful slaughter: "To many of them, livestock was a necessity and it meant survival. Some people consider livestock as sacred because it is life's necessity. They think of livestock as their mother."

Stock reductions left the Navajo Nation impoverished. The loss of goats forced families to eat their Navajo-Churro breeding stock. Families could no longer get credit from the trading posts because they had no lambs or wool to sell, and it was difficult for women to find enough fleece to weave their valuable blankets. Some would scrape the wool from their bedding pelts to have something to weave. Many families were on the brink of starvation. To offset the poverty caused by the loss of their livestock, Collier introduced wage work, including New Deal conservation efforts, which paid out nearly $800,000 in wages to Diné workers. But this work only benefited young, healthy men. Women and the elderly traditionally found wealth, power, and stability through the ownership of their livestock. Ethnographer Laila Shukry was told by a Diné woman, "You know, when we had lots of sheep, we don't care when the husband go away and don't send money. We butcher sheep and sell lamb. We make rugs and have money that way." But after stock reduction, "we don't have no sheeps now."

At the end of stock reduction, grazing permits were issued. The permits included a maximum number of animals, dependent on their impact on the range, that a certain district could contain. The permit also regulated a family's grazing area to one or two fixed locations, usually between a permanent farmstead and summer grazing grounds in the lush Chuska Mountains. Some Diné refused the permits, immediately throwing them away; others burned them in protest; some were jailed for refusing to accept the papers. The grazing permits were given to the heads of families—which the government assumed were men—but the permits were often immediately turned over to the wives, the real owners of the sheep. The permits were passed down matrilineally, often divided between multiple children, until the number of animals allowed per family holding was too small for sustenance. The grazing permits leveled wealth; no one family could become a wealthy stockholder with a large flock. Many families turned to cattle as a more reliable source of income than sheep.

Howard Gorman, the former tribal council member, said, "I think that the drastic stock reductions in the 1930s and 1940s was one of the worst things that ever happened to the Navajos because it ruined them economically. It cut off their livelihood. It ruined many Navajos to the point where they had to get relief. To this day, I think many of them have never recovered from it."

\* \* \*

STOCK REDUCTION HAPPENED all over the United States, with preference given to cattle ranchers over shepherds. Shepherds were largely Indigenous or Latine, while cattle ranchers were Anglo. The shepherds were systematically forced out off their grazing grounds to make way for cattle ranchers.

In the 1970s, Lyle McNeal founded the Navajo Sheep Project.

McNeal, then an animal science professor at Cal Poly, would become the Sheep and Wool Science professor at Utah State University. He spent the late 1970s seeking Navajo-Churro throughout the reservation and added them to his breeding flock; in 1982, he began repatriating the sheep to willing Diné ranchers and weavers. In the late 1980s, the NSP began providing educational support for breeding sheep and marketing wool, and the organization works with Navajo-Churro breeders to this day. The NSP was the first organization to focus money, education, and advocacy on rebuilding Navajo-Churro stock; it was followed by Diné-based Sheep Is Life and national organizations like the Livestock Conservancy and Slow Food. As a result, raw Navajo-Churro wool is selling for over one dollar a pound, an increase of over 2,000 percent in the past twenty years. When the wool has been hand-processed, spun, and dyed, it can be sold for as much as $100 a pound. And although the price for Navajo-Churro meat has also steadily gone up, lamb and mutton still remain rare in America's grocery stores.

On my last day in the Navajo Nation, I decided to visit a restaurant dedicated to serving Navajo-Churro meat: the Turquoise Room at the La Posada hotel in Winslow, Arizona. To get there, I drove west from Shiprock over the Chuskas and down the other side of the ridge into Arizona. Considered the more traditional side of the reservation, every sign was in two languages, English and Diné. Winslow is just outside the boundary of the Navajo Nation, on historic Route 66.

The driveway to La Posada was, tellingly, also the entrance to the Amtrak station. La Posada is a restored Harvey House. At the turn of the twentieth century, entrepreneur Fred Harvey built restaurants and hotels along the railroad, which are now considered the first chain restaurants. He used local architectural styles in his restaurants and hotels, famously worked with architect Mary Colter, and decorated the spaces with art purchased from Indigenous peoples.

Dim and cavern-like, the Turquoise Room was a relief from the relentless sun and heat outside. Diné weavings line the walls, as well as newspaper clippings from both the hotel's days as a Harvey House and its current incarnation as a destination restaurant. I sat in a window booth overlooking the train tracks and ordered a sloe gin fizz and the Churro lamb posole, a traditional Mexican soup made with meat, hominy, vegetables, and red chilies. The broth was made with mutton bones and the rich flavor took me right back to my weekend grilling ram over an open fire.

# The Turquoise Room Navajo-Churro Lamb Posole

You can toast the whole cumin and coriander seeds and grind them yourself for better flavor. The posole is even tastier the next day, and can be stored in the refrigerator for up to a week.

SERVES 8 AS A MAIN COURSE

INGREDIENTS
4 pounds lamb neck bones, shoulder, or shanks
¼ cup fresh garlic, chopped
1 large onion, diced
1½ cups fresh poblano peppers, diced
2 dried ancho chilies, roasted and seeds removed
4 dried guajillo chilies, roasted and seeds removed
1 dried Oaxaca chili, roasted and seeds removed
1 tablespoon dried Mexican oregano
½ teaspoon ground cumin
½ teaspoon ground coriander
½ teaspoon freshly ground black pepper
1 tablespoon sea salt
2½ cups cooked hominy (canned or homemade)

OPTIONAL GARNISHES:
diced onion, shredded cabbage, lime wedges, thinly sliced radishes, more dried oregano, hot sauce, soft tortillas or tortilla chips

1. Place the lamb in a 6- to 8-quart stock pot and cover with cold water. Bring to a boil, then remove from the heat. Dis-

card the hot water and wash the lamb with cold water. This blanching step ensures a clear broth with no off flavors.

2. Place the lamb back in the pot and once again cover with cold water. Bring to a boil and then reduce the heat to a simmer. Add garlic, onion, whole dried chilies, oregano, cumin, coriander, black pepper, and salt. Simmer, covered, until the meat starts falling off the bones, about 2–3 hours. Remove from heat.

3. Remove the meat and bones from the broth with a slotted spoon and skim fat from the broth. Puree the broth with an immersion blender until smooth.

4. When the lamb is cool enough to handle, strip all the meat from the bones and return it to the broth.

5. Add the cooked hominy. Simmer until heated through. Adjust seasoning to taste.

6. Serve with a variety of garnishes.

\* \* \*

THE TURQUOISE ROOM'S FAMED CHEF, John Sharpe, made a commitment to serve Navajo-Churro at every meal. He buys whole Navajo-Churro lambs and uses the entire animal, serving lamb empanadas, "Navajo tacos" of fry bread stuffed with grilled lamb meat, lamb meatballs, lamb shank, lamb shoulder chops, roast leg of lamb, and a Moroccan lamb tagine. Chef Sharpe arrived at my table as I was finishing up my posole. He's a dashing British man in his early seventies, in chef's whites and a jaunty red neckerchief. He ordered an espresso; I got a pot of tea.

A local writer and heritage food advocate originally pointed Chef Sharpe toward Churro meat about eighteen years ago. He bought a few lambs from a local Diné shepherd and did a tasting.

"I was astounded," Sharpe told me. "I realized that this was very good meat." Herbaceous and mild, it was a completely different experience from Colorado or New Zealand lamb.

He began buying more local lambs and butchering them at the restaurant. Since then, he's streamlined the process, working only with Diné shepherd Irene Benally and a Latino rancher, Antonio Manzanares, the owner of Shepherd's Lamb in New Mexico. All the lamb he buys is raised on wild forage, which he believes plays a big part in the flavor, as opposed to commercial lamb raised on hay and feed. And now, instead of processing the lambs at the restaurant, he has them slaughtered at a USDA-inspected processor in Durango, Colorado.

Sharpe works with Slow Food and the Navajo-Churro Presidium to do demos at local meetups showcasing the meat. He's won over other local chefs, who don't just order a few favored cuts, but work with the whole animal. James Beard Award-winning Chef Charleen Badman, co-owner of FnB in Scottsdale, Arizona, bought a whole Navajo-Churro lamb after attending a demo with Sharpe. The meat regularly appears on her menus, and she served a Navajo-Churro lamb loin with manti, yogurt, sprouted coriander and Urfa butter at a James Beard House dinner in New York.

Sharpe originally envisioned a network of breeders and butchers that would be able to distribute Navajo-Churro meat across the country. But sadly, there were too many logistical issues preventing shepherds from reliably getting the animals to slaughterhouses, many of which are in Colorado.

"Is their vehicle roadworthy? Can they leave their animals? Can they get a trailer or the tires? Can they afford the petrol?" Sharpe explained. So many daily problems become insurmountable in remote areas that lack infrastructure.

A mobile slaughterhouse could solve many of these issues; even a stationary slaughterhouse on the Navajo Nation could make a huge difference in getting the product out of the Southwest and bringing more revenue to shepherds. In 2023, the USDA announced a new Indigenous Animals Harvesting and Meat Processing Grant program that could potentially fund these solutions. Aretta Begay, Sheep Is Life coordinator and head of the Navajo-Churro Presidium, also suggested a wool mill on the reservation to further support shepherds. Both Aretta and Chef Sharpe agree that a process of certifying and labeling traditionally raised Navajo-Churro would make a difference. However, the Navajo Nation tribal government gives more support to cattle ranching, which they see as a more promising route to financial success than sheepherding.

"I try to be hopeful," Aretta told me on the phone after I came home from my visit to the Navajo Nation. "I just hope that one day we do have someone in our tribal presidency seat or tribal administration office who has the ability to see and recognize the importance of sheep producers."

In the meantime, those in the know can enjoy the meat in restaurants like the Turquoise Room. And the truly fortunate can make their way to Sheep Is Life, and perhaps trade a day of dishwashing for grilled mutton wrapped in a handmade tortilla. The secret to its incredible flavor is not just the sprinkle of salt on top. It's eating it in the shade of a tree, while cedar smoke curls through the air and elders trade stories nearby. That is the true flavor of the meat.

FOUR

# Sxwo'le

## STRAITS SALISH REEFNET FISHING

In August 2019, I drove north from Seattle to Lummi Island in the waters of the Salish Sea, a part of the Puget Sound less than 25 miles from the Canadian border. Lummi Island is the only place on the planet where commercial fishers practice an ancient, Indigenous method of salmon fishing: *Sxwo'le* (*sxole*), or reefnet fishing. This stationary system, which catches schooling salmon by funneling them into an underwater net, was invented by the Native peoples of the Salish Sea thousands of years ago; it is unique to the Straits Salish peoples. Today, reefnet is considered the most humane method of catching salmon and delivers the highest quality fish to market.

I was originally drawn to reefnet fishing as an Ark entry because it was the only listing I came across that commemorates a process rather than an ingredient. Although it has since been renamed "Reefnet Caught Wild Pacific Salmon from North Puget Sound" in an Ark editorial overhaul, the idea of preserving food processes as much as the ingredients themselves is a reminder that ways of making and doing are intangible, but important, signifiers of culture.

Before I fished on one of these reefnet gears, I tasted some of the catch of the previous fishing season at Copperleaf Restaurant at Cedarbrook Lodge in Tacoma, Washington. The restaurant buys directly from Lummi Island Wild, a fishing collective that processes the fish from reefnetters—in this case, smoking pink salmon—before selling to local restaurants and markets. The smoking process condenses the flavor of the salmon: the pink fillets start three inches thick and reduce to one inch by the end of the process. The smoke adds a pleasant sweetness.

Chefs Adam Stevenson and David Mitchell serve the smoked salmon on Copperleaf's brunch menu: a thick salmon fillet that's somewhere between jerky and lox, with goat cheese, hearty slices of in-season tomatoes, and mustard dressing. Chef Mitchell was accommodating and served my table a salmon brunch platter at dinnertime. The smoked fillets melted on my tongue, deeply savory with a touch of oceanic brine. Chef Mitchell also served us a special dish, a smoked salmon fillet dressed in cucumber and a sprig of dill, shaved pickled beets, and warm "salmon milk"—salmon skin-infused whole milk—which he poured around the fillet. At first I was like, "Get out of here with your salmon milk," but I ended up appreciating the dressing, creamy with fat, salty and intense.

* * *

LUMMI ISLAND IS ONLY ACCESSIBLE by ferry; the terminal is at the tip of the Lummi Nation, a reservation created in the 1850s. My guide into the world of reefnet fishing was Riley Starks, the technique's most passionate advocate and a longtime resident of Lummi Island. I stayed at Nettles Farm—Riley's home, AirBnB, and a functional farm—while I visited his reefnet gear.

The morning was cool but sunny when I climbed into Riley's gray Kia Soul. I gently moved Stella, his white dog with a sad-sweet face, out of the passenger seat, and she complied with a harrumph. Riley was all business, the excitement of the imminent start of the fishing season apparent in his bubbling energy. He is in his seventies but moves his lean frame with youthful strength and energy. As we drove down the forested lane toward the Salish Sea, I asked him what had brought him to Lummi Island and made him a passionate advocate for reefnet fishing.

"Reefnetting was the culture of this island," he said. When Riley arrived on Lummi Island in 1992, he wanted to be a part of it.

Riley graduated from Western Washington University in Bellingham in 1969. He was twenty-three, and all he had ever cared about was getting straight A's. He got into law school at the University of Oregon, but had six months to kill before the program started. A friend of his had bought a fishing boat; Riley needed to earn some money and his friend needed a deckhand. The experience ended up being an epiphany. "Oh God, I have to do this," Riley thought. So he dropped out of law school, sold everything he owned, and bought a boat.

The day he bought the boat at a marina in Everett, Washington, his family and financier gathered to wish him good luck. But Riley realized he didn't know how to turn the boat around to sail out. To avoid embarrassment, he backed up a mile as his family waved goodbye.

Then he got lost. He ran aground. Once he got his boat free, he tied it up at a slip, went home, and didn't come back for a week.

His disastrous start in boat ownership had paralyzed him with fear. But Riley's motto in life has always been, "If you fear something, you have to face it." When he finally found the courage to go back, his boat had half sunk. Panicked, he turned to a fisherman sitting on a boat nearby.

"And I was like, 'My boat is sinking, what do I do?'" Riley recreated the scene for me. "So he reached down and got a number 10 can [about three quarts]. And he said, 'Here, bail it out!' Of course they had a pump at the port office. I didn't know that. And he didn't give a shit. So I spent the whole day bailing it out with a number 10 can." Riley chuckled in embarrassment at the memory.

Somehow, Riley recovered from his mortifying first few weeks as a fisherman and made fishing not only his career but his passion.

We had been following a road around the edge of the island, the Salish Sea to our right. When we rounded a bend, I could see for the first time the reefnet gears lined up in the bay. When Riley first bought his reefnet gear, there were at least fifty licensed gears in the waters of the Salish Sea. Now there were twelve. I saw seven pairs of floating platforms stretching out to sea in a C shape, with two more gear pairs farther north, closer to the mouth of the Fraser River. That river mouth was where the salmon were headed, coming in from the open sea to breed. The Fraser is the longest river in British Columbia, and one of the most important and prolific salmon spawning locations in the world. The reefnet gears were located in the path of schooling salmon. A strong tide moves like a river through the bay, propelling the fish along their journey and hopefully into the fishers' nets.

We pulled onto property owned by the Salish Center for Sustainable Fishing Methods, the not-for-profit Riley founded to advocate for reefnet-caught fish and other sustainable fishing in the Salish Sea. The site is where the reefnet gear is stored in the off-season and launched via a set of rails that slope down into the water. Once the gear is dragged into position—a licensed parking spot in the bay, essentially—it remains anchored there for the remainder of the season.

We put on our life jackets, and Riley left his car door open so Stella could wander in and out as she pleased. "We have a routine," Riley said of himself and Stella. Riley called his crew on his cellphone to pick us up on shore. We crunched down the gravel beach to wait, picking our way over and around enormous trunks of driftwood, bleached gray in the sun. The water of the Salish Sea was like glass, clear but reflective; a mirror of the sky, islands, and pine forests around it, but with fish visible deep below the surface.

One of Riley's crew, Olivia—in her early twenties, tall and blonde—arrived in the skiff. I jumped in first and Riley pushed the skiff off the shore, jumping in after. His gear was in the seventh space, farthest out from shore, so we passed the gears of other fishers on our way. Each gear was a little different; there is no reefnet gear factory, so each is built to the whims and specifications of the gear's captain or their predecessors. But each operates with the same basic structure. Reefnet gears are made of two floating platforms each about 40 feet long, with a 55-foot-wide net strung between them. Each pair of floating platforms had up to four crow's nests on either end of the plat-forms. I could see people standing in these crow's nests, 20 feet in the air, silhouetted against the morning sun, their eyes glued to the clear water below as they looked for the schools of salmon.

"Sometimes they're clear as day, sometimes just a color change in the water, or a feeling," Riley told me about spotting the fish. As the captain of the gear, he would be in the crow's nest when it came time.

The spotters in the crow's nests were assisted by another crew member in a small cabin below, keeping an eye on monitors with video from four underwater cameras. Today, the crews were testing their gears; state officials had not given the go-ahead to fish. When the gears are active, you periodically hear a shout, and the spotters in the crow's nest pull a lever or grab a cord to engage solar-powered winches that lift the net spanning between the two platforms out of the water. Fishing days are punctuated by the sound of these winches, a rattle like a roller coaster being dragged up its first hill. Then the deck crew spring to life, some manning another winch to position the net, some dragging in the net manually, and finally hauling the net— containing several hundred pounds of fish—on to the deck by hand. The flopping fish tumble into a live well, a rectangular metal mesh cage set into a hole in the deck where seawater flows through it. The salmon swim in the live well and calm down, which allows the lactic acid in their muscles to disperse and results in a better-tasting fish.

In this live well, the catch is sorted, and any "non-targeted" species are released, with less than .5 percent mortality. This by-catch often includes protected species of salmon, because multiple salmon spe-cies commonly school together. Protected species are salmon whose populations are dangerously low, such as chinook salmon, another Ark of Taste entry. The gentle handling of reefnet fishing means the non-targeted fish are returned to the water healthy, ready to continue their journey to spawn. The targeted fish are bled by hand before being iced and sent to the Lummi Island Wild processing facility in Bellingham.

No other commercial fishing process is this selective, or this gentle, on the fish. The fish aren't damaged; they have all their scales when they come to market, and the flesh isn't bruised. And when they are caught in salt water, their meat is fatty and firm, characteristics which change once the fish hit freshwater rivers. Additionally, because the gears are stationary (and otherwise solar-powered), the whole process uses very little fossil fuel.

This season we were fishing for pink salmon, a species that runs in odd years. Riley feels that pinks are key to the future of wild salmon fishing. While other species of salmon are depleted, pink runs are abundant, larger now than at any other time in history. A more enthusiastic embrace of pinks would take the pressure off other species, like sockeye and chinook. But pink salmon is much maligned, thought to be too soft for cooking and only suitable for canning. Some fishers I talked to said they only fed it to their dogs. It's true that pink salmon doesn't hold up well to high heat—it gets mushy in a sauté pan. But Riley—and a growing number of chefs—know that, especially with the gentle handling of reefnet fishing, the pink is a delicate, flavorful, premium fish.

Riley has been championing pink salmon for years, and in 2013 he landed a large buyer: Patagonia Provisions. The food department of one of the nation's largest outdoor gear purveyors, Patagonia Provisions provides sustainably sourced and "regenerative" food that's also shelf-stable and ready to be packed up for an adventure. They sell Riley's reefnet-caught pink and sockeye salmon smoked and vacuum-packed, lightly flavored with black pepper or lemon pepper. This year, Patagonia contracted to buy 225,000 pounds of pink salmon from Lummi Island Wild, and the pressure was on to provide the fish.

Riley had a hired crew of three college students from his alma mater: Olivia (who was piloting the skiff), Natalie, and Ben. They were majoring in fishing and wanted to do this work for a living. Even though they were "green," meaning this was their first year on the water, Riley felt confident in their abilities. They loved the work, and Riley hoped to find funding to keep them over the winter, so they'd be available next season. The crew is paid based on the fish caught: .65 cents a pound per person. A pink salmon will weigh 3 to 5 pounds, so a fisher will make about two to three dollars a fish. A few volunteers would also come aboard when it was time to fish, including myself.

"Do you do much boating?" Riley asked me as our skiff pulled up to his gear.

"Nope," I replied. That was an understatement; I had probably been on less than a dozen boats in my life. Unfortunately, I get really seasick and was only managing that day because a friend had told me about the seasickness patches that are prescribed on cruise ships. I had slapped one on my neck that morning.

"So you don't know your knots?" Riley followed up.

"I don't—it's interesting to watch, though," I offered. Riley was inspecting one of the lines that extended in front of his gear into the bay.

"Pretty critical in this fishery." I could tell Riley was beginning to doubt my usefulness.

We pulled up to one of the platforms and the rest of the crew greeted us. Ben—tall, skinny, and generally the quiet type—jumped aboard the skiff with Riley, and they left to go fuss with the long ropes that extended "upstream," the direction the tide and the salmon would be coming from. These ropes were the visible element of the most critical and ingenious part of the reefnet: the reef.

The reef is a web of rope which guides salmon both up from the ocean floor and in toward the net, like a funnel. The reef starts with two 200-foot rope lines that extend upstream from the platforms; the lines float with the help of buoys. The ends of these lines are about 80 feet apart at the upstream end, and narrow to the width of the net between the two floating platforms. Ropes are tied at intervals horizontally between these two main lines. At the upstream end, these horizontal ropes are anchored 80 feet below the surface of the water, nearly at the bay's floor. Gradually, the ropes slope upward until their depth matches the opening of the net strung between the platforms.

Onto these horizontal ropes are tied blue or green plastic ribbons that shimmy in the tide and look like underwater plants. The ribbons trick the salmon into thinking that they are swimming safely on the ocean floor up a shoal, a natural shallowing of the bay.

"And so the fish swim up from 80 feet and they think that they're in their little ecosystem with grass," Natalie explained. Charged with giving me a tour of the gear, she was slight, with brown hair in a low ponytail, young, and incredibly knowledgeable. She tromped around deck in shorts and galoshes. "And then they're slowly brought up to 20 feet and then right into the net."

Salmon schooling in the sound move fast, pushed along by the tide at four knots or more. As they come into the funnel of the reef, they're moving too fast to notice that they're swimming away from the true bottom of the sound. Even if they did, with the tide pushing them forward it's difficult for them to turn around. Suddenly, they're in the net.

The spotter sees the salmon entering the reef, or perhaps it's the crew member watching the camera feed that sees them swim past. The cue is given—traditionally "Give 'em hell!" but Riley often shouted, "We've got fish!" The nets are pulled up, the fish hauled on deck.

As Natalie pointed out to the reef, a salmon leapt out of the water near the reef's opening in the bay. "Oh, there went one!" I squealed.

"A jumper? Nice." Jumpers mean that a big school of fish is just below the surface.

When Riley returned from adjusting the reef, a fisher from another gear came by on a skiff, asking if we'd seen any schools of salmon yet. Riley paused his work to chat with him.

"That's one of the things about this fishery. It's convivial," Riley said to me later, as we climbed back into the skiff. The equipment had been checked, fixed, and set. We were ready to fish. "There's not another fishery like this. People come back and forth, they bring their whole families, everybody's on the boat." Since the gears are stationary, there's no missing the boat, so to speak.

"And there's no competition," I observed.

"Noooo, there's no competition," Riley affirmed. "That's the thing. You're happy whenever someone catches fish. Whereas in all the other fisheries that I've ever fished, you lie about everything, never tell where you get the fish, how much you catch. There's nothing to hide here. You can't do anything about it. You can only do a good job where you are."

"And think," Natalie added, "there used to be rows and rows and rows of these all up and down the Salish Strait. All the way up to Canada, all the way down to Puget Sound."

Riley smiled warmly at his young crew as we pushed off from the gear. "These guys have never fished, but they are just terrific," he declared. "I don't think I've ever had a better crew." Natalie, Ben, and Olivia beamed.

"Really, I think we're ready. I think it's going to be a good season." Riley looked out at the sound, then turned the skiff to shore.

* * *

FOSSILS OF THE EARLIEST SALMON, *Eosalmo*, have been found from Washington to northern British Columbia. Dating to about 50 million years ago, the skeletons and fin impressions look like salmon, although there are some subtle differences between modern fish and their ancestors. The five modern species of Pacific salmon are pinks (also known as humpbacks), chinook (also known as kings), sockeye, chum and coho.

Salmon are anadromous: they are born in freshwater, spend most of their lives in the ocean, and then return to freshwater to spawn. Every salmon species has its own pattern of anadromy. Pinks migrate like clockwork, every other year. Two-year-old pinks run in odd years, like 2019, in August or September. Chinook, on the other hand, run in both the spring and fall, and can stay out to sea anywhere between three and eight years before returning to spawn. A chinook will also travel far inland, to high-mountain tributaries, up to 2,000 miles from the ocean.

After the fish spawn, that is the end of their life cycle. They don't eat after they return to freshwater, dying in droves after mating. I was in Anchorage, Alaska, once during the end of spawning season, and the banks of rivers and streams were carpeted with the bodies of rotting fish. But the salmon's death is a vital part of the ecosystem: scavengers enjoy a fish feast and the rotting salmon add vital nutrients back into the soil that feeds the West Coast's forests.

Salmon are fished primarily when they return to freshwater rivers, not just because they're conveniently close to land, but because they store up enormous reserves of fat before they make the journey. Fat salmon, caught just before they hit freshwater, are considered the tastiest.

For the Native people of the Pacific Northwest, the salmon are not only a food source but are seen as kin, integral to their Indigenous identity. The Saanich of Vancouver Island, in present-day British Columbia, believe that long ago the salmon lived in a faraway land. During a time of starvation, two brave men got into their canoes and rowed out to sea, searching for food for their people. After journeying for three and a half months, they dragged their canoe ashore in an unfamiliar place. A man approached them and said, "You have finally arrived." This man was one of the Salmon People, who would accompany the Saanich back to their homeland.

The Saanich are one of at least four tribes that traditionally practiced reefnet fishing, including the Lummis of northwest Washington State, the Samish, and the Songhees. All of these tribes belong to a broader group called the Straits Salish, who historically intermarried and interacted extensively, speak a common language, and share cultural traditions and beliefs. Archeological evidence shows that the Straits Salish have lived around Puget Sound for at least 14,000 years, having arrived during the end of the last ice age. In the belief system of the Straits Salish, they have been there since the dawn of creation, placed beside the water by the creator Xals. All Straits Salish territories border and include Puget Sound, and many of their foods and customs revolve around the sea. There are about 57,000 Straits Salish people today; it is not known how many existed before European contact.

Historically, Straits Salish homesites were clusters of cedar-plank longhouses, each containing a family group connected through a patriarch. The family worked collectively on food gathering and fishing—like reefnet—but each son and his family kept their own food stores and cooked separately. Before being confined to reservations, Straits Salish traveled seasonally to gather shellfish, forage edible plants, and hunt waterfowl and sea mammals. But fishing was the primary source of sustenance; pre-contact consumption is estimated at about 600 pounds per person per year of salmon.

The Straits Salish, and other Indigenous people of the Pacific Northwest, invented at least six major fishing techniques as well as dozens of types of hooks, nets, lures, traps, spears, and harpoons to fish in different locations for a wide variety of fish. Reefnet fishing, swxo'le in the Straits Salish language, developed specifically among the Straits Salish because their territories focused on coastal areas. They didn't have as much access to spawning rivers, so they relied on fishing techniques effective in the sound.

The Sannich believed the reefnet was given to the Straits Salish by the Salmon People. A salmon spirit in the form of a man met a beautiful Saanich woman on the beach one day and decided he wanted to marry her. Her family requested that the young man live with her family for a time after they were married. He did, and while he was there he asked that the family bring him all the materials needed to construct a sxwo'le. He showed the people how to process the raw materials into a net to catch the salmon schools that migrated through the sound. One day, he said it was time for him and his wife to leave. They loaded up their canoe and rowed out into the water, and then vanished.

The sites for reefnetting, or swálet, were inherited. A family "belonged" to the location and took care of it. Usually the male head of household was considered the caretaker of the swálet, and the captain, or ȼenályen, the caretaker of the reefnet gear. A crew of family housemates, and perhaps extended kin, would work the site together and share the catch. There were at least thirty reefnet swálet used by the Lummi and twenty-nine Saanich sites.

The traditional reefnet gears of the Straits Salish looked much different than the modern gears I saw off Lummi Island. But the principle has not changed in thousands of years—just the materials. A white American, traveling through the San Juan Islands in August of 1853, observed a group of Lummis fishing:

> In the tide-ways toward the Sound's mouth, the Indians anchor two canoes parallel, fifteen feet apart, and stretch a flat net of strips of inner bark between them, sinking it just below the surface . . . Salmon . . . come swimming in shoals across the suspended net. Whereupon every fisher, with inconceivable screeches, whoops, and howls, beats the

water to bewilder the silver swimmers, and, hauling up the net, clutches them by dozens.

Dr. Nick Xemtoltw Claxton, a member of the Saanich tribe from Tsawout on Vancouver Island, began researching the practice of reef-netting while in the MA program at the University of Victoria. When he went on to get his PhD in 2015, he successfully built a reefnet gear and took it out into the waters of the Salish Sea. He completed his project with the help of his family, his community, and his Lummi neighbors. It was the first time in over seventy years that the Saanich had set a reefnet gear.

Despite being banned by the Canadian government in the early 1900s, reefnet fishing was still in living memory of the Saanich people when Claxton started his work. "The sxwo'le, or Reefnet Fishery . . . was the 'backbone' of our W̱SÁNEĆ society," Claxton wrote in his dissertation. "This knowledge system was demeaned, degraded and dismantled through legislation, coercion and the effective colonizing assimilationist tools of Western education and schooling."

"This project is about bringing the reef net fishery back to life. It is about making it living again," he continued. "By returning to our ancient reef net locations and putting our gear back in the water we will be reconnecting to the essence of what it means to be Straits Salish."

Claxton's uncle Earl, a respected elder in the community, remembered going with his family to a swálet as a boy for the summer. Inspired by Uncle Earl, who had wanted to create a reefnet curriculum to be taught in tribal schools, Claxton worked with faculty and students at the ȽÁU,WELṈEW̱ tribal school to build a ceremonial reefnet. It would be a scale model of a historical gear, made using traditional materials and methods.

The word sxwo'le comes from the Straits Salish word for the inner bark of the willow tree; fishing nets were historically made from this pliable bark. Traditionally, families worked on net sections over the winter, then assembled them at the swálet during the summer fishing season. The fishing canoes for a reefnet were 35 to 40 feet long, carved from hollowed cedar logs. The reef was made from cedar-bark rope, with the bark stripped from only one side of the tree so that it would survive and produce bark again. The bark was twisted into "a strong, yet, fine two-ply cord." The fake reef was anchored to the ocean floor with rock weights, and the sides were held up by cedar-log buoys. The ropes across the bottom and sides of the reef were threaded with dune grass.

At the tribal school, the tiny net was hung between two scale-model canoes. The symbolic sxwol'e was celebrated in a sacred ceremony that was held on August 6, 2014, "to acknowledge and bring back the spiritual practice of Reefnet Fishing."

Just three days later, on August 9, Claxton and a group of community members launched their own full-sized sxwo'le. They had obtained a small grant to purchase materials: nylon nets, ropes, and lines instead of willow and cedar bark; steel anchors instead of stone; plastic buoys instead of logs; and blue ribbon instead of dune grass. They borrowed a traditional dugout canoe from their own Tsawout First Nation community and a fiberglass canoe from the nearby Tsey-cum First Nation, also part of the Saanich tribe. Next they had to figure out how to put it all together into a working reefnet gear. It was halfway through July; they had only a few short weeks to assemble the gear before the salmon runs in August.

Claxton reached out to "our Lummi relatives." The Lummis are just across Puget Sound from the Saanich, although separated by the international boundary between Canada and the US. The Lummis had embarked on their own reefnet restoration project a few years before and had helped Claxton and the Saanich build their ceremonial model. Now, they crossed the water to build a full-sized gear with the Saanich. They arrived and "immediately drew a blueprint," Claxton wrote. "Under the guidance of the Lummi Fishermen, we were able to build the whole gear in one day."

Although Claxton's reefnet gear was made with modern materials, it incorporated Saanich and Lummi tradition. In particular, the team created a *shelis* in the net, an open ring made from stiff willow branches. This ritual hole in the net allowed some salmon to escape and continue to their spawning grounds. Claxton wrote about the practice: "This is more than just a simple act of conservation. . . . It represents a profound respect for salmon. It was believed that the runs of salmon were lineages, and if some were allowed to return to their home rivers, then those lineages would always continue."

Once the sxwo'le was built, it was time to take it to the water. Just like today, the historical gears had to be anchored anew at the swálet every year because the structures would disintegrate if left in the water year-round. The swálet were in locations that intercepted the migrating salmon and took advantage of the tide to push them into the nets: the mouth of a bay, a channel between islands, or in front of an estuary. Claxton chose a site called Sxixte, at the mouth of Bedwell Harbour on South Pender Island on the Canadian side of the sound. Claxton's advisors believed this site was one of the Saanich's original reefnet fishing sites, if not *the* original.

Claxton and his team took to the water in the early morning of August 9, 2014, from Tsawout, two canoes packed with equipment and a crew of eight. Their intent was to row the 12 miles to South Pender Island, but after struggling against the tide for hours, they accepted a tow from a Parks Canada boat the rest of the way. As they arrived at Bedwell Harbour, the fishers saw a "pod of orcas travelled along the shore of Pender Island, through Bedwell Harbour, and directly over our Reef net site at SXIXTE." "The visit from the pod of orcas, while it could be dismissed as merely coincidence, was characterised by an elder advisor as a spiritual occurrence," Claxton wrote. "The elder explained that killer whales are our relatives in our worldview, and they were there to help us."

Since the crew lacked the intergenerational knowledge of an experienced ¢enályen, Claxton used a GPS chart plotter to determine where to set the main anchors. The Parks Canada boat helped them set the reef, stretching out its trapezoidal shape in front of the canoes. Then the team realized that the reef was twisted, and they couldn't fix the issue with the ropes in the water. So they hauled the whole thing in again, took it to shore, untwisted it, and then took it back out to reset it. The team anchored the reef close to the ocean floor, attached the downstream end to the canoes, and stretched the net between the two canoes. The net bagged out in the tidal flow as it should, a pocket waiting for a school of salmon.

"It was really amazing to set the net and have all of the gear in the water, working properly in the flow of the tide," Claxton wrote later. They watched two bottom-swimming fish, a flounder and a rockfish, follow the slope of the reef up from the ocean floor and swim over the net, just like they were supposed to.

Historically, a reefnet gear would be crewed by eight to ten people, although during busy runs, up to fifteen men were needed to haul in the net. Spotters were stationed at the front of the canoes, watching for the silvery bodies and jumpers that signaled approaching salmon. They gave the cue for the crew to spring into action. The crew slackened lines that attached the canoes to the rear anchors, which let the tide push the canoe ends together. The net was pulled up at the downstream end first to trap the salmon, then at the upstream end, and then hauled on board. A "klootchman"—who could be any gender—rowed out from shore in a third canoe to transport the catch to be processed by the women and children. Summer villages were set up near the swálet for families to live in while the salmon was smoked or dried in batches for preservation.

Claxton's spotter kept his eyes on the water. The crew was poised to haul in the net. But there were no salmon to be seen, not even jumping or finning farther out in the sound.

While it was disappointing not to catch any fish that day, Claxton still felt the trip was a success. They had built a reefnet gear and watched it work as it should in the waters of the Salish Sea. As Claxton recounted in his dissertation, "There are things that I learned that could have only been learned by experiencing it, by doing it, by living it." The learning is in the doing.

Had they pulled in a big sockeye salmon that day, it would have been cause for celebration. Traditionally, fishing activity halted when the first sockeye salmon was caught in a reefnet—not just for the family that caught it, but for everyone in the tribal network. For the Lummi and Saanich, the fish was celebrated as a "special guest" and "the King of All Salmon." "Saanich traditional philosophy maintains that all living things were once people who were transformed by the Creator," Claxton explained, "and then given to the Saanich peoples as gifts, and thus they must be respected accordingly." The salmon guest was cooked and everyone in the community had a bite. Then, its skeleton was returned to the water where it was caught, so its spirit could tell all the other salmon how it had been honored.

The festival lasted up to ten days; and while the people partied, schools of fish swam past the unmanned gears and up into their spawning rivers. Allowing the salmon to spawn ensured that the salmon stocks would perpetuate and the salmon would run again for years to come.

Until the late 1800s, a thousand salmon a day could be caught in a reefnet, and sometimes as many as three to four thousand fish in one day. A single day of work at the reefnet gear could provide enough fish to feed three dozen people for a year. The fish were divided among the crew and their families first, and the remainder went to the owner of the reefnet site. There are no histories that tell of a year when not enough salmon were caught to feed everyone. It never happened.

## Roast Salmon on Sticks

This traditional salmon preparation is still used all over the Pacific Northwest, and visitors might be lucky enough to see it at a First Salmon Ceremony. I tried this one at home—in my parents' backyard—adapted from a recipe written by Agnes E. Pilgrim (Yurok Tribe) in 1974.

I built a big fire—bigger than you would for normal sitting-around-the-fire activities—and let it burn down. I didn't shift, stoke, or add more wood, just waited until I saw hot coals glowing in the center.

While I waited for the fire to burn down, I cut scions with a hatchet—thin, straight, new growth from an apple tree—each one 2–3 feet long. Some sources suggest cedar or redwood, but any nontoxic green wood will do. I used a utility knife to cut off any side shoots until I had one smooth skewer, then sharpened both ends to a point.

I pushed the thin end of my sharpened applewood skewer through a salmon fillet, underneath the skin but close to the surface. My fillets were relatively small, so I was able to fit three on a skewer. I dusted the flesh side with salt and pepper.

Here's the most important trick of the process: I held my hand open toward the fire and found the spot where I could hold my hand for thirteen seconds before it felt too hot and I had to move it. That space is approximately 2–3 feet from the center of the fire. I disturbed the ground slightly to loosen the soil and pushed the thick end of the skewer into the earth at a slight angle, so the fillets leaned toward the fire. The skin side of the fillets should face away from the fire, the flesh toward the fire. It is important to cook the salmon slowly at a low heat to get a "silky smooth texture and juicy interior." I had to resist the temptation to move the fillets closer to the fire, and ignored comments from the peanut gallery (my parents) that the skewers were in the wrong place.

Leave the fillets for 45–60 minutes, depending on their thickness. To check for doneness, brush the skin side with your fingers; when it feels dry, the salmon is cooked. The salmon flesh should be opaque and flaky, but the center slightly translucent. The finished salmon is juicy, slightly smoky, and has the pure taste of the sea.

\* \* \*

THE FIRST EUROPEAN SHIPS passed through Puget Sound in the 1770s; the first smallpox epidemic struck the Straits Salish in 1782. The Indigenous population was decimated, and later explorers noted the abandoned villages and smallpox scars on the survivors.

The Strait of Juan de Fuca was claimed and named by Spanish explorers in 1787. The British came in the 1790s, searching for fur-bearing animals, beavers mostly, to trap and sell. Early colonists were uninterested in salmon. Europeans viewed salmon as abundant but abhorrent, as a "food of last resort, not as a staple source of protein." Salmon was used as hog feed and fertilizer, literally shoveled onto the fields—even through the nineteenth century—by white farmers. The earliest attempt at developing a commercial salmon industry was founded in the 1830s by the Hudson Bay Company, British traders who focused on furs. The company salted salmon and shipped it to Hawaii, where it was bought by sugar planters to feed their workers.

The Pacific Northwest didn't attract white settlers in significant numbers until the Treaty of 1846 divided the territory between the United States and Great Britain. Seen as the realization of America's "manifest destiny," the treaty split the Straits Salish territory. The Lummis were on the United States side, while the Saanich ended up on the British side. Tempted by the US government's promise of up to 640 acres of free land for families, 53,000 white settlers arrived in the Oregon Territory between 1840 and 1860 and settled as far north as Bellingham by the 1850s.

White settlers wanted land and fishing rights, so the United States began to work out treaties with the Straits Salish. It's in this moment that the Straits Salish were divided into separate tribes; until the mid-nineteenth century, the Straits Salish had thought of themselves as one interconnected community. Several treaties in the 1850s confined groups who were accustomed to migrating seasonally to specific reservations. The Treaty of Point Elliott, signed in 1855, defined reservation lands for the Lummi and six other tribes. The treaty also guaranteed the Indigenous peoples "the right of taking fish at usual and accustomed grounds and stations." This single line would be hotly debated for the next 130 years.

A white "resident farmer" was assigned to live on the reservation and teach the Lummis "civilized pursuits." Fishing and foraging were considered uncivilized by the US government. Farming and ranching were the accepted way to thrive in America. The Lummis took to potato growing but worked their farms only as long as it wasn't fishing season. As soon as the tide was low enough to gather shellfish, or the salmon were running in the summer, they left their farms, much to the frustration of the resident farmer. Fish remained the focus of the Lummi's daily diet.

The advent of canning in the middle of the nineteenth century created a salmon industry in the Pacific Northwest. Salmon canners were established around Puget Sound in the late 1870s, and by 1883, there were at least fifty-five canneries on or near the Columbia River and Puget Sound. That same year, the Northern Pacific Railroad completed its cross-country track, connecting the Pacific Northwest to the rest of America. Now, canned salmon could be shipped nationwide for sale.

Salmon quickly became one of America's most popular canned foods. But the length of the salmon spawning runs—about two weeks—forced the canneries to both obtain and package their entire annual output in a very short time. Canning factories became fully mechanized to maximize efficiency between 1864 and 1914. According to Patrick W. O'Bannon, a scholar of the history of salmon processing mechanization, "Salmon were delivered to the cannery, butchered, cleaned, and cut into can-sized pieces. The cans, fabricated prior to the start of the fishing season, were then filled with these pieces, fitted with tops, and washed, cooked, lacquered, labeled, and boxed for delivery to market." While machines that filled, soldered, heated, and labeled the cans were brought from the East early on and adapted, the much trickier process of butchering and cleaning the fish was performed by human hands until about 1905. Even after the introduction of the Smith Fish Cleaner, a large vertical wheel "with salmon attached along the rim," which "carried the fish past a series of knives and brushes that removed the fins, and split and cleaned the body cavity," cans of salmon still contained many bits of skin and bones until the mid-twentieth century. It was up to the consumer to either pick out these bits or enjoy the extra crunch.

Although Native people were hired to work in the canneries, they were more valued for their fishing skills as well as their knowledge of salmon migration patterns. In the 1890s, nearly a quarter of all fishery employees were Indigenous. Although the Lummis had previously been discouraged by the Bureau of Indian Affairs from fishing and foraging off their reservation in lieu of farming, the BIA did encourage them to take cannery work. Lummis who weren't working in or for the canneries were selling surplus salmon to the canneries. In 1895, Native reefnetters on San Juan Island sold 419,960 pounds of salmon to the canneries, and reefnet fishers around Point Roberts—the most northern US land in Puget Sound—sold 184,239 pounds and took another 350,805 pounds of salmon for their own use. Native fishers were paid less for their fish compared to white fishers: five to eight cents a pound, compared to the 10–15 cents that went to white fishers.

The profitable, if prejudiced, arrangement between the canneries and Straits Salish had degraded by 1900. The canneries hired immigrant workers instead of Native people and paid these new hires poverty wages. The canneries also began to infringe on the Salish's ability to fish for themselves. On the American side of the sound, canning companies set up "fish traps," stationary nets that blocked salmon traveling on known migration routes and funneled them into a holding pen, where they would be periodically "hauled out with a dip net." Some of these traps blocked a mile-wide stretch of sea, and were often set up in front of Lummi reefnet sites, scooping up the salmon runs before they made it to the reefnet locations.

But the Lummis were litigious and challenged the presence of the traps based on the Point Elliott treaty. In 1894, the tribe petitioned the Commissioner of Indian Affairs to intervene:

> Several years ago white men began to encroach on our ground. We were willing to have them share with us the right to fish but not satisfied with equal rights they have yearly made additional obstructions preventing our catching fish, by setting traps, and placing piling along the grounds. They have driven us from our camping ground on the beach and have so treated us that we feel we must appeal to you for assistance. In our treaty with the government we were given the first right to hunt and fish on our grounds and we know too well that the good government

that has so far protected our rights will not permit us to be trodden upon simply because we are Indians.

When the BIA did nothing, the Lummis took the matter to court. A Washington state judge ruled against them. The judge's interpretation said the treaty gave Lummis "equal fishing rights, not special fishing privileges such as permanent protected locations." The Lummis appealed in 1897, and the case went all the way to the US Supreme Court, which dismissed the appeal. The Lummis were emotionally crushed, writing, "we now find ourselves excluded from earning an honest living for ourselves and our families." Although the courts told them there were still plenty of fish in the sea, the Lummis knew by their empty nets that they had to abandon the open waters. They fished the Nooksack River on their reservation.

The fish traps were so effective that salmon populations plummeted. The Canadian government banned trap fishing in 1915 as part of a salmon conservation law and included reefnet gears in the ban, thus outlawing the Saanich's native practice. On the American side, the 1893–94 Fish and Game Protector Report stated: "For a third of a century, Oregon has drawn wealth from her streams, but now, by reason of her wastefulness and lack of intelligent provision for the future, the source of that wealth is disappearing and is threatened with complete annihilation."

The state of Washington established an agency to oversee fishing. By treaty law, Native peoples were exempt from state laws, but the state fishing agency enforced regulations against them anyway, resulting in monetary penalties and arrests. Native people seen fishing after the commercial season had closed were arrested, even though the salmon runs didn't cross their reservations until after the commercial season closed. Over 40 percent of fishing violation arrests in 1915 and 1916 were of Lummis, for fishing after the season closed, fishing without a license, or fishing in prohibited waters. Many of these Native fishers also had their gear confiscated upon arrest.

In 1934, Washington state banned all "fixed gear"—traps, weirs, and reefnets—in an attempt to curb overfishing. Although Straits Salish were explicitly exempted because of their federal treaty rights, the state government enforced the new restrictions against them. In 1939, this law was refined to relegalize reefnet fishing, but the Lummis were simply not told about the revision. The best reefnet sites were claimed by white fishers before the Lummi even knew they were available.

\* \* \*

THE DAY AFTER HEADING OUT to the reefnet gear with Riley and his crew, I returned to Seattle to await The Call. Riley needed the OK from the Pacific Salmon Commission—run jointly by Canada and the United States—to start fishing. Once Riley got The Call, he would let me know it was time to join the crew.

The delay in the start of the fishing season was caused by a rock-slide up the Fraser River in Canada, which was blocking the salmon's path to their spawning grounds. The entire industry was in a panic. The slide had occurred in late 2018, but in such a remote area that it wasn't discovered until June 2019. By that point, it had already been blocking the migrations of spring salmon. Spring chinook, coho, and sockeye salmon had been "battering themselves to exhaustion trying to scale the new five-metre waterfall blocking their routes," according to reporting for *Maclean's* magazine in Canada. The salmon, driven by millions of years of instinct and evolution, would either make it over the waterfall, or die trying. Over 89 percent of endangered spring chinook died attempting their migration.

The Canadian government was working furiously to clear the river. But the situation was too dire and the timing too tight, so workers began moving fish above the blockage by hand and helicopter. As a temporary solution, what is professionally called a "passage portal" and colloquially called a "fish cannon" was installed: a pressurized tube that safely shot salmon over the impassable area.

But once again, fishing for pinks proved advantageous: although the Fraser hosts one of the largest pink runs, the pinks don't swim as far upriver as other salmon species and did not need to pass the rockslide area.

Finally, late Saturday afternoon, Riley got the word that they could fish the next day. I was scheduled to fly out the next morning at 5 a.m. Six hundred painful but priceless dollars later, I had rebooked my flight for 10 p.m. Sunday night, and I was waiting impatiently in my rental car for the ferry to Lummi Island. It was already 10 o'clock on Sunday morning, and although I was not worried about missing the boat—impossible, as I've said, in reefnet fishing—I was worried about somehow missing the tide and the fish. Riley, Ben, Natalie, and Olivia had camped out on the Salish Center land the night before and woke up at 5 a.m. so that they would be ready to fish by daylight. But Riley had assured me the tides were long, sometimes constituting a ten-hour workday on the gears.

I also hoped to head over to Kyle Kinley's gear that afternoon. Kyle and his family were running the first Lummi-owned reefnet gear to fish these waters in over eighty years. This was their debut season, and their second day out in the sound—Indigenous fishers had been allowed to start the season one day earlier.

Thirty minutes later I pulled up next to Riley's parked car, strapped on the life jacket he had left for me, gave Stella a scritch on her head, and walked down to the beach. I was wearing battered running shoes, yoga capris, an old tank top, and the polarized sunglasses Riley had recommended for combating ocean glare. The weather was perfect: calm, warm, and clear. I texted Riley that I had arrived, and in a few minutes Olivia pulled up in the skiff.

"Kyle is going to be the one in the tower right now," Olivia told me as we passed his gear, in the first position closest to shore. "He's the captain." I looked up to see a figure silhouetted by the sun. The gear had *Spirit of Sxwo'le* painted on the side in blue lettering.

I looked out over the bay of reefnet gears buzzing with activity. Unlike the quiet day when we had prepped the gear, this morning every gear crawled with crew. I could hear captains yelling orders, their words unintelligible on the breeze but the urgency of their commands clear. As schools of salmon were pulled to the surface in nets, the sound of hundreds of flopping fish was like the splashing rain of a heavy thunderstorm. Sunlight struck droplets of water tossed up by the slapping fish, lighting them up like a sea of diamonds. The bay was alive with this ancient practice.

The skiff pulled up to Riley's gear, Natalie shouted "Hi, Sarah!" as we approached. I jumped on board and said my hellos and shouted up to Riley in the crow's nest. His eyes watched the water for silvery shapes. On board were Ben, Olivia, and Natalie, plus Sean and Benoit, friends of Riley who were volunteering for the day. The crew were all dressed in waterproof boots, bright yellow waterproof overalls, and life jackets. There would also be a steady stream of spectators over the course of the day. Riley opened the invitation to anyone he thought could make a positive impact on the future of reefnet fishing.

Recognizing that the crew was busy, I wanted to help. I knelt by Sean, who was on his knees in front of the live well, grabbing fish out of the water with his bare hands. The well was nearly empty—only three salmon left, with plenty of room to swim.

"These are the hardest to catch," Sean told me. He instructed me to reach in and grab a fish just behind its head. I leaned over and plunged my hand into the water in the well—it was shockingly cold. I felt the firm, fleshy bodies of the salmon slip past my fingers. Each one shot out of my grasp and splashed me with its tail, soaking me with salty water that ran into my eyes.

Natalie saw me flailing and came over. "See those little fins, in the front?" She pointed down at a salmon in the well. "Aim for just in front of those and apply a lot of pressure."

I focused on my target and shot my hand into the water, aiming as Natalie had shown me. I connected with the fish and squeezed my thumb and index finger around it as hard as I could. I lifted a two-foot-long pink salmon out of the water.

"Yeaaaaaaaah!!!!!" I roared, the victor over the fish. The boat's crew and spectators joined me in my cheer. Then, realizing what my victory meant for the fish, I apologized. "Sorry, fish," I said, before looking at Natalie. "What's next?"

What was next was bleeding the salmon. The gills are pulled out by hand, which breaks one of their arterial blood vessels. Then they're sorted into another well to swim until they bleed out, dying peacefully in the water. The flowing water of the sound also helps to wash out all the blood, which can cause an off flavor in the fish. This method is considered the most humane way to kill fish, instead of throwing them directly on ice or letting them suffocate on deck.

The salmon, a five-pound, slippery sock of pure muscle, struggled in my right hand. It took all the strength in my hand and forearm to hold it. I slid open one gill slit with my left hand, hooked my middle and index fingers into the bony white rings of the gills and pulled hard. When the gills gave way with a pop, I tossed the fish into one of three holding wells to bleed out. I caught the last two salmon swimming in the live well one after another, bled them, and tossed them in the holding wells.

Each holding well was lined with a "brailer," a mesh bag that looked like a big laundry bag. When a holding well was filled, the brailer full of fish was lifted by a pulley and placed on the skiff in a large plastic tote filled with slush ice. Each tote would hold 400–500 pounds of fish. A crew member in the skiff ran the totes to the tender, a boat waiting to receive the catch from all the gears. The tender weighed the catch for each gear, stored the fish on ice, and then took them to Lummi Island Wild's facilities in Bellingham, where they were processed and sold to Patagonia.

As it turns out, that was the last time that day the live well would be empty. No sooner had I torn out the last fish's gills than Ben called from the cabin under the crow's nest: "Fish in camera one!" Riley gave the signal and pulled the winch that hauled the net out of the water.

Riley shouted directions to his novice crew from the crow's nest: "Get behind it, get behind the net! Pull, pull right there!" Sometimes he would climb halfway down the ladder to yell at us by name. As we heaved the nylon net out of the water, I was directed to use my feet to pin the edge of the net to the deck, so when the fish were hauled on board they couldn't slip back into the water. But I had to be careful: the weight and the strength of the fish in the net could pull me right off the deck and into the water, and crew members wore gloves to prevent rope burn if the nylon net slid through their hands. The final heave-ho pulled the 100-pound pocket of fish on deck. The platforms float just a few inches above the water to make this part as easy as possible. The wet salmon bodies were dumped over my feet, a mass of flopping fish that spilled into the live well behind me. I was soaking wet and ankle-deep in fish.

"That was a good one, guys," Natalie said, breathless.

Another school came four minutes later. So we got up off our knees—three or four of us were at the live well processing the last haul—and brought in another net of salmon. Five minutes later, Riley yelled, "We've got fish!!" We pulled the net in again.

"Fish camera three and four!!" Olivia shouted two minutes later.

"All right, I see it!" Riley called back before engaging the net.

"Here we go again," I commented as we spun around to haul the net out of the water.

And that's how our afternoon progressed: Riley in the tower, Olivia on the cameras, Ben and Benoit running fish to the tender, and me, Natalie, and Sean processing the fish. And it wasn't only us in constant motion. The gear next to us and the one behind us were pulling in huge numbers of fish as well. "Maybe a record year," Riley commented. We could hear people cheering on other boats. There was something special happening that day.

After I'm not sure how many hours, I stood up briefly to stretch my back, give my knees a break, and warm up my hands. Although the air was 80 degrees, the water was cold enough that my fingers were numb, making me less nimble as I tried to grab the fish. I called up to Riley in the crow's nest to ask if I could join him for a few minutes.

"Was this worth the wait?" I asked, smiling when I got to the top.

Riley laughed. "Yeah!"

"How many pounds are going to Patagonia?"

"225,000."

"Think you'll make that today?"

"Nooo," Riley said, dismissing the idea. But they would come close.

Riley's gear alone would end up catching nearly 6,000 pounds of pink salmon that day. On that Sunday in August, the nine gears on the water would pull more fish out of the Salish Sea than on any other documented day in history.

# Riley's Baked Whole Pink Salmon

Riley, an unabashed advocate of pink salmon consumption, passed along his favorite recipe for pinks. It's very quick to throw together, feeds a crowd along with some sides, and the acids in the lemon and mustard complement but don't overpower the salmon.

SERVES 2–4 AS A MAIN

INGREDIENTS
1 whole pink salmon, 2-3 pounds
Black pepper
2 lemons, zested then sliced
2-4 tablespoons Dijon mustard
2 tablespoons salted butter, softened

1. Preheat oven to 350°F. Line a full sheet pan with parchment.
2. Rinse the fish well and pat dry. Make 4 shallow slits, ¼ inch deep, through the skin on each side of the fish.
3. Sprinkle freshly ground black pepper into the cavity, then place the lemon slices along the length of the cavity. Fill the skin slits with lemon zest, then with butter. Coat both sides with Dijon mustard. Lay fish on sheet pan.
4. Bake for 20 minutes, then turn the heat down to 250° and cook for another 10 minutes, or until a thermometer inserted into the thickest part of the fish reads 130°. Let the fish rest for 10 minutes.
5. Carefully peel back the skin with your fingers or a pair of tongs. With a fork and a spatula, lift the top fillet off the bone. Remove any pin bones from the fillet. Take off the head and bones by pulling the tail up (discard or save for stock), revealing another boneless fillet beneath.

Riley's recipe is intended for a small, whole pink salmon. For a larger fish, increase the ingredients and the cooking time. For fillets, halve the ingredients and spread the mustard on the flesh side first, then layer with black pepper, lemon zest, butter, and finally lemon slices. Cook at 350°F for 20 minutes.

\* \* \*

IN 1962, THE LUMMIS ASKED for help from the Bureau of Indian Affairs to reclaim their reefnet sites. This original petition grew into a lawsuit as the Lummis joined with twelve other tribes to sue the federal government for violation of the 1850s' treaties. The suit specifically sought clarification of the hotly debated language that tribes were guaranteed fishing at "all usual and accustomed grounds and stations . . . in common with all citizens of the Territory."

In February 1974, federal district court judge George Boldt decided that wording in the treaties should be interpreted to mean that the treaty tribes were entitled to fish wherever they had traditionally fished—their "usual and accustomed grounds"—whether on or off their reservations. "Members of the Lummi Tribe are entitled to and shall have, as a matter of *right*, the opportunity to fish with reef nets in such areas," Judge Boldt wrote in his decision. "While non-treaty fishermen when licensed by the State to fish in reef net areas have the *privilege* of fishing in those areas 'in common with' Lummi Tribal members, they do not have the *right* to do so." Boldt ruled that included in these Native fishing rights was a guaranteed percentage of the total allowable seasonal catch, which he set at 50 percent. From now on, half of all fish were the guaranteed right of Native peoples, and the other half were a privilege granted to non-Native fishers.

The ruling, which became known as the Boldt decision, was appealed by Washington state and heard by the US Supreme Court, which upheld Boldt's decision in 1979. The Supreme Court added in its ruling that "the state of Washington had the responsibility to manage the fishery so that the treaty Fishers would be given a fair chance at harvesting their allocation."

For white fishers, the Boldt decision meant that 50 percent of the fish they felt entitled to, and relied on to make a living, would be taken away. The anger created by economic uncertainty expressed itself in racist attitudes and actions against Indigenous fishers. In addition to protests and harassment, white fishers lashed out in criminal acts. On several occasions, white men shot at Lummi fishers, and in one instance targeted a fourteen-year-old boy. White fishers would vandalize Native boats docked at marinas, cutting cables and pouring sugar into gas tanks.

Despite the harassment they faced, by the mid-1980s the Lummi Nation were the most successful Native fishers in the region. Their fleet consisted mostly of gill net boats, a trolling system that uses a net sized specifically to entangle only certain species of fish. At the time of the Boldt decision, there were forty-three registered reefnet gears fishing off Lummi Island, but not one of them was owned by an Indigenous fisher. Still, the cultural and spiritual attachment to reefnetting never disappeared. It was seen as the center of Lummi culture even decades after the last Lummi reefnet was shut down.

Finally, in 2012, the Lummi Nation launched the first traditional reefnet in a century. Made of two canoes and a net built by hand, the gear was anchored off Cherry Point, *Xwe'chi'eXen*, a site that's thought to have been a reefnet location at least several hundreds of years old. Tribal Council member Jay Julius said of the event, "To us, culture is fish and fish is culture. It's more than a privilege, it's who we are." Claxton, helped by the Lummi, launched his reefnet two years later.

The next step, some Lummis felt, was to bring back reefnet as a commercial fishery. Larry Chexanexwh Kinley, the longest-serving Tribal Chairman of the Lummi Nation, was the most outspoken believer in a future for commercial Lummi reefnet, so much so that he built one for himself.

Kinley was a legend in the Lummi community, a powerful voice for the preservation of traditions. He grew up in the small community of Marietta, Washington, on the banks of the Nooksack River, a spawning ground for salmon. His mother fished in the river; his father was a commercial fisher who traveled to Alaska for work.

Kinley eventually left Marietta to serve in the Vietnam War, then attended college at Chaminade University in Honolulu, graduating in 1970. Like his father, he began a professional career in commercial fishing. He later said he was able to fish the whole West Coast, from "Alaska to Costa Rica," an experience that informed his work as an advocate for Native peoples in the same areas.

Kinley became Lummi Tribal Council Chair and served on the Lummi Indian Business Council in the 1970s and 1980s. During his tenure, he established Fisherman's Cove, a convenience store across from the Lummi Island ferry that provides much-needed basic services like access to bait, snacks, and gas. He helped open a fish processing plant on the reservation and a blackjack hall that grew into the Silver Reef Casino and Spa. The casino now provides three times the profits of fishing for the Lummi community. Profitable or no, Kinley knew that fishing was at the heart of the Lummi identity, and of his own identity.

Kinley met his wife, Ellie, while they were both working as fishing crew leads. Ellie later said that as a lead you "spent a lot of time sitting in coffee houses—kind of like designated drivers—keeping a sober eye on their crews while they were off duty." It was during these long hours in coffee shops that Kinley and Ellie fell in love. They got married in 1993, and had two sons, Lucas and Kyle.

As of 2015, there were still no Lummi-owned and operated commercial reefnets; Lummis tended to use gill nets or purse seiners. Kinley and his family decided to change that. He knew that reefnetting resulted in a better-quality product than other commercial fishing techniques. "There's minimal handling, so we can sell the fish for more," he told a reporter from the Northwest Treaty Tribes website in 2016.

Perhaps more important, Kinley wanted to bring back the reefnet to reconnect the tribe's children to their heritage. "There's a real active side when you set up the gear, that it can get dangerous at times," Kinley admitted. But as a stationary, place-based fishery, "there's another side that's very passive and it's a safe place. And we think that's a real opportunity . . . for a lot of the children that haven't come from the more recent active fishing families to be able to get back a little bit more about who they are, where they come from. I also believe being on the water, that that would also help them in terms of their own wellness." Ultimately, Kinley hoped to make reefnetting part of the curriculum in local schools and colleges.

Working with Lummi Island Wild—and friends' boatbuilding company Strongback Metal Boats—Kinley designed a modern reef-net gear: aluminum platforms, underwater cameras, and all the latest technology. He named that craft the *Spirit of Sxwo'le*.

The Kinleys anchored their reefnet off of Cherry Point in 2016, the same fishing site that the traditional reefnet had fished in 2012. Ellie monitored the underwater camera, while their son Lucas was in the crow's nest; nineteen-year-old Kyle helped, too. But they spotted very few fish, especially the sockeye salmon they were there to catch.

The lack of results didn't bother Kinley. "There's a lot of times we don't catch any fish at all. And right now we're not catching very much fish. But we're just going out on the water because we love it there. We love it. Our culture's so tied to it, there's a lot of spirituality with us."

"We're looking toward next year," Larry Kinley told *Northwest Treaty Tribes*. "Nobody's fished this area for a long time; we don't have a gauge for how many fish come through here."

In February 2018, Kinley died of cancer at the age of seventy-one.

\* \* \*

I HAD BEEN FISHING ON RILEY'S GEAR for four or five hours when I asked Ben and Benoit to take me in the skiff. We stopped by the tender to deliver another 400 pounds of pink salmon, and then they dropped me off at Kyle Kinley's gear. This gear was the *Spirit of Sxwo'le*, the gear Larry Kinley built, now captained by his younger son. It was the first Indigenous-owned commercial reefnet on the water in at least eighty years.

"One of you guys must be Kyle?" I asked the two men on deck as I clumsily climbed onboard.

"I'm Kyle!" the man in the live well, literally waist-deep in fish, singsonged back. "Welcome aboard!"

Kyle, twenty-two, was dressed in a soaking wet black T and khaki shorts, even his dark brown hair was wet and spiky. He had a big, warm smile and a scruffy beard.

Kyle was performing the Sisyphean task of bleeding hundreds of salmon on his own, while more kept getting dumped in the live well from the net. As opposed to the crowd staffing Riley's boat, Kyle's boat was crewed only by him, his older brother, Lucas, and his mom, Ellie, who was watching the cameras in a hutch on the opposite platform.

Lucas, twenty-six, had golden brown hair that fell below his shoulders, light eyes, and, like his brother, he smiled and laughed easily. Lucas worked as a commercial fisher and was usually in Alaska at this time of year, but he had stayed back this season to help Kyle get the reefnet going. In 2019, when I met him, he was serving on the board of directors of the Salish Center for Sustainable Fishing; in 2020, he became its president. Kyle was also involved with the Salish Center, although not officially. As he put it, "I put in my two cents whenever they ask."

I kneeled down and started pulling fish from the live well, and asked Kyle why he had decided to get his dad's reefnet gear up and running again.

"It wasn't in the water last year and I really didn't like it. It didn't feel good. So it only feels right to be out here and it's workin' out." Despite the fact that Kyle had never fished commercially or owned a boat, he had spent more time on the water than not in his life. When he decided to captain the gear, he secured the spot off of Lummi Island.

"It just feels right for this time of year. It's like tradition, basically."

I asked the Kinleys if they thought reefnetting was the future of salmon fishing.

"The future?" Kyle asked back. "It is what we have always done, or that was always done, I guess? The future, yeah. I could see it being the future of fishing due to changing times but . . . I know Riley would definitely say that . . ."

"Riley!" Lucas laughed. We all did, knowing Riley's unabashed passion and advocacy for the reefnet. "Riley's an extreme reefnetter."

"He told me a few nights ago," I said, "that he's just a placeholder. He said, this is for you—you're the future." The two men smiled.

"I would like to see a lot more tribal gear out here," Kyle agreed. "There's the interest, but the lack of resource for people . . ."

"Not a whole lot of the younger generation is interested," Lucas added.

"No. My brother and I are one of the few young ones that have moved our way up to owning boats."

"Well, we kinda grew up on them. But a lot of people aren't getting into it or staying in it."

"Why do you think that is?" I asked.

"Western culture is too enticing." Lucas shrugged. "Money . . ."

"Yeah, it really comes down to not being able to make enough a year to survive," Kyle added. "Whereas us, we just kinda do it just to do it."

"Oh, I love chasin' salmon," Lucas, the commercial fisher, agreed. "It's one of my favorite parts of the year."

Kyle hoped he could get young Lummis interested through local colleges, and then maybe younger kids in the tribal school. He's thought about building a second gear as a learning center and setting up a summer "fish camp" for students to stay near the water during the salmon season and learn how to reefnet.

"But right now, we're just trying to catch fish," Kyle added with a laugh. "This is the first day everybody's actually really caught anything."

Suddenly, Ellie screamed from across the water. I looked up, but the brothers didn't seem alarmed. They calmly turned around and prepared to drag in the net, so I did the same, and we hauled aboard another hundred pounds of fish.

"What does your mom yell when she sees fish?" I asked, startled.

"AAAAAHHH!!!!!" Kyle and Lucas both mimicked in unison.

"What??" Ellie cried innocently from across the water.

"We're talking about your little war cry," Kyle shouted back. "It's either 'Fish' or just 'Aaaaaah!' " he told me.

"I said, 'Give her hell' that time!" Ellie protested.

We had pulled in a chinook salmon in the last load and Kyle scooped it out of the holding well, cradling it in his arms for a moment before gently tipping it back into the sea. "There you go, little buddy!" He gently encouraged the chinook as it swam away.

Ellie would let out her war cry two more times in the next fifteen minutes, but we were coming to the end of the tide and the constant onslaught of fish was slowing down. Lucas joked that this type of fishery was like a nine-to-five job because it was totally based on the tides.

As the net was reset after our last haul, two harbor seals swam between the floating platforms. Ellie laughed as they came near her, happily playing in and around the gear, even biting and tugging on the ropes. They swam off down the bay, splashing and rolling in the water. Those seals felt like our blessing. This method of fishing was so undisruptive, so unthreatening, that two seals could play around it without a care in the world.

Kyle was practically glowing.

"This is a fun day. I'm having a lot of fun," he declared.

"I am, too, actually," Lucas agreed, beaming.

"I just built a boat," Kyle declared with a bit of awe. "It's like I'm officially a boat owner, as well. Lots of learning to do, and I'll be better next year."

Then Kyle corrected himself. "No, I already know it." He was Lummi; reefnetting was in his blood. "I just need to remember it."

# FIVE

# *Manoomin*

## ANISHINAABE WILD RICE

US Highway 41 skirts the southern shore of Lake Superior on Michigan's Upper Peninsula. The UP is so remote that the residents refer to the rest of the country as "down below," as in, "Are you going down below?" Through the dense forest beyond the two-lane road, I could see glittering lakes, and even though August hadn't quite ended, the leaves of the staghorn sumac trees were bright red and the tips of the sugar maples were starting to change. Trucks loaded with fresh-cut timber passed me, and a blob of porcupine roadkill appeared on the shoulder. I slowed down to watch a family of sandhill cranes, prehistoric birds with blood-red plumage around their eyes, cross the highway in front of me. One of the cranes whirled around and began to approach my car aggressively. I apologized and sped off.

I was due at a rice camp, a multiday class led by Ojibwe elders that would teach attendees how to harvest *manoomin*, or wild rice. Wild rice is the common name for plants in the genus *Zizania*. It's an aquatic grass, most closely related to corn, classified as a cereal grain. It's not *Oryza sativa*, the Asian plant commonly called rice in English.

Wild rice has many names in Anishinaabe dialects. The Ojibwe—

sometimes known outside the community as Chippewa—are one of the culturally and linguistically related tribes of the Anishinaabeg. *Manoomin* is the Ojibwe word for wild rice; its many dialectal cousins include *mannomin, mnomiin, mnomen,* and *manohmen.* Its name is most commonly translated as "the good fruit" or "the good berry," but some translate it as "spirit delicacy." The full moon of late August is known to the Ojibwe people as Manoominike-giizi, the Ricing Moon. Manoominike-giizi meant the rice would be ripe before the next full moon, and the Ojibwe would begin the harvest of their sacred food.

Manoominike-giizi had passed, and brought me to the UP to learn the necessary skills to prepare to harvest wild rice. By the next full moon, I'd be at Roseville, Minnesota's wild rice soup festival, gorging myself on fry bread dipped in wild rice soup with a side of wild rice-stuffed sausages, before heading north to witness the manoomin harvest.

Tribes of the Anishinaabeg and their neighbors, the Sioux (Dakota and Lakota), are the only two contemporary Native groups that harvest wild rice. They collect it in the waters of upstate Wisconsin, Minnesota, Michigan, and in parts of Canada bordering the Great Lakes. In Minnesota alone, Native peoples consume an average of 350,000 pounds of wild rice annually, about six pounds per person per year. It is the most commonly consumed traditional food. But manoomin is a spiritual food as well, essential to *mino-bimaadiziwin,* the concept of living a good life. It's the first solid food fed to Ojibwe infants and it is one of the foods present at funeral ceremonies.

A Presidium for Anishinaabe Manoomin was created by Slow Food and well-known Ojibwe activist and water protector Winona LaDuke to "promote consumption of traditionally harvested and prepared wild rice." LaDuke continues to coordinate the presidium, working with local conservation initiatives as well as nationally famous chefs to preserve and promote the grain. Sean Sherman, Oglala Lakota chef and founder of Owamni restaurant in Minneapolis, gave a traditional wild rice cooking demo at the 2016 Indigenous Terra Madre Slow Food gathering, which was attended by "148 indigenous food communities from 58 countries in Africa, the Americas, the Arctic, Asia, Europe, the Middle East, Russia and the Pacific" and 60,000 members of the public in India. He prepared the manoomin with maple syrup and dried berries.

Even though I'm a born and raised Midwesterner, I had no idea that wild rice was native to the Great Lakes region. I was drawn to this topic in part because *Zizania palustris*, the most commonly harvested variety of wild rice, hasn't been spotted in my home state of Ohio since the 1990s. The range of *Zizania palustris* has been shrinking northward due to climate change: the seeds need a deep winter freeze to germinate in the spring, and warming temperatures have shortened this dormancy period. Additionally, waterfront industrialization, invasive plants, and pollution have destroyed manoomin beds—a bit like a canary in a coalmine, the sudden disappearance of manoomin can warn of pollutants from mining or sewage runoff.

Manoomin doesn't only feed humans. It's a staple food source for waterfowl as a young plant in its "tender floating leaf stage" in the spring, and for migratory birds when it is seeding in the fall. Both Indigenous people and European colonists stewarded wild rice beds for the purpose of attracting waterfowl to hunt. And the plant's large root masses provide a breeding ground for fish as well as hold sediment in place. Manoomin stems slow wind on the water's surface, stopping organic matter from mixing in the water, which can contribute to algae blooms.

It's also an extremely genetically diverse plant. It adapts to the water and soil it grows in, meaning that every lake, river, and marsh has its own unique variety. One study of wild rice genetics even found differences between the east and west ends of a single lake. In my travels, I saw manoomin from the Mississippi River, long grains that were almost black; rice from Lindsey Lake in upstate Minnesota that was straw-colored and short; and rice from Lower Rice Lake that ranged in color from toasty brown to tan. Researcher Margaret Lehman, writing for the Manomin Research Project, said, "They taste like a lake. But not the same lake. Equally delicious, but unique from each other. There is beauty in that."

Currently, there are four plants in the genus: *Z. latifolia* grows in Asia and is the only member of the genus found outside the US. *Z. texana* is endangered, and only grows in the San Marcos River in Texas. *Z. aquatica*, also known as river rice or Southern wild rice, grows over most of the eastern United States, but it's a "threatened" species in most states. *Z. aquatica* is not commonly harvested, because it often grows 12 to 16 feet tall, in dense patches along the edges of rivers, and its grains are relatively small. A few groups of Ojibwe in southern Michigan make the effort; they press wooden board-walks into the rice beds and bend the stalks down with long shepherd's crooks. One manoomin processor told me he likes river rice best because it is more flavorful: the smaller grains take on more woodsmoke during the parching part of processing.

*Z. palustris*, also known as lake rice or northern wild rice, is the "just right" of the wild rice world. It grows two to three feet above the waterline and is spaced enough that a canoe can pass through the rice bed. The stems are thin with narrow leaves, and the flowers that bloom at the top look like a mini-Christmas tree, male flowers spiking out laterally and female flowers in a tassel called a panicle at the top. The panicle is where the grains form, darkening as they ripen, the tassel drooping as the kernels get heavier. It's traditionally harvested from a canoe that a "poler" pushes through the rice beds like a gondolier, while a "knocker" uses two lightweight cedar sticks to bend the grass over the hull and gently knock off ripe rice. Since wild rice doesn't ripen all at once, the process of tapping the stalks loosens only the ripe grains. Most of the grains fall into the canoe; the rest hit the water and reseed the plant, ensuring another generation of manoomin.

The harvested manoomin is traditionally dried in the sun, then parched in a metal washtub or cast iron cauldron over an open fire. The hulls are removed by "dancing" on the dry grains in a pit and then winnowed by tossing the grains into the air with a birch bark basket; the hulls fly away in the breeze, leaving the clean grain behind. Many Ojibwe still process small amounts of wild rice for home use by this traditional method. The modern commercial processors—still small and family-owned—copy this traditional pattern with custom mechanized equipment.

While manoomin has strict preservation protections in place in

Minnesota and Wisconsin, no such regulation exists in Michigan. Rice camps, like the one I was attending sponsored by Keweenaw Bay Indian Community Natural Resources Department and Michigan Technological University, have popped up to train Native and non-Native participants how to respectfully harvest wild rice.

After a night in the Twin Lakes Motel in Michigamme, I woke up the day of the rice camp to drizzling rain and temperatures barely over 50 degrees. Having just come from working on the reefnet gear, where temperatures were in the 80s, I was unprepared. I pulled on a few thin layers and shivered my way to the Ford Forest Center. Now a museum and nature center, it was a former logging camp and processing facility established shortly after the First World War by Henry Ford to produce the wooden accents for his famous cars.

The camp met in a large hall with fluorescent lighting and a linoleum floor; plastic stackable chairs were arranged in a circle. About forty people were in attendance, predominantly Ojibwe families, but also Native and non-Native professors from Michigan State University and other locals. A few kids ran around, and one of the organizers announced, "If the little ones need to take a nap, put them underneath a table. I've got a blanket in the car. It's important that they're here just to hear these things. We want to welcome everybody."

Roger LaBine, an elder from the Getegitigaaning Ojibwe Nation, or the Lac Vieux Desert Band of Lake Superior Chippewa, welcomed the attendees. Short, plump, with a little gray in his black beard and an uproarious laugh, he's considered one of Michigan's wild rice experts. He's particularly engaged with education to keep ricing traditions alive. He began our meeting with a prayer.

"For our people that are gathered here today, these individuals that have come and have that earnest desire to learn about the sacred gift that you've given to us as Anishinaabe people, give me the words that I can answer their questions, I can give them the knowledge that they seek. These medicines, these foods, this way of life that was once ours that we can fall back on so that we can learn and become healthy again.

"I thank you for bringing these people here safely today. I'll ask that as they gain this knowledge and they go back to their communities, that they take this knowledge. They do not keep it to themselves, but they share it."

Roger went over some of the basic regulations for harvesting rice in Michigan, and what regulation tools looked like. Then he cleared his throat and said, "I'm going to give this teaching to you now.

"Our ancestors here, my ancestors, we were not native to this area. Years ago, the Three Fires People were actually located up at the mouth of the St. Lawrence Seaway. Our oral history talks about that you could go stand on a hill or a mountain and no matter which direction you looked, all you'd see was the fire of the Three Fires People."

The Anishinaabe people belong to the Algonquian language group; the Algonquians are found along the East Coast, from northern Quebec to North Carolina. Many Algonquian language family words have become pan-Native words, such as totem, moccasin, and powwow; others have been adopted into American English, such as toboggan, chickadee, and moose. Many of the places they inhabit have maintained their Algonquian names, including Michigan—from *mishigami* or *meicigama,* meaning large lake.

The Anishinaabeg emerged as a distinct group about 1,500 years ago. About AD 800, they began migrating west.

"The Creator presented us with seven prophecies," Roger told the rice camp. "The first prophecy told us that we needed to move. There was an *ikwe*, a woman, who had this dream, she was standing on the back of a turtle and she was facing the setting sun. The spiritual people told her that we needed to leave. We needed to migrate because if we didn't, we were going to be facing death and destruction."

Over several hundred years, the Anishinaabeg traveled along the St. Lawrence Seaway and the shores of the Great Lakes. As they migrated, they encountered other Native groups, and warfare between these groups is one of the factors that may have kept them moving. While some Anishinaabeg stayed and settled, others kept pushing west.

"The Third Prophecy says that we were going to head in the direction of the setting sun," Roger continued. "We needed to come to this place where we were going to find the food that grows on the water. And when we find the food that grows on the water, we know we will be home."

The "food that grows on the water" is manoomin.

## Manoomin in Birch Bark

I wanted to experience what some of the earliest Anishinaabe dishes with wild rice were like, so I decided to try out a recipe written by Renee "Wasson" Dillard of the Little Traverse Bay Bands of Odawa Indians, as published in *Manoomin: The Story of Wild Rice in Michigan* by Barbara J. Barton:

> Get a bed of hot coals with some steady rocks on the bottom. Rocks hold up the birch bowl.
> Soak ½ cup of rice for about an hour. Place the rice in the bowl on the coals with 3 cups of water. Bring to a boil. Put in 1 cup diced cattail shoots. Add 1/4 cup diced wild leeks. Add a handful of winter berries. Add 1 1/2 cups diced fillet fish. Simmer until fish is cooked. Take the birch bowl off the rocks. Some of the birch bowl edges may have burnt and fallen into the soup, which adds flavor. Eat hot and enjoy!

This recipe could be a challenge for a modern cook, since every ingredient is foraged. Luckily, I have a frequent collaborator for foraged meals: Mark, a friend since high school.

On a sunny August day, we began by sifting through a forest floor of rotting leaves to find earthworms for bait. We sat by a shady fishing hole on the Black River in Lorain, Ohio, and fished in amicable silence, pulling small perch and sunfish out of the freshwater. Then we stuck our hands in the squelching muck to pull out crisp cattail shoots and a few cat-

tail rhizomes just for fun. The rhizomes we roasted directly
on hot coals. They had a taste and texture almost exactly like
mashed potatoes.

We collected wild garlic on the hike back home, and Mark
had ramps in his freezer from earlier in the year. I had brought
wild rice with me, purchased from the White Earth Nation
in Minnesota, and a bag of dried blueberries. I even had a few
birch baskets to cook in—although I hadn't thought to seal
them, with spruce pitch or by another method, and they leaked
water and put out my fire.

So I turned to cast iron, boiled the water and manoomin
as we prepped the other ingredients, and then tossed in our
handfuls of alliums, cattails, and blueberries. Finally, I nestled
the fish—headless, gutted and cleaned of scales but otherwise
whole—into the thick stew. When the fish was white and flaky,
it was time to eat.

The broth of the soup had the color and taste of a tea, flavored by the nutty wild rice. The manoomin was the heartiest, most filling part of the dish. The flavor of the garlic was
key to bringing the soup alive, and the sweet-and-sour pop
of the plumped blueberries was enormously pleasant. The
still-crunchy cattail shoots gave it the texture it needed, and
the fresh fish tasted of lake and lemon. The only element that
betrayed that this wasn't a modern dish was the lack of salt. Perhaps I'm too used to highly salted food, but a dash made the
flavors blossom. Historical Anishinaabeg ate well, but the entire
process took six hours from start to finish, and we didn't even
harvest and process the rice ourselves.

\* \* \*

THE OJIBWE'S NEW HOME was in Lakota territory. While these
two communities were enemies at times, they were allies at others,
and it's likely that the Ojibwe learned how to harvest and process
manoomin from the Lakota. Today, wild rice is now extinct in much

of the Lakota territory. Those who want to harvest it usually travel to Ojibwe lands.

In the oral history of the Ojibwe, it was their hero Wenabozho (also Waynaboozhoo, Nanaboozhoo or Nanabozho) who discovered that manoomin was edible. Wenabozho is sometimes thought to be the Original Man, but he is more often described as a spirit with humanlike characteristics. In some versions of the stories he has a twin brother and in others he has a wolf companion, which is sometimes also considered his brother. Wenabozho was a teacher to the Ojibwe, bringing them skills that bettered their lives.

There are two different versions of the story of Wenabozho's discovery of manoomin. In one, Wenabozho worried about how this new migrant nation would feed themselves over the winter. He fasted in isolation, then had a dream where he walked along the edge of a river and saw dancers over the water, decked out in the feathered headdress of Ojibwe men. Wenabozho asked if he could dance, too, and joined the celebration on the water. When he woke up the next morning, he looked out over the water and saw the seed tassels of ripe wild rice dancing in the wind. He dreamed again of how to prepare the manoomin, then shared the knowledge with his people.

In the second version of the story, Wenabozho returned to his campsite after a luckless day of hunting to find a duck perched on the edge of his cooking basket. The duck dropped grains of wild rice into the basket of boiling water before it flew away. Wenabozho tasted the cooked grain and thought it was delicious. The next day, he followed a flock of ducks to a lake, where he saw manoomin plants. The Wild Rice Spirit spoke to Wenabozho and told him that manoomin was good to eat.

The Ojibwe believe that the manoomin has a spirit. In the Ojibwe language, manoomin is referred to as "him" or "her," not "it." So an important step of the harvesting season is to ceremonially offer tobacco to the manoomin. As Roger LaBine told his rice camp students: "You want to talk to that manoomin spirit out there and tell him that you're coming, why you're coming, thanking him if you're harvesting. I do not go in there unannounced."

Roger has been ricing since 1972, when his grandparents would take him out in their canoe. It's most common for pairs to rice together—one to knock the rice into the canoe with cedar sticks, the other to pole the canoe through the shallow water and navigate toward ripe rice.

As Roger addressed the crowd, one of the attendees spoke up: "Should married couples split up?" The assembled laughed.

"My wife and I cannot get in a canoe together," Roger replied.

Roger turned his attention to the tools we would have to make: poling poles, *gaandakii'iganaak*, and ricing sticks, *bawa'iganaakoog*, otherwise known as knockers. A pair of ricing sticks should be carved from cedar and be 36–39 inches long, with a combined weight of no more than one pound. Heavier sticks risk breaking the manoomin stems, wasting any unripe seeds.

"You need to have one stick done by lunchtime to get lunch," Roger warned us. "If you're solo, then you know what that means."

"Two sticks by lunch!" someone shouted. More laughter. Roger agreed.

"And you better have all ten fingers when you come for lunch, too," he scolded.

We adjourned outside to an area covered against the rain. Two women in attendance took pity on me and offered up the rain gear they always keep in their trunk—a habit of any wise Upper Midwesterner.

Roger assigned me to work on a pole. I laid the straight trunk of a tamarack pine, at least twice my height, between two picnic tables. Roger showed me how to use a tool to strip off the bark, plane it smooth, and beat the knots flat with a mallet. Then the splinters needed to be sanded away until the entire surface of the pole was perfectly smooth. Crooks of hardwood were laid out on a picnic table, looking like slingshots for Huck Finn. Roger helped me secure one to the end of the pole with pegs, and then wrap the joint in twine. Historically, the twine would have been made from spruce roots or the inner bark of cedar trees—the same type of rope used by the Lummi to make nets for reefnet fishing. The forked end of the pole would find purchase in the mucky bottom of the wild rice beds without damaging the roots of the plants.

Attendees sang as they worked, shared jokes and laughed; one young Ojibwe man practiced the drum and traditional songs. Before lunch, Roger paused our work so he could demonstrate how the poles are used out on the water. He showed us how we would stand up in our canoes—breaking the first cardinal rule of canoeing, but key to wild rice harvesting. We'd lean on our poles to find purchase in the mucky bottom, then slide our hands up the pole until the tip was at chest level, pushing the canoe forward. Then we'd lift the pole, but not out of the water, before plunging it into the muck again. In Michigan, Ojibwe polers stood in the bow on the boat, and the ricers worked behind them. In Minnesota, they did it "backwards," Roger joked, with the poler in back and the knocker in the bow in front of them.

The next day, during canoe training, we'd learn how not to tip the canoe. If the canoe tips, worse than getting wet, you dump all of your wild rice. The manoomin seeds have "beards" or "awns," a tail that works like a rudder. When the seed hits the water, it sinks straight down and sticks in the muck, ready to propagate a new generation of plants.

"So, what do you do if your canoe tips over and you lose all of your rice?" Roger asked the crowd of future ricers. No one knew the answer.

"Well," Roger said with a shrug. "The spirit thanks you for the gift."

I finished my pole before the end of the day, with all ten fingers intact, and racked it on a trailer next to the canoes.

The next morning dawned, just as chilly and wet, as we gathered on the shore of Lake Superior for canoe training. In blue-green fiber-glass canoes on dry land, we learned how to get in (stay low), fall out (grab the gunnel as you tip), and stand up (carefully). Later, after lunch, we'd drill by tipping the canoe into the lake and learning how to get back in. In the shallow, mucky areas where wild rice grows, there's no walking back to shore; if you fall out, you've got to get back in your canoe. Everyone tips at least once in their ricing career.

During break, as I slowly chewed my turkey sandwich, one of the program assistants came over to me and asked, "Are you OK?"

"I'm just so cold," I responded pathetically. I left shortly after and slept sixteen hours in my motel before I had to drive the ten hours home to Cleveland. I still regret not going out onto the lake, but I hope my pole served someone well that day. And I hope it's still out there, teaching others how to rice.

\* \* \*

THE MODERN-DAY RICE CAMP was named after the historical practice of Ojibwe camping near the rice beds for the one or two weeks during harvest. These campsites were used for generations, a tradition that lasted well into the twentieth century.

Historically, before the season began, an appointed rice chief would go into the rice bed to inspect the rice. They'd watch for changes in color, particularly a darkening of the grain to indicate ripeness, and snap a kernel in half, checking for a firm white center, not soft and juicy. And they'd tap the panicles to make sure the ripe kernels released easily. If they still clung to the plant, they weren't ready. The rice chief would signal to the community when the rice was ready and it was time to camp for harvest.

To start the harvest, the rice chief selected a pair of ricers to harvest a few pounds of rice. This ceremonial rice was processed, cooked, and brought to the rice chief, who would take a handful and lead a prayer. After that, a taste of the rice was given to all the assembled Ojibwe. Only then could teams of ricers take to the lake and collect rice.

Two weeks after rice camp, in mid-September, I made my way to Minnesota for the start of the rice harvesting season. My first stop was Roseville, a town just outside Minneapolis, for the annual Wild Rice Festival. The Saturday festival took place at a nature center, and I had just the right person to bring along: Caley, a former colleague of mine at the Lower East Side Tenement Museum in New York City, had moved back to her hometown of Minneapolis. An artist and educator, she gleefully accompanied me as we attended the honey extraction demonstration—that hot knife slicing the honeycomb is always so satisfying—spun the gears of a cider press and tasted the results, and attended an Ojibwe language class. We dutifully repeated back our vocabulary words—*miigwetch* (thank you) and *boozhoo* (hello)—to the young teacher. The word boozhoo is taken from Nanaboozhoo, because the spirit is still here on earth. Anyone (or any animal) you might encounter could be Nanaboozhoo. So you ask.

In the nature center, we were invited to taste samples side by side of true manoomin and what is known as "paddy rice." Although this product is labeled "wild rice" in grocery stores, it is not wild at all. Paddy rice has been selectively bred for commercial farms; it is grown in cultivated paddies in Minnesota and California and harvested by machine. While manoomin grains vary in length and color, paddy rice is a uniform length and black. The only "wild" rice most Americans have ever seen is paddy rice. The paddy rice had a firmer texture, but the manoomin had a far superior flavor. The true wild rice was nutty and smoky with a whisper of freshwater lake.

Caley and I headed over to the rice processing demo, in a shady field along a tree line. A volunteer—a cheerful older man—parched wild rice in a cast iron kettle tipped at an angle over a wood fire. The large kettle—picture a witch's cauldron—contained about a gallon of green rice, which gave him plenty of room to stir it with an old canoe paddle, continuously scraping the grains up from the bottom and giving them a little toss, until the rice toasted brown and had a nutty smell.

But before the rice is parched, it has to be dried. "I like to dry it three days," the demonstrator told us. Historically, the rice was air-dried on woven mats or animal skins, and, after it was spread out, it was picked clean of stems, rice worms, and spiders. Air-drying the rice helps prevent mold and shortens the parching process. This step is called *baate manoomin*.

*Gidasige manoomin* is the parching process, which removes moisture to preserve the grain. Before the Ojibwe started trading with French fur trappers for iron kettles in the 1500s, rice was dried on woven mats suspended over beds of hot coals. Parching removes the rest of the moisture, which makes the manoomin shelf-stable, kills the germ so the grains don't sprout, and loosens the hulls.

"Whenever it starts to brown, you want to keep it moving so it doesn't pop, otherwise you have popcorn," the volunteer said as he vigorously stirred the rice with the canoe paddle. Popped rice is a popular snack, so if you overtoast your rice, it doesn't go to waste. A small batch of rice like his takes 30–60 minutes to get appropriately browned.

Then the rice is threshed—*mimigoshkan manoomin*—to remove the hulls. A blue tarp was laid on the ground—historically, this would be a pit lined with animal skins—and a young woman "danced" the rice. She wore knee-high deerskin moccasins to protect her feet and legs from the rice hulls; the rice beards are covered in sharp barbs that are itchy irritants. The threshing dance is a little like the Charleston, a twisting that starts at the knees and smashes the rice with the balls of the feet. Sometimes, poles were set up by the threshing pits so a dancer could grab on for balance.

Finally, the rice had to be winnowed, *nooshkaachige manoomin*. Hope Flanagan, an Ojibwe elder, cultural educator, and wild plant expert, showed us how to winnow the rice using a shallow tray made from folded birch bark. The tray was curved on one side—"to make room for the tummies of the grandmas," Hope joked. Using her stomach to support one side of the tray, she tossed the rice into the air. The much lighter hulls, or chaff, blew away in the breeze while the rice grains fell back into the tray. Finally, the rice would be spread out one last time, for the oldest and youngest in the group to sort through and pick out bits of chaff or bad kernels.

Much like reefnet fishing, the method of harvesting and processing wild rice has stayed the same over time, but the Ojibwe have adopted different tools to make the job easier. Cast iron kettles and plastic tarps have replaced woven mats and animal skins; canoes are now fiberglass instead of birchbark; and work done by beavers to flood the rice beds is now performed by dams built by the Army Corps of Engineers. And just as the salmon were guaranteed to the Salish in their treaty rights, the right to harvest wild rice is guaranteed in the treaties between the US federal government and the Ojibwe.

\* \* \*

WAVES OF EPIDEMIC DISEASE hit the Ojibwe before they made first contact with white colonists, the deadly illnesses passed from white communities in the East through tribal connections. France built a military outpost—Fort Detroit—at the edge of Ojibwe territory in 1701 and declared the area New France. By the time French fur traders and Jesuit priests made inroads deeper into Ojibwe lands in the early eighteenth century, the Ojibwe population had recovered and was on the rise. The Ojibwe expanded over the next century from their post-migration base around Lake Superior, eastward to Lake Michigan and Lake Huron and westward into Dakota territory. The French and Ojibwe traded heavily, mostly furs in exchange for muskets and the metal kettles the Ojibwe used to parch rice and boil maple sap. The French and Ojibwe also frequently intermarried; even today, more than one-third of Ojibwe in Minnesota have French last names.

Later, larger settlements, often of fur trading companies, relied on wild rice as food. The *Detroit Gazette* wrote in 1820, "The fish and the wild rice are the chief sustenance of the traders, and without them the trade could scarcely be carried on." Another early nineteenth-century source mentioned buying wild rice from the Ojibwe at $1.50 a bushel.

The area was ceded to the British by the French in 1763, and then signed over to the United States after the Revolutionary War. Congress organized it as the Northwest Territory in 1787 and encouraged white settlement. Ohio was the first territory admitted to statehood in 1803, followed by Indiana in 1816 and Illinois in 1818. As white colonists moved into Michigan, Anishinaabe tribes were forcibly removed to reservations, often far from the ricing beds of their homelands. After Native groups were removed, industrial development destroyed the natural landscape of Michigan within fifty years and the wild rice was decimated.

While furs had been profitable in the eighteenth century, in the nineteenth century the industry was collapsing because of changing tastes in fashion. Entrepreneurs in Michigan turned to logging. Trees cut inland were transported down rivers to be shipped over the Great

Lakes. Rivers were dredged and dammed to create deep channels for these floating logs, drowning manoomin beds. The river bottoms became coated with sawdust and bark, which smothered seeds and young plants. The water became cloudy with sediment, and acidic and dark from the release of tannins from rotting wood. Sunlight couldn't penetrate to the bottom, so manoomin didn't germinate.

Meanwhile, the Ojibwe in the Minnesota territory were signing the first of many treaties with the federal government: the Treaty of 1837, or the White Pine Treaty. The collapse of the fur industry had also affected them. The tools they traded for had become a part of their daily lives and made work more efficient and life more prosperous. When they could no longer trade furs, they bought these tools with the sale of land. As the Ojibwe were moved farther from their ancestral lands, they had less access to the resources that supported them and they became more reliant on the sale of land. The system was rigged so the Ojibwe were always in debt, which left them further vulnerable to pressure to sell land to pay those debts.

The land the US wanted was timberland that could be logged, just like in Michigan; hence, the "White Pine" treaty. But the treaty included a clause that allowed the Ojibwe to continue to use the land they sold: "The privilege of hunting, fishing, and gathering the wild rice, upon the lands, the rivers and the lakes included in the territory ceded, is guaranteed to the Indians." It was unusual for a plant like wild rice to be mentioned specifically in a treaty.

By the late 1850s, the Ojibwe had sold off millions of acres of land in the Minnesota Territory. After Minnesota became a state in 1858, Natives were further pressured to cede land and move north to the White Earth Reservation. As the Ojibwe were moved to reservations, the government "assisted" by distributing foods like lard, flour, and sugar. But as the Fond du Lac Band of Lake Superior Chippewa noted in a report on tribal health, "it was also a strategy for weaning indigenous people away from their reliance on the natural and traditional foods so that they could become 'civilized.'" Boarding schools were established to further disintegrate the Ojibwes' link to their own culture. The boarding schools taught exclusively in English and imposed Christianity. In 1883, the Bureau of Indian Affairs issued a "Code of Indian Offenses" that banned traditional dances, feasts, and religious gatherings. Local BIA agents were empowered to actively suppress these activities on the reservations. Ojibwe historian Anton Treuer observed, "It is painfully ironic that the U.S. government was ostensibly created in large part to protect freedom of religion and incorporated that idea into the First Amendment to the Constitution but actively suppressed the religious freedom of the land's first inhabitants."

The notable exception to the government's assimilation campaign was the Red Lake Reservation. An Ojibwe band in Minnesota's far north, their reservation was created around their traditional lands. Connected to their homeland, they were more empowered to reject aspects of assimilation, particularly religion. Treuer wrote, "The Catholic Church twice tried to build a church, mission, and school, only to have tribal members burn all buildings to the ground each time. To this day there has never been a Christian funeral in the community, as all members steadfastly hold to traditional Ojibwe religious beliefs." Red Lake also retains the highest Ojibwe language fluency rate to this day.

In Michigan in 1857, the state put 5,680,054 acres of swampland up for sale. This land could be purchased by any citizen "on the condition [it] would be drained by the purchaser" and "turned to productive use." Draining the swamps to create farmland was called "reclaiming" the land, "a term that implies the land was taken from the colonizers somehow and they were taking it back as theirs," scholar Barbara Barton points out in her book *Manoomin: The Story of Wild Rice in Michigan.*

The results of the channeling, polluting, and, finally, draining of the waterways in Michigan meant that manoomin had largely disappeared from the state by the end of the nineteenth century. Although there were some attempts by sport hunters to reseed it, as ducks and other birds fed on the plants, they were largely unsuccessful. Large parts of Michigan's ecosystems had been thoroughly destroyed, and the rice beds with them.

\* \* \*

THE DAY AFTER THE Roseville Wild Rice Festival, I checked into the Shooting Star Casino in the White Earth Nation. The hotel and casino is situated on the banks of the Wild Rice River in Mahnomen, a town of about 1,200 located 235 miles northwest of Minneapolis. The casino also functioned as a conference center and performance venue, hosting touring acts as diverse as Willie Nelson and A Flock of Seagulls. It was also the only hotel in the area. I waited to check in behind a long line of elderly Minnesotans who had arrived on a luxury coach to gamble for a few days.

In 1987, the US Supreme Court ruled in *California v. Cabazon Band of Mission Indians* that neither county nor state governments had the authority to regulate gambling within a sovereign nation. The ruling opened up gambling on reservations across the country. By the early 1990s, all Ojibwe reservations had established some kind of gambling operation, and, as result, tribal unemployment dropped from 50 percent to 20 percent—still a high number, considering that the national unemployment rate rarely goes above 6 percent. But the casinos have done much to combat poverty in places like the White Earth Nation.

After I dropped my bags, I made my way across the casino floor to the Traditions Buffet for dinner. My room had displayed a little advertisement, advising me to "Try Traditions Buffet Homemade Blueberry Oat Cake! Made with our own White Earth wild rice flour." And I did. A moist, dense, deep-brown sheet cake dotted with blueberries under a snow-white layer of cream cheese frosting, the cake was absolutely killer. A large number of dishes at the buffet included local wild rice, from simple pilafs cooked with nuts and berries to creamy Midwestern chicken and wild rice casseroles. With the amount of cheese, cream cheese, and sour cream I saw at that buffet, it's clear that the Upper Midwest is singlehandedly keeping the American dairy industry in business. At breakfast the next morning, next to the hotel pan of oatmeal was an equal-sized pan labeled "bacon grease." I was told by a local, "The old folks like it on oatmeal, but it's good on just about everything. Cooking oil, rub it on a sore spot." I think the last part was a joke. I thought I was from the Midwest, but they were really out-Midwesterning me up there.

# Manoomin Porridge

Probably the most beloved way to enjoy wild rice in the Upper Midwest is in a sweet breakfast porridge. The recipe is flexible. The rice camp in Michigan sent out a recipe for manoomin with *minan* (wild blueberry), *mashkigimin* (cranberry), *bagaan* (hazelnuts), and *zinzibaakwad* (maple sugar) in 2020, instead of an in-person meeting that year. The recipe recommends adding a tablespoon each of dried cranberries, blueberries, hazelnuts, and maple sugar (two tablespoons if you are using maple syrup) to the raw rice and cooking water and heating it all together. This process gives the manoomin a lovely fruity and nutty flavor throughout.

For a different spin, I like to mimic the wild rice porridge from the now-closed Farmer's Daughter restaurant in Minneapolis. Hearty and textural, the wild rice is perfumed with a nonnative spice, cardamom. Cook the rice, then top with a splash of milk or cream, toasted walnuts, chopped cooked apple, fresh blueberries and a dollop of cardamom butter. The cardamon butter is 4 tablespoons butter, 1 tablespoon sugar, 1 tablespoon milk and ½ teaspoon ground cardamom, whipped together with a stand or hand mixer or food processor.

\* \* \*

LOWER RICE LAKE, a tribal ricing lake, had been declared ready for harvest a few days before my arrival. My visit had been facilitated by Tracy Nicole Goodwin, the Market Manager and Marketing Coordinator for the White Earth Nation. Tracy managed the White Earth Nation store, which buys tribal-made and -harvested goods and packages and sells them to the general public. White Earth maintains contracts with the USDA and relationships with grocery stores like Whole Foods, which carries White Earth rice in Minnesota.

In the morning, I met Tracy at the casino, which also functions as a tribal bank. Tracy withdrew $150,000 to buy rice for the next few days. I met her parked out front of the hotel. Passionate about bettering her community through the tribal store, she was also a hands-on mom of six. She was dressed that day in a black tank top and a long and breezy skirt, her brown-blonde hair up. Although it had been 48 degrees and raining just a few days ago, today we were expecting a high of 86.

After Tracy got the cash, I followed her and her police escort to the parking lot of the Rice Lake Community Center. A parked pickup truck with an empty 18-foot trailer was waiting to be stacked with bags of manoomin. An attendant would weigh the rice on an industrial scale, then write out a ticket that the ricer would take to Tracy to get paid. Four armed conservation officers from the tribe oversaw the entire process.

The buying point opened at 11 a.m.; the office was a folding table and chairs set up in the back of a box truck. A few teams of ricers who had been out early in the morning were already waiting to sell. "It's best to go out there in the morning; it falls better," one ricer advised me. Truck beds and sedan trunks were piled with white bags of rice, and the parking lot smelled like the fresh water that dripped from them, along with gas and oil from old cars and cigarette smoke.

Tracy taped a sign at the entrance of the field office: "$3 a pound. Most tribe has ever paid. Please bring clean rice." It was an excellent season for rice. The days had been hot, the nights cool, and no bad storm had come along and knocked off all the rice. And, with an increasing interest in wild rice as a health food, the tribe could offer a higher price per pound than ever before.

"There's some real dedicated guys out here who bring in some big numbers, like six and seven hundred pounds," Tracy told me. That's a $2100 payout, split two ways, for a few hours of work.

"There's a big joke that goes around, 'I'll get you when big rice opens!'" Tracy said. "This is a big payday for everyone." Manoomin season is a time for communities to pay down debts, buy school supplies and clothes for their kids, fix vehicles, and, if they're lucky, put a little away for the rest of the year.

\* \* \*

AL FOX, WHITE EARTH'S Department of Natural Resources Chief Conservation Officer, took me out in his truck to see the boat launches at Lower Rice Lake. Tall and uniformed, Al was in his mid-fifties, and curls of black and gray hair poked out from under his baseball cap. We rode down packed dirt roads through the forest, and he stopped to show me the water management system that is carefully monitored all season long. The water level needs to be low enough in the spring to protect the delicate new manoomin leaves and high enough in the fall that canoes can navigate the beds.

The conservation officers watch over the rice buying and check to make sure the rice coming in is "clean." That means that there's only rice in the bags, not broken rice heads caused by harvesting too forcefully, or other items thrown in to up the weight. If they discover fraud, the conservation officers will often dump the bags out publicly. The threat of embarrassment in front of tribal peers usually dissuades any thought of offending.

The officers were also down at the docks checking for permits and making sure the ricers on Lower Rice Lake were tribal members. While there were plenty of other sites where non-Natives could rice, you had to be a tribal member to rice anywhere within the bounds of the reservation. And, under Minnesota's strict ricing regulations, the officers even check to make sure ricing equipment is regulation, in particular, that the knockers are the correct weight, length, and shape.

Al pointed out to me the site of a traditional rice camp, where he remembers spending a week each summer as a kid with his extended family. The tribe would camp out in tents and teepees, harvesting and processing the rice.

"Come down in the morning, the sky would be a blue haze from woodsmoke," he told me, from women parching rice.

The site had been used for hundreds of years. "The gophers will push up pieces of pottery and stuff like that that they used to carry their rice in," Al told me.

We arrived at the canoe launch. Looking out across Lower Rice Lake, the dense rice bed looked like a field of wheat on the water, gold-green and undulating in the breeze. Lower Rice Lake was about four miles long and 98 percent covered in rice. I could just see the heads of polers, their long poles sticking up above them as they navigated the beds. There were three landings on the lake and each dock was marked by color-coded flags—because, as Al told me, once you're out in the rice it's easy to get lost. Even the poler, standing in the canoe, may not be able to see shore. You can get disoriented and end up at the wrong dock, or simply get lost on the lake for hours. Ricing was only open from sunrise to sunset for that reason; people have gotten lost on the lake all night.

Ricers had banked their canoes and were packing rice by the fist-ful into the white sacks provided by the tribal government. Rice worms and spiders scattered from the grain mounds, some meeting their ends in the beaks of the wrens and other birds that flitted by, waiting for an easy lunch. Some of the canoes were densely packed with manoomin from stern to prow, a fuzzy straw-green mound, with barely the space to spare for the knocker and poler. It was mostly pairs of middle-aged men who worked, long hair with streaks of gray tied back with bandannas, jeans covered in rice grains clinging by their awns. They wore wellies to keep out the wet and long-sleeved shirts to protect them from the irritating rice beards. There were teenage boys out with their dads and uncles, too, and I met a team of sixteen-year-old girls who would come out after school to make extra cash.

The ricing season in any one location lasts about two weeks in total. Once the tribal government has purchased all they've allotted for the year, the teams will come back to rice for themselves. A ricer will harvest about 200 pounds for personal use, often processing this small amount in the traditional way.

On the way back to the scales, Al pointed out the truck window to a low ranch house.

"My aunt and uncle live there. My uncle lives in that tan house there." Al's family has been in White Earth for a long time, living on that property. His ancestors used to be rice chiefs. "They would go down there and check the lake, then people would get together and say, okay, now the rice is ready."

Up until a few years ago, the Minnesota Department of Natural Resources would decide when the lake was ready for ricing. But with a renewed local interest in manoomin, White Earth brought back the rice chiefs. "We decided we're going to assign two people from each village to come up here, test the lake, get together, majority rules," Al told me. He had noticed in the past few years that more teams of young Ojibwe were showing up, like the high school girls who had been out ricing that day.

"Before, it was people just getting older, there was nobody filling in behind them. But now, all of the schools and the colleges and all that stuff are reintegrating the cultural significance of manoomin. The Good Berry."

When we returned to the scales, a line of trucks and sedans filled the parking lot. Teams of men and women were coming in sore and tired, sunburnt and sweaty, maybe damp and drippy if they'd fallen in. Tracy counted money out loud and passed it across her table to waiting ricers. This was the end-of-day rush before they shut down at 4pm. By the time Tracy closed the cashbox, the tribe had bought 24,000 pounds of manoomin. Last year, 109,000 pounds of rice was bought in the entire season; this year, in a single week, Tracy had bought 140,000 pounds.

Tracy hoped that the tribal council would release more money. When you deal with a wild food, you have to create a stockpile in the good years to provide a steady supply in bad seasons. More rice meant more annual contracts, which meant more money back into the community. There was still green rice out in the lake, so Tracy was hoping to buy 200,000 pounds or more.

\* \* \*

IN THE 1960S, RESEARCHERS AT the University of Minnesota began breeding wild rice, selecting for traits that would thrive in a manmade, machine-harvested paddy. By the 1970s, farm-grown wild rice had flooded the market, and by the year 2000 Minnesota was producing $40 million worth of paddy rice annually. California produces even more paddy-grown rice than Minnesota. In 1999, geneticists at the University of Minnesota mapped the wild rice genome, with the intent of using it for "cloning and crop improvement studies." But Winona LaDuke wrote in her pamphlet *Our Manoomin Our Life*: "While the future uses of such scientific data are at present unknown, we can be relatively assured as to who will most likely reap the benefits of this knowledge. The $21 million wild rice business is largely dominated by just a few paddy rice firms. Their interest in genetic work on wild rice stems largely from their own economic interests, not environmental, humanitarian, or tribal interests." Today, more than 95 percent of the rice on the market is paddy-grown, and NORCAL Wild Rice in Woodland, California, has patented a wild rice variety for the first time.

Many Native people believe that labeling paddy rice "wild rice" is simply dishonest. True wild rice is often three times the cost per pound of paddy rice; and if a consumer is not educated to know the difference—or if labeling isn't controlled to emphasize that difference—Native wild rice harvesters have difficulty finding a market for their product. Minnesota and Wisconsin require paddy rice be labeled as "paddy" or "cultivated," but there are no labeling laws of this kind at the federal level.

Most important, the Ojibwe feel that it isn't right for humans to breed wild rice. The rice, many of them believe, was a gift to the Ojibwe from the Creator. It is sacred in its wildness; it is not a farm crop and should not be treated as a commodity. In the Ojibwe mindset, the rice you have harvested is your own, while the rice in the lake belongs to all.

Not all Ojibwe share this view. The Red Lake Nation, considered one of the most traditional Ojibwe bands ("When you want to learn things about being Ojibwe, the language or the ceremonies, you go up there," Tracy told me), also cultivates and sells paddy rice. They dub their product Minnesota Cultivated Wild Rice. I had reached out to Red Lake for a visit, but they were unavailable in the busy ricing season. Tracy told me she was also curious to visit. We had this conversation on my last day in White Earth, a sunny Tuesday morning, as we drove to Dewandeler, one of the processors that handles the hundreds of thousands of pounds of wild rice White Earth brings in. As the golden September sun streamed between the reddening leaves, a bald eagle swooped across the road. Tracy whispered *"Bozhoo, migizi!"* She always said hi to the eagles, she told me.

We rolled down a gravel drive behind a farmhouse, parked on the grass, and a sweet old mutt named Buddy came out to greet us with the owner of the processing facility, Aaron Dewandeler. In his mid-thirties, bearded, in dusty work clothes and a baseball cap, he looked tired from the many hours of work processing rice. Aaron will barely see his family for two weeks or more during ricing season; he sleeps in a camper next to the processing facility. The Dewandeler business has been here—in this barn behind their farmhouse—for forty-five years. It was started by Aaron's grandfather, then passed on to his father, Richard, who still works with his son in the busy times.

The three of us crossed the threshold of the wood barn, the air pine-scented from the fires. The cement floor was covered with their custom equipment and rolling bins of rice, organized by client and location where the rice was harvested. Dewandeler served both large clients like White Earth and small, family orders.

All of the equipment is engineered and customized by the Dewandelers, from converted corn silage elevators to salvaged mobile home wheels. There's nowhere you can go out and buy a rice parcher; it had to be custom-built. Sunlight peeked through a huge vent in the roof and illuminated the steam billowing out of an enormous barrel parcher. The parchers were on tracks so they could be rolled off the fire if they need to cool down. It's just like how I cook over an open fire on a small scale: since you can't turn the temperature up and down like on a kitchen stove, you control heat through proximity to the fire. Pots—or parchers—are moved closer to get hot and away to cool. Blades like the paddles of a steamboat churned inside the parcher's barrel, continuously moving the rice. A second parcher was outside under a shed extension. Both were going full blast, a raging hot pine fire burning underneath.

"After all the steam's out, the rice itself starts to smoke. So, it's burnt a little bit. That's where the flavor comes along," Aaron told us as he walked us through the process. The rice first toasts brown, then turns yellow, and then, when all the water is out of it, it burns a little and turns red.

Aaron uses a laser thermometer to check the rice's temperature, but otherwise his methods are the same his dad and grandfather used. Aaron watches the color of the smoke coming off the toasting rice and is tuned in to the smell of the cooking grain.

"If I'm sitting in the front of the building talking to somebody, and, all of a sudden, I'll smell the rice, then I know that it's close to being done. I got to go."

He opened the parcher and the smell of the toasting rice wafted out. It smelled like breakfast cereal.

At another station, a thresher beat toasted rice with rotating paddles in a barrel and an exhaust system blew the hulls away. One metal bin, filled to the top with finished rice, bore a tag that read "WE Lower Rice." The bin held finished rice from this season, which Tracy would soon be packaging and shipping across the country.

Tracy and I drove away from Dewandeler and back to the community center parking lot, where there would be ricers waiting for her to open up her field office. She and I talked about a lot of things on our drive: our families, being in our thirties, having a career. But there was something she said about the manoomin that stuck with me; it wasn't even what she said, it was how she said it: stern, pleading, powerful:

"It's so precious to us. It's our gold. The food that grows on the water."

* * *

BACK AT THE COMMUNITY CENTER, Al greeted us with good news: he had reached out to the tribal council on my behalf and they had given me permission to go out on the lake with a team of ricers. But since I was non-Native, I could not touch any of the ricing tools or participate in the ricing.

Al took me down to one of the launches. The heat of the day was made more bearable by a moody cloud cover and a strong wind. Many of the ricers were coming in after working for hours in the cool morning, but we managed to catch a pair who were just heading out. Joey and Noodin were friends in their early twenties. Joey worked nights at the casino, so they were late starters. I climbed into the middle of the canoe and sat on my shins—the bottom of the canoe is always a little wet, with a few wild rice grains kicking around and a few spiders making their escape. Joey used his pole to push us off the earth launch. Noodin was in front of me with his pair of knockers. "He keeps us in rice and I keep ya in the boat," Joey said.

In minutes my entire view was water and rice. I quickly realized that without the flags marking the docks, it would be impossible to find your way back. At water level, there is only endless rice in every direction. It's quiet and cocooned. Some ricers bring radios out with them to combat the isolation and the repetitive nature of the task. Others just slide along in the silence.

As Joey poles, he looks for patches of ripe rice. "You can tell how ripe they are by, see how brownish the heads are?" Noodin used a knocker to part the grass on the left side of the canoe like stiff hair, bent the stems over the stern, then gave them a firm tap with his other knocker. The ripe rice released with a rattle and fell into the canoe. He continued and switched sides, developing a rhythm. Occasionally, he used his knockers or the canoe paddle to compact the rice at the front of the canoe. Noodin's arms were fully covered in a red work shirt and gloves. He showed me the welts on his wrists, an allergic reaction to the barbs on the rice beards. I got a single grain down my shirt and had an angry red welt on my chest for over a week.

"If you get one stuck in your eye, the only thing you can do is stick a piece of gum in there and try to get it out, or go to the hospital," Noodin warned. They always carry gum with them.

"You can chew it, too, because if you open your mouth and one gets in there . . . I don't know, you can't really grab them. Best thing you can do is eat bread."

We canoed on a bit more, talking and laughing, before Joey located the orange flag of the launch and navigated us to shore. I jumped out and wished them good luck the rest of the day. They disappeared back into the rice. The two of them had been out as a team three times this season; Joey had gone out with another poler once who tipped the canoe. They're a little slower than some of the more experienced ricers, but for six to eight hours of work they pull in about $600 each.

When I returned to Tracy at the community center, there was more good news: the tribal council had approved unlimited funds for her to buy rice this year. The rice was so plentiful and of such good quality that they took her advice and decided to keep buying. She'd be able to expand their vendor relationship, and for any tribal member that wanted to keep ricing, it would be a good year financially. Not every year would be so bountiful.

\* \* \*

THE OJIBWE HAVE SAID that the extinction of the wild rice would signal the end of the Ojibwe as a people—or even the end of the world. In 2018, the White Earth Nation passed the Rights of Manoomin to protect the remaining wild rice. The law was modeled after the work of the International Rights of Nature Tribunal: much like the legal rights given to corporations under US law, the Rights of Nature grant a natural resource guaranteed rights as a living entity. Under the Rights of Manoomin, wild rice is guaranteed the right to clean water, free from industrial pollution; the right to a "healthy, stable climate free from human-caused climate change impacts;" and the right to be free from patenting and GMO cross-pollination. The law declares that harvesting manoomin is a right, guaranteed in treaties between the Ojibwe and the United States. If the wild rice becomes extinct and can no longer be harvested, then the treaty has been violated. Through this law, the Ojibwe have declared—legally—that they will fight for manoomin's survival.

The first court case to enforce the Rights of Manoomin was brought to the tribal court in August 2021. That summer, Lower Rice Lake was nearly devoid of water as ricing season approached. Enbridge, a Canadian energy company, was in the process of building an oil pipeline that crosses Upper Minnesota in Anishinaabe territory. Not only are spills a concern—the pipeline will cross 79 miles of wetland and 200 bodies of water—but the company was pulling "up to 5 billion gallons of groundwater" during an unprecedented drought to build the pipeline, draining wild rice lakes. Water protectors have been organizing protests, blockades, and hunger strikes since December 2020, as well as appealing directly to President Biden and Secretary of the Interior Deb Haaland. Because the destruction of the rice is a treaty violation, action can be taken at the federal level. The Rights of Manoomin court case seeks to stop Enbridge's water use and stop the pipeline as a whole; the case is ongoing.

Lower Rice Lake did open for the August 2021 season, but many tribal ricing lakes needed their boat launches extended to reach water deep enough to float a canoe. The tribe was offering $4 a pound for what rice could be gathered. Ricers were only able to bring in a little less than 10,000 pounds.

* * *

WILD RICE IS AS RESILIENT as the Indigenous peoples who steward it. Its seeds stay viable in the mucky sediment for a long time, maybe a century or more in the right conditions. And given the chance, it will grow.

One of the reasons I was attracted to the story of manoomin was because it's native to my home of Ohio. There are records from the late nineteenth century of wild rice at the mouth of the Cuyahoga River in Cleveland. But as the lakefront was industrialized, the wild rice disappeared. Lake rice has not been spotted in the state of Ohio in over twenty years. River rice is rare in the state. I started asking around and learned from a forager friend that wild rice had been spotted at Mentor Marsh.

Mentor Marsh is a nature preserve of almost 700 acres along Lake Erie. Originally a river channel that became a marsh, then a swamp forest, it's considered one of the "most species-rich sites on the Great Lakes shoreline," hosting a huge number of birds, fish, mammals, and plants. But the land wasn't always so healthy or bountiful. The preserve was pieced together from lands donated by the nearby Morton and Diamond salt mines, after the mines had dumped 250,000 tons of salt-contaminated waste into the marsh throughout the 1960s. The saline waters killed the native marsh plants and swamp forest trees, leaving the area desolate. The destruction of the native plants left the marsh vulnerable to salt-tolerant invasive plants, in particular, the ecosystem-destroying trio of purple loosestrife, narrow-leaf cattail, and, worst of all, phragmites.

Invasive phragmites, a genus of reed grasses, arrived on the East Coast in the early nineteenth century, probably from Europe. Phragmites spread rapidly with the construction of the highway system in the 1950s, its seeds latching on to cars and semi trucks and spreading to susceptible areas like the depleted Mentor Marsh. If you've ever driven on a highway, you've seen phragmites; one of its favorite habitats is the polluted ditches alongside roadways. It's very recognizable by its feather-duster-like seed heads. It's often over 14 feet tall and grows in dense patches, choking out native vegetation, creating a monoculture and biological desert. Season to season, the old stems and roots die, but don't rot. All of the dead material is highly flammable, and Mentor Marsh—which abuts a residential area—was plagued by destructive fires. One particularly devastating fire in 2003 burned over 400 acres of the marsh and wooden boardwalk. But this costly disaster ended up being a boon.

In order to prevent the wooden boardwalk from burning in the future, the park decided to remove phragmites in a 10-foot buffer zone on either side of the boardwalk. They targeted the invasive plants with herbicides and crushed dead material into the marsh to promote rot. Much to their surprise, the following spring, dozens of native plants burst from the marsh. Freed from the strangling phragmites, plants that had lain dormant in the earth—the "seed bank"—sprung up from the mud. Over sixty different native plants returned along the restored boardwalk. Drone footage of the park from this time shows a vein of bright green with the boardwalk in the center, cutting through the brown of the phragmites.

Based on the results of the first efforts, Mentor Marsh was able to secure funding and community support for a full restoration across the marsh. Herbicide was sprayed by helicopter and by a targeted ground crew. Then a Marsh Master—a semi-amphibious vehicle on treads—was used to press the dead material into the marsh. Since the project's completion in 2018, 180 native plant species have returned to the marsh.

I learned much of this story from Becky Donaldson, a naturalist at the marsh, on a public tour. An entomologist by trade, Becky walked our group along the boardwalk, pointing out clusters of native ladybugs and catching a giant invasive praying mantis in a jar. A few weeks before, Becky had spotted a patch of wild rice growing in the marsh. After the public tour, I hopped in Becky's Subaru to see the rice for myself. She took me behind a locked gate and on a dirt road on the edge of the marsh's western basin. It was lined with swamp trees with buttressed roots; bright pink swamp mallow and native burr reed grew in patches. Wood ducks and great white egrets grazed in the water while a bald eagle swooped overhead. The increased plant diversity meant more birds, insects, and fish had come back to the marsh. The scene was unlike anything I had ever seen in Ohio; it reminded me of wetlands in South Carolina or even Florida.

"So, the first clump I saw had three heads in it." Becky pointed at a clump of three out in the marsh. After a careful examination of samples taken to the Cleveland Museum of Natural History herbarium—and archived forever with Becky's name on them—the rice was identified as Southern wild rice or river rice. The rice had been in the seed bank since at least the 1960s, when the salt dumping occurred, but it may have been there longer. It may have been over a century since the wild rice had the right conditions to grow. A careful survey was done of the marsh that fall, and forty-two wild rice plants were counted.

"This is one of the coolest things that has happened to me in my professional life," Becky glowed as we gazed on her discovery from the shore.

\* \* \*

BECAUSE OF THE COVID-19 PANDEMIC, it was nearly two years later when I slid a rented kayak off a launch with the intent of paddling into Mentor Marsh. I checked in with Becky in the intervening year and was pleased to hear that the stems of wild rice had nearly tripled, to 120. I was there to check on the status of wild rice from water level, to see if the number of stems had increased again. It was August 2021, a perfectly sunny day but not too hot, and I had brought along a wetland ecologist friend named Ben. Since I'd never been in a kayak, it was mostly Ben who navigated us through the channels between stands of marsh plants, although I did provide some muscle.

There was a distinctive ecological line between the lagoon where we launched the kayak and the marsh, between a vast monoculture of phragmites and stunning diversity. It wasn't long before I excitedly pointed out the first stand of river rice towering over us. The male flowers were in full bloom, tiny green blossoms. As we followed the channel farther east, there was another stand of rice, and then another. Within about 100 feet we saw over 1,000 stems of river rice. And as we continued, it became evident that there were more likely tens of thousands. In some places, what had been a stand of three stems had turned into a full rice bed.

I felt emotional. Humans have the capability to deeply mess up their environment. But with the investment of time, money, and effort, we can un-mess it up, too. Nature recovers if we give it the chance. I was paddling through the proof.

# Heirloom Cider Apples

In late March 2019, I set out for Angry Orchard Cider House in Walden, New York. Walden is an old agricultural town in the Hudson Valley, an area that was historically part of the Dutch colony of New Amsterdam. It was a gray and chilly day as a nor'easter swirled up the coast, dumping rain and snow in the higher elevations. I drove twisting, narrow roads that still bore names like Wallkill—"kill" being an old Dutch word for a creek. I followed these lanes around the tops of old mountains and down into valleys where tiny waterfalls splashed. This was *Legend of Sleepy Hollow* country.

When I finally rolled up the long driveway from the road, the bright red barns of the cidery and tasting room at the top of the hill were a welcome splash of color. The old orchard trees on the property, still leafless in the early spring, twisted and bulged. They looked exactly like the famous Angry Orchard logo, a crabby apple tree. However, many of these old trees—largely grocery store apples like Red Delicious—were being pulled out and replaced with varieties of heirloom apples, used for making cider. Eventually, around 5,300 cider apple trees will be planted on-site. Much like heading to Napa to drink wine in the vineyards, Angry Orchard feels that coming to their cidery should connect their product with the orchard.

I had come to Walden to watch the first steps in making a single-varietal cider from Newtown Pippins, an apple of local origins praised for cider making since before the Revolutionary War. The international Ark of Taste lists over 150 rare apples; about 25 are rare American apples, and at least nine of them are cider apples. Picked off the tree and eaten fresh, cider apples are often considered "spitters": painfully tannic, unpleasantly bitter, or mealy-textured. And frequently, their appearance is lacking: they might be russeted—brown and scaly like a russet potato—or speckled with black dots, misshapen and lumpy, or as tiny as a cherry. But these apples make exceptional cider. And when I say "cider," I don't mean fresh-pressed, sweet cider. I mean *cider*: fermented, alcoholic, and as flavorfully complex as any California wine.

Cider was considered America's national drink for hundreds of years. For the earliest colonists, apples were easier to grow than grains like rye or barley and they could be fermented into cider and distilled into apple brandy. Americans developed thousands of apple varieties that suited regional climates and soils. In 1905, the USDA published a bulletin titled *Nomenclature of the Apple: A Catalogue of the Known Varieties Referred to in American Publications from 1804 to 1904*. This pamphlet lists over 14,000 unique American apple varieties, many of them cider apples.

Today, there are fewer than 100 apple varieties grown commercially. Cultural shifts in the mid-nineteenth century led Americans to embrace beer, and the temperance movement and Prohibition were cider's death knell. By the 1920s, apple growers focused on only a few varieties of "culinary apples" designed to succeed in grocery stores. Currently, only about 7 percent of the apples grown in America are for cider making. Nationally, the US produces about 50 million gallons of cider, a drop in the bucket compared to 5.6 billion gallons of beer.

But the cider industry has grown tenfold in ten years. In 1991, there were ten cideries in America; by 2009, there were 100; by 2019, over 1,000. Today, it's a $1.5 billion industry. A positive result of folks drinking more cider is that rare apples are being found, reclaimed, regrown, and saved.

Most of Angry Orchard's cider is not produced in Walden. Angry Orchard's nationally distributed products are made in Cincinnati, Ohio, fermented from pressed apple juice concentrates. But Angry Orchard purchased their 60-acre property in 2016, four years after the company launched. The cidery at Walden is a place for experimentation, bold projects, and lovingly crafting long-lost apples into unique cider. The ciders made here are available at the onsite tasting room and restaurants down the Hudson Valley and into New York City, as well as in other foodie cities like Chicago, Seattle, and Austin.

I had met head cider maker Ryan Burk in the parking lot, both of us a little bleary on this gray day. Ryan is probably the most famous face of the contemporary cider world. Bearded and tatted, he's appeared in commercials for Angry Orchard, as well as served on industry boards. After pouring two cups of coffee from the office drip, he showed me around.

Ryan grew up in Williamson, New York, less than five miles from the shore of Lake Ontario. He made cider with his friends in high school.

"I'm not supposed to say that on the record, but I just did it," Ryan admitted. "I will say it with a caveat: we do not want to promote underage alcohol production and drinking. But whatever. I was a punk kid."

Before coming to Angry Orchard in 2015, Ryan ran production for Virtue Cider in Michigan. Before that, he was in law school in Chicago.

"I dropped out of law school for cider," he told me.

While he was in Chicago, Ryan became a "serious" home brewer and cider maker, and simultaneously became active in the local Slow Food chapter. He started as a low-level volunteer and ended up on the board. It's through Slow Food that he met Greg Hall, founder of Virtue Cider, and landed his first gig as a professional cider maker.

Slow Food, and more specifically the Ark of Taste, continues to inspire Ryan's work at Angry Orchard. Deciding to feature the Newtown Pippin as a single-varietal cider is part of that. In different incarnations of the brew's packaging, a historical drawing of a Newtown Pippin has graced the front of the bottle, and the story of the Newtown is included in the labeling text. It's all in an effort to connect the drinker with the apple's history.

The cider making space was a modern room with high ceilings, red I-beams and bare wood siding, filled with shiny metal pressing and fermenting equipment. Cryptically labeled oak barrels aged liquid treasures inside. And the Newtowns—electric yellow-green apples with a pink blush—tumbled along conveyor belts. They had been harvested the previous November, but they're a starchy apple when fresh. The longer they sit in cold storage, the more those starches are converted to sugars. By the early spring, they are at their best. Legendary pomologist Tom Burford wrote that "the long storage time imbued . . . an extraordinary taste that lingered on the tongue." And elevated sugar means elevated alcohol; a cider made with Newtown Pippins will have around an 8% ABV.

After the Newtown Pippins are picked and aged, they go through a visual inspection and rotten ones are pulled. Then they are rinsed, ground, and pressed for their luscious juice. Ryan rarely pitches yeast, relying on the yeast on the skin of the apples and in the air to create fermentation.

Some of the fermented juice will go into oak wine barrels to age, some into metal fermenters. That way Ryan can get different flavor profiles from the same juice to blend back together. The team also makes ice cider, a process that freezes the apples to concentrate the sugar, to have the flexibility to blend more sweetness into the final product.

Newtown Pippins were never as threatened as some of the other Ark of Taste apples because there is a demand for them even in the twenty-first century: they are an important ingredient in Martinelli's sparkling cider. Martinelli's was a hard cider company in the nineteenth century and switched to a sparkling, non-alcoholic blend around the time of Prohibition. Over half of the apples in Martinelli's all-juice sparkling cider are Newtown Pippins. I grew up drinking

Martinelli's at my teetotaling family's Thanksgivings, feeling fancy pouring it from its 750ml champagne-style bottle. But I didn't realize that the product preserved a colonial apple. Orchardists must have a market for the apples they produce; if no one is buying historical hard cider apples, no one will plant them. Martinelli's pays growers well above the market rate for the tons of Newtowns it presses. If they didn't pay a competitive rate, local orchardists would abandon the historical apple in favor of a more profitable contemporary supermarket favorite like Gala or Honeycrisp.

"If Red Jacket didn't have a market to sell Newtown Pippins, then they would plant something else," Ryan told me about the orchard where he purchases apples for his cider. "I mean, why would anyone grow bittersweet or bitter-sharp apples if it wasn't for cider? You can't eat them. I mean, for me this whole thing is about keeping trees in the ground. So if we do that, then I think we're doing something good for our land."

In Walden, many of the properties have been in the same hands for generations. But small farming, especially out East, has fallen on hard times. The unpredictability of farming in a warming climate has led many orchardists to throw in the towel, selling their land to real estate developers. The outlines of new McMansions, as Ryan called them, were appearing on one of the hillsides past the Angry Orchard property. According to CNBC, New York state has lost 471,000 acres of farmland to real estate development.

"And obviously it has a great story," Ryan said of the pippin. "We're in New York, it has a New York story, it's unique and it makes a great single-variety cider. It allows us to get people to think about the fact that apples are in this drink and that they can be special. In my opinion, the Newtown Pippin is one of the best ciders we make."

We walked to the tasting room. The 2018 Newtown Pippin was on tap, along with Angry Orchard's famous rosé cider; Baldwin, another heirloom apple single-varietal cider; and the Crisp Apple and Albany Post blends. In a connected retail space, 750ml bottles of their specialty ciders lined shelves.

Ryan poured me a pint of the Newtown Pippin. The pale-yellow liquid was slightly effervescent and had a fresh apple smell, a result of the slow fermentation which helps retain volatile apple aromatics. But there was a deeper odor, and flavor, too. I asked Ryan to describe his cider.

"I get a ton of green apple peel, which I sort of associate with fresh and bright and sorta grassy and sort of springtime." He swirled his cider and thought. "I grew up next to a creek and I always sort of associate this smell with what that smelled like. Like when everything's starting to bloom and blossom and the grass is coming up and the mud is wet."

I was brought back to being a kid on my family's property in Ohio, and how at the first muddy thaw I would feel liberated from the house and trudge into the woods. I often sat by a creek, really an agricultural runoff ditch, that was bursting with water from snowmelt. The newly warmed earth smelled a particular way. That transportive scent was now in this glass.

* * *

APPLES MAKE UP THE GENUS *MALUS,* which evolved before the continents split. There are apple trees all around the world. There were apples in the Americas when the first Europeans arrived, *Malus coronaria* and *Malus ioensis*, some of the oldest apple species on the planet. Today, these species are commonly known as crabapples. Modern culinary and cider apples, *Malus domestica*, descended from *Malus sieversii*, which grow in the mountain forests of southern Kazakhstan. Many of these forests are near Almaty, formerly known as Alma-Ata, or "father of apples." Apples feature heavily in the cuisine of this region, as in the traditional *plov*, a rice dish made with lamb, carrots, onions, and apples.

The fruits in the mountain apple forests reflect the full genetic diversity of *Malus*; they "range in size from marbles to softballs, in color from yellow and green to red and purple." The Russian agronomist Nikolai Vavilov was the first person to identify these wild apples as the domestic apple's forebear in 1929. He discovered that the "center of origin" for a species is where you find that species's highest genetic diversity. After the fall of Communism in 1989, a botanist and former student of Vavilov invited a group of American botanists to Kazakhstan to see the wild apples. An elderly man, he was seeking help to preserve the apple forests from deforestation for farmland and real estate development, two factors which still threaten them today. The wild apples' habitat has declined by over 70 percent in the last thirty years.

The American botanists were astonished by the apple forests. One witness recounted that when you looked "at these apples [you] felt sure you were looking at the ancestor of the Golden Delicious or the Macintosh." Hundreds of thousands of seeds and other genetic material was collected on this trip. Seeds were planted and stored at the USDA's living apple library in Geneva, New York, and distributed to researchers and breeders all over the world. Local activists continue to battle to preserve the wild apple forests, including a branch of Slow Food.

Ancient trade routes connecting Europe and Asia ran through the *sieversii* apple forests. It's likely that travelers would have picked some of the most beautiful and tasty fruit, carried its seeds both west and east, and planted it when they got home. There's evidence of apples being cultivated in Mesopotamia and Persia at least 4,500 years ago. Chinese orchardists figured out grafting about 4,000 years ago. Grafting is the process of propagating apple trees by taking new growth, called scion wood, from one tree and binding it to the rootstock of another tree, where it produces fruit identical to the scion's parent tree. In commercial orchards today, scion wood is grafted onto rootstocks that control how big the tree will grow. And in urban environments, it's not uncommon to see the work of guerrilla grafters, who add limbs of edible fruit to ornamental street trees.

The Greeks grew apples, and a few Roman apple varieties still exist: the little Lady apples that are in stores around Christmastime are believed to be a Roman variety. When it comes to cider, the first indisputable documents relating to cider making come from northern France in the eighth century, northern Spain in the year 803, and England in the eleventh century. These three regions have a similar climate, cool and wet, which made it difficult to grow grapes for wine or grains for beer, so apples became the primary source of alcohol. The climate of New England is comparable, which put early colonists in a similar position.

Puritans, despite their reputation, were big drinkers. They consumed 15–54 gallons of 4–6% ABV cider per person per year. Although the early colonists brought grafted trees with them, these trees quickly succumbed to the harsh New England climate. Devastating winters killed them outright, or late frosts froze off their flowers. But successful trees grew from apple seeds.

Apples are extreme heterozygotes. A heterozygote's offspring is a combination of the parents' genetic traits, rather than an exact copy. Humans are heterozygotes and contain about 30,000 different genes; apples have 57,000. Every apple tree (typically) has hundreds of fruits; each apple has five seeds; each seed has 57,000 genes in a unique combination. The incredible genetic diversity of an apple seed allowed the species to quickly adapt, through survival of the fittest, to an entirely new landmass and climate. The first generation of apple survivors would produce seeds even more well suited to the environment. Some trees may have naturally hybridized with the American crabapples, a technique still used today to add disease resistance to European plants. Some of the trees would produce fruit good for eating, baking, cooking, or drying, but the vast majority of apples would be good only for cider.

The Newtown Pippin is from Elmhurst, Queens, a neighborhood formerly known as Newtown. The apple originated on the estate of an English colonist, the Reverend John Moore. He was the first pastor of the First Presbyterian Church of Newtown, founded in 1652, today Queens's oldest congregation. Reverend Moore's son Gershom planted over 500 apple trees from seeds on the estate. The Newtown Pippin was discovered among these trees sometime in the late seventeenth or early eighteenth century. Newtowns were found to be a crisp, fresh eating apple and a bright, acidic baking apple.

Because Newtowns were great for eating, cooking, and cider, they became very popular in colonial America. By the end of the eighteenth century, there were orchards full of Newtowns all along Long Island and up the Hudson River Valley. George Washington and Thomas Jefferson both had Newtown Pippins on their plantations. Benjamin Franklin took bushels to England in the mid-eighteenth century, when he was there as the representative of the Assembly of Pennsylvania. They remained popular in England for another century. Queen Victoria, a particular fan of the Newtown Pippin, suspended import taxes on the apple. American entrepreneurs made fortunes shipping Newtowns to the UK. Rowan Jacobsen, author of *Apples of Uncommon Character*, wrote of the Newtown, "Like Forrest Gump, the Newtown Pippin has managed to intersect with an improbable number of historic personages and places over the course of its career, and has shown a knack for effortless success at whatever it was called upon to do."

In the early colonies, much of the work of growing and processing apples and fermenting cider was performed by Black and Indigenous laborers. Darlene Hayes, editor of *Malus* magazine, uncovered seventeenth-century records from the estate of Nathaniel Sylvester that give a glimpse into what cider making season might have been for farmers like the Moores. Sylvester's estate was on Shelter Island on the east end of Long Island. Slavery did not end in New York state until 1827, and Sylvester owned "Tammero, Oyou, Black John, J:O, Maria, Jenkin, Tony, Nannie, Japhet, Semenie, Jaquero, and Hannah" as well as their children. In addition to enslaved labor, his son Giles hired local Manhasset men to work during the fall, including a man named Henry. Henry "was paid for 55 days of cidermaking one year."

Indigenous people had been involved in orcharding since the early days of colonization. Farther north, the Haudenosaunee tended apple orchards in the Finger Lakes region of New York, until their plantings were destroyed in 1779. George Washington perceived the tribe as allies of the British and decimated their orchards, farms, and homes, pushing them as refugees to British-controlled Canada. In their absence, the new American government parceled out their lands to veterans of the Revolutionary War.

Jefferson had at least four dozen Newtown Pippin trees at Monticello, his Virginia plantation. The apples thrived in the South and became known there by the name of the county where Monticello sits: the Albemarle Pippin. Jefferson called his orchard the Fruitery and had about 600 fruit trees, mostly apples and peaches. Its location in Virginia's rolling hills east of the Blue Mountains was ideal for growing apples, "high enough that, during the spring and fall months as cold air settles in the bottomlands, the warmer air rises over the mountain—effectively preventing frost damage to blooming trees," according to research by Monticello's historians.

We know something of the lives of two of Jefferson's cider makers, husband and wife George and Ursula Granger. Their stories are peppered throughout documentation Jefferson left behind, but more importantly they appear in an oral history with their son Isaac Granger Jefferson in 1847. Isaac Jefferson was living as a free man in Petersburg, Virginia, at that time, and dictated some of his life story to a local pastor, the Reverend Charles Campbell. Campbell's handwritten notes were published a century later.

George and Ursula arrived at Monticello with their sons, George Jr., fourteen, and Bagwell, five, in January of 1773. Jefferson had attended an estate auction after pressure from his wife, Martha, to acquire "a favorite house woman of the name of Ursula." Jefferson collected Ursula and her sons for £210, then purchased George Sr. from a different plantation to reunite the family. Isaac was born at Monticello. The family would spend the next twenty-five years at the plantation, some remaining in forced labor their whole lives, others gaining their freedom.

George Sr.—who was often listed in Jefferson's books as "Great George" or "King George"—began agricultural work almost immediately, in particular managing the orchards and supervising the pressing and fermentation of cider. Jefferson preferred ciders made from the Hewes Crab and Taliaferro apples, the latter a long-lost apple that may be extinct. The cider was pressed in the fall, and George would have overseen the harvesting and visual inspection of apples, before the fruit was ground and pressed and the juice stowed in wooden casks. The cider aged in the casks until March, then Ursula oversaw the tricky bottling process.

Ursula—who was nicknamed Queen Ursula—reigned in the Monticello kitchens. Isaac recalled that Martha Jefferson would sit in the kitchen "with a cookery book in her hand and read out of it . . . how to make cakes, tarts, and so on." Ursula may not have been able to read and write, but she was a master of baking and pastry, employing incredible skill at crafting the household's dinner party desserts. Ursula also managed the smokehouse, supervising meat preservation in the fall, and the washhouse, where all the clothes and linens of Monticello were cleaned and ironed. She gave birth to nine children over about twenty-five years, six of whom died young.

Ursula was the only person Jefferson trusted to supervise the annual bottling of the plantation's cider. He wrote to his son-in-law on February 4, 1800, "I must get Martha [Jefferson's daughter] or yourself to give orders for bottling the cyder in the proper season in March. There is nobody there but Ursula who unites trust & skill to do it. She may take any body she pleases to aid her." One account remembers the process taking two weeks and a team of six women to store the cider in stoneware bottles.

By 1793, Great George was a foreman, the highest labor position on the farm, directly under the white overseer. And in 1796, when a newly hired overseer never turned up to work, George was appointed to the position. He was the only Black man to ever hold this position at Monticello, and it was rare to have a Black overseer anywhere. George oversaw more than fifty enslaved men and women who produced Monticello's cash crops, like tobacco. George received a salary of $67 a year, half of what a white overseer made.

For George, it was a difficult position. He was caught between two worlds: his community of Black men and women who were forced to work the plantation and the paid responsibilities normally given to a white worker. Although George struggled in his first year of management, his second was a huge success, producing a tobacco crop "so extraordinary," wrote Jefferson, "that I may safely say if there ever was a better hogshead of tobacco bought or sold in New York I may give it to the purchaser."

On November 1, 1799, Jefferson turned to George for advice for the last time: "70 bushels of the Robinson & red Hughes . . . have made 120 gallons of cider. George says that when in a proper state (there was much rot among these) they ought to make 3 galls. to the bushel, as he knows from having often measured both." The next day George Granger was dead. He was sixty-nine.

George died of an undiagnosed illness that would also take the lives of George Jr. and Ursula a few months later. The Jeffersons provided medical care and hired doctors for the Grangers, but the treatment seemed to speed the process of the disease. Jefferson's daughter Martha wrote in a letter, "Ursula is I fear going in the same manner with her husband and son, a constant puking, shortness of breath and swelling first in the legs but now extending itself."

George and Ursula's son Bagwell remained in bondage the rest of his life. With his wife Minerva, he labored on the plantation for Jefferson and then Jefferson's grandson. Isaac trained as a tinsmith, nailmaker, and blacksmith. He eventually gained his freedom, likely buying himself out of enslavement. He was still working as a blacksmith in the 1840s when Reverend Campbell documented his memories. Isaac was also documented in another way: he's the only member of his family who was ever photographed. He stands strong, looking younger than his years, his heavily muscled chest and arms visible under his work smock and apron.

After Jefferson's death, 200 enslaved men, women, and children were auctioned off to pay Jefferson's debts. Families were split apart and shipped away from the land they had lived on for three generations or more.

* * *

PAUL GIDEZ GOT INTO HEIRLOOM APPLES in the early 1970s, when he was in graduate school for neurobiology. "It was important to me to make good sweet cider," he told me over the phone, "because I thought that the sweet cider at the time wasn't that good."

Paul researched apples in his university library and came across the seminal pomological encyclopedia *A View of the Cultivation of*

*Fruit Trees and the Management of Orchards and Cider,* written in 1817 by William Coxe, Esq. Coxe wrote extraordinary praise of one cider apple in particular, the Harrison: "This is the most celebrated of the Cider apples of Newark in New Jersey . . . the flesh is light, yellow firm and tough; the taste pleasant and sprightly . . . it produces a high coloured, rich, sweet cider of great strength, commanding a high price in New-York."

Paul asked around at orchards, even the USDA collection at Geneva, but no one had a Harrison tree or had even heard of the Harrison. So he decided to look for it himself. In September 1976, he drove from where he was living in New Hampshire to New Jersey, deciding to search Essex County west of Newark. His first stop was a little strip mall in the town of Livingston.

"I inquired at a bagel shop about any old cider mills in the area. And he directed me just to go up the street and that I would find one." Paul headed up a hill and found Nettie Ochs Cider Mill, a site long known in the community for its fresh-pressed sweet cider and apple pies. It had been established in 1867, so it was exactly the kind of place Paul had been looking for.

"To the left and behind the house, I could see a tree full of yellow apples," Paul told me of that moment. "And I was pretty certain that it was a Harrison tree, even though I'd never seen one—just from Coxe's description. So I knocked on the door and I told the owner that I was looking for some Harrison trees and he pointed to that tree and said, 'That's the last one that I have.' His grandfather had planted it at the turn of the century. . . . He was about to cut it down, to make room for his vegetable garden."

Paul took cuttings of scion wood and propagated the tree on his property. When the trees did well and lived up to their reputation to make both sweet and hard cider, Paul planted Harrisons in orchards for friends and clients.

"It's very rich and quintessentially apple," said Paul in praise of the Harrison's juice. "And it's the right balance of sweet and tartness."

Because it had been so easy to locate a Harrison, Paul had no reason to think it was a rare tree. It was over a decade before he realized what he had discovered. In 1989, he heard about the work of an esteemed pomologist named Tom Burford. Burford was a champion of heirloom apples and on a mission like Paul's: to find and propagate old varieties of apples at risk of extinction.

Paul sent Harrison cuttings and a bushel of apples to Burford. Burford was elated and said that his father had spent his whole life looking for Harrisons. Burford confirmed both that the apple had been lost and that the cuttings Paul had propagated were in fact Harrisons.

Food writer Rowan Jacobsen wrote, "It's as if a legendary grape called Pinot Noir had been rediscovered, and we were the first generation in more than a century to taste its wine."

Burford has been credited with almost single-handedly fueling a revival of the Harrison, propagating trees from Paul's cuttings and another tree later found in Paramus, New Jersey. Burford became a consultant for historical orchards, including the recreated orchard at Monticello, and curated orchards for new cider makers. Burford always insisted that Harrisons should go in the ground. When the Ark of Taste was created, Burford nominated the Harrison for inclusion. It was an apple he never wanted lost again.

Burford died in March 2020. In his obituary, the *Washington Post* called the revival of the Harrison "his greatest contribution" to American agriculture.

\* \* \*

FROM THE SEVENTEENTH CENTURY onward, Newark, New Jersey, was the major cider producer in America. As early as 1682, the colonial governor noted that more cider was made in Newark than anywhere in New England. By 1810, Newark and surrounding Essex County produced nearly 200,000 barrels of cider, which sold for twice as much money as any other American cider.

The Harrison apple was first cultivated in New Jersey around 1712. It's a small, round apple, with a bright yellow or yellow-green skin speckled with black dots. Originally called the Osborne after the South Orange, New Jersey, family that cultivated it, it was obtained by landowner Samuel Harrison in the early eighteenth century. Harrison, a prominent citizen and industrialist as well as a member of one of the founding families of Newark, planted some of the first orchards in Essex County. By the late eighteenth century, Essex County—specifically, in and around Newark, New Jersey—became known for the Harrison apple and the high-quality cider made from it. The drink was known around the country as Newark cider or even Newark Champagne.

Newark's secret: consistency. While some wealthy plantation owners like Jefferson used the same select apples for their cider year after year, most cider makers—whether for sale or home use—pressed whatever variety of pippins grew in their orchard. Newark cider revolved around the much-revered Harrison, blended with a combination of Campfield, Graniwinkle, and Poveshon apples. One apple hunter I interviewed referred to these apples lovingly as the Newark Four.

I've tasted Harrison cider from several cideries and several vintages, and the taste has run the gamut from sweet and acidic to tannic and bitter; the flavors funky, floral, fruity, and, in one case, like the forest floor in the fall. It's remarkable to get all that dimension from one apple.

## The Jersey Cocktail

This cider-and-bitters cocktail is a favorite of mine, pulled from the pages of the first cocktail recipe book, Jerry Thomas's *How to Mix Drinks*, published in 1862. Although I've been making it for years, it was a mystery to me why a cider cocktail shared its name with the Garden State until I delved into the history of cider for this chapter.

The drink is like a mulled cider for summer: crisp, cool, and sweet. The simple syrup is entirely optional; use it only if you're in the mood for a sweet drink. While the cocktail is excellent with any cider, it seems fitting to make it with a Harrison apple cider if you can get it!

MAKES ONE COCKTAIL

*recipe continues >>*

**INGREDIENTS**
1 teaspoon simple syrup

I mix simple syrup 1:1. For example, 1 cup sugar and 1 cup water, placed in a tight-lidded mason jar and shaken until the sugar has dissolved.

2 dashes aromatic bitters
Cider
Lemon twist (the peel of a lemon, with only the yellow skin and as little as possible of the white pith)

Fill a rocks glass with crushed ice. Add simple syrup and bitters. Fill the glass with hard cider. Stir until the glass becomes very cold and condensation appears. Twist lemon peel over the top of the drink, then add it to the glass. Serve immediately.

\* \* \*

DESPITE ITS FAME, by the dawn of the twentieth century, the Harrison apple had nearly disappeared. The January 1918 issue of the New Jersey Historical Society magazine noted that "Twenty-five years ago many Harrison apple trees still flourished on the outskirts of Newark and in the surrounding towns, but where are they today? Houses are built where they formerly grew."

The roots of the Harrison's disappearance were planted by the temperance movement. Although America was colonized by many observant Christian communities, by the time of the Revolutionary War only 17 percent of Americans went to church regularly. But they were drinking: by 1830, the consumption of pure ethanol from all alcoholic beverages was just short of four gallons per person per year, about twice today's average. About 10 percent of that total was from hard cider and more than half was from distilled spirits, including apple brandy.

Let me bust a big myth here: I've often heard it said that "people drank a lot back then because the water was bad." My favorite retort is, "Is that why *you* drink?" Although there were issues with muddy water in some rural areas and contaminated water in cities, other parts of America were renowned for their good water. Sewers and aqueducts became more common in the nineteenth century, solving many water crises—and yet people still drank. Historical Americans drank for all the same reasons we drink today: community, entertainment, a preference for a variety of beverages, and to escape a tumultuous time.

When the US was a young republic, the economy often went through booms and busts. The country was frequently at war, whether with Britain or with Indigenous nations. There were no labor laws to protect factory workers and no government support to assist farmers on the frontier. Andrew Jackson, who was considered even in his time to be violent, aggressive, and polarizing, was elected to two terms as president. Many Americans turned to alcohol both for escape and for a feeling of control.

The temperance movement—a religious motivator for sobriety— was concieved of in 1813 by Calvinist students at a Massachusetts seminary. The many temperance societies that followed sought to provide the same feeling of control and social outlet that drinking served, but through family-focused events, pledges, and religious celebrations. Americans' consumption of alcohol dropped to less than a gallon a year per capita by the 1840s.

The shift away from cider specifically came in the mid-nineteenth century, triggered by another cultural change. Millions of German immigrants came to America between the 1840s and 1900, so many that today one in four Americans has German heritage. This mass immigration changed American culture, including our drinking habits. The Germans brought with them traditional lager beer. Beer was easier to brew in America's growing urban environments, the Midwest was colonized and became America's breadbasket, and the development of railways made it cheap and convenient to ship grain around the country.

Prohibition in the 1920s was the final death knell for cider. Having an apple tree was not illegal; even fermenting the fruit from that tree for home use was not forbidden. But in the eyes of the temperance movement, it was shameful. Many farmers cut down their trees to avoid suspicion or embarrassment. Orchardists switched to sweet dessert apples that had a guaranteed market in grocery stores. The industry worked hard to disassociate apples from cider and associate them with health and wellness: the slogan "an apple a day keeps the doctor away" was created in this era.

Additionally, a refrigerated rail system made a national market for fruit possible. Apples could be grown in far-off regions with ideal conditions and shipped into major markets. The apple industry "decided it would be wise to simplify that market by planting and promoting only a small handful of brand name varieties." With no need for the tannic, bitter, sour, and ugly apples used for cider making, the grocery industry focused only on appearance and sweetness. The Red Delicious became the de facto grocery store apple.

So, over the twentieth century, many historical apples were lost. The Harrison apple was long forgotten and destined never to be fermented again—until Paul Gidez made his fateful stop at a New Jersey bagel shop.

* * *

I WAS ABLE TO WITNESS Paul Gidez's and Tom Burford's impact firsthand. In August 2019, around the time I was learning about reefnets in the Puget Sound, I took a side trip to the apple-growing region of the Yakima Valley in central Washington state.

I drove through the heavy pine forests of the Cascade Mountains and descended into a valley with a sign that bragged "Welcome to Yakima! The Palm Springs of Washington!" And strangely, the landscape strongly resembles the arid Coachella Valley. Like SoCal, Yakima is a major agricultural area. Washington is the number one apple-growing state; more than half of the apples grown in the United States are grown in Washington, and 85 percent of all organic apples come from central Washington. Organic apples can be grown there because the climate in Yakima is arid, so fruit trees don't have to be treated for the fungus and blights that plague the humid East.

And because there are a lot of apples in Yakima, there are also a lot of cider makers: as of 2019, there were 120 cider makers in the state. I visited one of the first, Tieton Cider Works.

I met Marcus Robert and Craig Campbell at the latter's house, a concrete and steel piece of modern architecture. We sat on a covered porch that overlooked a vast dry valley patterned by irrigated circles and squares of bright green. Craig—tall and wiry, dressed in farmer's garb of a baseball hat and a blue neck gaiter—founded Tieton Cider Works in 2008 with his wife, Sharon. In his own words, Craig "loves to grow things," and planned to supply all of the apples for the cidery from his Harmony orchard, on land that had been in his family since the 1920s. In 2010, they brought on Marcus Robert, an orchardist and winemaker from nearby Natchez, to be their cider maker.

In the beginning, they had to figure out which of the heirloom cider apples would thrive in the western climate. Apple varieties often only grow well in a limited region; Paul Gidez's Harrison trees in his Vermont orchard never did as well as Jersey Harrisons. Craig and Marcus ended up pulling out almost half of the trees they put in the ground. But the Harrisons were happy and healthy. They got their trees from Diane Flynt, a legendary orchardist and cider maker, who got her trees from Burford, who got his original cuttings from Paul Gidez.

We got in Craig's truck to go down to the orchard. It was harvest season for the early varieties, and dozens of wood boxes were stacked throughout the orchard, ready to be packed with fruit. Craig's modern orchard looked vastly different from anything I had seen growing up in the Midwest or living in New York. It was designed on the tall spindle system: the trees grew along a trellis, short—a foot or two above my head—and skinny. The trellises were made up of five or six strong wires stretched between posts, and flatten the growth of the trees, allowing as much sunlight as possible to hit the leaves. The trees clung to the trellis like an ornamental bush, their apples revealed on either side, exposed and easy to pluck from the branches. The trees had been grafted onto size-controlling root stock that dwarfs the trees, which makes the fruit easier to harvest, and the trees produce fruit earlier—at around five years old—and quit around twenty.

We hopped out of Craig's truck at the Harrison orchard; more than

10,000 Harrison trees stretched to the horizon over seven acres. It was their fifth growing season; the trees were producing fruit, but they wouldn't be harvested until October. The small apples were unmistakably Harrisons, with their tell-tale black specs.

In addition to their cider blends, Marcus makes three single-varietal ciders: Ashmead's Kernel, Golden Russet, and, of course, Harrison. The Harrison makes a cider with a rich mouthfeel, golden color, and notes of ginger, honey, peach, and cherry.

"They've probably never heard of a Harrison," Marcus said of the drinkers who might pick up his cider. "But it's intriguing to go: what does that apple taste like by itself?" And Marcus loved the historical connection of once again making cider from Harrisons.

"Supposedly it demanded the highest price for a cider apple in the US," Marcus added as we admired the trees.

I wondered if the Harrison would ever be made into the famed Newark cider again, blended with the other famous New Jersey apples into an elixir not tasted in over a century. The problem was, one of the Newark Four apples was believed to be extinct: no one had seen a Poveshon apple in modern memory.

\* \* \*

HOPEFUL POMOLOGISTS, CIDER MAKERS, and orchardists hunt for old apples, referring to them as Lost Heritage Apples. These are apple varieties established before 1930 that have since gone missing. In Washington and Oregon, volunteers with the Lost Apple Project "consult historical maps, records from 19th-century county fairs, newspapers, and sales ledgers to pinpoint former orchards," then search the grounds for old apple trees. In North Carolina, apple conservationist Tom Brown founded AppleSearch.org. Brown has gained recent fame from a viral Reddit and Facebook post of him at one of the many festivals he visits with his heirloom apple collection. Brown claims on his website that over 1,000 trees have been rediscovered since the founding of his project in 1999.

If you should find an Unknown Apple, Brown recommends showing it to a commercial orchardist. "They probably can identify it if the apple is a Modern Apple or one of the more common Known Heritage Apples." If that does not yield results, he says, "You can also show the apple to older people at area stores where 'locals' hang out. Showing the apple to no more than six elderly people should result in its identification."

If the apple is identified, it can then be compared to historical descriptions and images, like Coxe's book and the 1905 USDA guide. Furthermore, a DNA sample sent to the USDA Plant Identification Lab at UC Davis can help match trees to their namesakes in the living collections. If there's no match, that potentially means a Lost Heritage Apple has been found. At this point, apples and scion wood are often sent to apple experts across the country to confirm the discovery.

If a Lost Heritage Apple has been found, scions are grafted and the tree is propagated and sold from commercial orchards or donated out to repopulate the variety. If the apple was discovered far from where it originated, an effort is made to return it to regional orchards.

A lot of luck and perseverance is involved when it comes to finding old apples. I was fortunate enough to watch one of these rediscoveries play out firsthand.

In mid-September 2019, I followed the shore of Lake Erie through the Seneca nation, past "Bear Crossing" signs, to the tiny town of Woodhull in western New York. Early fall upstate meant hillsides dotted with white and purple flowers and monarch butterflies flitting by on their steady, determined path south. From the highway, a rough road took me to a packed-dirt road, then directly over a mowed meadow and up a steep hill.

I got out of my car at the property of Wesley and Robin Stokes, overlooking rolling pastures and plots of woodland. A few trees whose leaves had changed to bright orange dotted forests that were otherwise still a deep green. Wesley and Robin lived near Newark, New Jersey, but their vacation cabin and property in upstate New York were beginning to take on a legendary reverence in the apple-hunting community.

After introductions and cracking a few cans of La Croix, we settled ourselves in lawn chairs and the couple told me their story. They bought their 37-acre property about twenty-five years ago. They came up once a month in warmer weather and brought their grandkids over the summers. They were aware of the four geriatric apple trees at the brambly edge of their woods but had never thought much of them.

"The apples were always nice," Robin told me. "I'd make pies, I'd make apple sauce."

In the fall of 2015, Wesley and Robin came up to the cabin with friends. They invited their guests to pick apples from the trees and filled a few shopping bags of their own to take back to New Jersey. Back at home, Robin had just launched a salad dressing business, and had picked up a copy of *Edible Jersey* to research the local food scene. She had left it on the coffee table, where Wes picked it up and started flipping through it.

In that issue, journalist Fran McManus had written an article about a newly opened cidery near Newark called Ironbound Farm. Ironbound's goal was to recreate the lauded Newark cider, but it was stuck without the lost Poveshon apple. McManus included in the article a sort of "wanted" poster, an image and description of the Poveshon from William Coxe's nineteenth-century guide: "The size is small, the form flat, the skin smooth and of a deep red with rich yellow flesh, which is sweet, and uncommonly dry. The skin of this apple is full of dark red blotches running longitudinally, with small white spots."

McManus concluded her article: "Charles Rosen, [Ironbound's] owner, holds out hope that a Poveshon tree still stands in an abandoned orchard or farmyard somewhere in the Garden State, waiting to be found and brought back to Newark."

Wes got one of the apples he had brought back from Woodhull and compared it to the watercolor in the article, which had been painted by one of Coxe's daughters.

Wes reached out to Charles Rosen via the Ironbound website. "I said, 'I think I might have your apple,'" Wes told me. "And then we were off to the races."

McManus collected apples from Wes and distributed them to three pomologists. One agreed that the sample matched the physical description of a Poveshon; one did not. Tom Burford, after examining the apples, wrote, "Yesterday, I examined the fruit repeatedly and all indicators and documentation coincides to indicate it is the Poveshon . . . Congratulations . . . to Wes Stokes, who now is guardian of the tree from which all other Poveshons will come." Later, Fran McManus would tell me that his determination surprised her, because "he was typically very cautious about making pronouncements." Additionally, a DNA sample sent to the USDA Plant Database didn't match anything in the collection. Without a living sample to compare it to, there is technically no way to be sure these trees are Poveshons.

Wes walked me down the hill from the cabin and through a brambly hedge into the woods, while Robin opted to stay behind in the meadow. In the woods, two enormous, elderly apple trees kept each other company. Their trunks were 30–40 inches in diameter and, unpruned for ages, they had grown 20 feet tall. Old scars marked where enormous branches—and parts of the trunk—had died and fallen away, while other branches thick as my thighs still offered up fresh growth. Knobbly bark the color of stone was covered in moss and lichen, the trunks were bent and corkscrewed, and roots pushed out of the ground and undulated across the soil.

A tree the Stokeses had named Hazel was the oldest and the most sculptural. Wes had lovingly constructed supports for her long, heavy limbs, crutches that kept them propped up and stable. Hazel was completely hollow: the center of her trunk had rotted away and a two-foot-wide window had opened straight through to the other side. It was incredible that these trees were still alive, let alone producing apples.

Flat, moss-covered rocks encircled the base of the tree, in an eighteenth-century method of orchard management called stone mulching. The flagstones stopped weeds from growing at the base of the tree and acted as a heat sink for the winter. The stumps of equally old and enormous trees, now dead, patterned the woods with their flagstone rings, marking a much larger orchard that was once here. It's been estimated the orchard was planted in the 1850s, meaning that the Poveshon trees were about 170 years old. Wes had decided to plunge into genealogy to learn more about the nineteenth-century property owners. In the 1850s, the family that owned the property happened to be from New Jersey, the Poveshon's home. In fact, all the surrounding properties were owned by Jersey families, some of whom had come from Newark.

Wes handed me an apple to try. The Poveshon apples were fairly small and slightly flat, the size and shape of a clementine orange, with coloring that ranged from blood red to pale pink, with highlights of orange, yellow, and green. I took a bite of the raw fruit. The tannins dried my mouth in that tooth-squeaking way, but the sugar was there too. It missed the bite of acidity, and the texture was a bit mealy.

"It's a very odd apple. It has a lot of tannins but almost no acid in it," Robin told me. "And so what happens is it gets like to molasses brown when they press the cider."

"It oxidized almost instantly," Wes added. It's now thought the Poveshon was blended into Newark cider not just for its tannins but for its deep caramel color.

A few apples adorned Hazel's higher branches and she was still producing scion wood, meaning that cuttings could be harvested and grafted. She and her sisters had been found before the apple was lost forever.

I petted a branch four times the thickness of my arm and whispered, "You got this, Hazel. You've made it this long."

* * *

AFTER MEETING THE STOKESES AND HAZEL, I made my way downstate. I traveled through Geneva to visit the USDA apple collection, and I stopped in Esopus to visit a few commemorative Esopus Spitzenburg trees, another heirloom and Ark of Taste apple variety. Three days later, I found myself in a diner in Livingston, New Jersey. I sat at the counter sipping tea and considering a bear claw. I was down the block from where Paul Gidez found the Harrison apple tree in the 1970s.

I was waiting for Fran McManus, the journalist who had helped bring the Poveshon to light, and who now worked as a consultant for Ironbound Farm. In her role as "cultural strategist," she wove together the story of Newark's historical apples, Ironbound's commitment to workforce development, and the farm's use of regenerative agriculture. We had an appointment at Ironbound that afternoon, but had planned a few apple adventures first.

I recognized Fran immediately when she came through the diner doors: slender with short gray hair, wearing a lavender zip-up activewear shirt and a Fit Bit on her wrist. She had an easy energy and a contagious fascination for apples. We went out to the parking lot and I popped my trunk, revealing bags of Poveshons Wes had given me. She plucked an apple out of the bag, held it close to her face, and asked it, "What is your story?"

It was promising to be a hot day as we marched up the hill to the site where Paul Gidez had found the Harrison. Fran laughed when she called Paul "an enigma. I don't know anyone who has ever met him."

I knew the Nettie Ochs Cider Mill was closed; when the last owner passed away in 2005, the remaining family decided to sell the property to developers. There was a fight on Facebook and in the Livingston town hall to designate the property as a historical landmark or to sell it to a private individual who would restore the mill. Some locals fought because they wanted to preserve a part of Livingston's history; others feared the "affordable housing" that would be built there. "More affordable housing?? Meaning low-income rentals?" one resident gasped on Facebook. "If you can't afford to live in Livingston you shouldn't. It's a classy town, hope it stays that way," another protested.

"We wish town people would stay out of our property sale," one of the Ochs descendants retorted.

Even knowing all this, I wasn't prepared for what we found at the top of the hill. The historical mill had been razed. Fran and I stood in front of a field of dirt, a squad of bulldozers digging out the basements of future townhomes. A large sign announced the name of this new development: Cider Mill Townhomes. Livingston's "classy" residents had no reason to despair: the townhomes were promised to be "the Ultimate in Luxury Rental Living."

We headed back down the hill.

"After working on that story," Fran told me about her Harrison

196 | ENDANGERED EATING

article, "it has forever changed the way that I pass through Newark on the train. I take a moment to look at the bend in the river and think about the settlers coming. Would they even be able to imagine what it is today? Probably not. But they were enterprising anyway, so they might be proud to see a huge city on that land. I feel that our state gets a bum rap around things like food and agriculture when we actually have a really rich history, as well as, I think, a very vibrant culture."

Fran took me to a living Harrison tree outside a high school in Maplewood, New Jersey. Tall, tri-trunked, and replete with yellow apples, the fruit looked even more golden in the autumn light. Then we headed farther east to Alexandria, to the site of Ironbound Farm. Ironbound is located more than 50 miles from its namesake neighborhood in Newark, but cideries in New Jersey are subject to the same laws as winemakers, including having their business adjacent to the agricultural land where their raw materials are produced. So while there are dreams of one day opening a tasting room and retail outlet in Newark, currently Ironbound is a destination in the countryside.

Coming down the long drive from the road, we passed Ironbound's eighteenth-century farmhouse and barn, the latter housing the tasting room and farm-to-table restaurant as well as the cidery and kitchen. A sloping hill was covered in young apple trees and the property ended in a wood edged by a lake.

When I stepped out of my car, Charles Rosen, Ironbound's founder and CEO, was working with the kitchen staff on a few enormous barbecue grills outside the lower level of the barn. Before even saying hello, he thrust a chunk of fresh-baked bread slathered in rendered pork fat at me, insisting I needed to try it. I did.

The idea for the cidery came from Charles's motivation to invest back in Newark. He wanted to create a business model that addressed income inequality, racial division, and food systems injustice. A longtime resident of a Newark suburb, he felt there was no better place to create the business than in the city he loved.

He met with Cory Booker, then the mayor of Newark, and Booker's Director of Sustainability Stephanie Greenwood, to discuss where he should invest his money and what kind of business should be built.

It was Greenwood who suggested bringing back the Harrison apple; she went into her office and grabbed a copy of *Edible Jersey* containing an article written by Fran on the history of the Harrison. Fran had included an argument as to why the apple should be returned to its home soil: "Perhaps, emulating New York City's recent efforts to reestablish the Newtown Pippin, the mayors of Newark and West Orange can promote the planting of this apple that is so intertwined in the history of their cities."

When he read those words, the direction of Charles's life changed. He had come, in part, from an ad agency background. He had run campaigns for Mike's Hard Lemonade, Svedka vodka, and Fat Tire ale. He knew cider was a rapidly growing industry. But after he connected with Fran and learned more about her research, he loved that cider had deep roots in Newark.

While Charles was initially frustrated that he had to build his cidery far from Newark, he soon saw it as an opportunity to regrow these historical apples. Charles bought his land in 2015 and vowed to do just that. The property, a farm since the eighteenth century, had lain fallow for more than twenty years. The barn had been made "practical" in the 1980s with vinyl siding and drop ceilings. Charles's team peeled it all back to reveal the original hand-hewn beams. The old barn doors were replaced with the roll-up garage doors you find at Brooklyn restaurants.

The afternoon Fran and I arrived at Ironbound was warm and those doors were up, allowing a view from the tasting room to the outside dining space and enormous fire pit, and beyond to the rolling hills of the farm. Ironbound's farm dog, Finn, chased a groundhog in the distance around rows of fall vegetables. Beyond him, young apple trees pushed their way skyward.

Fran and I sat at one of the wide wood tables on high stools, flights of cider appearing before us. Charles produced a carboy of a new product they were working on, a cider made from heirloom Golden Russet apples infused with foraged American spicebush and fortified with American apple brandy—all three Ark of Taste ingredients—and sweetened with the farm's own honey. The result was a rich golden beverage that reminded me of a dessert wine or after-dinner liqueur, redolent with the caramel-apple qualities of Golden Russet and the cinnamon, nutmeg, and allspice flavor of the spicebush. The apple brandy had come from Laird's, the oldest distillery in the country, which is located in nearby Eatontown.

## Two Fortified Cider Cocktails

Ironbound isn't the only cidery trying its hand at fortified ciders. Angry Orchard released a French-style "pommeau," aged in oak barrels, and Eden Specialty Ciders in Vermont makes fortified "aperitif" ciders, infused with a variety of herbs and spices. They can all be consumed straight or on the rocks, but here are two modern cocktails that highlight fortified cider, created by Ironbound's bar team.

### HARVEST MOON

MAKES ONE COCKTAIL

INGREDIENTS

10 ounces Ironbound Hard Cider Devil's Harvest, or another rosé cider

2 ounces Ironbound Golden Russet Orange Fortified Cider, or another fortified cider

Orange slice, for garnish

Serve over ice in your preferred glass.

### THE ONE-SEATER

INGREDIENTS

1.5 ounces Cognac

¾ ounce Ironbound Golden Russet Orange Fortified Cider, or another fortified cider

¾ ounce lemon juice

Lemon twist, for garnish

Combine all ingredients and shake with ice. Strain and pour into a sugar-rimmed coupe glass and garnish with lemon twist.

\* \* \*

IT WAS A LITTLE AFTER 3 P.M. and Ironbound's farmers were ending their shift, gathering in the barn and at the bar, getting loud and jovial. Alex Gioseffi, the farm manager, came in from the field with a baseball cap full of apples, and sorted out five tiny Harrisons. Still green, with a red blush, lumpy and covered in constellations of black speckles, these apples would never see grocery store shelves. But they would one day make incredible cider.

Derek Blackwell and James Williams came in from the dirty work of setting up new greenhouses for winter produce and sat at the bar for a breather. Both were lifelong Newark residents who had been with Ironbound since the beginning. They had come on board never having farmed a day in their lives, hired through Ironbound's workforce development program focused on job creation for the chronically underemployed, including the formerly incarcerated. In Newark, one in four Black men "have been involved in the criminal justice system." As Williams put it, most employers are "looking at your criminal background and saying 'no, no, no.'" And it's not just prejudice against the formerly incarcerated; employers have to work to meet the needs of the recently released. The formerly incarcerated may need access to reliable transportation, assistance getting important forms of ID like driver's licenses reinstated, and flexible schedules so they can meet with a parole officer or be a caretaker for children or elderly family members. At times, Ironbound has even provided local housing for those that couldn't make the forty-five-minute commute from Newark every day.

The team faced many setbacks when they first began. Clearing the acreage was brutally slow. When trees went into the ground they suffered, and had to be pulled out three years later. To the novice farm team at Ironbound, it felt like a deep cut. "It was devastatingly hard to envision the future," Charles told me.

But then Charles got some advice from one of the orchard consultants brought onto the project. "He said, 'Stop approaching this like the aggressive New York Jew you are and slow the fuck down.'" For the record, Charles is originally from Canada, but he has become as much of a place as his historical apple trees. "And I said, 'But I've got to get my trees in the ground, these guys need jobs now.' He's like, 'You can't rush your trees.'"

While the team learned to take their time with the trees, they also integrated crops that would show more immediate results. They began to grow the herbs and spices that Ironbound infused into its ciders, like gooseberries, ginger, hops, and lemon verbena. They grew the vegetables served at the restaurant, and added livestock: pigs, goats, sheep, and chickens. The goats cleared land quicker than chainsaws and pickaxes, and the chickens roamed the fields, managing pests and depositing fertilizer.

The change in pace and expectations of farming had been tough for both Derek and James, but over the years they had made a deep connection to the land. Derek now headed the poultry department and James was crew chief and head grafter. They both worked on the training program for new employees, drawing on their own experiences to help a new generation of farmers.

When not on the farm, James managed Ironbound's greenhouses in Oldwick, New Jersey, propagating apple trees. He had grown out the Poveshon scions to hundreds, then thousands, of trees. "I took to the grafting because it was about patience," James told Fran McManus in an interview in the farm's early days. He saw his work restoring these trees as something that would outlast him.

"I'll be dead and gone, but looking down, and I'll be like, 'Yeah, that's my work—thousands of trees.'"

Ironbound has propagated far more trees than they have space for on their acreage. "Our goal is to give away thousands and thousands of trees. I give them to growers in New York, Pennsylvania," Charles told me. All of the Newark Four have gone to surrounding orchards; the farmers get the raw materials for free and sell the apples back to Ironbound. Charles wants the entire region to benefit from his cidery, and it also diversifies his own risk. If his farm gets hit with a blight or a pest, one of the other orchards growing his trees may still be producing.

The farm and cidery had come a long way. But so far, there was no Newark Cider. The team had more than 10,000 Harrisons, Poveshons, Campfields, and Granniwinkles planted on Ironbound Farm and other orchards, but the trees would need another three years or more to produce enough apples. In the meantime, Charles and his team purchased apples to create their inaugural cider blends. A Newark Cider is still in the plans.

"We're going to make a New Jersey cider, a Newark Cider," Charles told me. "It's still the heart of this company. It's important to bring this back and honor history."

Charles walked us down to the orchards, rows of skinny young trees just beginning to produce apples. Between the rows of trees, the farmers had planted flowers to attract pollinators, a riot of scarlet, purple, orange, white and pink. Hundreds of monarch butterflies shared the space with the farm's honeybees, flitting from bloom to bloom for a sip before continuing their weary way to Mexico.

Charles was on the phone with his farm manager while Fran and I marveled at the paradise before us, illuminated in the red light of the setting sun.

"We need to do something to get rid of the butterflies, though," Charles deadpanned into the phone. "Too many fucking butterflies. They're all over the place."

Charles was hosting Rosh Hashanah dinner at the farm the next night, for his family, staff, and their families. It was the first holiday he and his siblings would be celebrating without their parents, as Charles's mom had just passed away. On Rosh Hashanah, the Jewish New Year, it's traditional to eat apples and honey, in hopes of a sweet year to come.

"And then it just hit me," Charles exclaimed. " 'Oh my God, I have an orchard and we have our bees. I have my own honey. It's our own apples. We're going to be on the farm eating our own apples with our own honey." After four long years of labor, his family and his farm staff would enjoy Ironbound's very literal fruits on a very special day.

As we said our goodbyes, Charles invited Fran and me back the next night for the celebration, but we both had other obligations. I had one more stop to make on my apple journey: a church in Elmhurst, Queens.

* * *

EARLY THE NEXT MORNING, I wound through the neighborhoods of east Queens, finally parking at a familiar intersection. Across the ten lanes of Queens Boulevard traffic was the stadium-shaped Queens Place Mall. When I lived in Long Island City in the 2000s, I used to take two trains to get to the Target in this shopping center. Despite all the trips I had made out here, I had never once noticed the old stone church across the street: the First Presbyterian Church of Newtown. This was the church of Reverend John Moore and the birthplace of the Newtown Pippin.

Made from rough-hewn, quarried stone blocks, the current building was erected in 1895. The yard was fenced in wrought iron and the gate locked, but in the side yard I could spot what I was looking for: a grove of twenty-year-old Newtown Pippin apple trees. In the mid-2000s there was a flurry of effort to establish Newtowns as New York City's official apple. A Newtown Pippin nonprofit was briefly formed to plant the Newtowns as street trees in the city. They succeeded in planting orchards both at Queens College and here, to commemorate the 350th anniversary of the congregation's founding. Slow Food NYC also acquired scion wood from orchards in Virginia and gave away grafted trees to New York orchards.

Pressing my face through the bars of the fence, I knew that the future of these Newtown Pippins—and other heirloom apples like the Harrison and the Poveshon—were brighter than at any time in the last century.

SEVEN

# *Kombo Hakshish*

## CHOCTAW FILÉ POWDER

Seeking out the foods on the Ark of Taste meant chasing an endless summer. By October 2019, fall was deep up north; the leaves had turned red and frost coated the grass on chilly mornings. But on a plane bound for New Orleans, I peeked out the window to see the Mississippi snaking below, a silver thread winding through a lush green landscape. After we landed, I stepped out of the airport into the hazy, subtropical atmosphere.

Although the temperature would hit 91 that day, the recent dip below 100 degrees meant that it was officially "gumbo weather." Gumbo weather heralds the coming of fall and the time to make the meaty stew that should accompany it, flavored and thickened with a few tablespoons of electric green filé powder.

Filé is made from the dried, ground leaves of the sassafras tree, *Sassafras albidum*, a member of the odorous laurel family that includes bay and cinnamon trees. The deciduous tree is native to North America and grows all over the eastern United States, from Maine to Texas. It's easy to identify; the leaves grow in three different shapes: oval, mitten-shaped, and three-lobed. Additionally, the perfume of the tree is unmis-

204 | ENDANGERED EATING

takable. If you brush past a sassafras in the woods, perhaps breaking a branch, you'll notice the slightly lemony smell of the leaves as well as the root beer-scented bark. Pull a sapling out of the ground and its unique smell fills the air, an explosion of vanilla, cinnamon, and spearmint.

Filé is an Ark of Taste food that isn't necessarily endangered, although the tree is at risk of disappearing from Louisiana, where it is culturally significant. Sassafras is affected by laurel wilt disease, a pathogen that is carried from tree to tree by an invasive insect, the red-bay ambrosia beetle. The bug bores into sassafras trees to feed and lay eggs, and the laurel wilt pathogen catches a ride on the insects and is introduced into the interior of the tree. Once a tree is infected, it cannot be saved.

"It is truly a tragic story," I was told over email by Louisiana Forestry and Wildlife Extension Agent Robbie Hutchins. "Both sassafras and redbay are now in danger of becoming extinct throughout Louisiana . . . neither redbay nor sassafras is a commercially important species. Because of this it seems that only people like scientists (foresters and botanists), people that understand the importance of sassafras to our environment (wildlife biologists), and people that understand the importance of sassafras to our culture for both filé and folk medicinal uses (historians and naturalists) seem to understand the seriousness of the situation." The redbay beetle is not yet found throughout sassafras's entire native range, and the beetle is less destructive in colder climates.

Filé ended up on the Ark because the use of it is so localized; few Americans outside of Louisiana, or the Gullah Geechee areas of coastal Georgia and South Carolina, have ever heard of it. It's a defining ingredient of Cajun and Creole cuisine and is emblematic of what food historian Jessica Harris calls "the Braid": the weaving together of Indigenous, Black, and European culinary cultures in America. Filé began as an ingredient used by Indigenous peoples, then it was incorporated into a West African stew that was served to European colonists.

It's the traditional way to make filé which the Ark also sought to preserve, but has probably already been lost: "the time-honored fashion of hand harvesting, drying and curing the sassafras leaves before pounding them with a pestle in a traditional cypress mortar." Fresh, handmade filé from a traditional maker is matcha-green and smells like spearmint tea, cracked peppercorns, and lemon zest. According to Louisiana journalist Morgan Randall, commercially processed filé "has the color, consistency, and arguably the flavor of sawdust." The drying methods, as well as the time the product sits on the shelf, mean that the filé loses flavor and color. And commercial filé is often not pure and contains other spices like bay leaf and thyme.

But just because no one is out there pounding leaves in a cypress mortar doesn't mean that the tradition is entirely gone. My journey into the local foodscape began, as it often did, at the rental car counter. While the agent got my paperwork in order, we chatted about my trip and my filé powder research.

"Well, I didn't know it was endangered," the agent exclaimed. "My house is full of it!"

I asked her how she made it.

"You put the leaves in a pillowcase and put it in the dryer. I grind mine in a marble bowl." A mortar and pestle? "Yes. My mother's bowl was wood, I remember that."

When I got in the car, I drove west, away from New Orleans, on Interstate 10, a highway elevated over the edge of Lake Pontchartrain. The lake is an immense estuary where inland freshwater and saltwater from the Gulf of Mexico meet. High waves crested on the lake on my right and broke on the buttressed roots of trees in the Maurepas Swamp on my left.

I took the highway exit into La Place, a bit of dry land that fronted the Mississippi River. I drove past shrimp stands, andouille shops and sugarcane fields; I smelled smoked meat and saw people fishing in the spillways. This was Acadiana, a unique culinary landscape within America. The Acadiana region starts about 100 miles west of New Orleans, on the other side of the Mississippi River and the vast wetland of the Atchafalaya Basin. The area was settled by French Acadians—or Cajuns,[*] as they came to be known—after the French

---

[*] Until the twentieth century, the word "Cajun" was considered an ethnic slur. Acadians were derided for their rural ways and heavily accented English. It wasn't until Louisiana had its first Cajun governor, Edwin Edwards, who proudly called himself a Cajun, that the word became reclaimed.

lost the territory of Nova Scotia to the British in 1710. The French residents refused to accept British rule, and were deported starting in 1755. This mass expulsion was known as *le Grand Dérangement*. The Acadians first went to French colonies in the Caribbean, and some made their way to French Louisiana.

Cajun food was simply prepared and seasoned, and heavy on local game and plentiful seafood, like shrimp, crab, oysters, and crawfish. Cajun cuisine is extremely community-oriented: big pots of gumbo are made, a whole hog is roasted, or a crawfish boil cooks up hundreds if not thousands of shellfish. These are not just meals; they're events that bring people together.

Although Acadiana technically starts on the far side of the Mississippi, I was headed to Wayne Jacob's Smokehouse and Restaurant in La Place, which had been declared "as Cajun as it comes" by local food personality and advocate Poppy Tooker. An unassuming brown brick, one-story building, its storefront pressed right up to the country road, Wayne Jacob's has been around since 1950. It was originally a grocery store, serving the workers who manned the surrounding sugarcane fields. When chain stores threatened to put it out of business, it became a smokehouse only open from October to February, making sausage during gumbo season. Today, under the ownership of chef Jarred Zeringue, Wayne Jacob's still hand-makes traditional Cajun smoked meats like andouille, boudin, and tasso, as well as cracklins and head cheese. It sells multicolored eggs from its own chickens, citrus and pecans from its own trees, honey from its own bees, and locally grown onions and tomatoes. It also operates as a restaurant seven days a week.

I parked and came in a side door, near the butcher counter topped with a mountain of reddish andouille, a stack of at least sixty of the wrinkly sausages. The dining room took up the front half of the space, dark wood four-tops, maybe ten or fifteen tables in total. The walls were covered with framed newspaper and magazine articles from the restaurant's past, along with photos of the generations of owners. Spices, hot sauces, and pickles for sale were stacked on shelves by the front doors, alongside little plastic jars of filé for $7 a pop. I picked up a jar and shook the contents: a fluff of particles as green as the shag carpet in my grandparents' house, or green like the first new grass in a snowy wood.

Wayne Jacob's resident filé maker is known only as Coco. When Chef Jarred bought the place five years before, Coco came with it. When I met Coco, he was eighty-one years old. He walked in the front door of Wayne Jacob's for our interview in dark blue jeans belted over a tucked-in white T-shirt. An LSU baseball cap covered wisps of white hair, and a bright gold watch contrasted against his sun-darkened skin.

"Coco! How ya doing today?" I asked.

"Well," Coco responded, "I'm not under the ground yet."

Coco was born in the house that still stands across the street. Even though he has since moved "a mile or two" away, he still stops by the store every day but Sunday—sometimes just to sit and chat, sometimes to help out. On Sundays, he stays home and cooks for his children and grandchildren: big boiling pots of red beans and rice, spaghetti, or chicken and andouille gumbo made with his own filé.

Coco's uncle, Nolan Jacobs, built this store. His dad used to deliver groceries to the town's residents and was the smokehouse's first filé maker. His mama was in a photograph on the wall, in red lipstick, a denim dress, and an oatmeal-colored cardigan, standing in front of a butcher's station with a hunk of meat ready to be sliced.

I asked Coco how long he'd been making filé for the store.

"Woo, Lord! . . . After my daddy quit, after he got too old. I guess it was twenty-five, thirty years ago. I saw him make it, long time ago, when they had a big hollow log, a big log, and they'd hollow it out and beat it by hand." Coco guessed his dad's mortar was at least 150 years old when his dad used it. "And then they'd pass it through a screen until it got fine. Just by beating it, just by hand. That was before they had food processors and blenders all that. But if I had to do it that way . . . " He shook his head.

"At one time I was making, like, three hundred, four hundred bottles," Coco told me. "This year I made a hundred bottles. . . . There's no trees around here!"

Southern Louisiana is on the very edge of the sassafras tree's southerly range, and laurel wilt disease had been affecting local trees. Coco walked me across the street, behind the white house he was born in, to show me his trees. In the middle of a field, near a cypress-wood shed that Coco called "older than time," was a stand of sassafras trees. But because of their purpose, these were shaped like topiary. On the oldest, there were no branches or leaves on the bottom six feet of the trunk. Higher on the trunk, perhaps a dozen thick branches leaned out laterally, then reached up to the sky. The leaves stuck out of the ends of these branches in Seussian tufts. A handsaw attached to a long pole leaned against the trunk, a handmade tool designed to prune high branches off the elderly tree.

Little trees were popping up in the grass; sassafras can propagate by seed, but more often it sends up shoots from its roots. Coco had marked the young trees with rods so he didn't run them down with his lawnmower. He even fertilizes his trees, but said they often stayed stunted and small. Any trees he had transplanted had died.

After Coco trimmed new growth, he left the leaves on the branches to dry. Part of the key to making traditional filé is to air-dry the sassafras leaves in the dark. Coco puts them in his greenhouse and covers them with cardboard or dries them in the heat of his attic. This process means that the leaves retain color and flavor. After the leaves air-dry, Coco crushes them by hand and picks out any large stems, then stores them in a five-gallon bucket with a lid. Whole or partially crushed filé leaves retain their flavor, so Coco prefers to grind them as he needs them.

When it comes time to grind for the store, Coco sets up out back of Wayne Jacob's with a tabletop grain mill. The leaves go through the mill once, then they are sifted to remove stems before being ground a second time. Then they're bottled for sale.

When Coco and I walked back across the street and into the restaurant, chef Jarred had just come back from running an errand. "He don't talk like it, but he's a Cajun," Coco informed me. "Originally, because he comes from across the river."

"So, you got a lot of information out of him?" Jarred ribbed us as I crossed the restaurant to shake his hand. Jarred was maybe forty, bearded, baseball-capped, and wearing a branded Wayne Jacob's T-shirt.

We sat to talk a bit more about the particulars of gumbo, the dish in which filé features most prominently. There is a lot of debate concerning which gumbos filé should go into and at what point in the cooking process. Coco brings his gumbo to a rolling boil and adds filé, letting it cook for a few minutes to thicken up before serving. Most Cajun folks like to add their filé at the table, sprinkling it on top and stirring it in. Coco's son, however, "He would put it in there until it was—oh gawd—it was green! I mean he used too much."

Coco's way of cooking follows popular and traditional knowledge. If filé is cooked too hard and long it tends to get "stringy," adding an unpleasant texture to the soup. As Poppy Tooker once said to me, "filé powder can become tragically slimy." In fact, the origin of its name in French Creole probably comes from this texture: *fil* in French means "thread."

Jarred adds some filé near the beginning of cooking. "I sauté my vegetables and my smoked meat, so that it renders some of the fat and you get more of the smoke flavor out of it. And I put a little bit of filé in there."

And Coco warned me, "You don't want it too thick. You eat in New Orleans, the gumbo in New Orleans is gonna be too thick. Gumbo is supposed to be thin. Stews are thick, gumbo is thin."

Jarred theorized that New Orleans gumbo was thicker, in part, because it looks prettier. "With the thicker roux, the stuff sits up in it, you know, and doesn't just fall down in it. And it looks good when you present it on the plate, you know?" But often the most delicious dishes are not good-looking. "When I serve certain things in my restaurant, I know people are gonna love it, but when they get it, it's just going to look like a bowl of slop."

Coco uses a roux to start his gumbo. Roux is cooked flour and fat—a French culinary technique used to thicken stews and sauces, but many Louisiana cooks will tell you it's more about "adding a rich, roasted flavor." In New Orleans, the roux is cooked nearly black, but west of the city, in Acadiana, the roux is lighter. Coco then adds onions and parsley—"Like my mama used to make it. Only onions and parsley in the gumbo."

Okra can also be used as a thickener. But there are rules about which gumbos use okra and which use filé; they are never used together.

"We never really mixed like sausage and shrimp and okra and all that kind of stuff," Jarred added. "My grandmother used to make an okra and shrimp gumbo."

"That's it," Coco agreed.

"And then she made chicken and andouille gumbo, which had filé but didn't have any okra."

"Okra is for seafood gumbo, not in andouille and chicken gumbo," Coco confirmed. "In New Orleans you might find that, but not in this area. I use chicken, andouille and smoked sausage. I use all three. Some people like smoked turkey necks or they use smoked chicken."

Coco never eats gumbo in a restaurant, not even at Wayne Jacob's. He only makes his own. "I like it the way I make it. And if I want gumbo, I'll cook a pot of gumbo for the week." But he will buy his andouille from Jarred.

Coco said his goodbyes and Jarred headed back to the kitchen to fill orders. Of course, I got a bowl of gumbo before I left. Although the restaurant was empty when I sat down at 11 a.m., it was completely full twenty minutes later.

On every table was a bottle of hot sauce and a shaker of Coco's filé. When the server approached with a menu, I apologized for photographing the filé at my table. The server busted out her Instagram to show me the photos she'd taken the day they bottled it. "You can't help it, it's so pretty!" she gushed.

When my lunch arrived at the table, the gumbo was deep brown and dense with shredded chicken, served over a scoop of rice that just broke the surface of the soup. I sprinkled on filé, like a covering of moss on a log, and then stirred it in to thicken and flavor. The gumbo thickened, but not to the gelatinous thickness I expected; it created a smooth suspension, a liquid like plush velvet. The flavors floated in this emulsion, smoke up front—pure campfire—then a red-pepper heat at the back of my throat, then a mouth-coating savory taste.

"Good and gone, right?" my server said as she whisked away my empty bowl.

* * *

SASSAFRAS HAS BEEN TRADITIONALLY used in many food preparations by Indigenous peoples. The roots have been used to make a cooling tea consumed in the hottest months of the summer. Barbacoa cooks—the ancestry of modern barbecue—would burn different types of wood to flavor cooking meat, sassafras being one. Sassafras removes the gamey flavor from meats, and small strips of sassafras could be inserted into roasts for this purpose. Spits were made from sassafras wood, which would perfume the meat as it was rotated over the fire.

In the Choctaw language, the sassafras tree is called *iti kvfi*. It was the Choctaw who introduced filé to the European and African cooks of Louisiana.

The Choctaw people are the third largest Native American tribe, currently comprising about 200,000 members, including the Mississippi band of Choctaw Indians, the Jena band of Choctaw Indians in Louisiana, and the Choctaw Nation of Oklahoma. Before the Choctaw tribe was pushed to a reservation in "Indian Country," or Oklahoma, in 1831, their homeland was located in what is now western Alabama and eastern Mississippi. Their origin stories say the Choctaw people emerged from Nanih Waiya cave, located in present-day Winston County, Mississippi, along with the Muscogees, Cherokees, and Chickasaws. The archeological record shows the existence of Choctaw ancestors in eastern Mississippi for at least 14,500 years—since the end of the last ice age, when mastodons would have roamed the region.

The earliest-known name for powdered sassafras leaves is *kombo hakshish*. Although "kombo" is very similar to the word "gumbo," it did not give the stew its name. In fact, it happened the other way around: sassafras powder became so known for its use in gumbos that it influenced the Choctaw language.

Choctaw historian Dr. Ian Thompson printed a traditional recipe for kombo hakshish, pieced together from historical sources, in his book *Choctaw Food*:

> In the fall, pick red sassafras leaves that are free of dark blotches. Arrange them on a flat basket and set them in the sun for several days until the leaves are fully dry. Pound the dry leaves in a mortar. Sift to remove woody bits, then pound leaves into a very fine powder. Due to the lightness of the leaf powder, this should only be attempted on a calm day to prevent the powder from blowing away. Traditionally the powder was stored in deep, narrow river cane baskets lined with a piece of buckskin or cloth.

Although this recipe uses red leaves, in modern memory, filé is, and has always been, green. *Native American Recipes*, a cookbook printed in 1986 by the American Indian Church of Louisiana, notes under its recipe for filé: "Old Folks say: 'Better to gather leaves the second week in September.'" As the tradition of making filé shifted from Native communities to Creole and Cajun folks, the sassafras leaves were harvested around August 15, marked by the Feast of the Assumption, a Catholic holiday. More recently, the date has shifted later, possibly due to climate change—but most traditional makers are tight-lipped about the right time to pick sassafras for filé.

The Choctaw mortar and pestle used to process kombo hakshish is called *kiti micha kitvpi*. It was used for a variety of tasks, like processing corn and acorns, pulping fresh fruit, making flour from dried roots, and "kneading dough to make bread and dumplings." Before contact with Europeans or Africans, Choctaw would make the mortar from a tree trunk "laid horizontally on the ground, with a depression made into the top side of the trunk," according to Thompson. The mortar would usually be made "from Hickory or Black Gum, hardwoods which would impart a pleasant taste to the food."

This mortar would change after First Contact, influenced by the habits of the enslaved Africans who cooked in the kitchens of the colonists. The Choctaw mortar and pestle shifted to a vertical style, reminiscent of mortars from western Africa that are still used today. A section of log 30 inches long and at least 14 inches in diameter was flipped on its end. A depression was made on the top end of the log by carefully controlled glowing coals from a fire that were used to burn away the wood, which was then chiseled out with iron tools. The depression would end up about 10 inches wide and 8 to 12 inches deep, often with a second, narrower depression burnt into the bottom of the first, as a place for the finer particles of food to settle. Pestles were made from hardwood, left thick at one end and whittled narrow at the other. The entire pestle was anywhere from 4 to 10 feet long. This style of mortar and pestle, called a *pilan et pilé* in French Creole, was used from at least the eighteenth century to the early twentieth century. For a long time, it was the best tool for grinding corn and red pepper, for knocking the husks off rice, and, of course, for pounding filé.

The crossover of Choctaw and European food began in the sixteenth century. The Spanish were exploring Mobile Bay as early as 1500, but the first documented contact between conquistadors and Choctaws was in 1528. A Spanish army led by Pánfilo de Narváez had traveled westward from Florida with the intention of subjugating, colonizing, and exploiting native communities. It failed. A chronicler of the next attempted conquest, led by Hernando de Soto in 1540, wrote: "It was impossible to rule such bellicose people, or to subjugate such bold men. Neither by force nor by persuasion could they be brought under the authority and dominion of the Spaniards; they would allow themselves to be killed first."

French colonists began to settle on the Gulf Coast in 1699. When New Orleans was founded in 1718, Europeans began trading directly with the Choctaw. The Mississippi River facilitated trade, and the first market was tucked into a curve of the river, where the French Market in New Orleans still stands today. Some Native traders came into the New Orleans area seasonally; others stayed all year. Europeans traded cloth, metal tools, guns, and other labor-saving goods to the Choctaw for land rent, military aid, animal hides, and food.

The Choctaw and other Indigenous groups would bring to market duck, venison, and other game, as well as snakeroot, sage, tarragon, sarsaparilla, persimmons, plantains, muscadine grapes, hickory nuts, pecans, livestock like horses and pigs, and kombo hakskish. French colonists and the enslaved were documented using Choctaw filé by the early 1700s.

Throughout the nineteenth century, a Choctaw community remained in Louisiana, across Lake Pontchartrain, at Bayou Lacombe. The 1901 *Picayune Creole Cook Book* said that Choctaw women "bring the filé to New Orleans to sell, coming twice a week to the French Market, from the old reservation set aside for their home on Bayou Lacombe." These women were such an iconic part of the market that there are images of them. A black and white sketch from 1870 shows three Choctaw women seated on the market's flagstone floor, wrapped in blankets, baskets filled with sassafras in front of them. A photograph from the 1880s shows a mother seated much the same way, with a little boy and girl on the ground next to her. She stares defiantly downward, away from the camera lens, at her sack of ground filé. The sack is rolled back so that the powder is visible, a large spoon placed on top to dole out portions. The sack is flanked by bundles of dried bay leaves on the branch.

The French Market is the oldest continually operating market in the United States, although there are no longer any filé vendors inside. As for filé's place in Louisiana cuisine, Mary Land wrote in her 1954 cookbook *Louisiana Cookery*, "the folk of Louisiana have clung to the first Native herbs their forebears learned and loved."

* * *

THERE ARE MANY DIFFERENCES between the cuisines of the Cajuns and the Creoles, but gumbo is one of the dishes they have in common. The term "Creole" has been used by several different communities in New Orleans. Historically, it tended to mean the American-born descendants of European immigrants who settled the area in the eighteenth century. Today, it is often used by those who are descended from white Europeans and Black Americans of African or Caribbean descent.

Starting in 1719, French colonists brought enslaved Africans to New Orleans from their colonial outposts in the Caribbean or directly from Africa. By 1721, half of the city's population was Black. By 1743, more than 6,000 enslaved Africans had been brought to New Orleans. The captives were brought to the city and the surrounding area and compelled to "clear land, build the city, and serve as domestic servants."

Either by birth or by heritage, most of the enslaved's roots were in the Senegambia region of western Africa. They grew a variety of crops, in particular indigo and rice, and were valued by enslavers for their agricultural knowledge. Their culinary expertise was soon introduced to Louisiana kitchens, alongside the ingredients of the Choctaw and the preferences of the French.

Gumbo is thought to be based on West African soups, like Sauce Gumbo from Benin, a dish of okra stewed in tomatoes served over a starch, or *soupe kandia*, a Senegalese stew made with okra and palm oil and served over rice. The word "gumbo" comes from Bantu, a language family spoken by about 5 million people throughout the African continent. The Bantu word for okra is *ki ngombo* or *kigombo*. *Gombo* became the word for okra in French.

The earliest references to gumbo are for dishes of okra stewed with tomatoes, such as in a 1764 court testimony where it's called *gombeau*. This is the first known usage of the word in America, discovered by historian Gwendolyn Midlo Hall. *The Virginia House-wife*, one of America's earliest cookbooks, published in 1824, has a recipe for "Gumbo—A West India Dish," that is for okra stewed until tender and served with melted butter.

Okra is only available fresh from July through October, so it's used to thicken summer gumbos. In the winter, cooks use filé. Food historian Lolis Eric Elie told the *Washington Post* in 2019: "Even when I was growing up [in New Orleans] people would say, 'Make okra gumbo in the summer and filé gumbo in the winter when there was no okra to be had.'" Poppy Tooker wrote in her book *Louisiana Eats! The People, The Food, and Their Stories* about Delores

Lombard, a Black woman who cooked for one of New Orleans's elite families in the mid-twentieth century. For Delores, "The seasons dictated her gumbos. She cooked okra gumbo from late spring through early fall, redolent with tomatoes, fresh and smoked sausage, shrimp, crabs, oysters, and occasionally the chicken feet that Delores loved. And in the winter, filé powder replaced the okra with much the same list of ingredients, except she never put tomatoes in her filé gumbo."

Gumbo can contain a multitude of ingredients depending on the chef and the season. I've seen gumbo recipes that include smoked rabbit, squirrel, turkey, ham, crab, shrimp, oysters with their juice, veal, beef brisket, capon, duck gizzards, and moorhen (also known as swamp chicken). There's also gumbo z'herbes, the green, meat-free gumbo served at Lent. Poppy told me, "Some people use chicken hearts and chicken gizzards and any sort of protein at all. This one old New Orleans guy who was a cameraman at WYES [New Orleans public television] talked about his mother's gumbo and how she made weenie gumbo. There were *actual* hot dogs."

Most modern gumbos start with a roux. Although prevalent today, roux wasn't added to gumbo until the late nineteenth century. Journalist Robert Moss was able to pin down the earliest use of roux in seafood gumbos in the 1880s. Even in the 1920s, cookbooks presented gumbo recipes with and without roux, and not until the 1950s did roux become the standard. A very dark roux—chocolate-colored or black—came into style in the late 1970s, when Cajun chef Paul Prudhomme took over the kitchen at the New Orleans restaurant Commander's Palace. Prudhomme shook up the traditional French menu of Commander's Palace by adding Cajun classics and changed the gumbo by making it extra dark and thick. Prudhomme told the *Times–Picayune* in 2005, "To my knowledge, it had never been done before. It was chicken and andouille, down-and-dirty Cajun. It was what Mama used to do." And with Prudhomme's rising fame via his cookbooks, TV shows, and spice blends, this thick gumbo soon became the expectation, copied by every restaurant in New Orleans.

Perhaps the biggest difference between gumbo served in New Orleans and in Acadiana is that in New Orleans it's always served over rice, while in Acadiana it's just as common to serve it over a scoop of potato salad. Perhaps descended from the traditions of German settlers in the region, cold, creamy potato salad cuts through a heavy gumbo with tangy mustard.

# Filé Gumbo

I've assembled this recipe by looking at three early twentieth-century cookbooks: *Cooking in Creole Days: La Cuisine Créole à L'usage des Petits Ménages* by Célestine Eustis (1903); *A Collection of Créole Récipés as Used in New Orleans Prepared for use with Herbs and Seasonings of New Orleans, Kiskatom Farm, Mandeville, LA* by Caroline D. Weiss (1941); and *Louisiana Cookery* by Mary Land (1954). It's an old-fashioned rouxless gumbo, which makes it lighter, but it's still hearty enough to be a meal. You can adjust the spice level by reducing the number of cayenne pods. The soup may be salty for those of you in northern climes, but in the hot and humid Gulf Coast, it's just right. This gumbo is deeply savory and spicy, with a hint of smoke from the sausage and floral vegetal notes from the filé.

SERVES 8 AS A MAIN

**INGREDIENTS**
2 tablespoons butter or lard
¼ pound lean ham, cut into small cubes
½ pound andouille sausage, sliced
2 large onions, chopped
½ teaspoon garlic salt
1 teaspoon table salt
1 teaspoon dried thyme
2 bay leaves
3 dried cayenne peppers, stem and seeds removed
3 quarts any combination of water, stock, and/or oyster water, heated to boiling

*recipe continues >>*

**4 pounds chicken, on the bone, light and dark meat, rubbed with salt and pepper**
**3 dozen oysters, shucked (optional)**
**1 scant tablespoon filé**
**Cooked white rice or potato salad (optional, for serving)**

1. Add the butter or lard to a very large stock pot over medium-high heat. When melted, add the ham and sausage. Cover and fry for 5 minutes.
2. Add the onions, garlic salt, table salt, thyme, bay leaves, and peppers. Stir occasionally until the onions are well browned, then add three quarts of hot liquid.
3. Drop in the chicken and turn heat to medium. Cook, uncovered, for 90 minutes, or until the chicken is tender and comes off the bone easily.
4. Remove the chicken and set aside on a cutting board to cool. Remove peppers and bay leaves and discard.
5. When the chicken is cool enough to handle, shred the meat and add it to the pot.
6. Turn heat to high and bring to a boil. Add oysters (if using) and boil for two minutes.
7. While stirring, add the filé. Boil for one minute more. Remove from heat.
8. Serve over a scoop of rice or potato salad, with a dusting of filé on top.

\* \* \*

HISTORY DOESN'T DOCUMENT the names of most of the Choctaw filé makers. But in 1978, Howard Mitcham wrote in his book *Creole Gumbo and All that Jazz:*

> On several visits to Bayou Lacombe a few years ago, I was fortunate enough to meet one of the last of those Indian filé makers. His name was Nick Ducré, and he was over eighty-five. . . . Once a month he would take a schooner across the lake to New Orleans and sell his filé and bay leaves at the market at the New Basin Canal.

Nicholas DuCré was born in 1885 and lived his entire life in St. Tammany Parish in Bayou Lacombe. He had ten siblings. His father, Drosin, and his mother, Rosalie Ordogne, were both born in Louisiana. His grandparents are given different places of birth on different documents: Louisiana, Virginia, Cuba, France.

DuCré never went to school but could read and write. He was working as a day laborer by age fifteen. Never once in his long life is he listed as "filé maker," but the seasonal pattern of filé-making would have fit into his life well, providing a little extra money to help him stay afloat.

DuCré died in 1969 at the age of eighty-five—perhaps shortly after he met Mitcham, who was inspired to memorialize him in his book. DuCré owned his own house and land, but seems to have never married or had children of his own. His neighbors were his siblings and nephews. Mitcham wrote of DuCré, "A great storyteller, he told us much about the good old days in the early part of the century."

Filé-making by hand persisted into the twenty-first century, and perhaps the best known filé maker was Lionel Key. It's because of Key that handmade filé is on the Ark of Taste. He took his rare vocation around to fairs and festivals, pounding filé fresh, and it's his passion for the product that got this food noticed. Key was so well known for the quality of his filé that he sold it to chefs at Commander's Palace and to culinary legend Leah Chase of Dooky Chase restaurant. It was always freshly made, super fine, and free from stems.

Lionel Key was born in Baton Rouge, Louisiana, in 1948. A photo of Key from 1993 in the Historic New Orleans Collection shows him looking about how he always looked. He's at an outdoor festival, under the shade of a canopy, pounding filé with a pestle, his arms muscular, fingers wrapped in athletic tape to prevent blisters. He's dressed in jeans held up by red suspenders over a T-shirt. He sports a mustache, those 1980s large-framed glasses that are back in style, and an afro tight on the sides and tall on top. In later images, he wears a dangly earring made of feathers and stones.

When Key recorded an oral history for the Southern Foodways Alliance in 2006, he described himself as making "a living by making gumbo filé."

"I employ mortar and pedestal," Key said in the interview. He always called the tools of his trade his mortar and pedestal. No hesitation, no correction. It was his pedestal to show off tradition. His great-great-uncle had made the huge cypress mortar by hand in 1904; when Key sat, the mortar came up to his waist, about three feet high. The pestle was about as long as a baseball bat with a block of heavy ash on one end, which he used to "break the leaves into smaller portions." Then he flipped the maul around and pulverized the leaves with the rounded cypress end.

After the sassafras leaves were pounded into a powder, Key scooped out the filé with a coffee cup into a flour sifter.

"I triple-sift it and go through three sifters: a flour sifter first and that way I'm able to shake it off and get all the big pieces of the stems and everything off of it, and then I take a splash screen which is real fine and I go through that process and it's able to get all the little fine pieces out, and then I got another screen that it goes through and that's it."

Key learned to make filé the traditional way from his great-uncle Joseph Willy Ricard. Ricard was blind but was able to raise four children by making mops, brooms, and filé powder. He had a twin sister he was close with, and, according to Key, "They used to celebrate their birthday together every year—eating gumbo and filé."

One day, when Key was in his thirties, he was visiting his aging uncle and he decided to ask how the filé was made. "I said, 'Uncle Bill, would you teach me how to make the filé?'

"The first thing he did was told me to sit there and pound the filé. So I went to pound it and he say, 'You're not hitting it in the middle.' I'm saying to myself, 'How does this old man know I'm not hitting something in the middle; he can't even see?' But it makes a distinct sound like a baseball hitting off the end of a bat or something like that."

Key's uncle passed away in 1985. From there, "I had to go on my own." At age thirty-seven, he stopped driving for UPS and turned to making filé full-time. He inherited Ricard's *pilan et pilé* and got to work. He named his business Uncle Bill's Spices to honor the man who taught him the trade.

Key harvested his sassafras one month out of the year; but which month? "Oh, that's a family secret. Uncle Bill told me don't tell nobody unless I tell somebody in the family." He pruned his cache of trees, much like Coco, then dried the leaves on the branches in his garage. The total curing time? Another family secret. He stored the leaves whole so he could pound fresh filé at festivals all over the state. He averaged about sixty sacks of dried leaves in a year.

He sold his spice in simply-branded glass jars. "You can use it for soups, sausage, gravies, stews—anything you want to thicken up," he said in the oral history. "Red beans, potato soup, shrimp and corn soup."

Compared to commercial filé, Key said of his product: "the texture is different; the smell is different. The thickness is different. The taste is different.

"I make it look like it's easy and people will say, 'Oh that's easy to do.' And I say, 'Well come on, have a seat, here you go.' And then they start pounding and the next thing you know—'This is hard!'

"Usually, they'll say somebody in their family did this when they were growing up but they don't do it anymore, because they're old and deceased now and nobody picked it up."

"It's a rarity," the interviewer commented.

"It's an art form," Key added.

Lionel Joseph Key, Jr., died on December 31, 2017, at the age of sixty-nine.

When I was in New Orleans, I sat down with a few people who knew Key. I met Poppy Tooker for lunch at Toups South, the restaurant inside the Southern Food and Beverage Museum. A lifelong New Orleanian, she formed the local Slow Food chapter in 1999, and worked hard to enshrine local food in the Ark of Taste. She was the one who nominated Key and his handmade filé for the Ark, and he came to the meeting where he would be inducted.

"I remember when he lugged upstairs what he called his mortar and pedestal," Poppy told me. "It was a log. It was an upright, like a tree stump hollowed out. Mortar and pedestal. He was such an interesting man, such a great guy. He didn't have to drag that big thing around, but that was part of what would draw people to him."

I also bumped into Elizabeth Williams, founder of the museum and author of *New Orleans: A Food Biography*. "When Lionel did it, it was theater," she said of Key's live filé demonstrations. "And that is the real loss. But it's also more important that the ingredient continue."

\* \* \*

IN OCTOBER 2021, I BOARDED A PLANE to Dallas, Texas, on my way to the Choctaw Nation in Oklahoma. Oklahoma was the name given to "Indian Territory" when it became a state; it's a Choctaw phrase, "Okla Humma," meaning "People Who Don't Retreat." I was going to meet Dr. Ian and Amy Thompson. Ian studied archeology and anthropology and got his doctorate from the University of New Mexico in 2008. He met Amy, and the two of them started teaching cultural camps for Choctaw kids. They had been married eleven years when I met them. Today, he's the Tribal Historic Preservation Officer, the Senior Director of the Historic Preservation Department, and chair of the repatriation review committee at the Smithsonian National Museum of Natural History. Our plan for the weekend was to cook several traditional recipes using filé over an open fire.

Oklahoma is a long way from the Choctaw homeland. After the Revolutionary War, treaty negotiations began in good faith between the Choctaw and the United States government. But even this early, the United States planned to bury the Choctaw people in debt, eventually forcing them to sell off their land. The Choctaw became dependent on trade goods, and no matter how much they brought in to trade, they always seemed to end up at a deficit. From 1800 to 1830, the U.S. government requested the Choctaw sell off land at least forty times, "under the pretense of extinguishing Tribal debt that accrued through the hide trade," Ian wrote in his book *Choctaw Food*. This was the same tactic used to buy land from the Ojibwe up north.

In 1820, at the Treaty of Doak's Stand, the US government offered Choctaw groups land if they moved farther westward: 13 million acres in Arkansas and Oklahoma in exchange for 5 million acres of land in Mississippi. The offered lands already belonged to the Caddo, Wichita,

Comanche, and Kiowa peoples. And for the Choctaw, leaving their homeland was not an option. In 1830, the United States threatened genocide if the Choctaw did not move west. As the story is told at the Choctaw Cultural Center in Calera, Oklahoma, "Facing impossible circumstances, we invested in the future. . . . Ultimately, our leaders did sign, wanting a better life in the West, away from American society. . . . Through the process of treaty negotiation, we gave ourselves a foundation for sovereignty in our new home."

The Choctaw were the first Indigenous people removed from the Southeast to Indian Territory. Again, Thompson writes, "Newspaper accounts from the time describe Choctaw women as they set out, gently touching the trees of their beloved Homeland and telling them goodbye. In the form of small traditional clay eating bowls, many literally carry pieces of their Homeland with them on the journey as reminders of their connection to it. One of the American agents involved in the Choctaw removal wrote that 'it is impossible not to love a people who exhibited such attachment to their native land.'"

Between 1830 and 1833, about 16,000 Choctaws attempted the 550-mile walk to Indian Territory, "often without supplies promised by treaty, they faced hunger, record-cold temperatures, and disease." This exile became known as the Trail of Tears and Death. Four thousand Choctaw died along the way.

Those Choctaw who resisted removal were beaten or murdered and had their homes and crops destroyed. Some were able to stay, showing incredible bravery and persistence in the face of racism, violence, and homelessness. Today, two Choctaw tribes still remain in Mississippi and Louisiana, the descendants of those who were able to resist at all costs.

As with all Indigenous groups, the cost of removal is a loss of connection to the homeland. It's a forced disintegration of all the elements of culture, including language, religion, and foodways. But Choctaw anthropologists and archeologists seek to revive traditional knowledge. Ian wrote in *Choctaw Food*, "Many contemporary Indigenous people hold the view that sleeping traditional knowledge is never really gone. It can be reawakened when modern people put themselves in the same place as their ancestors."

Nan Awaya Heritage Farmstead, Ian and Amy's recently purchased 160-acre plot, sits in the heart of Choctaw land. They built
their own house and are restoring the prairie around it. They also
practice traditional arts and foodways, raise a herd of bison, and grow
heirloom crops.

Ian grew up in suburban Missouri, but his grandfather told him
stories about his Choctaw heritage and the self-sufficient household he
had grown up in.

"When I was seven, my uncle said, 'Hey, let's make some arrowheads.' So we picked up some flint and he started teaching me how to
chip arrowheads. That interest in culture just caught fire for me from
a young age. So instead of going to the movies or whatever, when I
was a kid, I was out in the woods, making arrows and bows and brain
tans and all that kind of stuff."

"Can't say that on my end," Amy added. "I was born and raised in
Oklahoma and basically *just* started learning about all this." Amy felt
like, growing up, she had a pan-Indian identity but didn't really know
what it meant to be Choctaw. When she and Ian started dating, they
began cooking traditional recipes over an open fire. He kindled her
interest in Choctaw culture, and she became an expert and a teacher
in her own right. "Personally, I think it's important to remember what
our people was back before pre-European civilization. They were
very knowledgeable people because they had a lifeway of their own.
Growing up in the Choctaw community, we never really had that
knowledge except in the church."

Amy grabbed her Choctaw hymnal from the other room to show
me. The first Choctaw hymnal was produced in 1829; today, church
is one of the few places where the endangered Choctaw language is
spoken. Additionally, church community gatherings often mean the
preparation of modern versions of Choctaw food. Next to the "Spam
and Hamburger Helper," there's *bvnaha*, a tamale-like corn bread that
can be made with beans, hickory nuts, Choctaw squash, or black-
eyed peas. Another standard is *tanchi labona*, a hominy stew made with
meat, usually pork. Or *walakshi*, dumplings smothered in a grape juice
sauce. Ian and Amy have since made a more traditional version of

walakshi with muscadine grapes and hand-ground, parched corn. Ian called these "ancestral foods."

While we planned our day in their kitchen, Amy boiled the bark from sassafras roots in water to make tea. The space was now scented with the mint and cinnamon spice of the sassafras. She poured the tea into thermal cups and iced it, so we'd have something cooling to drink while we worked. One sip and the complicated flavor washed over me: nutmeg, root beer, and lemon.

We were going to prepare two dishes that used filé powder: a rabbit stuffed with blackberries and dusted with filé, then roasted in an underground oven; and catfish fillets covered in torn sassafras leaves and wrapped in clay.

"So, we're going to start with building an earth oven today," Ian told me as we headed outside to the shade of a broad oak. We were joined by their cat, Chinche, a pleasingly rotund orange tabby, who supervised from under a tree. We dug a square pit about one and a half feet deep in the sandy soil, and then the three of us pressed a thin layer of wet clay along the sides. We started a fire in the pit with torn paper and small sticks and slowly added larger branches, so it got hotter a little at a time. The fire would dry out and cure the sides of the pit. The clay, after it was cured, would both keep the sandy walls in place and retain heat. It was a process, but one that would not have to be done from scratch every day. A much larger pit would be made to cook a lot of roots or meat, and the pit could be reused many times. Ovens like these were found all over archeological sites in the Choctaw Homeland.

"It's kind of like a slow cooker," Ian explained. "Most Choctaw food is cooked in clay pottery. This is an older style of cooking before pottery. It was really common, say 3,000 years ago, and it began in the early archaic period, maybe like 8,000 years ago. It was most commonly used with resilient root crops, ones that have to cook for a very long time. Things like laurel greenbriar, American groundnut, cattail bulbs."

"So, what does it feel like for you when you're doing something that's 3,000 years old?" I asked him.

Ian paused to think. "Sometimes it feels so familiar. Like the first time we cooked lambsquarter seeds. It's like, man, that's such a familiar smell that we'd never smelled before."

While the oven cured, we took a walk on their property to collect some ingredients. Their farmstead was on true Oklahoma prairie, the great grass ocean I had only read about. Though their land had been overgrazed by cattle, they're working to restore it and have seen 207 native plants come back. I was surprised by the variety of texture and color, an undulating ocean of greens, pale blues, late summer yellows, and orange-reds. As we walked the property, Ian pointed to each plant, telling me its name and what it was used for. Bull nettle, goldenrod, muscadine grapes, sand plums, cottonwood, river birch. We saw raccoon prints in the mud by a stream, a wild boar wallow in a hollow, and a long black rat snake calmly sunning itself.

We stopped to pick broad sycamore leaves to use as wrappers in cooking the food. The leaves were pale green, but spotty with brown and yellow from a long summer of service. We chose leaves bigger than my hands, some twice as big. Our second stop was to collect handfuls of still-green sassafras leaves to spice our dishes. Ian stopped to pick some fresh leaves from a native prairie yucca to use for tying up the food packets.

When we got back to the house, Ian went down to the creek to collect some fist-sized sandstone chunks. These would go into the fire to further absorb heat. Amy and I unpacked and washed the rabbits. The historical recipe was intended for squirrel, but neither Ian nor I had been able to procure a squirrel. So, instead, I had ordered two frozen whole rabbits. These were farmed rabbits, not wild, so their meat was pale pink and white and would lack the gaminess of a wild bunny. But they would do.

After the rabbits were washed inside and out, we filled the cavities with fresh blackberries and sprinkled the skin generously with filé. I had brought some of my own filé, which I had made in Ohio. Then we wrapped the rabbits in large sycamore leaves, tying the package off with the strips of yucca. Ian noted that grape leaves would be a good option, and in the Homeland, the Choctaw would have used enormous umbrella palmetto leaves. We wrapped the second rabbit in tinfoil, figuring that if the traditional method didn't work out, we'd still have something to eat for dinner.

The fire had been burning in the clay oven for about two and a half hours. We shoveled sand over the glowing coals and sandstone, then nestled the packages of rabbit on top. Then we built a lid: "We're going to go cut a whole bunch of little sapling trees with leaves on them and pile them on there with two sturdy ones so that we can lift it off," Ian explained. "Then we're going to take that sand and put it on top. And then we're going to build a fire on top of that." Again, in the Homeland, Ian would have used palmetto fronds.

While the rabbit cooked, we headed back inside and sat around the kitchen table, prepping the catfish fillets.

## Clay-Cooked Filé Fish Fillets, a variation of *Nvni Hoponi*

Ian had begun preparations for this dish earlier that week by digging clay out of the ground at a construction site nearby. Depending on where you live, you might be able to pull clay from the ground as well—my home of northeast Ohio is famous for it, much to the chagrin of local gardeners. But pottery clay will work well, too.

We rinsed the catfish fillets and patted them dry, then sprinkled the flesh side with torn fresh sassafras leaves. You may want to add a sprinkle of salt as well. We used more of the large, soaked sycamore leaves to wrap the fillets and tied them with strips of yucca, like tamale packets. You can also use corn-husks or grape leaves to wrap the fillets, and strips of corn husk or kitchen twine to tie them off.

Then we coated the little packets in wet clay, ¼ to ½ inch thick. We made sure there were no gaps in the clay, which would make the fish dry out.

*recipe continues >>*

When all the fillets were wrapped in clay, we headed back outside and built up the fire on top of the oven. We set the clay packets in the glowing coals, then sat quietly under the tree in the reddening light. Cicadas and crickets chirped and the fire crackled, while Ian and Amy talked gently to each other in Choctaw.

The thin fillets were done in about ten minutes. We used tongs to pull them from the heat, and cracked them open to find juicy fish, redolent with the lemony perfume of sassafras. We ate scraps of fish with our hands; the flesh tasted like citrus and fresh water, bitter and sweet.

This recipe can also be prepared with a whole fish. In this case, fill the cavity with torn sassafras, salt, pepper, and, if desired, cayenne pepper pods.

\* \* \*

"I CAN TELL this is definitely work that would have been done by a group of people sitting around talking," I commented while we prepped the catfish.

Ian agreed. "Choctaws, especially Choctaw women, are always razzing each other, laughing when they do stuff like this. It's just like constant laughter."

"Growing up, the main place I wanted to be was always the kitchen," Amy added. "They're always laughing and talking; you hear all kinds of stuff in the kitchen. Didn't you say," she asked Ian, "that there's actually a historical account in which Choctaw women were busy doing something, but there's like a whole bunch of laughing and talking coming out of the kitchen or something like that?"

"It was a sad one," Ian acknowledged. "It was this European guy writing about when, after the Trail of Tears, when the last Choctaw village moved, he said that 'the sound of laughter from the Choctaw women that had echoed through the hills forever went silent.'"

About six hours after we had put the rabbits in the oven, we debated whether or not to take them out. "I hope we don't pull it out and it's still raw," Ian worried.

Ian and I grabbed the sapling trunks that held the pile of green, leafy branches and the live fire. We lifted up and over, set the lid on the ground, and peered into the open oven. Immediately, I could see that the meat of the rabbit legs had pulled back from the bone and its juices were running clear. Good signs.

When we pulled the packets out of the coal and ash, the meat was sizzling juicily and we could smell the sassafras. We unwrapped the leaves to reveal a gorgeous—if a little sandy—roast rabbit. I stole a taste of tender meat off the thigh: it was as flavorful as the best roast chicken and exploding with the citrus-like flavor of the handmade filé.

We took the rabbit inside and I cooked a pot of manoomin, a gift Ian and Amy had been sent by a friend. Ian commented that the Choctaw ancestors had harvested wild river rice in the Homeland; preserved kernels of *Zizania aquatica* had been found in archeological sites. As we sat down at the dinner table, the sun set on a very long day.

* * *

INDIGENOUS CHEFS ACROSS AMERICA are working to preserve traditional foods by reviving Native cuisine. The history of displacement and forced cultural assimilation has meant that much of Indigenous food is "careening towards extinction," as Cherokee chef Taelor Barton was quoted as saying in an *Atlas Obscura* article. Barton and her mentor, Cherokee chef Nico Albert, serve an annual all-Indigenous menu at Duet restaurant in Tulsa, Oklahoma, each November. Their work had caught my eye because one of the dishes they prepared was "rabbit legs seasoned with dried sassafras leaves and braised with cedar fronds in wild sunflower oil, served over a bed of pitseed goosefoot grains and the plant's sautéed leaves and okra-like milkweed seed pods." A high-end modernization of Native cuisine, yes, but using traditional ingredients and traditional preparation methods, like rabbits dusted in filé, the several-thousands-years-old dish I had just cooked with Ian and Amy.

Like Choctaw church food, sometimes evolution helps preservation. I did wonder what it would be like to feel the weight of an ash-wood pestle and hear the resonant thud of it pounding sassafras leaves in a cypress mortar. I wondered if I would ever taste filé ground that way and if it would hold the wood's aroma as well as its own citrus bouquet. I don't think I ever will. It's a tradition that has passed from the hands of artists into museums, the tools once used in daily life now a display of the past.

Does it matter that the thump-thump of a *pilan et pilé* has been replaced by the grinding whirr of a food processor? Filé isn't gone, it's transformed, which has helped it stay an indispensable part of a highly local cuisine. If food is always held to a standard of the past, sometimes it becomes history.

EIGHT

# Carolina African Runner Peanuts

It's estimated that 75 percent of vegetable varieties worldwide have been permanently lost, while 95 percent of America's historical produce is gone. But every once in a while, one of those "extinct" veggies is plucked from the void.

The Carolina African Runner peanut, called "the South's ancestral peanut" by historian David Shields, was the first peanut grown in North America. Peanuts are indigenous to South America, but there's no evidence they were grown farther north than Mexico and the Caribbean before European contact. Peanuts were exported to Europe, then Africa, then crossed the ocean once again on ships carrying the enslaved. A nutritious and spoilage-resistant food, peanuts were prized on transatlantic voyages. The nuts were called African Runners and later Carolina Runners; after the state that produced the largest crop.

After arriving in the United States, peanuts were at first grown only in the gardens of the enslaved, but, by the mid-nineteenth century, they had become a cash crop. Although Carolina Runners were the peanut used for any confection, soup, or peanut butter until the twentieth century, they were no longer planted by the 1930s. A relatively small nut, they were discarded for larger varieties that were easier to harvest. By the mid-twentieth century, it was believed that these peanuts had disappeared forever.

Cut to 2003. Glenn Roberts, now the head of Anson Mills—a celebrated purveyor of heirloom grains—wanted to revive the cuisine of the South Carolina tidewater region. He approached scholar and researcher David Shields to compile a list of the lost ingredients of the "Carolina Rice Kitchen," the Lowcountry cuisine based around another lost heirloom, Carolina Gold rice.

What Shields thought would be a six-month project sent his life in an entirely new direction. He has spent nearly twenty years restoring long-lost crops to the South. Although the Carolina Runner was on his list, Shields thought it would never be found. But after dozens of phone calls, forty peanuts were located in a cold storage seedbank at North Carolina State University—the last Carolina Runner peanuts on the planet. Half of the remaining peanuts, a mere twenty, were divided out and put in the ground, and fingers were crossed. The peanuts sprouted.

Many believe the Runners should be on the finest dining tables. According to the National Peanut Board, the Carolina Runner is "denser, sweeter, smaller, and has a higher oil content than the peanuts we eat today." However, not many chefs have been able to cook with the peanuts yet. Charleston chef Forrest Parker said the Carolina Runner "has the most intense peanut flavor I've ever experienced, and continues to be a revelation every time I taste it." He used it in a dessert of toasted peanuts and roasted banana curd topped with bacon and a reduction of hot sauce and molasses, all inside a puff pastry. Sean Brock, formerly executive chef and part owner of Charleston's Husk and McCrady's restaurants, is one of the biggest purchasers of the Carolina Runners. He told *Food & Wine* magazine in 2018, "These are black truffles to me. You have to peel the skin off of each one. One falls on the floor, we don't throw it away. We go wash it and put it back in the pile. We are so thankful and grateful to be able to eat them and cook with them. I keep them in a bowl in my house and eat them all day."

Aside from the fabulous luxury of eating them as a household snack, Brock has pressed them for oil and used it to make a vinaigrette with peanut puree, which he has served over fresh local produce and Tennessee ham. The Carolina Runner is especially high in oil, which, when pressed, is golden-hued and aromatic with a "rich peanutty scent." Oil pressed from green runners of other varieties has recently become popular in Southern cooking; the *New York Times* described the green oil as "buttery, slightly vegetal," and another potential outlet for a Carolina Runner crop. Peanuts are not a nut, by the way, but a legume like peas and beans. Fresh, they taste more like their bean brethren.

Food historian Andrew F. Smith called peanuts "an American culinary emblem." The quantity of peanuts Americans consume, and the diversity of ways in which they use them, is unmatched by any other country. So, is there a place in American cuisine today for the original, allegedly most delicious, peanut?

The easiest way to get the chance to try this still rare ingredient is to grow them yourself. I was able to order seeds online, and since I live in the cold northern climes of Cleveland, I had to start my peanuts indoors in April. I watched little twin-leafed seedlings push up through the soil while there was still snow on the ground outside. I transplanted in May, digging the babies into a sandy hillside in my small urban garden. The peanuts grew in the heat of the summer, eventually expanding in a three-foot radius. Most peanuts grow vertically, in a bush, but a runner spreads out into a lush, green ground cover. They were a remarkably pretty plant; the deep green leaves grew in sets of four like butterfly wings and folded up in the evening like they were tucking themselves in bed. They flowered all summer long, cheery yellow blossoms.

The most unusual part of the peanut plant is its long pegs or peduncles: thin appendages that grow out of the fertilized flowers and push down into the dirt. A peanut grows at the ends of peduncles, unseen, underground. Peanuts are in the genus *Arachis hypogaea,* from the Greek meaning "underground chamber." If they are left unharvested, new plants grow from these underground seeds in the spring. A truly unusual way for a plant to fruit, there is only one other plant on the planet that propagates in this fashion: the Bambara groundnut of West Africa, a legume that looks a bit like a hazelnut or a black-eyed pea.

I checked on my peanut children every few days, lifting up the green canopy to see the peduncles. But I would have to wait months for the reveal; I couldn't pull them up until after the first frost—October or November. That would be after I had returned from my trip to South Carolina to see the Carolina Runner's home in person.

*  *  *

PEANUTS ARE INDIGENOUS to the Pantanal, the world's largest wetland, in modern-day Brazil, Paraguay, and Bolivia. This origin spot was deduced the same way Nikolai Vavilov determined the homeland of apples: it is the site of the greatest genetic diversity of peanuts. It's believed peanuts were first cultivated in Bolivia, where they are still frequently used in local cuisine, including ground to flavor drinks, and eaten whole, shell and all, when they are underripe.

The oldest physical example of peanuts comes from a 3,800-year-old burial site in Peru, where well-preserved peanuts were found in terra-cotta jars. At least 2,500 years ago, the Inca ate roasted peanuts. Other Indigenous peoples cured peanuts with smoke, or ground them to a paste and blended it with chocolate. Peanut cultivation moved northward into the Aztec Empire and then to the Caribbean, where peanuts were cultivated by the Arawak people. Europeans encountered the plant in the early sixteenth century. Portuguese women living in Brazil replaced almonds in confectionery with roasted peanuts, candying them with sugar. French colonists in the Caribbean used peanut oil as a replacement for almond oil and made peanut marzipan. Peanuts eventually became the traditional nut in North American sweets.

Colonists exported peanuts back to Europe, and from there they were taken to Asia and Africa, along with other crops from the Americas like tomatoes, corn, chilies, and cassava. Peanut plants thrived in the sandy soils of West Africa, in what is modern-day Senegal. The legume had landed in the only other place in the world with a similar crop, the Bambara groundnut. So, farmers in this area knew how to grow peanuts before they arrived. Peanuts quickly became a dominant crop in West Africa because they were easier to grow than Bambara groundnuts, produced more fruit, and had a higher oil content. Many American words for peanuts are derived from West African cultivation: "goobers" comes from the Kimbundu word *nguba*, and "pindars" from the Kikongo word *mpinda*.

Ground, roasted peanuts—what in America we call peanut butter—is used in a huge variety of West African food preparations, including as a base for soups and stews and as a sauce for meat. Groundnut stew is the most popular; as culinary historian Jessica Harris writes, "It is served along with large bottles of cold beer in the outdoor cabarets of Ghana." In Senegal, the stew is called *maafe* and is made with ground peanuts, meat, root vegetables, and tomatoes. In the Gambia it's *domoda*, a thick stew of ground peanuts, tomatoes, vegetables like potatoes, carrots or eggplant, and hot chilies. In Sudan, *shorba* is made with lamb bones, garlic, vegetables, and peanut butter.

The smell of roasting peanuts perfumes the streets of Senegal. The smell, called "celestial" by food historian Andrew F. Smith, is created by the Maillard reaction, an interaction between the peanuts' proteins and sugars that creates hundreds of new flavor compounds. Jessica Harris wrote in her book *Iron Pots and Wooden Spoons: Africa's Gifts to New World Cooking*, "you will see women sitting on the curbside selling tiny cornets of peanuts they have roasted to a deep mahogany color . . . When I inquired about the secret that gave the peanuts their delicious taste, I was answered in one word: sand. The peanuts are roasted in sand."

## Sand-Roasted Peanuts

If you ever get a chance to taste the Carolina Runner or another heirloom peanut, you may want to prepare it as simply as possible. Sand-roasted peanuts are a fantastic way to experience pure peanut flavor. The peanuts are mixed with sand and roasted under high heat for a short time. Sand roasting makes the peanuts particularly puffed, crunchy, aromatic, and flavorful.

Although normally roasted in a wok-like skillet over an open flame, this variation, I adapted from *Iron Pots and Wooden*

*Spoons*, is a simpler way to do it in a home kitchen. You can get "clean" sand from a home-improvement store or landscaper, but sifted beach sand should also do the trick.

FEEDS FOUR AS A SNACK

INGREDIENTS
1 pound raw peanuts in the shell
3 pounds clean, dry sand

1. Preheat oven to 400°F.
2. Fill a deep baking dish or casserole with half of the sand. Add peanuts. Pour in remaining sand, then mix peanuts and sand together with your hands.
3. Place baking dish in the oven, uncovered, and bake for 30 minutes.
4. Pluck a peanut out of the sand (with a fork or slotted spoon) and test for doneness: peel and taste. If not roasted to perfection, put baking dish back in the oven for another 15 minutes.

\* \* \*

NO ONE IS ABSOLUTELY CERTAIN how peanuts got to North America. Plenty of white families came to the South from the Caribbean; migrants from Barbados settled in Charleston. The enslaved were forced to migrate with them, perhaps bringing peanuts along to plant in their own gardens. But most scholars seem to think peanuts came with the enslaved directly from Africa. During the transatlantic slave trade, peanuts became the provision of choice for enslavers because they were familiar to West Africans and stored well on long voyages. There is documentation of the enslaved being fed peanuts in transport as early as 1601. The enslaved that survived the journey to America planted peanuts in their gardens along the Atlantic coast. Peanuts were so closely associated with the newly enslaved that most scholars who wrote about the peanut throughout the eighteenth century assumed that it had originated in Africa.

* * *

ON MY FIRST MORNING IN COLUMBIA, South Carolina, I wandered the Soda City Market, an outdoor farmer's market with food vendors. It was late October, and the city was quiet on this Saturday morning. The weather—a chilly 46 degrees with a solid gray sky that occasionally spat a fine mist—was keeping most residents indoors.

Next to pints of perfect blackberries and luscious-looking watermelons, I found the Anson Mills stand. I picked up bags of "18th century Style Toasted Stone Cut Oats" and Carolina Gold Rice. Glenn Roberts's grist mill, one of the long-term results of his plan to bring back the Carolina Rice Kitchen, is located in Columbia.

I walked from the market a mile to the Robert Mills House and Gardens to meet David Shields. The historic home—a brick Greek revival mansion—was built in the 1820s. First used as a private residence, it was later a campus for various educational institutions. I had been directed to meet David in the historic gardens.

David looked like a tall Truman Capote in a raincoat. A professor and author—and a distant cousin of the Shields of the Coachella date garden—he was the chair of the Ark of Taste's southeastern regional nominating committee and the Carolina Gold Rice Foundation, which has been organized to continue the revival of Southern ingredients. He greeted me cordially and walked me around the manicured gardens, symmetrical beds lined with gravel paths and trimmed hedges. David pointed out plants he had helped onboard to the Ark of Taste: tan-colored Dutch Fork pumpkins peeked out between green and white speckled leaves; bolls of Sea Island cotton dribbled from dried, star-shaped seed pods; and ripe Carolina Gold rice clung to its stems, radiating its signature yellow color. There was also Palmetto asparagus, a late-nineteenth-century variety now so rare that it's considered functionally extinct. Green-stemmed and known as exceptionally delicious, this plant was perhaps the only one in the ground, and there were some seeds in storage at the USDA. Then we came to half a bed lushly covered in vibrant green Carolina Runners. A gentle tug on the mass—the runners had threaded themselves together—and

David pulled up its treasures from beneath the soil: dirty little nubbins, the rarest peanuts in the country.

"It took six years for the seed to acclimate itself to the soil," David told me. In the early years, the plants were highly susceptible to disease and insect damage. Since the peanuts had been removed from the environment for a century, it took them time to adjust. But thanks to phenotypic plasticity—the ability of a plant's genotype to shift and adapt—this year's crop had thrived.

The weather had turned misty again, so we jumped in David's car and headed to a coffee shop. When we were tucked at a table with our beverages in the warm and clamorous cafe, I asked David how his quest to locate lost Southern culinary plants began. He traced the movement back to chef Alice Waters in the 1970s. She had inspired chefs to seek out produce that *tasted* like something, often heirloom varieties.

"Grains and vegetables created since the early twentieth century were not sensory tested," David explained. "Taste was always a secondary consideration to productivity, early maturation, processability, disease resistance, pest resistance. There was this call, where are the *ingredients?*" He said Waters insisted on "asserting the primacy of taste over other qualities in a plant."

One of the people who heard that call was Glenn Roberts of Anson Mills. Glenn approached David at a conference in 2003 and pitched his plan: "I want to bring back Carolina Gold and I want to bring back all its co-crops, all the stuff that was part of the rice kitchen." Much like New Orleans, the area around Charleston—known as the Lowcountry—had its own cuisine, special ingredients and dishes prepared by both restaurant chefs and home cooks. But Glenn felt the cuisine had become lost as the traditional crops were lost; it needed a reboot. The ultimate goal was to provide these heirloom ingredients to chefs. He said to David, "The problem is we've lost so much we don't know what to bring back. You do research, you could help us."

"In a kind of profound ignorance, I was thinking, maybe I can go spend a month in the libraries looking up stuff and getting a list, and maybe get free dinners for the remainder of the decade or something like that," David said. When I talked to him, he had been working on the project for seventeen years.

David came up with a master list of missing crops that gave their flavor to South Carolina cooking before the turn of the twentieth century. He combed through historical agricultural journals, seed catalogs, and recipe books. He sought plants that were not anomalies or "flash in the pan" hits, but those that had been "a steady seller" for fifty years or more. Two categories of ingredients still proliferated in South Carolina: collard greens and okra. Shields decided to focus on other fundamental items: benne seeds, purple ribbon sugarcane, African sorghum, white dent corn, and the Bradford watermelon, to name a few. Some plants turned up in germplasm banks, others were held by seed-saving organizations. Sometimes seeds were found in the freezer of a local old-timer who had tucked them away years ago. And some items David was still searching for, like white mammoth rye, the original grain used to ferment rye whiskey in America. He thinks he may have a lead in Canada, where it was grown until the 1990s.

But some ingredients are irrevocably lost: the Neunan's strawberry, the Ravenscroft watermelon, and—so he thought—the Carolina Runner peanut.

David called peanut growers for a decade asking after the Carolina Runner, with no luck. Eventually, he got a lead that Dr. Tom Isleib at North Carolina State kept a stash of historical peanuts in seed storage at the university. The collection had been started in the 1930s—the same time the Carolina Runner stopped being planted—to establish a seed pool for future breeding projects.

"When I inquired whether he had the Carolina peanut variety, he asked me to hold while he consulted a database," David recounted. "There was a two-minute pause. 'Yes, I do. Carolina number four and Carolina number eight.'"

David explained his research and his ultimate plan to restore the Carolina Runner. Isleib agreed to help; he had forty peanuts in storage and sent David twenty. David was able to compare those peanuts with images of an actual historical example: the Natural History Museum, London, has a pressing of a peanut plant from the 1680s. Its leaves,

stems, and peanuts in the shell were collected by physician and botanist Sir Hans Sloan from a plant in Jamaica; Sloan cited the provenance
of the parent plant's seeds to West Africa. David saw that his peanuts
were remarkably similar to the 340-year-old example. The twenty
Carolina Runners were passed to horticulturist Dr. Brian Ward at the
USDA Clemson Coastal Research and Education Center in 2013 to
be grown out.

"I don't think it'll ever become a huge mass commodity," David
told me of the Carolina Runner. "But maybe in the future, there'll
be a Carolina Runner peanut butter on the shelves at Whole Foods."

\* \* \*

THE FIRST AFRICANS arrived in the American colonies in 1619,
and were sold off as indentured servants, not into the chattel slavery that would later define the American economy. It's estimated
that 27,233 transatlantic trips were made between 1619 and 1860 and
that between 389,000 and 450,000 Africans survived the journey to
North America.

Culinary historian Michael Twitty wrote in his book *The Cooking Gene* that "the average slaveholder going to auction in Annapolis,
Charleston, or New Orleans had a greater understanding of African
ethnic groups than most Americans of any color do today." People of
different tribes were prized for different qualities, perceived or real,
and for their knowledge of various agricultures and culinary techniques—although, more often than not, this experience was portrayed
as a magical gift rather than a well-practiced skill. Most of the enslaved
purchased to labor in the Lowcountry were from Angola and Senegambia, areas known for growing rice.

Before the nineteenth century, peanuts were almost exclusively
grown by the enslaved. In addition to providing forced labor, the
enslaved were also required to produce most of their own food. Mary
Reynolds was 105 years old when she was interviewed by the Federal Writers Project in 1937. She had been enslaved in Louisiana. She
recounted: "Sometimes massa let n—ggers have a li'l patch. They'd

raise taters or goobers. They liked to have them to help fill out on the victuals. . . . The n–ggers had to work the patches at night and dig the taters and goobers at night. Then if they wanted to sell any in town they'd have to git a pass to go. They had to go at night, cause they couldn't ever spare a hand from the fields." She remembered that her enslaver handed out "pickled pork," cornmeal, peas, beans, and potatoes for the enslaved to eat, but "They never was as much as we needed." Other food came from fishing or foraging.

The enslaved planted American vegetables like peppers, sweet potatoes (a stand-in for African yams), and tomatoes that colored dishes red like the palm oil from home. Southern Spanish rice, made red with tomatoes, is the Black American version of jollof rice from Africa, cooked with red palm oil. They planted African vegetables as well, like okra, cowpeas, watermelons, and even Bambara groundnuts.

"These spaces were little landscapes of resistance," Twitty wrote of the gardens of the enslaved. "Resistance against a culture of dehumanizing poverty and want, resistance against the erasure of African cultural practices, resistance against the destruction of African religions, and resistance against slavery itself."

Frequently, the enslaved sold surplus produce to their enslavers. They were paid in "cash, trade goods, or bartered privileges like passes to visit relatives." Money earned would be put toward more food, household items, or saved to purchase their own freedom or that of a family member. Black men and women also sold produce, including peanuts, in public markets. Period accounts place Black peanut vendors on the streets of Wilmington, North Carolina—known as the United States peanut capital in the nineteenth century—before the Civil War.

By the end of the seventeenth century, the Black population of South Carolina outnumbered the white. More than half of the population of the state—57 percent—was enslaved, owned by about 26,000 white people. Between 1778 and 1808, South Carolina was the largest trafficker of Africans to the United States; more enslaved people arrived during this time than in all the years before the American Revolution. Sold off the boats and on the docks, the enslaved were taken as far north as New York City—which was the second-largest slave trade port—or south to New Orleans, and eventually west as far as Texas. By the start of the Civil War, there were 4 million enslaved people in the United States; 400,000 of them lived in South Carolina, and more than 40 percent of all trafficked Africans had passed through the port of Charleston.

* * *

Driving to Charleston from Columbia, I caught the edge of hurricane Nestor. I managed a stop at a local place for BBQ, but then fortified myself in my Airbnb on the outskirts of the city while the wind whipped and the rain lashed. The next morning was gray and chilly, but calm. I decided to visit McLeod Plantation on James Island, one of the few historical sites in the country that focuses on the stories of the enslaved, not the enslavers.

As I approached, McLeod looked like any other revered Southern mansion, its grand drive lined with elderly oaks, some 1,000 years old, dripping with Spanish moss. The house itself was imposing but stark, the facade mimicking a Greek temple. The site was a plantation starting in the early eighteenth century, but this Big House wasn't built until 1858.

Visitors milled around the small, modern visitor center and bookstore until the tour began; we gathered on the gravel drive in front of the house. Our guide, Mills, was a young woman with shoulder-length blond hair, dressed in a museum-branded blue rain jacket so large on her petite frame that it consumed her. Based on her appearance, one might think she would be easily intimidated. But when Mills began, she did not mince words.

"What is a plantation?" she asked—but didn't wait for an answer. "A plantation is a forced labor camp," she told the group, stripping away any illusions of *Gone with the Wind* romance. "The Big House residents' life of silk and luxury, of iced drinks on the veranda, was brought about on the backs of those trafficked and exploited to work here."

We would not be going into the Big House on this tour; it was

open for self-guided walkthroughs only and was nearly devoid of fur-
nishings. Instead, we would be looking at the former homes of the
enslaved, small cabins with brick chimneys now sprouting moss and
ferns. These buildings were original to the site. What had once been
homes for the enslaved became homes for sharecroppers; Black farmers
still lived in these primitive conditions through the 1980s.

Mills passed around a handbill advertising "Sixty-Five Valuable
Negroes" in a Charleston auction. Columns listed names and ages,
and in pencil along the lefthand side the prices that the enslaved sold
for. Young women garnered the highest prices, over $1,000. Another
document outlined McLeod's enslaved population in 1860: seventy-
four people were enslaved at McLeod and picked 21.76 tons of cotton that season, about 588 pounds per person: the Robinson family,
the Dawsons, "Delia and her unrecorded children," "Charles (1813–
1863)," Cephas, Patience, Frank—and many more.

Mills walked us over to a small agricultural building, constructed
from reddish-brown bricks and thick white mortar. Mills pointed to
one brick, about waist high. Three tiny fingerprints were pressed into
the rough surface. An enslaved child's small hands worked all day to
make these bricks. Their fingers slipped when they unmolded the wet
brick from the wood form, leaving an unintended signature, frozen
in time. I lingered behind the group for a moment as the tour moved
ahead. I touched my own fingers, ring, middle, and pointer, into the
divots. The fingerprints of the enslaved are all over Charleston, pressed
into the bricks of the city they built.

\* \* \*

THE FIRST CULINARY USES of the peanut in North America reflected
how West Africans used it back home. Roasting or boiling was the
most common, and ground peanuts were used as the basis for soups
and stews. Fresh, unripe peanuts boiled in a weak brine, sometimes
dusted in spice, are still popular in parts of the South. The first published recipe in America that used ground peanuts for the base of a
soup appeared in the cookbook *The Carolina Housewife*, written by

244 | ENDANGERED EATING

Sarah Rutledge and published in 1847: "Groundnut Soup.—To half a pint of shelled groundnuts, well beaten up, add two spoonfuls of flour, and mix well. Put to them a pint of oysters, and a pint and half of water. While boiling, throw in a red pepper, or two, if small." There was a tradition of making soup in Benin with peanuts and "the large black snail, a solid, meaty crawler," according to a nineteenth-century ethnographer. Oysters were substituted in the American adaptation.

In addition to the peanut soup, Rutledge included recipes for a pea-nut brittle she calls groundnut candy, "groundnut cakes," a meringue cookie made with brown sugar and ground peanuts, and "ground-nut cheese cakes," which have no cheese but consist of ground pea-nuts, brandy, eggs, and sugar baked in puff pastry. No one is certain when peanuts became an ingredient in white kitchens—likely via Black cooks—but Rutledge's book shows that peanuts were regularly consumed by white Southerners sometime before the 1840s. Peanuts caught on as a commercial crop when farmers realized that the plants thrived in sandy soil which wasn't good for other crops. Likely as a result of the nut's growing popularity, an expedition was made to Bolivia in the 1840s by a group of Virginians looking to steal the pea-nut industry away from South Carolina. They found a large peanut that became known as the Virginia; it is one of the most common peanuts grown in America today.

By the mid-nineteenth century, peanuts roasted in their shells were "so much the rage" in New York City that peanuts bought from the South were not enough and importers were bringing nuts from West Africa. Peanut imports went from 4.8 million pounds in 1865 to 11.5 million pounds in 1868. Peanut vendors were on street cor-ners, at train stations, at circuses (peddling "jumbo" nuts) and theaters. Roasted street peanuts replaced chestnuts and European visitors asso-ciated the peanut with American cities. By the 1880s, domestic peanut production hit "two million bushels, of which one-fourth were sold in New York."

After the larger Virginia peanut was introduced, it was used pri-marily for roasting in the shell, and the Carolina Runner was used almost exclusively in confectionery. It's a naturally sweet peanut, so it suited candies. The most famous Carolina Runner confection was known as the Charleston groundnut cake, actually a candy rather than a cake. An Ark of Taste item, it was sold on the streets of Charleston by Black women through the early twentieth century. Groundnut cakes were sold off trays alongside monkey meat, a coconut and molasses treat; benne twists, made with sesame seeds; and horse biscuits, a gingerbread cookie. All of these sweets were related to candies sold in the Caribbean, where you can still find monkey meat.

The *Charleston Evening Post* described groundnut cakes in 1895 as "Delightful, crisp and wholesome, the syrup boiled to just the right consistency, the nuts selected with care." David Shields told me the candies were made with molasses or cane syrup—although upscale versions sometimes used brown sugar and cream—with a little bit of lemon zest.

Molasses was a cheap sweetener, a by-product of the sugar-refining process that would have been easy to find in Charleston. Some accounts even say the molasses was "acquired" for free by enterprising women who went down to Charleston's wharves, where casks of semi-refined sugar arrived from the Caribbean. The women scraped molasses off leaking kegs, strained it, and boiled it into candy. The recipe for groundnut cakes would have been passed from mothers to daughters, who would have watched as their mothers mixed up the candies while carefully explaining the important steps.

"The secret of cooking the groundnut cake was the length of time you cooked the molasses," David wrote in an article on the subject. "A half hour for a substantial batch was frequently mentioned as a benchmark. But too short a cooking and the molasses would ooze in the sun, too long and it would be too thick to be manageable."

Food vending was one of the few socially acceptable ways Black women, free or enslaved, could earn money. Harris wrote, "African American vendors approached their task with a cacophonous zeal and were often argumentative, insubordinate, and rude." Vending was one of the few public spaces where Black women had the freedom to act fully human.

A surprising number of photographs and illustrations depict these women, and newspaper accounts describe their dress in great detail. According to the same 1895 *Post* article, a vendor was "always neatly dressed, her head gaily turbaned, a clean kerchief crossed over her bosom." Her candies were sold off "a clean sheet of brown paper spread over a waiter [a large, round platter], which the seller held on her lap." They usually had a fly whisk to keep the insects at bay. Each had her own street cry to advertise her wares.

For the most part, these Black women were talked about as an interchangeable group, most often referred to as Maumas, the Charleston-area equivalent of "mammy." A few names have survived time. Celia Wilson was a washerwoman who sometimes sold groundnut cakes near the corner of John and Meeting streets. A widow, she raised three children on her income. Wilson made the paper in 1893 because, while selling her wares, she witnessed a horse-drawn streetcar hit a young boy.

Chloe Jenkins was photographed with her waiter of sweets in 1897. She sits on her stool on a brick street, next to a stoop. She's dressed in a dark blouse and long skirt with a clean white apron tied over it. She's wrapped in a shawl and wears a narrow-brimmed straw hat to keep the sun out of her eyes. She presents her waiter covered in brown paper, four types of sweets neatly organized on the tray, benne twists and dark groundnut cakes clearly visible. She's about fifty-four in this photo but looks like she could be twice that age. Chloe was widowed young with three children and worked most of her days as a farm laborer. She passed away from dysentery two years after the photo was taken.

Black women began to sell groundnut cakes sometime in the 1830s, and the Federal Writers Project made note of them selling in markets in the 1930s. The treats, for most of their history, cost one penny. Shortly after the turn of the twentieth century, new sanitation laws made it more difficult and expensive for the vendors to produce and sell their wares. Similar laws targeted Black and brown vendors across the country, and many were driven out of business. Other vendors moved indoors and sold groundnut cakes at the intermission at theatrical performances and public celebrations. The recipe survived in both Black and white communities in Charleston until the 1930s, and the candies were whipped up for fundraisers, PTA and church meetings, and fairs. By the 1950s, they were the topic of nostalgia pieces in local papers.

Groundnut cakes seem to have been the inspiration for commercial peanut candies. In the mid-nineteenth century, candymakers produced a sweet known as flat bars, "composed of peanut pieces held together by melted sugar or molasses and pressed into the shape of a bar"—simply an industrialized groundnut cake. In 1905, the Squirrel Candy Company created the "Squirrel Brand Peanut Bar," and by the 1920s had launched a whole line of peanut-based candies, including Nut Zippers, a caramel peanut candy. In 1911, the Standard Candy Company of Nashville, Tennessee, launched Goo Goo Clusters, a combo of caramel, marshmallow, milk chocolate, and roasted peanuts. Hershey's released Mr. Goodbar in 1925, and Reese's—who originally made monkey meat-like molasses and coconut candies—came up with Reese's Peanut Butter Cups in 1928. Mars launched Snickers Bars—"nougat, peanuts, and caramel encased in milk chocolate"—in 1930. The treats made by Black women and sold on the streets of Charleston predated them all; they are the ancestors of all modern American peanut candy.

The preservation of groundnut cakes lies largely in maintaining the recipe and making these sweets at home. Gullah Geechee chef BJ Dennis worked on recreating groundnut cakes after a trip to Trinidad where he asked monkey meat vendors for tips on how to work with molasses. Charleston natives Matt and Ted Lee included a recipe for a Florentine-like version made with brown sugar and butter in their cookbook, *The Lee Bros. Charleston Kitchen.* When Jeni's Splendid Ice Cream established a new store in Charleston in 2014, they launched a tribute flavor: sweet cream ice cream with "pockets of blackstrap molasses and fistfuls of crunchy, roasted, and salted Virginia peanuts." Of course it was made with the popular Virginia peanuts, but perhaps someday they will be convinced to release a version with Charleston's own Carolina Runners.

# Charleston Groundnut Cakes

I'm going to be honest with you: I don't know if this recipe is "right." I consulted all the historical accounts and worked from the most-often-repeated recipe, from *The Carolina Housewife*, published in 1855:

> To one quart of molasses, add half a pint of brown sugar and a quarter of a pound of butter. Boil it for half an hour over a slow fire then put in a quart of groundnuts parched and shelled. Boil for a quarter of an hour and pour it into a shallow tin pan to harden.

Though one historical text describes the texture of these candies as "crisp," these are not crisp. They break apart easily, but they are chewy when it comes down to it. I couldn't help but feel like there was something missing—a step, an ingredient. Probably it was intentionally held back as a Black woman was pressed for her recipe for Charleston's favorite treats.

But this re-creation is still delicious. It has a deep molasses flavor you don't get in modern candies, and a rich texture from the butter. A sprinkle of sea salt over the top pulls the flavors together.

MAKES 25–50 CAKES, DEPENDING ON SIZE

### INGREDIENTS
1 jar (12 ounces) molasses
½ cup lightly packed light brown sugar
4 tablespoons (½ stick) unsalted butter
2 cups roasted and lightly salted peanuts
Sprinkle of sea salt or other large flake salt (optional)

1. Line a rimmed baking sheet with parchment paper.
2. In a 4-quart saucepan, combine molasses, brown sugar, and butter over high heat. Bring to a boil, then immediately turn temperature to medium-low. Continue to cook until a candy thermometer inserted into the mixture registers 165°F, 20–30 minutes.

3. Add peanuts and cook, stirring constantly, until the thermometer reaches 280°, another 10–15 minutes.
4. Remove from heat and stir. The easiest thing to do is to pour the molten mixture directly onto the parchment-lined baking sheet. For a more traditional candy, use a spoon or cookie scoop to make piles of peanuts and molasses.
5. Allow to cool to room temperature, about 30 minutes, then break apart like peanut brittle. Sprinkle with large flake salt, if you like.

\* \* \*

THROUGHOUT THE NINETEENTH CENTURY, most of the labor of peanut farming was done by hand. First, seeds were planted in hilled rows; then, after the seeds sprouted, "rows were hoed by hand to keep weeds down." Dirt was heaped by hand over the peduncles as the peanuts ripened. During harvest, ripe peanuts were loosened from the earth with hoes, dirt shaken off by hand, then the peanut plants were piled around seven-foot "stackpoles," stacked loosely so air could flow around the plants to dry them. Then, the peanuts were plucked off the plants by hand and finally sorted by hand. The workers were almost always enslaved.

Soon after the free, compulsory labor of the enslaved was abolished, the peanut-growing process was mechanized. By the 1880s, a peanut dotter made holes in the ground for peanuts to be dropped in, and a peanut plow covered those holes up. A scraper plow removed weeds. By the 1920s, plows released the peanut plants from the earth and a peanut picker plucked the fruits. The Eureka Peanut Sheller removed the shells and still more machines sorted and graded the peanuts. By this time, one-quarter fewer workers were needed than in the late nineteenth century. Still, all these workers were Black, and the work did not pay well. When the Great Migration drew Black workers north for better-paying jobs and more personal freedom in the 1920s and 1930s, the Georgia legislature attempted to pass a law to prevent African Americans from leaving the state.

The Carolina Runner peanut's small size made it harder to harvest by hand than newer cultivars, and the new machinery was designed for larger nuts. The Carolina Runner may have been the best-tasting, but out of convenience it was rapidly replaced by other varieties. The last Carolina Runner went into the ground in the late 1920s, and by the 1950s, it was thought to be not just functionally extinct but *extinct* extinct. Gone.

Then, nearly a century later, when David Shields was able to acquire twenty of the rarest peanuts on the planet, he sent them to Clemson University's Coastal Research and Education Center outside of Charleston. A partnership between Clemson and the USDA, the site includes the USDA Vegetable Laboratory and works to research specialty crops and educate the public. The site is part of Clemson's campus and hosts graduate students as well as USDA scientists. The land used to be a large plantation—at the turn of the twentieth century, the Carolina Agricultural Society bought the land and gave it to the USDA and Clemson. The cotton industry had collapsed as a result of a destructive pest called the boll weevil as well as exhausted soil, and the Agricultural Society wanted a research station to figure out how to save or replace it.

The Research Center occupies a two-story brick building. The main foyer leads to a labyrinth of labs and offices, and behind one door is a magical cold storage with (literally) a million different seeds. The buildings are surrounded by acres of fields growing a baffling variety of crops.

I was there to meet with the man entrusted with resurrecting the extinct peanut: Brian Ward, who came around the corner at a good clip to meet me. An assistant professor at Clemson and a horticulturist specializing in heirloom vegetables, Brian was dressed for utility, with both sunglasses and reading glasses strung around his neck.

Brian, in his words, has grown "everything from rice to watermelon to wheat." But peanuts were a new crop to him when he was given the twenty Carolina Runner seeds in 2013. "I didn't know what I had," Brian told me. David and Glenn were initially tight-lipped about the project. "They just said, 'Do your best job.'"

Brian grew the peanuts in his field lab, a patch of land just outside his office window where he could watch them all day. About half of the seeds sprouted, blossomed, and sent down peduncles. When it came time to harvest, David was there.

David said he knew this was the long-lost Carolina Runner the moment he saw the multitude of nuts hanging from the peduncles. They looked just like the historical images he had seen. Then he finally told Brian what had been on the line.

The first season, they harvested 1,200 peanuts. The Carolina Gold Rice Foundation provided the initial funding, and after the plants showed promise, the Peanut Commodities Board stepped in to support the project. Brian and his team planted 900 peanuts the following year and got 60,000 seeds back. By the third year, they had a million peanuts in storage.

With the seed stock built up, Brian started trying to generate interest in the Carolina Runner and reached out to candy companies. NPR picked up the story and Brian got requests from farmers around the country.

"I started packing five-gallon buckets, sealed and cleaned, and just giving the seed away all over the United States," Brian told me. He hoped farmers would pick it up as a specialty crop, something that would be valuable as a premium commodity. The endgame of the Carolina Rice Kitchen project was for farmers to provide these ingredients to high-end chefs and confectioners at a premium price.

"So the bottom line is, how can we make growers more profitable? Well, they need to make more money. How do they make more money? You offer them niche markets or a particular thing that they can do that nobody else has," Brian explained. "This peanut is one of the ways to do that."

There has been some interest from the federal government, too. The Carolina Runner is being studied to see if it lacks the proteins in modern peanuts that cause peanut allergies.

So far, there has been no Carolina Runner revolution. A few seed companies sell it, it appeared briefly on the menus of a few fine dining restaurants, but there are currently very few farmers growing it. The biggest issue is equipment.

"The shellers are not up to speed. The combine's not up to speed," Brian explained.

The Carolina Runner is such a tiny peanut that when it runs through these machines, only about 70 percent emerge. The rest are dropped to the dirt, mixed with the shells, or crushed. Brian believes that a few simply machined attachments could adapt modern combines for the Carolina Runner. But so far, no one has done it.

Brian took me to cold storage and shifted towers of sealed white five-gallon buckets until we found one labeled "African Runner." The lid came up with a plastic *plurp* and reddish peanuts jiggled around inside. I popped one in my mouth—my first taste of a Carolina Runner—and it tasted like a fresh green pea.

When I spoke to Brian in 2019, he'd spent five years on the project, growing out the peanut, providing it to farmers, and promoting it. "I can bring them like a horse to water but I can't make them drink. Ultimately, I've done what I can do. I've brought it back. I'm on to the next thing."

So, what's the next thing?

"Purple straw wheat."

\* \* \*

THE SINGLE MOST DEDICATED grower of the Carolina Runner is Nat Bradford of Sumter County, South Carolina. The morning of my last day in the South, it was overcast, warm, and thickly humid. I turned down a dirt drive and passed brown fall fields to park near the house. Nat bounced out with an old dog who was doing her best scary bark while her tail was wagging. Nat was in his early forties, with short hair that had probably been blond when he was a kid. He loved Tom Petty and had some of Petty's vibe: tall, lanky, and tightly muscled.

Nat's family has been in Sumter County since the eighteenth century and on the same land for generations. Nat had some recent fame for the restoration of the nineteenth century's greatest watermelon, the Bradford watermelon. It was one of his ancestors, Nathaniel

Napoleon Bradford, who created the variety. An Ark of Taste entry (naturally), it was called by NPR "the most luscious watermelon the Deep South has ever produced," a jewel so precious that historically "growers used poison or electrocuting wires to thwart potential thieves, or simply stood guard with guns in the thick of night." Its deep red flesh was exceptionally sweet, but the melon was also soft and easily crushed, so it couldn't be shipped. It fell out of popularity in the era of national grocery store chains.

The Bradfords kept it alive in their own backyard. They planted a patch every year and enjoyed it themselves, gave it to friends, and saved the seeds for the next year. The melon ended up on David Shields's list, and Nat discovered David's interest in it while researching the watermelon's history in college. They connected, which eventually led to Nat growing the watermelon commercially. He harvests and sells for ten days in the summer; the prized melons are reserved months before they're plucked from the vines. Melons that aren't up to par for retail sale are boiled into watermelon molasses or distilled into watermelon brandy.

A trained landscape architect, Nat had recently left landscaping to farm full-time, the watermelon's success being a tipping point for his career switch. Nat, his wife, and five kids moved to the family farm in 2015, and he currently manages 10.5 acres. Okra and collards make the farm profitable, but Nat has a particular passion for exploring long-lost heirlooms that have potential in the culinary world.

"Folks share seeds with me," Nat explained. "A lot of them are old people and they don't have anybody that's going to save their seeds anymore. And it's kind of their last hope of their family seed passing on or being safe." Nat grows out the seed with care, either storing the results so the seed is saved, or cultivating it into a saleable crop.

"This is a half an acre of peanuts," Nat said as he presented me the results of six seasons of growing out the Carolina Runner. The peanuts had been pulled out of the ground and were lying in mounded rows, drying. Runners continue to flower and set pegs until the first frost, but a farmer like Nat is looking to see that the central clump of fruits is 80–85 percent mature, about 120 to 160 days after planting.

He pulls up a few plants every day toward the end of the season to check for ripeness and for the ideal soil conditions, not too wet or dry. The peanuts sit in rows and dry for two to seven days, depending on the weather.

Every year, Nat watched the plants grow more robust. Nat grows organic, which means that he doesn't treat the plants with pesticides or fungicides, and handles weeds with the help of hired labor. After six seasons of adjusting to its environment, this year's crop had thrived.

"Anytime you're working with an heirloom, it takes a number of years just to understand the crop, identify its handicaps, why it went extinct. And then, can it be brought back? That's the big question. Can you do it? I think we reacclimated it. We've got it to where it's a viable landrace peanut again."

Nat plucked a pod and split it open; two rust-skinned peanuts nestled together inside, each the size of the tip of my pinky finger.

"They're dug and they're ready to combine," Nat told me. But Nat, as a small farmer, did not have his own peanut combine, which meant borrowing equipment from a neighbor. The large-scale farmers had to get their crops in first before Nat could get his hands on the equipment. The humidity of the recent hurricane had made the peanut plants swell with moisture and more rain was on the way.

"If we don't get 'em out in time, they'll either start to germinate or they'll rot in the field. It is what it is," he sighed.

The yield wasn't comparable to that of modern peanut varieties, but Nat expected to get 500 pounds from his half acre if he could get it combined. He'd have to hire labor to run a small sheller, since his crop wouldn't be large enough to take to a peanut-buying point for shelling—25,000 pounds is the minimum, one truck trailer full. For Nat to get production up to that level, it would take three to four years of growing peanuts and holding back the entire crop to build up seed volume. He would need to invest in cold storage for several thousand pounds of peanuts and he'd have to buy or lease 25 acres to plant them. Scaling an operation up takes money, an investor willing to stick with the crop and wait for the payoff.

"There's not anything out there for heirloom repatriation," Nat told me. Initial funding went into saving the crop, but as far as making it financially viable, there was no support. "It's a tremendous burden to put on the farmer to carry it to the next level. This is where it's stuck."

As a result of all the time and labor his crop requires, Nat has to sell the Carolina Runners for $20 a pound; commercial Virginias sell for $6 or less. A jar of peanut butter made with the Carolina Runner would cost $40. Even though a buyer is guaranteed—Sean Brock would scoop them all up—$20 a pound is only enough for Nat to break even on his investment.

"I think I'm at the top price point that a chef's willing to pay for these peanuts," Nat explained. "And I've kind of been telling them all along, if I can get these up to scale, the price will come down." The chefs believe in the peanut and love the story behind it, so they buy what they can.

"I'd decided after five years of growing it, and the amount of time that it consumes and the little amount that it generated to our bottom line, that this year I was just going to preserve the peanut. I was gonna grow enough and put some in the freezer."

So, for the moment, the Carolina Runner is saved. There are seeds in cold storage, there are seeds available through catalogs as a curiosity for home growers, but that seems to be as far as the peanut is going to get. "Some crops have a chance at survival in small patches in people's backyards," Nat offered, remembering his own family's watermelon.

The skies had turned an ominous purple: rain for sure. It wasn't looking good for the peanuts. I left with a gallon bag half-filled with Carolina Runners we had picked off the plants by hand. I packed them with care into my checked bag and flew home to Cleveland.

\* \* \*

WHEN I GOT BACK to my little urban garden, the first frost had come. I gently tugged my own Carolina Runner peanut plants out of the soil, not certain what I would find. The plant revealed its underground treasures: twelve peanuts.

Left outside, they would have been devoured by squirrels. It wasn't until I grew my own peanuts that I realized how many feral peanut plants are out there, the result of squirrels burying food for the winter. I let my plants dry on a sunny windowsill for a week, then cracked the shells open and, along with a few nuts from Nat's field, toasted the peanuts in a dry pan. I ate them with just a little salt. The Carolina Runners were as sweet as peanut brittle and the pure peanut flavor of their oil coated my mouth. In comparison, regular peanuts tasted like nothing, just salt and crunch.

This ritual in my Cleveland kitchen was all I had of the South's first and most delicious peanut. I quietly chewed each one until they were gone.

And that bothered me. I was particularly disturbed that it seemed like these peanuts were not getting back into the hands of Black farmers and chefs. The focus seemed to be on saving functionally extinct foods at all costs, primarily targeting high-end chefs and wealthy diners to ensure an ingredient's survival. But there was not an emphasis on making certain that those foods were returned to the communities where they are traditional. For farmers, growing peanuts as more than a novelty is impossible without financial support, since a commercial crop of peanuts requires specialized equipment to harvest and process. For Black chefs, even getting to try the rare ingredient was elusive. Chef Valerie Erwin, formerly of Geechee Girl Café in Philadelphia, spoke with David Shields about reviving groundnut cakes. But the plan never got off the ground. "Even sourcing the groundnuts seemed daunting," she told me.

During a trip to New York City, I called my colleague Tonya Hopkins and took her out for lunch. Tonya is the Food Griot, teller of Black culinary histories, and co-founder of the James Hemings Society, which is "dedicated to remembering, preserving, upholding and celebrating African American contributions to American food and drink." Tonya feels it is her duty to present a Black-centric culinary history because, as she told me, "Huge swaths of our population have not been learning inclusive history. We live in a world that has suppressed those authentic voices."

When we started talking peanuts, Tonya took a moment to set up some context for me. Many of the earliest Southern cookbooks were written by white women but filled with recipes created by Black cooks. Today, we look at these cookbooks through the lens of stolen, usually uncredited, culture. But as Tonya pointed out, the white cookbook author would have seen it much differently.

"She didn't steal. That was *her* house. She's got her own issues in terms of being oppressed and whatever; but it's her house and *her slave*. That's her kitchen, that's her pen and paper that she's using to observe her cook prepare her food the way she thinks she wants it. That's her shit. She owns all of that, including the woman creating that shit."

Tonya pointed out that the same attitude still permeates food culture today.

"What's yours is mine. And what's mine is mine. From their perspective, they are the victors. Everybody else lost, was defeated and enslaved and captured. It's unfair. It's infuriating, it's wrong.

"They didn't save it for us," Tonya said of the Carolina Runner peanut. "They didn't save it to survive Black culinary culture. They saved it for capitalistic reasons. They saved it because what these guys are conditioned to do is to find the next thing. They are explorers . . . they discover. It doesn't matter that somebody already lived here or that somebody else was already using this for millennia—it's new to them." I was reminded of the Food Explorers like David Fairchild, traveling the globe to find profitable crops. "So, they might introduce it on a level that profits them. It's capitalism. That's all it is.

"Capitalism has ruined every fucking thing."

# NOT THE END

On November 8, 2019, I drove an easy ninety minutes south from my home in Cleveland to Columbus, to attend the Ohio National Poultry Show. As soon as I pulled into the parking lot of the Ohio State Fairgrounds, I heard roosters crowing. Chickens were being unloaded out of trucks in crates, cardboard boxes, and cat carriers. That year, the Ohio National was the largest poultry show in the country, and the seventh largest in the history of the American Poultry Association's 150 years as an organization. It was also the largest showing for an Ark of Taste bird: the Buckeye chicken. A mahogany-red bird, it is the only American poultry breed known to have been developed by a woman: Mrs. Nettie Metcalf of Warren, Ohio.

The show occupied two buildings on the fairgrounds. The cacophony inside a football field-sized agricultural building housing 8,549 chickens, ducks, geese, turkeys, peacocks, and various fancy game birds is nearly indescribable, but it's a bit like a million souls screaming in hell. And then the smell hits you: slightly acidic and musty from the combination of poultry poop and wood shaving bedding.

To the right of the entrance were several long tables covered with hundreds of golden trophies, cups, plaques, and ribbons. To the left: pens on the floor for turkeys and geese, then thousands of stacked cages for smaller birds. Breeders walked around cradling chickens

under their arms, chasing escaped chickens down the aisles, or strok-
ing snuggly chickens asleep on their laps.

There were chickens of all variations of size and plumage. Leggy
chickens, stocky ones, and tiny bantam chickens the size of a kitten
with ludicrous crests of feathers or enormously fluffy butts. There were
adorable bantam ducks with beady black eyes that had quacks so loud I
had to plug my ears when I walked past. And there were many Ark of
Taste birds on display, too, like luminous Cayuga ducks. These ducks
originated in upstate New York and are a spectacular all-black animal:
black feet and bills with iridescent black feathers shimmering green,
teal, and blue. I spotted Sebastopol geese, large, pure white birds with
*curly feathers* that corkscrew out of their bodies like a luxurious feather
duster. As I was looking at the birds, many of them looked right back
at me, boldly and curiously, while clucking out a conversation.

The Ohio National is like the home game for the Buckeye chicken;
they show in the largest numbers here and their national chapter
meeting takes place the same weekend. Breeders had driven in their
birds from all over the eastern half of the country, from as far away as
Arkansas and Alabama.

If you're a football fan, you're probably familiar with the Ohio
State Buckeyes. The buckeye tree, an inedible cousin of the chestnut,
is Ohio's state tree. The smooth nuts the tree produces in the late summer are a deep red-brown color, the same shade as the ideal plumage
of the Buckeye chicken. Its feathers range from mahogany to deep gar-
net, sometimes slate or black near the skin and dark, iridescent green
in their tailfeathers. Glossy and incredibly soft, their plumage is unlike
that of any other bird. And their striking color is offset by their golden
yellow legs, upright carriage, and tiny pea comb, a little wrinkle of
red on top of the head. They're known for being cold-hardy, bred for
tough Ohio winters, and those legs and pea combs don't freeze even
in the worst weather. Full-sized Buckeyes are about the size of a basketball; bantam Buckeyes could fit comfortably in a purse.

Walking the show, I noticed the majority of poultry breeders were
white, many of them burly men with Walt Whitman–sized beards,
camo clothes, and farm equipment-branded baseball hats. But the

Buckeye breeders were a little different. This was one of the few breeds dominated by women breeders, perhaps because a woman originated it. And two of the show's most well-known breeders and officers of the American Buckeye Poultry Club were Christopher McCary and Michael Sullivan, a couple based in Alabama.

I spotted Chris, fit and blond, and Michael, trim and brown-haired, at the end of the aisle of the bantam Buckeyes. Michael was holding a hen while Chris massaged glycerin into her beak, comb, and wattle.

"It's their blush!" Michael told me. A common show bird trick, the oil brings out the color of their skin while taking away ashy dryness.

"Can you flip her?" Chris asked Michael, and the hen was rotated so her legs pointed toward Chris, who rubbed the glycerin into her scaly dinosaur feet. The hen didn't seem to mind, contentedly resting in Chris's hands while she accepted the rub-down. Buckeyes have a charming personality and have been described as dog-like and people-focused.

The Buckeyes are great egg-layers but are truly valued for their meat. Michael and Chris love raising bantam Buckeyes because they cook up like a little game bird: one is a great single serving. And they feel the bird's flavor is unparalleled.

"They have these huge, huge shanks and they have great connective tissue that breaks down," Michael told me about braising a Buckeye. "It has a very round, unguent mouthfeel, it completely coats your palette. The kind of consommé that you get from a Buckeye! You cannot find it commercially."

Michael's phone rang; it was a buyer inquiring about their birds for sale. He excused himself. Chris continued to apply the chicken "blush" on his own.

"I've been told that you have done more work on the history of the Buckeye breed than any other person," I said to Chris as he primped his birds. He laughed.

"I showed them back when nobody hardly had them," he acknowledged. He bought birds from a breeder, one of the few who kept Buckeye stock pure, in 2005. He was interested in them for their dual-purpose qualities as meat birds and egg-layers, but he ended up falling in love with the breed.

"I really liked their personality," Chris told me. "They love people. Most chickens run away from you—they would run to you." The happy hen cooed in his hands. "And I was also very interested in the history because they're created by a woman."

\* \* \*

IN 1879, AT THE AGE OF NINETEEN, Miss Annette "Nettie" Williams became Mrs. Frank Metcalf. She was born in Windham in northeast Ohio, and had only an eighth-grade education. After she got married, she moved to her husband's new property in Warren, almost at the Pennsylvania border. A search on Ancestry.com yielded a photo of her from this time: a sweet face with brows knitted in concern.

Metcalf's husband was the son of a physician born in New York state who graduated from medical college in Geneva, New York. Frank didn't go to medical school like his father; instead, he bought an old farm in deep disrepair.

Metcalf was listed as "keeping house" in early census records, a vague understatement for a farm wife. In fact, she took over the chicken hutch almost immediately. Chickens were often the domain of women in the early twentieth century—kept close to the house and fed on kitchen scraps. But Metcalf had a particular reason for taking on the chickens.

"I kept chickens on the farm in Ohio for the purpose of earning my own spending money," she wrote many years later. "I had been used to having my own pocketbook before marriage and every woman who has ever been independent in this way, always wants the same feeling of independence as to money all her life."

"When I took the neglected chickens in hand on the old Ohio farm," Metcalf wrote in *Poultry Success* magazine, "I had not the slightest idea that it was going to lead up to the originating of a new breed and a national reputation. . . . The fascinating thing about life is that we never know what is going to turn up next."

Metcalf tried in vain to work with the raggedy chickens on the property, but after some research in poultry books, she decided to try a different breed altogether. She tried several, without much success: one had white chicks that were easily spotted by hawks and scooped up; another breed had black feathers which made their carcasses look speckled and unappealing. Finally, she bought some Plymouth Rock chickens—black and white birds, one of America's oldest breeds—which she crossed with her neighbor's Buff Cochins—fluffy, golden-plumaged birds. She bred the next generation with Cornish chickens—a dark and muscular British bird—that had been crossed with Black Breasted Red Games, a "plucky" English bird with deep green and bright orange feathers. The result was "the first red chickens I ever saw, and I determined right then and there I would have a whole flock of red chickens."

One day when her husband went into town, she disassembled some seldom-used fence gates and used them to make two breeding pens. "Frank scolded, of course, but didn't take the gates away, so I didn't care about the scolding any."

Her neighbors laughed at her, particularly the men, for her ambition in becoming a poultry breeder—not a role usually taken on by the woman of the house. "You should have heard the ridicule I received from all sides," Metcalf wrote of that time. "One good neighbor quit laughing at me and decided to help me out by taking a pair and raising some to exchange with me, but her husband said, 'He wouldn't have one of Nett Metcalf's mongrels on the place.'

"So, I set to work to prove to these people that I not only could but would make a red breed of fowls." The ridicule only set her mind to it: "Whoever heard of a woman stopped for anything once her mind was made up."

The birds she bred were not only beautiful, they also had magnificent personalities. Because of the game bird in their ancestry, they were feisty and self-sufficient. They'd stalk mice and lizards.

"If something moves, if they can catch it they will eat it," Michael Sullivan told me. "I had one catch a chipmunk once." But the birds were also affectionate—personable with their caretakers, friendly and social. And Metcalf soon realized they were an ideal farm bird as well: cold-hardy, good mothers, self-sufficient, and decent egg-layers with tasty meat.

Metcalf's new breed quickly built a fan base. "As our place was very near the city"—not too far from Youngstown, Ohio—"we had regular customers for all the young chickens we could raise." The Metcalfs renamed their farm Red Feather Farm. Soon after, she started advertising her breed as Buckeye Reds.

Metcalf spent over twenty years perfecting her breed, at the same time taking care of her home and raising three children. Her youngest daughter, Dora, was born in 1899, when Metcalf was on the cusp of forty. Dora was still a toddler when Metcalf began the process of creating a breed standard and club with the American Poultry Association.

To make the Buckeyes a recognized standard breed, Metcalf had to show her birds under their name at three annual meetings of the APA. The first time Buckeyes showed was in 1902 in Cleveland. The second, in 1904, involved a daring car ride through a blizzard to Rochester, New York, with snow drifting several feet high. Frank Metcalf accompanied his wife, and she wrote that they got through the drifting snow by "backing up and running against the bank at full speed, while snow was swirling against the coach windows and the whole landscape a shroud of white." Frank was sick for a month after that trip. After one more showing, Buckeyes were admitted as a new breed in 1905.

Metcalf came up against some chicken drama from the Rhode Island Red breed club, which up until the creation of the Buckeyes had been the only American red chicken. But Metcalf was not a woman to be messed with. She wrote in her protest, "It is very brave and heroic in this powerful [Rhode Island Red] Club to try to undo the work of a woman, but if the Buckeyes should be dropped from the Standard it will be at their behest . . ." An agreement was reached: "Red" would be dropped from the newer breed's name, from Buckeye Reds to just Buckeyes. "Owing to the jealousy of the R.I. Red people, the name Buckeye Reds was dropped, as this autocratic body say no other Red shall be on the standard," Metcalf wrote.

When the battle with the Rhode Island Red club was over, Metcalf was exhausted. "The demand created for this breed caused me, the originator, such strenuous work that I gave all my time to chickens entirely and tried to supply the demand for Buckeyes until my health was breaking down."

By the time the first of her histories of the breed was published in *Pacific Fancier*, in 1909, Metcalf and her husband had moved to Inglewood, California, where they were some of the community's founding members. Metcalf had culled her flock down to a few choice specimens. "[I] have been enjoying the change from snow, slush and mud, ice and blizzards," Metcalf wrote of her move; it's hard to say if her cold-hardy chickens enjoyed the Southern California climate as much.

For a time, Metcalf remained president of the breed club and showed her birds locally. In 1907, the *Los Angeles Times* reported on the Los Angeles County Poultry Association show and noted that in the category of Peacomb Buckeyes, "All awards to Mrs. Frank Metcalf." But soon enough, she retired from all poultry-related public life. "I am content to let the breed go into the hands of others and stand or fall as their merits deserve," she commented. Frank took up ranching, while Metcalf worked as a real estate agent and served on the Los Angeles Board of Education. She also composed music, submitting copyrights for at least two songs, "My Home in Old Ohio" in 1907 and "Our Own Sunny Southern California" in 1920. She was still working at the age of seventy, now a widow, living with her youngest daughter, Dora, and helping out with her grandchildren. She passed away in 1945 at the age of eighty-five.

Without the force of Metcalf's personality, the Buckeye breed nearly vanished. She had created it just before commercial, factory-farm poultry production took off in America, and the breed fell out of favor as it was outcompeted by faster-growing birds that thrived in confinement. By the 1990s, the breed was almost extinct, with less than 500 birds in existence—one of the rarest chickens in the United States.

In 2005, the Livestock Conservancy, in collaboration with Slow

Food, received a grant to focus on reviving the Buckeye and sought out hatching eggs from the remaining Buckeye breeders. The first year of the project, about 200 chicks were hatched and raised by poultry farmers. The Livestock Conservancy trained the new breeders to select birds that met the traditional breed standards. The second year, 500 chicks were hatched, followed by 750 the third year. As a result of this project, rapid progress was made to recover and stabilize the breed. Today, between 600 and 1,000 breeding-age Buckeyes exist nationally.

And there's a very specific pride amongst Buckeye breeders for the plucky little birds they helped save. Every one of them knows the name of Mrs. Nettie Metcalf.

"Showing in numbers like this shows people that there's a community," Michael Sullivan told me at the Ohio National. The hope is that by seeing the energy and effort this community of breeders invests in these birds, more poultry farmers will consider taking a chance on the Buckeye. "So that they'll give them a try and find out: Good God! These are the most healthiest, most hardiest, toughest little birds."

My trip to see the Buckeye chickens wasn't the furthest distance I traveled for research. It wasn't the most foreign-to-me culture I immersed myself in. By the standards of this book, the trip was practically lazy. But I met people passionate about the food they raised, a bird they believed in so much they'd dedicated their lives to it. They felt the Buckeyes and their story was a legacy worth preserving.

You can use the Ark of Taste like I did, as a travel guide that will take you on some wild adventures. It will open doors to communities you may never have had a chance to engage with before, and if you're lucky, an opportunity to connect with people over foods they love. But the secret of the Ark is that you don't have to travel very far at all. Turn around and take a good look; there's probably a rare food practically in your backyard.

# ACKNOWLEDGMENTS

I'd like to thank my editors: Alane Mason, who brought this project to W. W. Norton & Co., and Melanie Tortoroli, who finished this book with me. Both have been so enthusiastic, invested, and encouraging. It's been an honor to work with them and the entire Norton staff.

I'd like to thank my long-time agent, Wendy Sherman, who has now guided me through two projects, as well as Callie Deitrick for her passion for my work. I look forward to what's next!

I'm grateful to the experts who shared their time and knowledge with me to give context to this project: Bill Bissell, Robert Dawson, Yara Elmjouie, Dan and Talia Haykin, Megan Larmer, Noa Kekuewa Lincoln, Denisa Livingston, Anna Mulé, Andi Murphy, Gregory Peck, Raffaella Ponzio, Susan Schenck, and Linda Ziedrich.

Thanks to my interns, Ashley Frenkel and Cecily Griesser, for all their hard work, and my research assistant, Dressler Parsons. A big thank-you to my fact-checkers: Ashley Frenkel, Kathleen Fletcher, Andrew Gustafson, Tammy Hart, Miranda Knutson, Karen Lohman, Laura Nesson, Dressler Parsons, and Jay Popham.

I was awarded an Ohio Arts Council Individual Excellence Award for FY 2020. This book was made possible by grants from PEN America Writers' Emergency Fund, Artist Relief, Author's League Fund, Curious Creators Grant, Libbie Agran, Ken Schneck Creative Journalism Fund, and my Go Fund Me supporters: Abigail Weiner, Adam

Weiner, Aimee Armour-Avant, Alex Lombardo, Amy and Misha Kligman, Ang Kopa, Angela Serratore, Arlyn Blake, Barry Underwood, Bleu Caldwell, Brian Wolf, Bryan DiFrancesco, Carolyn Cleveland, Carrie Russo, Cathy Nierras, Chip Hiebler, Dan Kalmus, Deborah Delare, Elizabeth Kaeser, Eva Ulz, Giovanni D'Amato, Jammy Tart, Jen Messier, Jennifer Zielinski, Jenny Blackwell, Jess Tsang, Jess Walters, Jessi Moths, Jessica Reed, Jessica Varma, Alex and Jonathan Anderson, Julie Brophy, Kate Conerton, Kate McCarthy, Kathleen Fletcher, Katie Watson, Kristen Harvey, Kristina Demain, Lauren Davis, Leo and Jordan McNeill, Madeline Earp, Mara Saxer, Margaret Weber, Mark Gondree, Matt Hamilton, maude burns, Melinda Montelauro, Michelle Zatta, Pat Williamsen, Pete Koomen, Renee Newton, Sharon Stadul, Shelly Fank, Shelly Felton, Steven Michalske, Tanya Washburn, and Terri Bate. I am grateful for the financial assistance that made this project possible.

This book was also made possible by a support group of friends and family that chased down obscure facts, let me sleep on their couch, took care of my cat, and provided many other forms of aid: Luke Anderson and Elisabeth Dobbins, Ashley Betton and Jeff Kurtze, Emily Bute and Kevin O'Leary, Brian and Danielle Carless Wolf, Josh Daley, Kat Dobbins and Greg Lohman, Maggie Dobbins and Jon Krop, Sue Erickson, Emily Fellner and Chris Zeig, Rich Fulkerson and Jonathan Nyquist, Samer Hamze, Dan Hendrock and Nick Torres, Sarah Litvin, Stan Mayer, Bo Mendez, Elizabeth Migliore, Kim Miller, Drew Pisarra, Michelle Sibio, Mark and Jessica Stadul, Dayna and Matt Sowd, Caley Vickerman, and Tanya Washburn.

If I have forgotten anyone who has been a part of this project, I owe you a sincere thanks and possibly a doughnut.

# FURTHER READING

If you'd like to take a deeper dive into the stories of these ingredients or the cultures that caretake them, here are some of my most valuable references.

## CHAPTER 1: DATES

Fairchild, David. *The World Was My Garden*. New York: Scribner's, 1947.

Seekatz, Sarah. *America's Arabia: The Date Industry and the Cultivation of Middle Eastern Fantasies in the Deserts of Southern California*. Dissertation. Berkeley: University of California Press, 2014.

———. *Indio's Date Festival*. Arcadia Publishing Library Editions, 2016.

## CHAPTER 2: SUGARCANE

Kamakau, Samuel. *Ruling Chiefs of Hawaii*. Honolulu: Kamehameha Press, 1961.

Liliuokalani. *Hawaii's Story by Hawaii's Queen*. Honolulu: University of Hawai'i Press, 2013.

Lincoln, Noa Kekuewa. *Kō: An Ethnobotanical Guide to Hawaiian Sugarcane Cultivars*. Honolulu: University of Hawai'i Press, 2020.

MacLennan, Carol A. *Sovereign Sugar: Industry and Environment in Hawai'i*. Honolulu: University of Hawai'i Press, 2014.

Mintz, Sidney W. *Sweetness and Power: The Place of Sugar in Modern History*. London: Penguin Books, 1986.

Vowell, Sarah. *Unfamiliar Fishes*. New York: Riverhead Books, 2012.

## CHAPTER 3: SHEEP

Chee, Patti, et al. *Oral History Stories of the Long Walk = Hwéeldi Baa Hané by the Diné of the Eastern Region of the Navajo Reservation; Stories Collected and Recorded by the Title VII Bilingual Staff*. Crownpoint, NM: Lake Valley Navajo School, 1991.

Denetdale, Jennifer Nez. *Reclaiming Diné History: The Legacies of Navajo Chief Manuelito and Juanita*. Tucson: University of Arizona Press, 2007.

Iverson, Peter. *Diné: A History of the Navajos.* Albuquerque: University of New Mexico Press, 2002.

Johnson, Broderick, and Ruth Roessel. *Navajo Livestock Reduction.* Tsaile, AZ: Navajo Community College Press, 1974.

Weisiger, Marsha. *Dreaming of Sheep in Navajo Country.* Seattle: University of Washington Press, 2011.

White, Richard. *The Roots of Dependency: Subsistence, Environment, and Social Change among the Choctaws, Pawnees, and Navajos.* Lincoln: University of Nebraska Press, 1988.

## CHAPTER 4: SALMON

Boxberger, Daniel L. *To Fish in Common: The Ethnohistory of Lummi Island Salmon Fishing.* Seattle: University of Washington Press, 2000.

Claxton, Nicolas Xemtoltw. *To Fish as Formerly: A Resurgent Journey Back to the Saanich Reef Net Fishery.* Dissertation. Victoria, BC: University of Victoria, 2015.

Cook, Langdon. *Upstream: Searching for Wild Salmon, from River to Table.* New York: Ballantine Books, 2017.

Poth, Janet, ed. *Saltwater People as Told by Dave Elliott Sr.: A Resource Book for the Saanich Native Studies Program.* British Columbia: School District 63 [Saanich], 1983.

Snively, Gloria, and Wanosts'a7 Lorna Williams. *Knowing Home: Braiding Indigenous Science with Western Science, Book 1.* Victoria, BC: University of Victoria, 2016.

## CHAPTER 5: WILD RICE

Barton, Barbara J. *Manoomin: The Story of Wild Rice in Michigan.* East Lansing: Michigan State University Press, 2018.

LaDuke, Winona, and Brian Carlson. *Our Manoomin, Our Life: The Anishinaabeg Struggle to Protect Wild Rice.* Callaway, MN: White Earth Land Recovery Project, 2003.

"Manoomin," https://www.1854treatyauthority.org/images/ManoominChapter.Appendices.2019.final.pdf.

Treuer, Anton. *Ojibwe in Minnesota.* St. Paul: Minnesota Historical Society Press, 2010.

## CHAPTER 6: CIDER

McManus, Fran. "Newark's Celebrated Cider," *Newark History Society,* Fall 2015. https://www.newarkhistorysociety.org/images/articles/past_programs/Cider%20Works%20EJ%20fall15.pdf.

———. "Lost & Found: The Search for the Harrison Apple," *Edible Jersey,* September 1, 2020. https://ediblejersey.ediblecommunities.com/food-thought/lost-found-search-harrison-apple.

Pollan, Michael. *The Botany of Desire: A Plant's-Eye View of the World.* New York: Random House, 2001.

Pucci, Dan, and Craig Cavallo. *American Cider: A Modern Guide to a Historic Beverage.* New York: Ballantine Books, 2021.

Rorabaugh, W. J. *The Alcoholic Republic: An American Tradition.* Oxford: Oxford University Press, 1979.

Stanton, Lucia C. *"Those Who Labor for My Happiness": Slavery at Thomas Jefferson's Monticello.* Charlottesville: University of Virginia Press, 2012.

Wiencek, Henry. "The Dark Side of Thomas Jefferson," Smithsonian Magazine, October 2012. https://www.smithsonianmag.com/history/the-dark-side-of -thomas-jefferson-35976004/.

## CHAPTER 7: FILÉ

Smith, Rebecca. "How Much Do You Know about Filé Powder? It's Used for More Than Just Gumbo . . ." *nola*, November 21, 2018. https://www.nola.com/ entertainment_life/article_61fbb8c2-26e8-5826-89b5-fe61c5f64b5f.html.

Thompson, Ian. *Choctaw Food: Remembering the Land, Rekindling Ancient Knowledge.* Durant, OK: Choctaw Nation Education Special Projects, 2019.

Williams, Elizabeth M. *New Orleans: A Food Biography.* Lanham, MD: AltaMira Press, 2012.

## CHAPTER 8: PEANUTS

Harris, Jessica B. *High on the Hog: A Culinary Journey from Africa to America.* New York: Bloomsbury USA, 2012.

Shields, David S. *Southern Provisions: The Creation and Revival of a Cuisine.* Chicago: University of Chicago Press, 2015.

Smith, Andrew F. *Peanuts: The Illustrious History of the Goober Pea.* Champaign: University of Illinois Press, 2007.

Twitty, Michael W. *The Cooking Gene: A Journey through African American Culinary History in the Old South.* New York: Amistad, 2017.

# REFERENCES

## INTRODUCTION: WHAT IS ENDANGERED EATING?

xiii    **As a part of their mission**: Raffaella Ponzio, interview by author, November 14, 2018.

xiii    **The Ark of Taste contains over 5,000**: "Ark of Taste," Slow Food Foundation for Biodiversity, http://www.fondazioneslowfood.com/en/ark-of-taste-slow-food/.

xiii    *su filindeu*: Chris Colin, "On the Hunt for the World's Rarest Pasta," *Saveur,* September 22, 2017.

xiv    **Slow Food International was founded**: "Our History," Slow Food, https://www .slowfood.com/about-us/our-history/.

xiv    **In the organization's own words**: "About Us," Slow Food, http://www.slowfood .com/about-us/.

xiv    **The Ark of Taste was launched**: Carlo Petrini, "The Ark of Taste Continues Its Journey," Slow Food, February 11, 2019, http://www.slowfood.com/the-ark-of-taste -continues-its-journey/.

xiv    **The list includes plants**: "Ark of Taste Nomination Form," Slow Food Foundation for Biodiversity, https://www.fondazioneslowfood.com/wp-content/uploads/2016/02/ ING_scheda_segnalazioni_compilabile-1.pdf.

xiv    **When an item is submitted**: Anna Mulé, interview by author, April 12, 2017.

xiv    **Once a nomination is approved**: Linda Ziedrich, notes on author's manuscript, July 20, 2019.

xiv    **There, the information about**: Ponzio, interview by author.

xiv    **They consider four factors**: "The Ark of Taste," Slow Food USA, http://slowfoodusa .org/ark-of-taste/.

xv    **cultural or historical significance**: Ziedrich, notes on author's manuscript.

xv    **The organization may begin**: Ponzio, interview by author.

xv    **Slow Food creates events**: Mulé, interview by author.

xv    **In general, the organization facilitates**: "Ark of Taste Products in United States," Slow Food Foundation for Biodiversity, http://www.slowfoodusa.org/files/files/ark-of-taste -nomination-process.pdf.

xvi    **Recaptured, they were a favorite**: "Heritage Texas Longhorn Cattle," Slow Food Foundation for Biodiversity, https://www.fondazioneslowfood.com/en/ark-of-taste-slow -food/heritage-texas-longhorn-cattle/.

xvii    **critically endangered**: "Texas Longhorn Cattle (CTLR)," Livestock Conservancy, https://livestockconservancy.org/heritage-breeds/heritage-breeds-list/texas-longhorn -cattle/.

# 1. COACHELLA VALLEY DATES

1   **Sometimes called the American Sahara**: The Kitchen Sisters and Lisa Morehouse, "Forbidding Fruit: How America Got Turned on to the Date," *The Salt*, NPR, June 10, 2014.

1   **It's not uncommon**: Jessica Duenow, interview by author, February 15, 2019.

1   **But aquifers run deep**: Sarah Seekatz, *America's Arabia: The Date Industry and the Cultivation of Middle Eastern Fantasies in the Deserts of Southern California*, PhD diss. (University of California, Riverside, 2014), 26.

2   **"wondered whether the government"**: David Fairchild, "Dates," unpublished manuscript (1931), 21, Fairchild Tropical Botanic Garden Center for Tropical Plant Conservation, Coral Gables, FL.

2   **the Cahuilla Indians**: "Agua Caliente Band of Cahuilla Indians, Cultural History," http://www.aguacaliente.org/content/History%20and%20Culture/; Erica M. Ward, *Coachella* (Charleston, SC: Arcadia, 2014), 7.

2   **When the Southern Pacific Railroad**: Denise Goolsby, "Southern Pacific Railroad Made Path through the Wild," *Desert Sun*, August 23, 2014.

2   **Many of the early settlers**: "Desert Land Act," http://en.wikipedia.org/wiki/Desert_Land_Act. Accessed February 15, 2020.

2   **over 90 percent of the dates**: Kitchen Sisters and Morehouse, "Forbidding Fruit."

3   **Laflin eventually took over**: Patricia B. Laflin, "The Story of Dates, Part II," *Periscope* (2007), Palm Springs Historical Society, 3.

4   **Dates are very sweet**: "ASU's Grove Is the No. 2 Collection in the U.S., Full of Rare Varieties Sold to ASU Community, the Public," Arizona State University, October 5, 2016, http://asunow.asu.edu/20161005-arizona-impact-asu-date-grove-harvest; "Dates, Medjool Nutrition Facts," NutritionValue, http://www.nutritionvalue.org/Dates%2C_Medjool_nutritional_value.html, accessed February 15, 2020.

4   **Additionally, a date contains**: Toby Amidor, "How and Why to Love Dates—the Fruit, That Is," *U.S. News & World Report*, February 2, 2018.

4   **The date palm originated**: Donald R. Hodel and Dennis V. Johnson, *Dates: Imported and American Varieties of Dates in the United States* (Oakland: University of California Division of Agriculture and Natural Resources, 2007), 13.

4   **They grow specifically in places**: E. Floyd Shields, *Coachella Valley Desert Trails, The Salton Sea Saga, and The Romance and Sex Life of the Date* (Indio, CA: Shields Date Gardens, 1957), 30.

4   **Dental calculus**: Amanda G. Henry, Alison S. Brooks, and Dolores R. Piperno, "Microfossils in Calculus Demonstrate Consumption of Plants and Cooked Foods in Neanderthal Diets," *PNAS* 108 (January 2011), 487.

4   **no wild varieties exist today**: "ASU's Grove Is the No. 2 Collection."

4   **The date palm has symbolism**: Michele Kayal, "Dates: The Sticky History of a Sweet Fruit," *National Geographic*, June 18, 2015.

5   **Suckers . . . fifteen years**: Shields Date Gardens, "The Romance & Sex Life of the Date," video, February 14, 2017, http://www.youtube.com/watch?v=HSHPQWyxZds.

5   **The male plants produce**: Duenow, interview by author.

5   **"In the first orchard"**: Fairchild, *The World Was My Garden*, 182.

5   **The trees are pollinated**: Shields, *Coachella Valley Desert Trails*, 30.

6   **Additionally, the center . . . don't ripen all at once**: Shields, *Coachella Valley Desert Trails*, 30, 32.

6   **Bracero Program**: Seekatz, *America's Arabia*, 42.

6   **Being a palmero**: Seekatz, *America's Arabia*, 44; Colin Atagi, "Ten Hottest Days in Palm Springs Area History," *Desert Sun*, June 20, 2016.

6   **For comparison, the hottest temperature**: Andrea Thompson, "What's the Highest Temperature Ever Recorded in the U.S.?" *Live Science*, July 8, 2011.

6   **A major selling point**: Fairchild, *The World Was My Garden*, 240.

7   **After the dates ripened . . . by the pound**: Fairchild, *The World Was My Garden*, 230.

7   **"They were probably the stickiest"**: Fairchild, *The World Was My Garden*, 181.

8   **"easily embarrassed"**: Amanda Harris, *Fruits of Eden: David Fairchild and America's Plant Hunters* (Gainesville: University Press of Florida, 2015), 3–4, 11.

8   **Fairchild would write later**: Fairchild, *The World Was My Garden*, 12.

8   **Swingle never fully lost . . . Arabic**: Frank D. Venning, "Walter Tennyson Swingle, 1871–1952," *The Carrell: Journal of the Friends of the University of Miami Library* 18 (1977): 8.

8   **"I am often criticized"**: Fairchild, *The World Was My Garden,* 204.

8   **"[Fairchild] suddenly realized"**: Harris, *Fruits of Eden*, 6–7.

8   **Within two years of his arrival**: Daniel Stone, *The Food Explorer: The True Adventures of the Globe-Trotting Botanist Who Transformed What America Eats* (New York: Dutton, 2019), 82.

9   **He sported a hard part**: Fairchild, *The World Was My Garden*, 26a.

9   **The name they came up with**: Venning, "Walter Tennyson Swingle," 83.

9   **After petitioning their boss**: Venning, "Walter Tennyson Swingle," 13.

9   **"Plant introduction has"**: Fairchild, *The World Was My Garden*, 206.

9   **The two scientists would eventually**: "Mission & History," Fairchild Tropical Botanic Garden, http://www.fairchildgarden.org/About-Fairchild/Mission-History.

10   **"It was Swingle"**: Fairchild, "Dates," 1.

10   **Fairchild collected many**: "Mission & History," Fairchild Tropical Botanic Garden.

10   **"which we kept always"**: Fairchild, "Dates," 1.

10   **It's unclear what book**: Janet Mosley, "Introduction of Phoenix dactylifera: Getting the Date Palm to the 'New World'," https://www.fairchildgarden.org/Science-Conservation-/Archives-Natural-History-Collection/Whats-New/Date-Palm-Introduction.

11   **"The idea of planting"**: Fairchild, "Dates," 7.

11   **The railroad access**: Maggie Downs, "How a Farming Experiment in the Palm Springs Desert Led to the Iconic Date Shake," *MIC*, August 17, 2018.

11   **"A new world . . . 95% of the suckers lived"**: Fairchild, "Dates," 2, 6, 15.

11   **"I mixed a liquid . . . Nile delta"**: Fairchild, *The World Was My Garden,* 180–81, 241.

12   **Unlike Swingle . . . heading to Baghdad**: Fairchild, "Dates," 10–11, 13.

12   **During his trip, Fairchild collected**: Fairchild, *The World Was My Garden*, 189, 236.

12   **The USDA established**: "The Salton Sea: A Status Update," Legislative Analyst's Office (California), https://lao.ca.gov/Publications/Report/3879l.

12   **When the inland sea's rising . . . hands-on work**: Laflin, "The Story of Dates, Part II," 3.

13   **The Coachella Valley . . . resembles**: Sarah Seekatz, "Harem Girls and Camel Races: Middle Eastern Fantasies in the Deserts of Southern California," KCET, February 5, 2013, http://www.kcet.org/shows/artbound/harem-girls-and-camel-races-middle-eastern-fantasies-in-the-deserts-of-southern. Accessed February 15, 2020.

13   **"a damn near carbon copy"**: Stan Mayer, interview by author, March 4, 2020.

13   **There were insect infestations . . . far less than what he had anticipated**: Venning, "Walter Tennyson Swingle," 17–18, 90.

14   **"Of course this is just"**: Fairchild, "Dates," 20.

15   **So, while the mother palm**: Sarah Seekatz, interview by author, February 15, 2019.

16   **His unusual, tasty dates**: Laflin, "The Story of Dates, Part II," 25.

16   **"the flesh is soft"**: "Honey Date," Slow Food Foundation for Biodiversity, http://www.fondazioneslowfood.com/en/ark-of-taste-slow-food/honey-date/.

16   **He advertised**: Laflin, "The Story of Dates, Part II," 36–37.

16   **The Pyramid date shop**: Kitchen Sisters and Morehouse, "Forbidding Fruit."

17   **Through these mission sites . . . favorite shops**: Seekatz, interview by author.

18   **Before the Shields family settled**: Shields, *Coachella Valley Desert Trails*, 5.

18   **The roadside knight**: Shields Date Gardens, "The Romance & Sex Life of the Date,".

18   **The store no longer shows**: Shields Date Garden, https://shieldsdategarden.com/. Accessed February 15, 2020.

19    **The sculptures include**: Carol Shuster, "A Trip through Shields Date Garden," *High Prairie Washington*, March 12, 2018.

19    **When these date palms**: Seekatz, *America's Arabia*, 14.

19    **The date industry . . . sex in the front**: Seekatz, interview by author.

20    **"that some Middle Easterners"**: Downs, "How a Farming Experiment."

20    **There is a popular recipe**: "The Health Benefits of Dates," *Teach Middle East*, June 25, 2015.

20    **sexual vitality . . . both released in 1922**: Katherine Marko, *Alternative Daily*, "Dates Can Rev Up Your Sex Life."

20    **"There was a time"**: Seekatz, email to author, January 4, 2020.

20    **Shields blends vanilla ice milk**: Downs, "How a Farming Experiment."

21    **"For the history and the legacy"**: Duenow, interview by author.

21    **"Tasting the quality of anything"**: Fairchild, *The World Was My Garden*, 241.

21    **By 1930, America was producing**: Fairchild, "Dates," 20.

22    **The earliest date cookbook**: Seekatz, "America's Arabia," 46.

22    **It included recipes**: *Dromedary Cook Book: Being a Collection of One Hundred Thoroughly Tested Recipes Selected from a Large Number Submitted in a Prize Competition and Employing Dromedary Dates and Other Superior Quality Dried Fruits* (New York: Hills Brothers, 1914).

22    **The first Coachella Date Festival**: May Sowles Metzler, *Date Cook Book: International Festival of Dates* (Coachella Valley, 1921).

22    **brown sugar and chopped nut date-drop cookies**: Shields, *Coachella Valley Desert Trails*, 38.

23    **Chock Full o'Nuts**: Leah Koenig, "Lost Foods of New York City: Date-nut Bread Sandwiches at Chock Full o'Nuts," *Politico*, July 16, 2012.

23    **This recipe withstands**: "Blast from Cafes Past!" *Chock Full o'Nuts*, https://www.chockfullonuts.com/cafe-locator/. Accessed March 10, 2020.

25    **"The presentation of"**: Shields, *Coachella Valley Desert Trails*, 13.

25    **Each year of the pageant**: Seekatz, *Indio's Date Festival*, 63.

25    **"Lots of chiffon"**: Kitchen Sisters and Morehouse, "Forbidding Fruit."

25    **The costumes were also**: Seekatz, *Indio's Date Festival*, 61.

25    **"They were literally"**: Seekatz, interview by author.

25    **In photos . . . "good girl"**: Seekatz, *America's Arabia*, 283.

27    **"And then in the larger"**: Seekatz, interview by author.

28    **Immigration from these countries**: "Countries of Birth for U.S. Immigrants, 1960–Present," Migration Policy Institute, http://www.migrationpolicy.org/programs/data-hub/charts/immigrants-countries-birth-over-time?width=1000&height=850&iframe=true.

28    **Ramadan now represents**: Kayal, "Dates."

29    **Mark Tadros**: Ricardo Lopez, "Are Coachella Valley Dates California's Next Superfood? They're Sweet and Healthy, But Not Visually Appealing," *Desert Sun*, September 20, 2019.

29    **The single-day festival . . . specializes in Bahris**: Mark Tadros, interview by author, January 14, 2020.

29    **But over the twentieth century**: Tadros, interview by author; Lopez, "Are Coachella Valley Dates California's Next Superfood?"

29    **A classic food festival**: "Date Harvest Festival," https://dateharvestfest.com/, accessed February 15, 2020; Tadros, interview by author.

30    **Sam Cobb**: Sam Cobb, interviews by author, February 17, 2019, and January 14, 2020; Sam Cobb Farms, http://www.samcobbdates.com, accessed January 28, 2022.

34    **"Again the scene of 1898" . . . 230 publications**: Fairchild, "Dates," 20, 22, 28, 30.

35    **"I've never heard anyone"**: Venning, "Walter Tennyson Swingle," 30.

35    **In California, the domestic industry**: Lopez, "Are Coachella Valley Dates California's Next Superfood"; "Dates," Agricultural Marketing Resource Center, September 2021, https://www.agmrc.org/commodities-products/fruits/dates. Accessed January 28, 2022.

35    **The date industry has shifted**: Seekatz, interview by author.

## 2. *KUPUNA KŌ*: HAWAIIAN LEGACY SUGARCANE

37  **"Work with the land"**: Hoapiono (@hoapiono), Instagram, May 28, 2020, https://www.instagram.com/p/CAuTOBljau6kA3IarKalbGiilvRtpyOaGIbsVc0/?igshid=1adveytdta4zg. Accessed October 29, 2022.

38  **commercial sugar production no longer exists**: Michael Keany, "The End of an Era: Hawai'i's Last Sugar Mill Closes Forever," *Honolulu*, December 21, 2016.

38  **For example, Halali'i is . . . or implacable"**: Noa Kekuewa Lincoln, "Description of Hawaiian Sugarcane Varieties," College of Tropical Agriculture and Human Resources, University of Hawai'i at Manoa, 2017, https://cms.ctahr.hawaii.edu/cane/Cane-Varieties. Accessed June 21, 2020.

38  **True to its grumpy name**: Noa Kekuewa Lincoln, "Hawaiian Uses of Sugarcane," College of Tropical Agriculture and Human Resources, University of Hawai'i at Manoa, 2017, https://cms.ctahr.hawaii.edu/cane/Hawaiian-Uses.

38  **Uahiapele means**: Lincoln, "Description of Hawaiian Sugarcane Varieties."

38  **Additionally, with housing and hotel**: Robin Robinson, interview by author, May 6, 2019.

39  **"was raised in the ocean"**: Anthony Deluze, interview by author, May 13, 2019.

40  **There are two wild sugarcane species**: Noa Kekuewa Lincoln, "General Cane Information: The Sugarcane Plant," College of Tropical Agriculture and Human Resources, University of Hawai'i at Manoa, 2017, https://cms.ctahr.hawaii.edu/cane/General-Info.

41  *S. officinarum* . . . **originated**: Sidney W. Mintz, *Sweetness and Power: The Place of Sugar in Modern History* (London: Penguin, 1986), 19.

41  **The cane was chewed**: "Sugarcane beverage," U.S. Department of Agriculture, https://fdc.nal.usda.gov/fdc-app.html#/food-details/789582/nutrients.

41  **It's since been bred**: Marvellous Zhou, "Sugarcane (*S. officinarum* x *S. spontaneum*)," in *Genetic Improvement of Tropical Crops*, edited by Hugo Campos and Peter D. S. Caligari, (Springer, Cham, 2017), https://doi.org/10.1007/978-3-319-59819-2_9.

41  **These canes can grow**: Lincoln, "General Cane Information."

41  **The earliest definite record . . . into Europe**: Mintz, *Sweetness and Power,* 23–24.

42  **By the end of the sixteenth century**: Lincoln, "General Cane Information."

42  **Polynesian people**: "Did the Polynesians Discover America?" *History*, https://www.history.com/topics/exploration/did-the-polynesians-discover-america-video; Michaeleen Doucleff, "How The Sweet Potato Crossed the Pacific Way Before the Europeans Did," *The Salt*, NPR, January 23, 2013;

42  **One boat could carry**: "Wayfinders: A Pacific Odyssey," PBS, https://www.pbs.org/wayfinders/polynesian2.html.

42  **They brought plant tubers**: Lincoln, "General Cane Information."

42  **These are the *kupuna***: Noa Kekuewa Lincoln, interview by author, May 8, 2019.

42  **There is anthropological**: Noa Kekuewa Lincoln, "Sugarcane in Ancient Hawai'i," https://cms.ctahr.hawaii.edu/cane/General-Info; Lincoln, interview by author.

43  **The flowers were also used**: Lincoln, "Hawaiian Uses of Sugarcane"; "The Art of Hee'holua," https://www.youtube.com/watch?v=i2qCXB78bkc&t=5s.

43  **Hawaiian creation chant**: "He pule hoolaa alii," https://www.sacred-texts.com/pac/lku/lku02.htm.

43  ***Manulele* means "flying bird"**: Lincoln, "Description of Hawaiian Sugarcane Varieties."

43  **Other canes were used . . . underground oven**: Lincoln, "Hawaiian Uses of Sugarcane."

44  **On January 18, 1778**: "225 Years Ago: January–March 1778," Captain Cook Society, https://www.captaincooksociety.com/home/detail/225-years-ago-january-march-1778.

44  **"several plantations of plantains"**: James Cook, *The Voyages of Captain James Cook* (London: William Smith, 1846), 233.

44  **The crew traded metal**: "January 18, 1778, Captain Cook Reaches Hawaii," *History*, https://www.history.com/this-day-in-history/cook-discovers-hawaii#:~:text=On%20January%2018%2C%201778%2C%20the,past%20the%20island%20of%20Oahu.

44    **"with a powerful blow"**: Samuel M. Kamakau, *Ruling Chiefs of Hawaii* (Honolulu: Kamehameha Publishing, 1992), 103.

44    **When Cook arrived**: Lewis Lord, "How Many People Were Here Before Columbus?" *U.S. News & World Report*, August 18–25, 1997.

44    **Forty years later**: Display text, Bishop Museum, Honolulu, Hawaii.

44    **European diseases . . . 70,000 individuals**: Carol A. MacLennan, *Sovereign Sugar: Industry and Environment in Hawai'i* (Honolulu: University of Hawai'i Press, 2014), 22, 26.

44    **"Today in some places"**: Kamakau, *Ruling Chiefs of Hawaii*, 235.

45    **Hawaiians started . . . raised and sold**: Catherine G. Ulep, "Women's Exchanges: The Sex Trade and Cloth in Early Nineteenth Century Hawai'i," MA diss., University of Hawai'i at Mānoa, 38, 40, https://scholarspace.manoa.hawaii.edu/items/5cee0716-e2f2 -4cb0-a56a-54003405b68b.

45    **Small farms of sugarcane**: Noa Kekuewa Lincoln, notes on author's manuscript, June 16, 2020; "History of Labor in Hawai'i," Center for Labor Education & Research, University of Hawai'i West O'ahu, https://www.hawaii.edu/uhwo/clear/home/ HawaiiLaborHistory.html.

45    **Port towns like Honolulu**: Ulep, "Women's Exchanges," 38.

45    **Hawaii also began to export . . . and Chamberlains**: Sarah Vowell, *Unfamiliar Fishes* (New York: Riverhead, 2011), 33, 40, 50, 60.

45    **The first sugar mill . . . in the black**: MacLennan, *Sovereign Sugar*, 85, 86.

46    **Laborers harvested cane**: "Sugarcane Machete," National Museum of American History, https://www.si.edu/object/nmah_1289290.

46    **Fresh-cut cane was carried**: MacLennan, *Sovereign Sugar*, 39, 133.

46    **Cane was fed into the side**: Mintz, *Sweetness and Power*, 27.

46    **The juice flowed out . . . dripped into the container below**: "Cane Grinder," "18th Century Style Sugar House," "La Grande," "La Batterie," display texts, and "Sugarcane," historical illustration, Baton Rouge, LA.

46    **two hundred Chinese laborers . . . catch their own food**: MacLennan, *Sovereign Sugar*, 133–34, 136–37.

47    **The introduction of Pacific Northwest salmon**: Kathy YL Chan, "Lomi Lomi Salmon," *Onolicious Hawai'i*, September 26, 2019.

47    **But with the North's supply**: MacLennan, *Sovereign Sugar*, 24.

47    **In 1860, there were**: Carol Wilcox, *Sugar Water: Hawaii's Plantain Ditches* (Honolulu: University of Hawai'i Press, 1997), 5.

47    **Trains hauled the cut cane . . . Alexander & Baldwin**: MacLennan, *Sovereign Sugar*, 37, 39, 72.

48    **In 1840, Kamehameha's son**: "Kamehameha," Wikipedia, https://en.wikipedia.org/ wiki/Kamehameha II. Accessed October 30, 2022.

48    **Great Mahele . . . 90 percent of Hawaii's land**: Vowell, *Unfamiliar Fishes*, 155–58.

49    **'Iolani Palace**: Charles Fowler, "Iolani Palace," *Atlas Obscura,* https://www.atlasobscura .com/places/iolani-palace; Charles E. Peterson, "The Iolani Palaces and the Barracks," *Journal of the Society of Architectural Historians* 22 (1963): 91–103; "A Place for Royalty," Iolani Palace, https://www.iolanipalace.org/history/a-place-for-royalty; Allison Marsh, "Why Hawaii Got Electricity Before Most of the Rest of the World," *IEEE Spectrum*, August 8, 2018.

49    **The table in the dining room**: Friends of 'Iolani Palace, "The State Dining Room in 'Iolani Palace," (Honolulu, 1982).

49    **A dinner in this room**: Iolani Palace dinner menu, February 14, 1883, Hawaiian State Archives.

50    **Money flooded into**: Peterson, "The Iolani Palaces and the Barracks," 91–103.

50    **The queen's birth name . . . volcano in Honolulu**: Liliuokalani, *Hawaii's Story by Hawaii's Queen* (Honolulu: University of Hawai'i Press, 2013), 3.

50    **At four years old**: Linda K. Merton, "A Christian and 'Civilized' Education: The Hawai-

ian Chiefs' Children's School, 1839–50," *History of Education Quarterly* 32 (Summer 1992): 213–42.

51   **King Kalākaua revived**: Meghan B. Kelly, "King David Kalākaua: The Original Most Interesting Man In The World," *wbur*, August 10, 2018.

51   **grandparents' worldview . . . not interested in acquiring the Islands**: MacLennan, *Sovereign Sugar*, 31, 73.

51   **ninety sugar plantations**: Wilcox, *Sugar Water*, 5.

51   **The Islands produced**: MacLennan, *Sovereign Sugar*, 124.

51   **It takes 500 gallons**: Wilcox, *Sugar Water*, 1.

52   **Native Hawaiians dug . . . massive reservoirs**: MacLennan, *Sovereign Sugar*, 48–49, 148–49.

52   **Lydia became**: "Liliuokalani," *History*, April 23, 2019.

52   **tender moment inspired her verses**: Jane Recker, "How the Music of Hawai'i's Last Ruler Guided the Island's People through Crisis," *Smithsonian Magazine*, March 26, 2019.

52   **The Royal Hawaiian Band**: Iolani Palace, "The Rise of Aloha Oe," Facebook, September 5, 2019, https://www.facebook.com/iolanipalace/posts/-the-rise-of-aloha-oe-onthisday-in-1883-the-royalhawaiianband-returned-from-a-tr/10162093700635234/. Accessed October 30, 2022.

52   **It was also played**: Vowell, *Unfamiliar Fishes*, 217.

52   **Lydia would write over two hundred**: Recker, "How the Music of Hawai'i's Last Ruler"; "Hawai'i Pono'ī," Wikipedia, https://en.wikipedia.org/wiki/Hawai%CA%BBi_Pono%CA%BB%C4%AB. Accessed October 30, 2022.

52   **"Having matured their plans"**: Liliuokalani, *Hawaii's Story by Hawaii's Queen*, 212.

52   **Bayonet Constitution**: MacLennan, *Sovereign Sugar*, 74; Vowell, *Unfamiliar Fishes*, 201.

53   **After Lydia received news**: Liliuokalani, *Hawaii's Story by Hawaii's Queen*, 207.

53   **By 1890, the king's health**: "Kalākaula," Wikipedia, https://en.wikipedia.org/wiki/Kal%C4%81kaua#Death_and_succession. Accessed October 30, 2022.

53   **"I was compelled . . . support the new government**: Vowell, *Unfamiliar Fishes*, 205–07, 244.

54   **Queen Lili'uokalani was arrested**: Liliuokalani, *Hawaii's Story by Hawaii's Queen*, 308, 311, 322, 345.

55   **President William McKinley**: Vowell, *Unfamiliar Fishes*, 221.

55   **"in island collections"**: Liliuokalani, *Hawaii's Story by Hawaii's Queen*, xii, xxxv.

56   **Now these workers . . . total population by 1930**: MacLennan, *Sovereign Sugar*, 171–72, 191.

56   **Blas Eugenio**: Chris Planas, "Interview with Blas Eugenio," 471, 478, 481, 483, https://scholarspace.manoa.hawaii.edu/items/00f83502-119e-4925-bac0-c84a7ddcf45b.

57   **Cutting and carrying cane**: Warren Nishimoto, "Tape Nos. 26-1-1-96 and 26-2-1-96 ORAL HISTORY INTERVIEW with Stanley C. Mendes (SM)," July 16, 1996, 279, https://scholarspace.manoa.hawaii.edu/handle/10125/30264.

57   **25 cents per day**: MacLennan, *Sovereign Sugar*, 133.

57   **There were twenty workers' strikes**: MacLennan, *Sovereign Sugar*, 174, 177.

57   **However, $22 was less**: Philip H. Douglas, "Wages and Hours of Labor in 1919," *Journal of Political Economy* 29 (January 1921), 78–80.

57   **Barrack housing also gave way . . . at 236,000**: MacLennan, *Sovereign Sugar* 190, 198, 45, 158, 32.

58   **They started by crossing**: Lincoln, notes on author's manuscript; Susan Schenck, interview by author, May 9, 2019; Lincoln, "Sugarcane Varieties."

58   **In the 1950s, cane hybrid**: Bob Gunter, interview by author, May 6, 2019; Lincoln, "Sugarcane Varieties."

58   **Sugar production doubled between**: MacLennan, *Sovereign Sugar*, 31–32.

58   **Hawaii could not compete**: Gunter, interview by author; Darren Hudson, "An Examination of Foreign Subsidies and Trade Policies for Sugar," International Center for Agricultural Competitiveness at Texas Tech University, May 2019, 5, https://sugaralliance

.org/wp-content/uploads/2019/07/Texas-Tech-foreign-sugar-subsidies-7-19-FINAL.pdf
. Accessed October 30, 2022.

59    **Cynthia Juan**: Holly Yamada, "Interview with Cynthia Juan," March 6, 1997, 181, 194, 195, 198, https://scholarspace.manoa.hawaii.edu/handle/10125/30257.

59    **HC&S**: Gunter, interview by author.

59    **ratoon cane**: Mintz, *Sweetness and Power,* 21.

60    **landmark water rights negotiation**: Mahealani Richardson, "Maui Water Rights Deal Praised as Step Toward Resolving Years-long Dispute," *Hawaii News Now*, November 19, 2019.

60    **Castle & Cook . . . $2.2 billion**: MacLennan, *Sovereign Sugar*, 278; L. Magin, "Castle & Cooke owner David Murdock plans to be hands-on with Koa Ridge," *Pacific Business News*, November 2, 2017.

60    **Currently there are thirteen distilleries**: Cat Wolinski, "The Differences between Soju, Shochu, and Sake, Explained," *VinePair*, August 29, 2018; "Hawaii—The Aloha State," Distillery Trail, https://www.distillerytrail.com/directory-distillery/locations/hawaii/, accessed June 30, 2020.

60    **The white or dark rum**: Wayne Curtis, "Are We Witnessing the Birth of American Agricole?" *Liquor.com*, November 16, 2017.

60    **It takes four tons . . . the cane was harvested**: Robert Dawson, interview by author, May 9, 2019.

62    **a market for farmers practicing diversified agriculture**: Lincoln, interview by author.

63    **kupuna kō should never be commercialized**: Robinson, interview by author.

## 3. *DIBÉ*: NAVAJO-CHURRO SHEEP

69    **Then, Talking God blew**: *A Gift from Talking God*, documentary by Peter Blystone, 2009.

70    **That's their wildness**: Aretta Begay, interview by author, September 27, 2019.

70    **"the pride, food, clothing"**: Broderick H. Johnson and Ruth Roessel, eds., *Navajo Livestock Reduction: A National Disgrace* (Tsaile, AZ: Diné College Press, 1974), 123.

71    **The sheep graze on plants**: Begay, interview by author.

71    **According to the Livestock Conservancy**: Jeannette Beranger, interview by author, November 24, 2020.

71    **The Navajo-Churro Sheep Presidium**: Begay, interview by author; "Lamb Presidium," The Navajo Lifeway, https://navajolifeway.org/lamb-presidium/. Accessed October 30, 2022.

72    **The Diné are Athabaskans**: Mark A. Scioli and Gary Holton, "Linguistic Phylogenies Support Back-Migration from Beringia to Asia," PLOS ONE, March 12, 2014.

72    **The Diné creation story**: Peter Iverson, *Diné: A History of the Navajos* (Albuquerque: University of New Mexico Press, 2002), 8, 11.

73    **The sheep described**: Blystone, *A Gift from Talking God*; Zefren Anderson, interview by author, September 21, 2019.

74    **Navajo-Churro have an inner coat**: "Wool and Weaving," Navajo Sheep Project, https://www.navajosheepproject.org/wool-and-weaving. Accessed November 30, 2020.

74    **The low lanolin content**: Marsha Weisiger, *Dreaming of Sheep in Navajo Country* (Seattle: University of Washington Press, 2011), 193–94.

74    **a dozen different natural colors**: Begay, interview by author.

74    **"handspun undyed"**: "Diné/Navajo artist, First-Phase Chief's Blanket, Handspun undyed and indigo-dyed Churro fleece and raveled lac-dyed bayeta, c. 1840," museum text, Art of Native America, Metropolitan Museum of Art, New York.

74    **Spanish Churra sheep**: "Morphological Qualification Manual," http://www.anche.org/pdf/manual-calificacion-morfologica.pdf, accessed November 30, 2020; "Navajo Churro Sheep," Livestock Conservancy, https://livestockconservancy.org/index.php/heritage/internal/navajo-churro. Accessed November 30, 2020.

74    **"vast amounts of livestock," "illegally," "legally"**: Anderson, interview by author.

75    **Franciscans wore a gray or brown habit**: "Franciscan Fabric of Faith: Rediscovering Sayal Wool, Part II," https://floridafriar.weebly.com/historical-habits/franciscan-fabric-of -faith-rediscovering-sayal-wool-part-ii.

75    **Awatovi**: "Awatovi Ruins: Arizona," National Park Service, https://www.nps.gov/nr/ travel/American_Latino_Heritage/Awatovi_Ruins.html.

75    **Some Navajo traded with**: "Awatovi Ruins: Arizona," 24; Anderson, interview by author.

75    **Only the toughest lambs**: Weisiger, *Dreaming of Sheep in Navajo Country*, 193.

75    **The Diné also bred for wool color**: Begay, interview by author.

75    **There are only five other breeds**: "Polycerate," https://en.wikipedia.org/wiki/ Polycerate. Accessed December 1, 2020.

75    **By the early eighteenth century**: Weisiger, *Dreaming of Sheep in Navajo Country*, 116.

75    **The weavings were utilitarian**: Iverson, *Diné*, 33; Anderson, interview by author.

76    **By the early nineteenth century**: Iverson, *Diné*, 33.

76    **They took the sheep**: Richard White, *The Roots of Dependency: Subsistence, Environment and Social Change Among the Choctaws, Pawnees and Navajos* (Lincoln: University of Nebraska Press, 1988), 224.

76    **Because they owned the livestock . . . winter forage for the sheep**: Weisiger, *Dreaming of Sheep in Navajo Country*, 81, 84–85, 124, 224.

76    **The Diné call it**: "Shiprock-Tse Bit A'i," https://fourcornersgeotourism.com/entries/ shiprock-tse-bit-ai/c6d040a9-c4ff-45a5-a7d8-5c2befa88573. Accessed December 1, 2020.

77    **176,600 Diné**: "Navajo Nation Profile," https://navajoprofile.wind.enavajo.org/. Accessed October 19, 2022.

77    **largest Indigenous tribe**: Simon Romero, "Navajo Nation Becomes Largest Tribe in U.S. After Pandemic Enrollment Surge," *New York Times*, May 21, 2021.

77    **On their sovereign land**: Jennifer Nez Denetdale, "Naal Tsoos Saní (The Old Paper): The Navajo Treaty of 1868, Nation Building and Self-Determination," *American Indian* 19, no. 2 (Summer 2018).

77    **maintain their cultural beliefs**: Denisa Livingston, interview by author, July 31, 2020.

77    **Diné is the third**: "This Map Shows the Most Commonly Spoken Language in Every US State, Excluding English and Spanish," *Business Insider*, https://www.businessinsider.com/what -is-the-most-common-language-in-every-state-map-2019-6. Accessed December 1, 2020.

81    **Miss Navajo Nation**: "Miss Navajo: A Documentary by Billy Luther," https://www.pbs .org/independentlens/missnavajo/aboutpageant.html.

81    **Unlike a cow's brisket**: Ron Garnanez, interview by author, June 14, 2020.

85    **Manuelito**: Denetdale, *Reclaiming Diné History: The Legacy of Navaho Chief Manuelito and Juanita*, (Tuscon: University of Arizona Press, 2007), Kindle locations 1123, 1135, 1142.

85    **His son, Naaltsoos Neiyéhí**: "Interview with Bob Manuelito," Native Oral History, https://www.nativeoralhistory.org/digital-heritage/interview-bob-manuelito. Accessed December 1, 2020.

85    **"Manuelito was born"**: Denetdale, *Reclaiming Diné History,* Kindle location 57.

85    **Juanita**: Denetdale, *Reclaiming Diné History*, Kindle locations 1145, 1558, 2371, 2393, 2404.

86    **Fort Defiance**: Iverson, *Diné*, 41.

86    **Conflicts arose . . . "contented people"**: Denetdale, *Reclaiming Diné History*, Kindle locations 1299, 1303, 1316, 1348, 1356, 1358, 1364, 1372.

87    **He gained renown**: Iverson, *Diné*, 51.

87    **"Go to the Bosque Redondo"**: Denetdale, *Reclaiming Diné History*, Kindle locations 1371, 1379.

87    **His troops destroyed**: White, *The Roots of Dependency*, 214.

87    **He made pacts**: Iverson, *Diné*, 51.

87    **Women and children were enslaved**: Denetdale, *Reclaiming Diné History*, Kindle location 1379.

87    **Carson waited for starvation**: White, *The Roots of Dependency*, 214.

87    **"My mother gave birth"**: Patti Chee et al., *Oral History Stories of the Long Walk = Hwéeldi Baa Hané by the Diné of the Eastern Region of the Navajo Reservation; Stories Collected and Recorded by the Title VII Bilingual Staff* (Crownpoint, NM: Lake Valley Navajo School, 1991), 17.

88    **By the end of 1863**: Denetdale, *Reclaiming Diné History*, Kindle location 1386.

88    **"Some of the old people"**: Iverson, *Diné*, 35, 52, 55.

88    **His resistance became . . . remaining on the run**: Denetdale, *Reclaiming Diné History*, Kindle locations 1425, 1430, 1701, 1709.

89    **A military outpost**: Iverson, *Diné*, 52, 57, 59.

89    **The Diné dug . . . cook their food**: Denetdale, *Reclaiming Diné History*, Kindle locations 1462, 1464.

89    **With much of the locally**: Kathy M'Closkey, *Swept under the Rug: A Hidden History of Navajo Weaving* (Albuquerque: University of New Mexico Press, 2008), 29.

89    **The government-provided rations**: Weisiger, *Dreaming of Sheep in Navajo Country*, 22; Iverson, *Diné*, 59.

89    **"bits of stale broken bread"**: Chee, *Oral History Stories of the Long Walk*, 13.

90    **calico or sateen skirts**: Weisiger, *Dreaming of Sheep in Navajo Country*, 67.

90    **They began to weave**: M'Closkey, *Swept under the Rug*, 29.

90    **"I usually chopped wood"**: Chee, *Oral Histories of the Long Walk*, 81.

90    **The Bosque Redondo prison camp**: Denetdale, *Reclaiming Diné History*, Kindle locations 1466–67.

90    **Civil War hero General William Tecumseh Sherman**: Denetdale, "Naal Tsoos Saní (The Old Paper)"; Iverson, *Diné*, 63.

90    **"I hope to God"**: Denetdale, *Reclaiming Diné History*, Kindle location 1478.

90    **On June 1, 1868**: Denetdale, "Naal Tsoos Saní (The Old Paper)."

90    **It is rare**: Iverson, *Diné*, 37.

90    **Treaty Day . . . nation**: Denetdale, "Naal Tsoos Saní (The Old Paper)."

91    **By the end of the month**: Denetdale, *Reclaiming Diné History*, 76.

91    **"The days and nights"**: Denetdale, "Naal Tsoos Saní (The Old Paper)."

91    **"When men and women talk"**: Chee, *Oral Histories of the Long Walk*, 99.

91    **When the Diné returned . . . survivial of the Diné in Anglo America**: Denetdale, *Reclaiming Diné History*, Kindle locations 1057, 1542, 1546, 1811, 1882, 1935, 2513.

92    **But Manuelito's words . . . an Anglo suit**: Iverson, *Diné*, 83, 91.

92    **To set a good example . . . never woke up**: Denetdale, *Reclaiming Diné History*, Kindle locations,1056, 1611–1612, 1631, 1716, 2100, 2624.

95    **After Bosque Redondo . . . Navajo-Churro sheep**: White, *The Roots of Dependency*, 215, 217, 219.

95    **The presence of water**: Denetdale, *Reclaiming Diné History*, 335.

95    **While some ranchers allowed**: Weiseger, *Dreaming of Sheep in Navajo Country*, 145.

96    **But the growing human population . . . maintain their traditions**: White, *The Roots of Dependency*, 227–29, 232, 234, 252–55, 272.

97    **Bosque Redondo was still alive . . . three dollars or more**: Weisiger, *Dreaming of Sheep in Navajo Country*, 164, 166.

97    **only old, unproductive animals**: White, *The Roots of Dependency*, 261.

97    **In total, 86,500 sheep**: Weisiger, *Dreaming of Sheep in Navajo Country*, 25, 167.

97    **It called for the removal**: White, *The Roots of Dependency*, 263.

97    **The BIA . . . flour at the trading post**: Weisiger, *Dreaming of Sheep in Navajo Country*, 168, 178.

97    **Goats provided milk . . . without asking**: White, *The Roots of Dependency*, 21, 263, 264.

97    **Many shepherds fled**: Johnson and Roessel, *Navajo Livestock Reduction*, 32.

97    **The intention was to send . . . on the brink of starvation**: Weisiger, *Dreaming of Sheep in Navajo Country*, 25, 46–47, 167, 174–77, 266, 300.

98    **To offset the poverty**: White, *The Roots of Dependency*, 259.

98    **Women and the elderly . . . source of income than sheep**: Weisiger, *Dreaming of Sheep in Navajo Country*, 21, 29, 32, 165, 206, 226, 259, 289.

99    **"I think that the drastic"**: Johnson and Roessel, *Navajo Livestock Reduction*, 69.

99    **The shepherds were systematically**: Lisa Fogarty, "After WWII, Mutton Fell Out Of Favor In The U.S. Can It Make A Comeback?" *The Salt*, NPR, November 26, 2019.

99    **The Navajo Sheep Project**: "News and Chronology," Navajo Sheep Project, https://www.navajosheepproject.org/news. Accessed December 1, 2020.

100   **When the wool has been hand-processed**: Blystone, *A Gift from Talking God*.

102   **John Sharpe**: John Sharpe, interview by author, June 18, 2019.

## 4. *SXWO'LE*: STRAITS SALISH REEFNET FISHING

105   **reefnet fishing . . . to market**: Nicolas Xemtoltw Claxton, "To Fish as Formerly: A Resurgent Journey Back to the Saanich Reef Net Fishery," PhD diss. (University of Victoria, 2015), 146, 172, https://dspace.library.uvic.ca/handle/1828/6614.

107   **"Reefnetting was the culture"**: "How Do You Tackle One of the Most Complex Food-Sourcing Challenges in the World?" Patagonia Provisions, https://www.patagoniaprovisions.com/pages/sourcing-salmon. Accessed April 10, 2021.

107   **Riley graduated from**: Riley Starks, interview by author, August 20, 2019; "Salish Center for Sustainable Fishing Methods," Salish Center for Sustainable Fishing Methods, https://salishcenter.org/. Accessed April 10, 2021.

108   **The Fraser is the longest**: Langdon Cook, *Upstream: Searching for Wild Salmon, from River to Table* (New York: Ballantine, 2017), 153.

108   **the same basic structure**: Cook, *Upstream*, 159.

109   **"Sometimes they're clear as day"**: Chris Malloy, "Unbroken Ground," video, Patagonia Provisions, 2016, https://www.patagoniaprovisions.com/blogs/films/unbroken-ground-film.

109   **the live well**: Cook, *Upstream*, 147, 164; "How Do You Tackle?"

109   **No other commercial fishing process . . . very little fossil fuel**: Claxton, "To Fish as Formerly," 217.

110   **While other species of salmon**: Cook, *Upstream*, 152.

110   **pink salmon**: "How Do You Tackle?"

110   **This year, Patagonia contracted**: Starks, interview by author, August 20, 2019.

110   **The crew is paid**: Natalie Lord, interview by author, August 20, 2019.

111   **The reef is a web of rope**: Cook, *Upstream*, 159.

112   **Salmon schooling in the sound . . . in the net**: Janet Poth, ed., *Saltwater People as Told by Dave Elliott Sr.: A Resource Book for the Saanich Native Studies Program* (British Columbia: School District 63 [Saanich], 1983), 58–59.

113   **The five modern species**: "Meet the 7 Species of Pacific Salmon," South Puget Sound Salmon Enhancement Group, https://spsseg.org/meet-the-7-species-of-pacific-salmon/. Accessed April 10, 2021.

113   **Salmon are anadromous**: Cook, *Upstream*, 11.

113   **Two-year-old pinks run**: "Life Cycle of Salmon," US Fish and Wildlife Service, https://www.fws.gov/refuge/togiak/wildlife_and_habitat/fish/salmon_lifecycle.html.

113   **Chinook. . . the West Coast's forests**: Cook, *Upstream*, 39, 20, 11.

113   **Fat salmon, caught just before they**: Paul Greenberg, *Four Fish: The Future of the Last Wild Food*. (London: Penguin, 2011), 17.

114   **For the Native people of . . . to their homeland**: Claxton, "To Fish as Formerly," 139.

114   **The Saanich are one of**: "Reefnets: A Northwest Original," Saltwater People Historical Society, February 1, 2014, https://saltwaterpeoplehistoricalsociety.blogspot.com/2014/02/reef-nets-northwest-original.html. Accessed April 10, 2021.

114   **All of these tribes belong**: Daniel L. Boxberger, *To Fish in Common: The Ethnohistory of Lummi Island Salmon Fishing* (Seattle: University of Washington Press, 2000), 12.

114   **Archeological evidence shows that the Straits Salish**: "The Bison at Ayer Pond on

Orcas Island Is Archaeological," *Northwest Coast Archaeology*, April 24, 2010; "The History of Samish Indian Nation," Samish Indian Nation, https://www.samishtribe.nsn.us/who-we-are/timeline. Accessed April 10, 2021.

114 **In the belief system of**: Claxton, "To Fish as Formerly," 24.

114 **There are about 57,000**: https://en.wikipedia.org/wiki/Coast_Salish. Accessed April 10, 2021.

114 **Historically, Straits Salish homesites**: Wayne Suttles, "Affinal Ties, Subsistence, and Prestige Among the Coast Salish," *American Anthropologist* 62 (April 1960): 296–305.

114 **But fishing was the primary**: Boxberger, *To Fish in Common*, 13.

114 **The Straits Salish, and other**: Gloria Snively and Wanosts'a7 Lorna Williams, eds., *Knowing Home: Braiding Indigenous Science with Western Science, Book 1* (Victoria, BC: University of Victoria Press, 2016), chapter 7.

115 **Reefnet fishing, *swxol'e***: Nicolas Claxton, "The Douglas Treaty and WSÁNEC traditional fisheries: A model for Saanich Peoples Governance," MA diss. (University of Victoria, 2003), 24, http://citeseerx.ist.psu.edu/viewdoc/download?doi=10.1.1.531.3534&rep=rep1&type=pdf.

115 **They didn't have as much access**: Poth, *Saltwater People,* 56.

115 **The Sannich believed the reefnet**: Claxton, "To Fish as Formerly," 151.

115 **The sxwo'le was the most important**: Boxberger, *To Fish in Common*, 13; Snively and Williams, *Knowing Home*, chapter 7.

115 **The sites for reefnetting, or *swálet***: Poth, *Saltwater People*, 56.

115 **A family "belonged" to the location**: Boxberger, *To Fish in Common*, 13.

115 **Usually the male head of household**: Claxton, "To Fish as Formerly," x.

115 **A crew of family housemates**: Boxberger, *To Fish in Common*, 14.

115 **There were at least thirty**: Boxberger, *To Fish in Common*, 14–15; Claxton, "To Fish as Formerly," 167.

115 **The traditional reefnet gears**: Snively and Williams, *Knowing Home*, chapter 7.

115 **"In the tide-ways"**: Theodore Winthrop, *The Canoe and the Saddle: or, Klalam and Klickatat* (Tacoma: John H. Williams, 1913), 27.

116 **Dr. Nick Xemɫoltw Claxton . . . traditional materials and methods**: Claxton, "To Fish as Formerly," i, 23, ix, 141, 172, 91, 142.

116 **The word *sxwo'le* comes**: Smith, *Indigenous and Decolonizing Studies in Education*, 220.

116 **Traditionally, families worked on**: Boxberger, *To Fish in Common*, 14.

116 **The fishing canoes**: Poth, *Saltwater People*, 59.

116 **carved from hollowed . . . two-ply cord**: Jacquelyn Martin, "Northwest Coast Canoes," Simon Frasier University, 2008, https://www.sfu.ca/brc/art_architecture/canoes.html#materials.

117 **The fake reef was anchored**: Snively and Williams, *Knowing Home*, chapter 7.

117 **The ropes across the bottom**: Poth, *Saltwater People*, 58.

117 **Just three days later . . . stiff willow branches**: Claxton, "To Fish as Formerly," 142, 182–83, xii.

118 **"This is more than just"**: Claxton, "The Douglas Treaty," 26.

118 **Claxton chose a site called Sxixte**: Claxton, "To Fish as Formerly," 168, 170.

118 **Claxton and his team took**: Suzanne Ahearne, "Reclaiming a Banned Saanich Fishery," University of Victoria, January 21, 2016, https://www.uvic.ca/news/topics/2016+reclaiming-the-reef-net-fishery+ring.

118 **"pod of orcas . . . help us"**: Claxton, "To Fish as Formerly," 194.

119 **"It was really amazing"**: Claxton, "To Fish as Formerly," 190–91.

119 **Historically, a reefnet gear . . . upstream end**: Kevin Bailey, "A Look at Sockeye Salmon, Native American Nets, and a Modern Fishery," *Grist*, December 23, 2015.

119 **and then hauled on board**: Poth, *Saltwater People*, 59.

119 **A "klootchman"**: Boxberger, *To Fish in Common*, 16.

119   **Summer villages were set up:** "Reefnets: A Northwest Original."

119   **Claxton's spotter . . . "by living it":** Claxton, "To Fish as Formerly," 192–93.

119   **not just for the family . . . "respected accordingly":** Claxton, "The Douglas Treaty," 27, 23.

120   **Then, its skeleton was returned:** "First-Salmon Ceremony," Northwest Power and Conservation Council, https://www.nwcouncil.org/reports/columbia-river-history/firstsalmonceremony.

120   **The festival lasted:** Snively and Williams, *Knowing Home*, chapter 7.

120   **Allowing the salmon to spawn:** Claxton, "The Douglas Treaty," 28.

120   **Until the late 1800s . . . never happened:** Boxberger, *To Fish in Common*, 15–16.

120   **adapted from a recipe:** Rayna Green, "Native Foodways: Roast Salmon on Sticks," Smithsonian Folklife Festival, 1991, https://festival.si.edu/blog/2016/native-foodways -roast-salmon-on-sticks.

121   **"silky smooth texture":** Cook, *Upstream*, 32.

121   **when it feels dry, the salmon is cooked:** "How to Cook Salmon in the Traditional Northwest Indian Way," Survival Common Sense, video, https://www.youtube.com/watch?v=muKtdzoD1U0.

122   **food of last resort":** Boxberger, *To Fish in Common*, 21, 18, viii, 31, 35.

122   **Tempted by the US government's promise:** "Oregon Territorial History," Oregon Secretary of State, https://sos.oregon.gov/archives/exhibits/echoes/Pages/history .aspx#:~:text=When%20he%20discovered%20the%20Hudson's,and%20John%20 McLoughlin%20were%20shareholders; Boxberger, *To Fish in Common*, 24.

122   **Several treaties in the 1850s:** Claxton, "To Fish as Formerly," 207.

122   **The Treaty of Point Elliott:** "Treaty of Point Elliott," Duwamish Tribe, https:// www.duwamishtribe.org/treaty-of-point-elliott#:~:text=The%201855%20Treaty%20 created%20a,represented%20by%20the%20Native%20signers; "Treaty of Point Elliott, 1855," Governor's Office of Indian Affairs, https://goia.wa.gov/tribal-government/treaty -point-elliott-1855.

122   **A white "resident farmer" . . . late 1870s:** Boxberger, *To Fish in Common*, 30–31, 36.

123   **and by 1883:** Cook, *Upstream*, 46.

123   **That same year, the Northern Pacific:** Workman, *We Are Puget Sound*, 116.

123   **But the length of the salmon . . . through the mid-twentieth century:** Patrick W. O'Bannon, "Waves of Change: Mechanization in the Pacific Coast Canned-Salmon Indus- try, 1864–1914," *Technology and Culture* 28, no. 3 (July 1987): 558–77.

123   **It was up to the consumer:** Diane Cooper, "How to Eat Canned Salmon," *San Francisco Maritime*, https://www.nps.gov/safr/learn/historyculture/how-to-eat-canned -salmon.htm.

123   **Although Native people were hired . . . Nooksack River on their reservation:** Boxberger, *To Fish in Common*, 40–60.

125   **The Canadian government banned:** Travis Patterson, "Saanich Nation Marks Return to Reef Net Fishing," *Saanich News*, August 11, 2015, https://www.saanichnews.com/ news/saanich-nation-marks-return-to-reef-net-fishing/.

125   **"For a third of a century":** Cook, *Upstream*, 47.

125   **By treaty law, Native peoples . . . were available:** Boxberger, *To Fish in Common*, 55, 90, 92, 103, 106.

126   **"battering themselves to exhaustion":** Aaron Hutchins, "The B.C. River Where Salmon Are Whisked to Safety in a Giant Pressurized Tube," *MacLean's*, July 13, 2020.

126   **Over 89 percent:** "'Almost Complete Loss' of Early Salmon Runs at Fraser River Slide Last Year: DFO," *City News* (Toronto), June 9, 2020.

126   **The Canadian government was working:** Hutchins, "The B.C. River."

126   **But once again, fishing for pinks:** Cook, *Upstream*, 270, 29.

129   **wash out all the blood:** Cook, *Upstream*, 29.

129 **This method is considered . . . sold to Patagonia**: Natalie Lord, interview by author, August 20, 2019.

130 **Riley's gear alone**: Riley Starks, email to author, April 13, 2021; Riley Starks, interview by author, September 22, 2019.

132 **In 1962, the Lummis**: Boxberger, *To Fish in Common*, 152.

132 **"all usual and accustomed"**: Cook, *Upstream*, 62.

132 **"Members of the Lummi Tribe"**: "Lummi Nation Holds Reef Net Fishery at Cherry Point," Northwest Treaty Tribes, September 17, 2013, https://nwtreatytribes.org/lummi-nation-holds-reef-net-fishery-cherry-point/.

132 **From now on, half of all fish**: Cook, *Upstream*, 67.

132 **The anger created by economic uncertainty**: Boxberger, *To Fish in Common*, 154–56.

133 **White fishers would vandalize**: Cook, *Upstream*, 57.

133 **Despite the harassment they faced . . . certain species of fish**: Boxberger, *To Fish in Common*, 167, 171.

133 **At the time of the Boldt decision**: "Lummi Nation Holds Reef Net Fishery at Cherry Point."

133 **Finally, in 2012, the Lummi Nation**: Ralph Schwartz, "Lummi Tribe Members say Fishing Is in Their DNA," *Columbian,* November 23, 2015.

133 **Cherry Point, *Xwe'chi'eXen***: "Lummi Nation Holds Reef Net Fishery at Cherry Point."

133 **"To us, culture is fish"**: Lummi Tribe Members say Fishing Is in Their DNA."

133 **Larry Chexanexwh Kinley**: "Huxley Speaker Series—Larry and Ellie Kinley, 2017-10-05," video, https://www.youtube.com/watch?v=Ro9vQ0gR2bk; Renai Ditmer, "In Memoriam: Larry Kinley—The Man, Not the Legend," *Native Business*, September 16, 2019; "Former Lummi Nation Chairman Larry Kinley Passes On at Age of 71," *Indian Z,* Febraury 21, 2018.

134 **Profitable or no, Kinley knew**: Tim Johnson, "Spirit of Sxwo'le: A Tribal Warrior Remembered," *Cascadia Weekly*, February 21, 2018.

134 **"spent a lot of time"**: Ditmer, "In Memoriam: Larry Kinley."

134 **As of 2015, there were still**: Kevin Bailey, "A Look at Sockeye Salmon, Native American Nets, and a Modern Fishery," *Grist*, December 23, 2015.

134 **"There's minimal handling"**: "Lummi Nation Holds Onto Tradition by Moving into the Future," Northwest Treaty Tribes, https://nwtreatytribes.org/lummi-nation-holds-onto-tradition-moving-future/.

134 **"There's a real active side"**: "Huxley Speaker Series—Larry and Ellie Kinley."

135 **Working with Lummi Island Wild**: Johnson, "Spirit of Sxwo'le"; "Lummi Nation Holds Onto Tradition."

135 **"There's a lot of times we don't"**: "Huxley Speaker Series—Larry and Ellie Kinley."

135 **It was the first Indigenous-owned**: Kyle Kinley and Lucas Kinley, interview by author, August 25, 2019.

## 5. *MANOOMIN*: ANISHINAABE WILD RICE

139 **It's not *Oryza sativa***: "Manomin Research Project," *NiCHE*, https://niche-canada.org/?s=manomin.

140 **Manoomin is the Ojibwe word . . . Ricing Moon**: Barbara J. Barton, *Manoomin: The Story of Wild Rice in Michigan* (East Lansing: Michigan State University Press, 2018), xix, 32; "The Ojibwe People's Dictionary," https://ojibwe.lib.umn.edu/main-entry/Manoominike-giizis-na.

140 **Tribes of the Anishinaabeg. . . per person per year**: "2018 Tribal Wild Rice Task Force Report," Minnesota Chippewa Tribe, https://mnchippewatribe.org/pdf/TWRTF.Report.2018.pdf.

140 **It is the most commonly . . . funeral ceremonies**: "The Effects of Wild Rice Water Quality Rule Changes on Tribal Health," Fond du Lac Band of Lake Superior

Chippewa Health Impact Assessment, 33, 16, http://www.fdlrez.com/rm/downloads/WQSHIA.pdf.

140 **A Presidium for Anishinaabe Manoomin**: Melissa Nelson, "Slow Food Turtle Island Association Takes Root: First Anniversary of a Promising Native American Association," Slow Food, March 31, 2017, https://www.slowfood.com/slow-food-turtle-island-association-takes-root-first-anniversary-promising-native-amercian-association/.

140 **LaDuke continues to coordinate**: "Anishinaabeg Manoomin," Slow Food Foundation for Biodiversity, https://www.fondazioneslowfood.com/en/slow-food-presidia/anishinaabeg-Manoomin/.

140 **"148 indigenous food communities"**: Megan Larmer, "Tasting Tradition for the Future We Want," Slow Food USA, June 30, 2016, https://slowfoodusa.org/tasting-tradition-for-the-future-we-want/.

141 **The range of *Zizania palustris***: Daniel Cusick, "Climate Change Threatens the Ancient Wild Rice Traditions of the Ojibwe," *Scientific American*, June 1, 2020.

141 **Additionally, waterfront industrialization**: Chris Malina, "New Research Aims to Bring Together Tribes, UW on Wild Rice Protection and Restoration," Wisconsin Public Radio, August 2, 2019, https://www.wpr.org/listen/1491461.

141 **Manoomin doesn't only feed humans . . . algae blooms**: Barton, "Manoomin," 13.

141 **One study of wild rice genetics**: Peter David, Lisa David, et al., "Manoomin" (1854 Treaty Authority, December 2019), 15, https://www.1854treatyauthority.org/images/ManoominChapter.Appendices.2019.final.pdf.

141 **"They taste like a lake"**: Margaret Lehman, "Cooking with Manomin: Comparing Regional Differences in Expression," *NiCHE*, June 26, 2020, https://niche-canada.org/2020/06/26/cooking-with-manomin-comparing-regional-differences-in-expression/.

141 **Currently, there are four plants**: David, "Manoomin," 6.

142 ***Z. aquatica***: Native Wild Rice Coalition, homepage, http://www.nativewildricecoalition.com.

142 **A few groups of Ojibwe**: Barb Barton, "Introduction to Traditional Foods Virtual Learning Sessions," online event, September 15, 2020.

142 **One Manoomin processor**: Aaron Dewandeler, interview by author, September 17, 2019.

142 ***Z. palustris* . . . the clean grain behind**: Barton, "Introduction to Traditional Foods."

142 **While Manoomin has strict preservation**: 2019 Wild Rice (Manoomin) Camp (L'Anse, MI), August 29, 2019.

144 **The Anishinaabe people belong**: Anton Treuer, *Ojibwe in Minnesota* (St. Paul: Minnesota Historical Society Press, 2010), Kindle locations 121, 127, 142, 191, 194.

144 **Many of the places they inhabit**: "The Library of Michigan Presents: Michigan in Brief," https://www.michigan.gov/som/0,4669,7-192-29938_30240_30250-56001--,00.html#:~:text=Web%20Sites-,MICHIGAN%20FACTS,meaning%20great%20or%20large%20lake.

146 **The Ojibwe's new home**: "2018 Tribal Wild Rice Task Force Report," 12–13.

147 **In the oral history of the Ojibwe**: Edward Benton-Banai, *The Mishomis Book: The Voice of the Ojibway* (Minneapolis: University of Minnesota Press, 2010), 30–31.

147 **In some versions of the stories**: "Native American Legends: Nanabozho," Native Languages of the Americas, http://www.native-languages.org/nanabozho.htm.

147 **Wenabozho was a teacher**: Bezhigobinesikwe Elaine Fleming, "Nanaboozwhoo and the Wiindigo: An Ojibwe History from Colonization to the Present," *Tribal College Journal*, February 19, 2017.

147 **There are two different versions . . . not "it"**: David, "Manoomin," 21–24.

148 **poling poles, *gaandakii'iganaak***: David, "Manoomin," 40.

149 **When the seed hits the water**: Barton, *Manoomin*, 5.

150 **Historically, before the season began**: Emily Hicks and Melody R. Stein, "Wild Rice Waters," *Places Journal*, June 2021.

150 **The rice chief would signal . . . assembled Ojibwe**: David, "Manoomin," 37–38.

151 **The word boozhoo**: Eli Baxter, "Reasons We Say Boozhoo," *Anishinabek News*, March 22, 2016.

151 **Although this product is labeled**: Amy Thielen, "The True Story of Wild Rice, North America's Most Misunderstood Grain," *Saveur*, August 10, 2019.

151 **Paddy rice has been selectively**: Winona LaDuke and Brian Carlson, *Our Manoomin, Our Life: The Anishinaabeg Struggle to Protect Wild Rice* (Callaway, MN: White Earth Land Recovery Project, 2003), 5.

151 **While manoomin grains vary**: Bonny Wolf, "To Find Truly Wild Rice, Head North to Minnesota," *The Salt*, NPR, September 16, 2012.

151 *baate manoomin, Gidasige manoomin*: David, "Manoomin," 43–44.

152 *mimigoshkan manoomin*: Barton, *Manoomin*, 152–53.

152 *nooshkaachige manoomin*: David, "Manoomin," 45.

152 **work done by beavers**: "The Effects of Wild Rice Water Quality Rule Changes," 46.

153 **Waves of epidemic disease . . . French surnames**: Treuer, *Ojibwe in Minnesota*, 195, 213, 226.

153 **Later, larger settlements . . . $1.50 a bushel**: David, "Manoomin," 27.

153 **The area was ceded . . . wild rice was decimated**: Barton, *Manoomin*, xvii.

153 **Entrepreneurs in Michigan . . . manoomin didn't germinate**: Barton, *Manoomin*, 173, 65.

154 **Meanwhile, the Ojibwe . . . life more prosperous**: "The Fur Trade," Minnesota Historical Society, https://www.mnhs.org/fortsnelling/learn/fur-trade.

154 **reliant on the sale of land**: Treuer, *Ojibwe in Minnesota*, 387.

154 **The land the US wanted**: "1837 Land Cession Treaties with the Ojibwe & Dakota," *Relations: Dakota and Ojibwe Treaties*, https://treatiesmatter.org/treaties/land/1837-ojibwe-dakota.

154 **But the treaty included a clause**: David, "Manoomin," 29.

154 **It was unusual for a plant**: Winona LaDuke, "The White Earth Band of Ojibwe Legally Recognized the Rights of Wild Rice," *Yes!*, February 1, 2019.

154 **By the late 1850s**: Treuer, *Ojibwe in Minnesota*, 413.

154 **"it was also a strategy"**: "The Effects of Wild Rice Water Quality Rule Changes," 44.

154 **Boarding schools were established**: Treuer, *Ojibwe in Minnesota*, 453.

155 **"Code of Indian Offenses"**: "Native Americans and Freedom of Religion," *National Geographic*, April 27, 2020.

155 **Local BIA agents were empowered . . . language fluency rate to this day**: Treuer, *Ojibwe in Minnesota*, 428–29, 436, 880.

155 **In Michigan in 1857 . . . largely unsuccessful**: Barton, *Manoomin*, xviii, 81, 105.

156 **In 1987, the US Supreme Court**: "California *v.* Cabazon Band of Mission Indians," *Oyez*, https://www.oyez.org/cases/1986/85-1708.

156 **unemployment rate rarely goes above 6 percent**: "United States Unemployment Rate," *Trading Economics*, https://tradingeconomics.com/united-states/unemployment-rate#:~:text=Unemployment%20Rate%20in%20the%20United,percent%20in%20May%20of%201953.

159 **The conservation officers watch over . . . two weeks in total**: Alfred Fox, interview by author, September 16, 2019.

160 **Once the tribal government has purchased**: Goodwin, email to author, October 14, 2021.

161 **There was still green rice**: Tracy Goodwin, interview by author, September 16, 2019.

162 **In the 1960s, researchers**: Thielen, "The True Story of Wild Rice."

162 **By the 1970s, farm-grown . . . than Minnesota**: Dan Gunderson and Chris Julen, "Wild Rice at the Center of a Cultural Dispute," Minnesota Public Radio, September 24, 2002, http://news.minnesota.publicradio.org/features/200209/22_gundersond_wildrice -m/.

162 **In 1999, geneticists**: Gary Johnson, "Should We Genetically Engineer Wild Rice?" https://minds.wisconsin.edu/bitstream/handle/1793/75918/Should%20 We%20Genetically%20Engineer%20Wild%20Rice%20by%20Josef%20Siebert .pdf?sequence=10&isAllowed=y.

162 **The $21 million wild rice business . . . first time**: LaDuke and Carlson, *Our Manoomin, Our Life*, 8, 11, 5.

162 **Many Native people believe . . . federal level**: "True vs. Cultivated Wild Rice," *Cook's Illustrated*, https://www.cooksillustrated.com/how_tos/5424-true-vs-cultivated-wild-rice; "2021 Minnesota Statutes: 30.49 Wild Rice Labeling," Minnesota Legislature, https:// www.revisor.mn.gov/statutes/cite/30.49; "2005 Assembly Bill 136," Wisconsin State Legislature, https://docs.legis.wisconsin.gov/2005/related/proposals/ab136/1/_14.

162 **Most important, the Ojibwe feel**: LaDuke and Carlson, *Our Manoomin, Our Life*, 11.

162 **It is sacred in its wildness**: Gunderson and Julen, "Wild Rice at the Center of a Cultural Dispute."

162 **Many Ojibwe have expressed**: LaDuke and Carlson, *Our Manoomin, Our Life*, 12; Gunderson and Julen, "Wild Rice at the Center of a Cultural Dispute."

162 **In the Ojibwe mindset**: Johnson, "Should We Genetically Engineer Wild Rice?"

163 **The Dewandeler business**: Thielen, "The True Story of Wild Rice."

166 **The Ojibwe have said**: "The Ways: Great Lakes Native Culture & Language," https:// theways.org/story/Manoomin.html. Accessed November 2, 2021.

166 **Rights of Manoomin**: LaDuke, "The White Earth Band of Ojibwe."

166 **The law declares that harvesting**: Hicks and Stein, "Wild Rice Waters."

167 **The first court case to enforce**: "First 'Rights of Nature' Enforcement Case Filed in Tribal Court to Enforce Treaty Guarantees," Stopline3, August 5, 2021, https://www .stopline3.org/news/manoominvdnr.

167 **Not only are spills a concern**: Associated Press, "Lawsuit Filed on Behalf of Wild Rice," Indian Country Today, August 6, 2021.

167 **"up to 5 billion gallons of groundwater"**: Lynn Sue Mizner, "Enbridge's Line 3 Is Putting Wild Rice at Risk—And Indigenous Water Protectors Are Taking A Stand," *Civil Eats*, May 18, 2021.

167 **draining wild rice lakes**: Timothy E. Wilson, "Canadian Pipeline Giant Accused of Paying U.S. Police to Harass Activists," *Canada's National Observer*, April 19, 2021.

167 **Water protectors have been organizing protest**: Mizner, "Enbridge's Line 3."

167 **The tribe was offering $4**: White Earth Nation, Facebook post, https://www.facebook .com/plugins/post.php?href=https%3A%2F%2Fwww.facebook.com%2FWhiteEarthNatio n%2Fposts%2F6520045114674136. Accessed November 3, 2021.

167 **Ricers were only able**: Tracy Goodwin, email to author, October 12, 2021.

167 **There are records from the late**: Becky Donaldson, interview by author, September 22, 2019.

168 **River rice is rare**: "BONAP'S North American Plant Atlas," http://bonap.net/ MapGallery/County/Zizania%20aquatica.png.

168 **Mentor Marsh**: "Mentor Marsh and Carol H. Sweet Visitor Center," Cleveland Museum of Natural History, https://www.cmnh.org/mentor-marsh..

168 **Invasive phragmites**: Jim Bissell, interview by author, December 17, 2019.

168 **One particularly devastating fire . . . brown of the phragmites**: "Mentor Marsh and Carol H. Sweet Visitor Center."

169 **Over sixty different native plants . . . forty-two wild rice plants were counted**: Donaldson, interview by author.

## 6. HEIRLOOM CIDER APPLES

172 **fewer than 100 apple varieties**: Tim Hensley, "A Curious Tale: The Apple in North America," Brooklyn Botanic Garden, June 2, 2005, https://www.bbg.org/gardening/article/the_apple_in_north_america.

172 **Cultural shifts**: Gregory Peck, interview by author, September 25, 2019; Hensley, "A Curious Tale."

172 **50 million gallons of cider**: "Cornell Research Benefits the Hard Cider Industry," Cornell Research, video, https://research.cornell.edu/video/cornell-research-benefits-hard-cider-industry; Jan Conway, "Beer Production in the United States from 1860 to 2020," *Statista*, April 15, 2021.

172 **In 1991, there were ten cideries**: Dan Pucci and Craig Cavallo, *American Cider: A Modern Guide to a Historic Beverage* (New York: Ballantine, 2021), 9.

172 **$1.5 billion industry**: Peck, interview by author.

173 **But Angry Orchard . . . and Austin**: Pucci and Cavallo, *American Cider*, 111.

173 **Ryan Burk**: Ryan Burk, interview by author, March 22, 2019; "Taking Tradition Forward at Angry Orchard Cider House," *Hudson Valley Wine*, June 2017.

174 **The longer they sit in cold storage**: J. A. Strub, "This Heritage Apple Is Coming Back to Queens," *Edible Queens*, January 26, 2018.

174 **"the long storage time imbued"**: Tom Burford, *Apples of North America: A Celebration of Exceptional Varieties* (Portland, OR: Timber Press, 2021), 122.

174 **And elevated sugar means**: Pucci and Cavallo, *American Cider*, 139.

174 **Over half of the apples in Martinelli's**: David Karp, "It's Crunch Time for the Venerable Pippin," *New York Times*, November 5, 2003.

175 **According to CNBC**: Emma Newburger, "'We're Fighting for Our Lives'—US Apple Farmers Endure Major Crop and Profit Losses as Climate Changes," CNBC, November 9, 2019.

176 **crabapples**: David Zakalik, interview by author, September 25, 2019.

176 **Modern culinary and cider apples**: Pucci and Cavallo, *American Cider*, 9.

176 **plov**: Mercedes Hutton, "The Birthplace of the Modern Apple," *BBC Travel*, November 18, 2018.

176 **"range in size from marbles"**: Michael Pollan, *The Botany of Desire: A Plant's-Eye View of the World* (New York: Random House, 2002), 11.

176 **Nikolai Vavilov**: Hutton, "The Birthplace of the Modern Apple."

177 **An elderly man**: Pollan, *The Botany of Desire*, 54.

177 **The wild apples' habitat**: "Sievers Apple," Slow Food Foundation for Biodiversity, https://www.fondazioneslowfood.com/en/ark-of-taste-slow-food/sievers-apple/.

177 **One witness recounted . . . all over the world**: Pollan, *The Botany of Desire*, 54.

177 **Local activists**: Hutton, "The Birthplace of the Modern Apple."

177 **It's likely that travelers**: Pollan, *The Botany of Desire*, 11.

177 **There's evidence of apples**: Burford, *Apples of North America*, 12.

177 **Chinese orchardists . . . Roman variety**: Pollan, *The Botany of Desire*, 12, 23.

177 **When it comes to cider . . . source of alcohol**: Pucci and Cavallo, *American Cider*, 7–8.

178 **They consumed 15–54 gallons**: Siddhi Lama, "Why Cider Means Something Completely Different in America and Europe," *Atlas Obscura*, January 7, 2019.

178 **heterozygotes . . . landmass and climate**: Pucci and Cavallo, *American Cider*, 10.

178 **Some trees may have naturally hybridized**: Pollan, *The Botany of Desire*, 13.

178 **Reverend John Moore**: "John Moore 1652–1657," First Presbyterian Church of Newtown, http://www.fpcn.org/history/pastors/25-moore.

178 **Reverend Moore's son**: Strub, "This Heritage Apple."

178 **Newtowns were found to be**: Karp, "It's Crunch Time."

178 **Because Newtowns were great**: Burford, *Apples of North America*, 122.

179 **George Washington and Thomas Jefferson**: Karp, "It's Crunch Time."

179    **Benjamin Franklin took**: Strub, "This Heritage Apple."

179    **American entrepreneurs**: Karp, "It's Crunch Time."

179    **"Like Forrest Gump"**: Rowan Jacobsen, *Apples of Uncommon Character: Heirlooms, Modern Classics and Little-Known Wonders* (London: Bloomsbury USA, 2014), 175.

179    **In the early colonies . . . "cidermaking one year"**: Darlene Hayes, "George and Ursula Granger: The Erasure of Enslaved Black Cidermakers," *Cider Culture*, May 13, 2021.

179    **parceled out their land to veterans of the Revolutionary War**: Pucci and Cavallo, *American Cider*, 102.

180    **the Fruitery**: "Overview of Fruits at Monticello" and "The Site of the Fruit Gardens," Thomas Jefferson Foundation, https://www.monticello.org/house-gardens/farms-gardens/fruit-gardens/.

180    **George and Ursula Granger**: Lucia C. Stanton, *"Those Who Labor for My Happiness": Slavery at Thomas Jefferson's Monticello* (Charlottesville: University of Virginia Press, 2012), Kindle location 2995; "The Granger Family," Thomas Jefferson Foundation, https://www.monticello.org/slavery/paradox-of-liberty/enslaved-families-of-monticello/the-granger-family/.

180    **Jefferson preferred ciders . . . bottling process**: "Featured Letter: Thomas Jefferson Requests a Sampling of Cider," Thomas Jefferson Foundation, https://www.monticello.org/site/research-and-collections/featured-letter-thomas-jefferson-requests-sampling-cider; Sararose Martin, "Man Searches for Famous Lost Apple Variety That Originated Near Williamsburg," *Virginia Gazette*, December 16, 2019.

181    **"I must get Martha"**: Hayes, "George and Ursula Granger."

181    **rare to have a Black overseer anywhere**: Hayes, "George and Ursula Granger."

181    **"so extraordinary"**: Stanton, *"Those Who Labor for My Happiness,"* Kindle location 2838.

181    **On November 1, 1799**: Hayes, "George and Ursula Granger."

182    **Isaac was also documented**: "Photographs of People Enslaved at Monticello," Thomas Jefferson Foundation, https://www.monticello.org/slavery/people-enslaved-at-monticello/gallery-enslaved-at-monticello/.

182    **After Jefferson's death**: "Slaves Who Gained Freedom," Thomas Jefferson Foundation, https://www.monticello.org/site/research-and-collections/slaves-who-gained-freedom; Henry Wiencek, "The Dark Side of Thomas Jefferson," *Smithsonian Magazine*, October 2012.

183    **"This is the most celebrated"**: William Coxe, *A View of the Cultivation of Fruit Trees, and the Management of Orchards and Cider: With Accurate Descriptions of the Most Estimable Varieties of Native and Foreign Apples, Pears, Peaches, Plums, and Cherries, Cultivated in the Middle States of America* (Pomona Books, 1976), 216.

183    **established in 1867**: "Evelyn Rahn Ochs Obituary," *Star-Ledger* (Newark, NJ), March 25, 2012.

184    **"It's as if a legendary grape"**: Jacobsen, *Apples of Uncommon Character*, 271.

184    **Burford has been credited**: Fran McManus, interview by author, September 10, 2019.

184    **In his obituary**: Adrian Higgins, "Tom Burford, Champion of the Heirloom Apple, Dies at 84," *Washington Post*, April 3, 2020.

184    **From the seventeenth century . . . any other American cider**: Pucci and Cavallo, *American Cider*, 153–54.

184    **The Harrison apple**: Jacobsen, *Apples of Uncommon Character*, 270; Pucci and Cavallo, *American Cider*, 75; Daniel J. Bussey, *The Illustrated History of Apples in the United States and Canada* (Mount Horeb, WI: Jak Kaw Press, 2016), 154.

185    **Newark's secret: consistency**: Bussey, *Illustrated History*, 153–54.

185    **One apple hunter**: Wesley Stokes, interview by author, September 24, 2019.

186    **"Twenty-five years ago"**: "Harrison Apples," *Proceedings of the New Jersey Historical Society* 3 (January 1918): 52.

186    **only 17 percent**: Pucci and Cavallo, *American Cider*, 144.

186    **by 1830, the consumption . . . tumultuous time**: W. J. Rorabaugh, *The Alcoholic Republic: An American Tradition* (Oxford: Oxford University Press, 1981), 9, 97, 125–46.

186 **about twice today's average**: Zoe Chevalier, "The Ten States That Consume the Most Alcohol," *U.S. News & World Report*, August 7, 2018.

187 **Andrew Jackson**: Daniel Feller, "Andrew Jackson: Impact and Legacy," Miller Center, University of Virginia, https://millercenter.org/president/jackson/impact-and-legacy; Donna M. Loring, "Andrew Jackson: The Father of Genocide of the South and Eastern Tribes," *Indian Country Today*, September 13, 2018.

187 **Many Americans turned**: Rorabaugh, *The Alcoholic Republic*, 151.

187 **The many temperance societies**: Pucci and Cavallo, *American Cider,* 144; Rorabaugh, *The Alcoholic Republic,*189.

187 **Americans' consumption of alcohol dropped**: Rorabaugh, *The Alcoholic Republic*, 9.

187 **The Germans brought:** Pucci and Cavallo, *American Cider,* 146.

187 **Beer was easier to brew**: Lama, "Why Cider Means Something Completely Different."

187 **Many farmers cut down**: Marcus Robert, interview by author, August 17, 2019; Rorabaugh, *The Alcoholic Republic*, 10.

188 **Orchardists switched**: Lama, "Why Cider Means Something Completely Different."

188 **"decided it would be wise"**: Pollan, *The Botany of Desire*, 9, 50.

188 **The Red Delicious . . . from central Washington**: Pucci and Cavallo, *American Cider,* 324–25.

188 **Organic apples can be grown**: Craig Campbell, interview by author, August 17, 2019.

189 **Marcus Robert**: Robert, interview by author; Marcus Robert, email to author, January 6, 2022.

190 **Lost Heritage Apples**: "How to Identify Unknown Apples," Apple Search, https://applesearch.org/?fbclid=IwAR1vyJKk_mAwNATsWCtvRapyEWvJ6n5amV6AJJwyXyD7nDr-9VFw9pIAOwk.

190 **"consult historical maps"**: Matthew Taub, "'Extinct' Apple Varieties Are Actually Everywhere," *Atlas Obscura*, April 17, 2020.

190 **Brown claims**: "The Search for 'Lost' Heritage Apples," Apple Search, https://applesearch.org/?fbclid=IwAR1vyJKk_mAwNATsWCtvRapyEWvJ6n5amV6AJJwyXyD7nDr-9VFw9pIAOwk.

191 **If the apple is identified**: Taub, "'Extinct' Apple Varieties."

192 **"The size is small, the form flat"**: Coxe, *A View of the Cultivation of Fruit Trees*, 110.

192 **"Charles Rosen"**: Fran McManus, "The Return of Newark Cider," *Edible Jersey*, September 1, 2015.

193 **"Yesterday, I examined"**: Fran McManus, email to author, January 10, 2022.

194 **"cultural strategist"**: McManus, interview by author.

195 **Some locals fought**: "You Know Your [*sic*] From Livingston, N.J. when . . .," Livingston, NJ, Facebook group,https://www.facebook.com/groups/njlivingston/permalink/1176791589006241/. Accessed January 13, 2022.

196 **Ironbound is located**: McManus, interview by author, September 10, 2019.

196 **A longtime resident**: Charles Rosen, email to author, January 6, 2022.

197 **It was Greenwood**: Charles Rosen, interview by author, September 27, 2019.

197 **"Perhaps, emulating New York"**: Fran McManus, "Lost & Found: The Search for the Harrison Apple," *Edible Jersey*, September 1, 2020.

197 **While Charles was initially frustrated**: Rachel Wharton, "Finding Lost Apples and Reviving a Beloved Cider," *New York Times*, October 15, 2018.

199 **"have been involved . . . no, no, no"**: Lela Nargi, "The Formerly Incarcerated Are Reviving Newark's Cider Industry at Ironbound Farm," *Civil Eats*, January 2, 2020.

200 **"I took to the grafting . . . trees"**: McManus, "Newark's Celebrated Cider."

200 **He saw his work**: Rosen, interview by author.

200 **The team had more than 10,000**: Rosen, email to author.

202 **Made from rough-hewn**: Melanie Melikian, "History: In the Beginning," First Presbyterian Church of Newtown, http://www.fpcn.org/history.

202   **They succeeded in planting**: Karp, "It's Crunch Time."
202   **Slow Food NYC**: Jacobsen, *Apples of Uncommon Character*, Kindle location 175.

## 7. *KOMBO HAKSHISH*: CHOCTAW FILÉ POWDER

203   **Filé is made from the dried**: Rebecca Smith, "How Much Do You Know about Filé Powder? It's Used for More Than Just Gumbo . . ." *nola*, November 21, 2018.
203   **The deciduous tree is native**: "*Sassafras albidum*," US Department of Agriculture, https://www.srs.fs.usda.gov/pubs/misc/ag_654/volume_2/sassafras/albidum .htm#:~:text=Native%20Range,to%20central%20Florida%20(8).
203   **It's easy to identify**: "Sassafras," Outdoor Learning Lab, Greenfield Community College, https://www.gcc.mass.edu/oll/plants/sassafras/#:~:text=One%20unique%20feature%20 of%20sassafras,lobed%20leaf%20(pictured%20here).
204   **"It is truly a tragic story"**: Robbie Hutchins, email to author, July 7, 2022.
204   **"the Braid"**: Poppy Tooker, interview with Jessica Harris, *Africa to America,* podcast, October 16, 2021, https://www.poppytooker.com/this-weeks-show/tag/Jessica+Harris.
204   **"the time-honored fashion"**: "Handmade Filé," Slow Food Foundation for Biodiversity, https://www.fondazioneslowfood.com/en/ark-of-taste-slow-food/handmade-file-2/.
205   **"has the color, consistency"**: Morgan Randall, "The Native-American Origins of Gumbo," *Atlas Obscura*, August 7, 2020.
205   **commercial filé is often not pure**: Burton and Rudy Lombard, *Creole Feast: Fifteen Master Chefs of New Orleans Reveal Their Secrets* (New York: Random House, 1978).
205   **Acadiana**: George Graham, *Acadiana Table: Cajun and Creole Home Cooking from the Heart of Louisiana* (Boston: Harvard Common Press, 2016), 6, 11; Williams, *New Orleans*, 53–54.
206   **Cajun food was simply prepared**: Bethany Ewald Bultman, "A True and Delectable History of Creole Cooking," *American Heritage*, December 1986; Graham, *Acadiana Table*, 11.
206   **community-oriented**: Graham, *Acadiana Table*, 11.
206   **Wayne Jacob's**: "About Us," Wayne Jacob's Smokehouse and Restaurant, https://wjsmokehouse.com/about/; Coco, interview by author, October 8, 2019.
208   **Southern Louisiana is on the very edge**: "Current Distribution Maps for Sassafras," USDA Forest Service, https://www.fs.fed.us/nrs/atlas/tree/v3/931.
209   **"adding a rich, roasted flavor"**: Robert Moss, "How Roux Made Its Way into the Gumbo Pot," *Serious Eats*, July 9, 2019.
211   **The roots have been used**: Amy Thompson, interview by author, September 25, 2021.
211   **Barbacoa cooks**: Ian Thompson, *Choctaw Food: Remembering the Land, Rekindling Ancient Knowledge* (Durant, OK: Choctaw Nation Education Special Projects, 2019), 156, 179, 186, 270, 172, v, vi, 3.
211   **Their origin stories say**: "Our Creation Stories: Earth Emergence," display text, Choctaw Cultural Center, Durant, OK.
211   **The archeological record shows**: Thompson, *Choctaw Food*, 3–4.
211   *kombo hakshish*: Thompson, *Choctaw Food*, 235.
212   **"In the fall, pick red sassafras"**: Thompson, *Choctaw Food*, 172.
212   **"Old Folks say"**: White Dove, *Native American Recipes; a Collection by White Dove 1986 Edition*," American Indian Church of Louisiana, 131.
212   **As the tradition of making filé**: Randall, "The Native-American Origins of Gumbo."
212   **The Choctaw mortar and pestle**: Thompson, *Choctaw Food*, 147–50.
213   **mortars from western Africa**: Pierre Thiam, "In Africa Mortar & Pestle Has Rich History and Use, Putting Food Processors to Shame," *Face2FaceAfrica*, April 24, 2014.
213   *pilan et pilé*: Sarah Roahen, "Lionel Key: Uncle Bill's Spices," Southern Foodways Alliance, July 14, 2006, https://www.southernfoodways.org/interview/uncle-bills-spices/; Tooker, interview with Jessica Harris.
213   **The Spanish . . . naive communities**: Thompson, *Choctaw Food*, 24.
213   **"It was impossible to rule"**: "Mabila," display text, Choctaw Cultural Center, Durant, OK.

213 **The Mississippi River facilitated**: Williams, *New Orleans*, 25.

213 **Some Native traders came**: Thompson, *Choctaw Food*, 39.

213 **Europeans traded cloth, metal tools**: "Treaty of Mobile, 1765" and "Relationships," display texts, Choctaw Cultural Center, Durant, OK.

213 **land rent . . . kombo hakskish**: Thompson, *Choctaw Food*, 37, 34.

214 **French colonists**: Smith, "How Much Do You Know about Filé Powder?"

214 **"bring the filé to New Orleans"**: "*The Picayune Creole Cookbook*," 18, https://archive .org/details/cu31924003574187/page/n21/mode/2up.

214 **A photograph from the 1880s**: Edward L. Wilson, *Filé vendor at French market*, 1884–85, Historic New Orleans Collection, 1982.127.188.

214 **"the folk of Louisiana"**: Mary Land, *Louisiana Cookery* (Jackson: University Press of Mississippi, 2005), 5.

214 **There are many differences**: Williams, *New Orleans*, 55.

214 **The term "Creole"**: Lolis Eric Elie, "The Origin Myth of New Orleans Cuisine," *Oxford American*, April 3, 2010.

215 **Starting in 1719, French colonists**: "The Arrival of the First Africans in Louisiana," Evergreen Plantation, May 7, 2020, https://www.evergreenplantation.org/evergreen -blog/2020/5/7/the-arrival-of-the-first-africans-in-louisiana#:~:text=The%20first%20 slave%20ships%20from,all%20embarking%20prior%20to%201730; Tim Carman and Shelly Tan, "Made in America: How Four Dishes with Roots in Other Lands Tell a Story of Immigration and Transformation," *Washington Post*, October 11, 2019.

215 **"clear land, build the city"**: Williams, *New Orleans*, 62.

215 **Gumbo is thought to be based**: Jessica B. Harris, *High on the Hog: A Culinary Journey from Africa to America* (London: Bloomsbury, 2012), 247.

215 *soupe kandia*: Carman and Tan, "Made in America"; "Kandia Soup: Okra Sauce with Palm Oil," *SeneCuisine*, October 4, 2018, http://senecuisine.com/soupe-kandia/.

215 **The word "gumbo"**: John T. Bendor-Samuel, "Bantu Languages," *Britannica*, https:// www.britannica.com/art/Bantu-languages.

215 **The Bantu word for okra**: Williams, *New Orleans*, 159.

215 **The earliest references to gumbo**: Robert Moss, "The Real Story of Gumbo, Okra and Filé," *Serious Eats*, August 10, 2018; Shane K. Bernard, "Gumbo in 1764?," *Bayou Teche Dispatches*, October 3, 2011.

215 **"Gumbo—A West India Dish"**: Mary Randolph, *The Virginia Housewife or Methodical Cook* (Baltmore: Plaskitt, Fite & Co., 1838), 81.

215 **Okra is only available. . . cooks use filé**: Moss, "The Real Story of Gumbo, Okra and Filé."

215 **"even when I was growing up"**: Carmen and Tan, "Made in America."

216 **"The seasons dictated"**: Tooker, *Louisiana Eats! The People, the Food and Their Stories* (New Orleans: Pelican, 2013), 54.

216 **"Some people use chicken hearts"**: Poppy Tooker, interview by author, October 8, 2019.

216 **"To my knowledge"**: quoted in Moss, "How Roux Made Its Way into the Gumbo Pot."

217 **a scoop of potato salad**: Graham, *Acadiana Table*, 17.

218 **"On several visits to Bayou Lacombe"**: Howard Mitcham, *Creole Gumbo and All That Jazz: A New Orleans Seafood Cookbook* (New Orleans: Pelican, 1992), 32.

219 **Nicholas DuCré**: "Nicolas Duarea in the 1900 United States Federal Census," https:// www.ancestry.com/discoveryui-content/view/6271123:7602; "Nicolas Duore in the 1930 United States Federal Census," https://www.ancestry.com/discoveryui-content/ view/35948106:6224?tid=&pid=&queryId=ee348e6b208ae4336989a89d3dac4df2&_ phsrc=qEG305&_phstart=successSource; "Nicholas Ducre in the U.S. Social Security Death Index, 1935–2014," https://search.ancestry.com/cgi-bin/sse.dll?dbid=3693&h=166 13129&indiv=try&o_vc=Record:OtherRecord&rhSource=6224.

219  **Lionel Key**: "Lionel J. Key, Jr., Filé Maker," Louisiana Folklife Center, September 5, 2017, https://louisianafolklife.nsula.edu/artist-biographies/profiles/125; "Lionel Joseph Key, Jr.," *Advocate*, January 8, 2017.

219  **A photo of Key**: Michael P. Smith, "Lionel Keys," [*sic*] Historic New Orleans Collection, http://hnoc.minisisinc.com/thnoc/catalog/1/299208.

219  **"a living by making gumbo filé"**: Roahen, "Lionel Key: Uncle Bill's Spices."

222  **"Okla Humma"**: "Oklahoma," display text, Choctaw Cultural Center, Durant, OK.

222  **Dr. Ian Thompson**: Ian Thompson, interview by author, September 25, 2021.

222  **After the Revolutionary War**: "1765," "Treaty of Fort Adams, 1801," and "Treaty of Doak's Stand, 1820," display texts, Choctaw Cultural Center, Durant, OK.

222  **"under the pretense"**: Thompson, *Choctaw Food*, 40–41.

223  **"Facing impossible ciurcumstances"**: "Treaty of Dancing Rabbit Creek, 1830," display text, Choctaw Cultural Center, Durant, OK.

223  **Between 1830 and 1833**: "Toward the West," display text, Choctaw Cultural Center, Durant, OK.

223  **Those Choctaw who resisted . . . "place as their ancestors"**: Thompson, *Choctaw Food*, 44–45, x.

224  **The first Choctaw hymnal**: "Farmsteading," display text, Choctaw Cultural Center, Durant, OK.

224  **church is one of the few places**: Thompson, interview by author.

224  ***bvnaha***: Thompson, *Choctaw Food*, 1.

227  **Clay-Cooked Filé Fish Fillets**: Thompson, *Choctaw Food*, 208.

229  **"careening towards extinction . . . seed pods"**: Eric J. Wallace, "The Cherokee Chefs Bringing Back North America's Lost Cuisine," *Atlas Obscura*, June 4, 2020.

## 8. CAROLINA AFRICAN RUNNER PEANUTS

231  **It's estimated that 75 percent**: "FAQS," Slow Food Foundation for Biodiversity, https://www.fondazioneslowfood.com/en/what-we-do/the-ark-of-taste/faqs/.

231  **"the South's ancestral peanut"**: David S. Shields, *Southern Provisions: The Creation and Revival of a Cuisine* (Chicago: University of Chicago Press, 2015), 320.

232  **"denser, sweeter, smaller"**: "A 1690s Peanut is Reborn," National Peanut Board, https://www.nationalpeanutboard.org/news/a-1690s-peanut-is-reborn.htm.

232  **"has the most intense"**: Jill Neimark, "The Lost Ancestral Peanut of the South Is Revived," *The Salt*, NPR, December 29, 2016.

232  **"These are black truffles"**: Maria Yagoda, "To Sean Brock, These Centuries-Old Carolina Peanuts Are More Precious Than Truffles," *Yahoo News*, January 17, 2018.

233  **The Carolina Runner is especially high**: April Blake, "Heirloom Peanut Brought Back from Extinction Ready to Order," *Free Times* (Columbia, SC), May 16, 2019.

233  **"buttery, slightly vegetal"**: Kim Severson, "Hatched from Peanuts, the South's Hot New Oil," *New York Times*, November 1, 2016.

233  **"an American culinary emblem"**: Andrew F. Smith, *Peanuts: The Illustrious History of the Goober Pea* (Champaign: University of Illinois Press, 2007), xvi, 2.

233  **Most peanuts grow vertically**: David Shields, interview by author, October 19, 2019.

233  **The most unusual part of the peanut plant**: Jon Krampner, *Creamy and Crunchy: An Informal History of Peanut Butter, the All-American Food* (New York: Columbia University Press, 2014), 2–5.

234  **Peanuts are indigenous . . . Arawak people**: Krampner, *Creamy and* Crunchy, 2–5.

234  **French colonists in the Caribbean**: Smith, *Peanuts*, 3–4.

234  **Colonists exported peanuts**: Jessica B. Harris, *High on the Hog: A Culinary Journey from Africa to America* (London: Bloomsbury USA, 2012), 11.

234  **Peanut plants thrived in the sandy**: Robert Voeks and John Rashford, eds., *African Ethobotany in the Americas* (New York: Springer, 2013), 28.

234 **The legume had landed**: Smith, *Peanuts*, 8.

235 **Many American words**: Krampner, *Creamy and Crunchy*, 7; Harris, *High on the Hog*, 181, 62.

235 **"It is served"**: Harris, *High on the Hog*, 120.

235 *maafe*: "Maafe: West African Peanut Soup," *Immaculate Bites*, https://www.africanbites.com/maafe-west-african-peanut-soup/.

235 *domoda*: Jessica B. Harris, *Iron Pots and Wooden Spoons: Africa's Gifts to New World Cooking* (New York: Simon and Schuster, 1999), 120.

235 *shorba*: "Catholic Recipe: Shorba," *Catholic Culture*, https://www.catholicculture.org/culture/liturgicalyear/recipes/view.cfm?id=1393.

235 **"celestial"**: Smith, *Peanuts*, 133.

235 **Maillard reaction**: Krampner, *Creamy and Crunchy*, 33; "What is the Maillard Reaction?" *Science of Cooking*, https://www.scienceofcooking.com/maillardreaction.htm.

235 **"you will see women sitting"**: Harris, *Iron Pots*, 21.

235 **Sand roasting**: A. J. Kora, "Applications of sand roasting and baking in the preparation of traditional Indian snacks: nutritional and antioxidant status," *Bulletin of the National Resource Centre* 43 (2019).

236 **No one is absolutely certain**: Smith, *Peanuts*, 11.

236 **Plenty of immigrants**: "Africans in Carolina," Lowcountry Digital Historical Initiative, https://ldhi.library.cofc.edu/exhibits/show/africanpassageslowcountryadapt/sectionii_introduction/africans_in_carolina.

236 **The enslaved were forced . . . as early as 1601**: Smith, *Peanuts*, 12–13.

236 **The enslaved that survived . . . had originated in Africa**: Voeks, *African Ethobotany*, 410, 53.

237 **A professor and author**: Shields, *Southern Provisions*, x.

237 **Green-stemmed and known**: "Heirloom Asparagus Varieties," *Mother Earth News*, https://www.motherearthnews.com/organic-gardening/heirloom-asparagus-varieties-zewz1304zsch/.

238 **phenotypic plasticity**: Brian Ward, interview by author, October 21, 2019.

238 **needed a reboot**: Shields, *Southern Provisions*, 16, 5.

239 **But some ingredients . . . "'number four and Carolina number eight'"**: Shields, *Southern Provisions*, 15, 320.

239 **images of an actual historical example**: "Data Portal," 266, Natural History Museum, London, https://data.nhm.ac.uk/record/612007dd-ce3f-4077-b745-793b9f4d780d/1542.

240 **The first Africans arrived**: Harris, *High on the Hog*, 33, 35; Michael W. Twitty, *The Cooking Gene: A Journey through African American Culinary History in the Old South* (New York: Amistad, 2017), 161.

240 **"the average slaveholder"**: Twitty, *The Cooking Gene*, 162.

240 **portrayed as a magical gift, knowledge of various agricultures**: Toni Tipton-Martin, *The Jemima Code: Two Centuries of African American Cookbooks* (Austin: University of Texas Press, 2015), 2, 163.

240 **Angola and Senegambia**: "Africans in Carolina," Lowcountry Digital Historical Initiative, https://ldhi.library.cofc.edu/exhibits/show/africanpassageslowcountryadapt/sectionii_introduction/africans_in_carolina.

240 **Mary Reynolds**: Timothy O'Sullivan and Mary Reynolds, "A Former Slave Recalls Slave Quarters and Moments of Leisure," American Social History Project, https://shec.ashp.cuny.edu/items/show/1570.

241 **fishing or foraging**: Harris, *High on the Hog*, 84.

241 **The enslaved planted American . . . "resistance against slavery itself"**: Twitty, *The Cooking Gene*, 180, 30, 232–33, 269.

241 **"cash, trade goods"**: Harris, *High on the Hog*, 84.

241 **Money earned would be put**: Twitty, *The Cooking Gene*, 269.

241 **Black men and women also sold produce**: Smith, *Peanuts*, 14.

241 **Period accounts place Black**: Shields, *Southern Provisions*, 307.

241 **By the end of the seventeenth century**: Ritu Prasad, "The Awkward Questions about Slavery from Tourists in the US South," BBC News, October 2, 2019.

241 **Between 1778 and 1808 . . . and eventually west as far as Texas**: Twitty, *The Cooking Gene*, 190, 182, 187.

242 **By the start of the Civil War**: Brian Hicks, "Slavery in Charleston: A Chronicle of Human Bondage in the Holy City," *Post and Courier*, April 9, 2011.

242 **McLeod Plantation**: "McLeod Plantation Timeline," Charleston County Parks, https://www.ccprc.com/1779/Historical-Timeline.

243 **Mills passed around a handbill**: "The Enslaved of McLeod," Charleston County Parks, https://www.ccprc.com/2020/The-Enslaved-of-McLeod.

243 **The first culinary uses**: "A 1690s Peanut is Reborn," National Peanut Board, https://www.nationalpeanutboard.org/news/a-1690s-peanut-is-reborn.htm.

243 **Roasting or boiling**: Cara Parks, "The Original Southern Peanut Was Thought To Be Extinct, But One Farmer Is Bringing It Back," *Modern Farmer*, January 12, 2015.

243 **Ground peanuts were still**: Smith, *Peanuts*, 14.

243 **Fresh, unripe peanuts boiled**: Harris, *High on the Hog*, 64.

244 **"Groundnut Soup"**: Sarah Rutledge, *House and Home; or, the Carolina Housewife* (Charleston: John Russell, 1855), 139, 102.

244 **"the large black snail"**: J. W. Watson, "A Trip to Dahomey," *Lippincott's Magazine of Popular Literature and Science* (United States: J. B. Lippincott, 1871), 45.

244 **Oysters were substituted**: David Shields, "Peanut Soup," Bradford Watermelon Company Facebook page, September 30, 2017, https://www.facebook.com/bradfordwatermelons/posts/carolina-african-runner-peanuts-now-available-for-the-first-time-to-the-public-w/283919975428872/.

244 **an expedition was made to Bolivia**: Parks, "The Original Southern Peanut."

244 **"so much the rage" . . . in 1868**: Smith, *Peanuts*, 22.

244 **Roasted street peanuts**: Shields, *Southern Provisions*, 307.

244 **"two million bushels"**: Smith, *Peanuts*, 24.

245 **monkey meat**: Smith, *Peanuts*, 24.

245 **"Delightful, crisp and wholesome"**: "The Bread You Eat!," *Charleston Evening Post*, May 24, 1895.

245 **Some accounts even say**: "The Bread You Eat!"

245 **The recipe for groundnut cakes**: Tipton-Martin, *The Jemima Code*, 2–3.

245 **"The secret of cooking"**: David S. Shields, "Issue 53, Sweets & Candies, Part 3: Old Southern Candies," https://davidsanfordshields.substack.com/p/issue-53-sweets-and-candies-part-0c7?s=r. Accessed June 25, 2022.

245 **"African American vendors"**: Harris, *High on the Hog*, 126.

246 **"always neatly dressed"**: "The Bread You Eat!"

246 **They usually had a fly whisk**: Shields, "Issue 53, Sweets & Candies."

246 **Celia Wilson**: "Celia Hall in the 1880 United States Federal Census," https://www.ancestry.com/discoveryui-content/view/42380875:6742?tid=&pid=&queryId=e3d6ff3a5ec810e8fc5c6d2aae78deb4&_phsrc=qEG360&_phstart=successSource; "The Enterprise Accident. Witnesses Testify to the Facts before the Coroner's Jury," *Charleston News and Courier*, July 24, 1893.

246 **Chloe Jenkins was photographed**: Jill Neimark, "The Lost Ancestral Peanut of the South Is Revived," *The Salt*, NPR, December 29, 2016.

246 **Chloe was widowed young**: "Celia Hall in the 1900 United States Federal Census."

246 **She passed away from**: "Celia Hall Death Record," https://www.ancestry.com/imageviewer/collections/8741/images/VRDUSASC1821_089181-00477.

246 **Black women began to sell**: Shields, *Southern Provisions*, 96.

246 **cost one penny**: Shields, "Issue 53, Sweets & Candies."

246 **new sanitation laws**: Neimark, "The Lost Ancestral Peanut."

246 **Other vendors moved indoors**: Shields, "Issue 53, Sweets & Candies."

247 **"composed of peanut pieces"**: Smith, *Peanuts*, 79–80.

247 **"Nut Zippers"**: "Squirrel Nut Zippers: The Vintage Candy That Tried to Make a Come-back," New England Historical Society, https://www.newenglandhistoricalsociety.com/squirrel-nut-zippers-return-to-massachusetts/.

247 **In 1911 . . . in 1930**: Smith, *Peanuts*, 80–84.

247 **BJ Dennis, Matt and Ted Lee, Jeni's Splendid Ice Cream**: Hannah Raskin, "Sweet Memories: Charleston Chef BJ Dennis Works to Replicate 19th Century Peanut and Mo-lasses Candy," *Post and Courier*, August 22, 2020.

247 **"pockets of blackstrap molasses"**: "Sweet Cream with Molasses and Peanuts," Jeni's, https://jenis.com/flavors/ice-creams/sweet-cream-molasses-peanuts/. Accessed June 25, 2022.

249 **Throughout the nineteenth century . . . to dry them**: Shields, *Southern Provisions*, 315; Krampner, *Creamy and Crunchy*, 23.

249 **Then, the peanuts were plucked . . . leaving the state**: Smith, *Peanuts*, 111, 83–84.

249 **The Carolina Runner peanut's small size**: "A 1690s Peanut is Reborn."

250 **A partnership between Clemson . . . how to save or replace it**: Coastal Research and Education Center, Clemson University, https://www.clemson.edu/cafls/research/coastal/.

250 **Brian grew the peanuts**: Neimark, "The Lost Ancestral Peanut."

251 **Then he finally told Brian**: "A 1690s Peanut is Reborn."

251 **The first season, they . . . peanut allergies**: Ward, interview by author.

252 **The Carolina Runner is such a tiny**: "A 1690s Peanut is Reborn."

252 **Nat Bradford**: Jill Neimark, "Saving the Sweetest Watermelon the South Has Ever Known," *The Salt*, NPR, May 19, 2015; Nat Bradford, interview by author, October 22, 2019.

253 **120 to 160 days after planting**: Smith, *Peanuts*, 112.

254 **The peanuts sit in rows**: Krampner, *Creamy and Crunchy*, 18.

## NOT THE END

259 **That year, the Ohio National**: "APA-Only National Meet," digital display, American National Poultry Show, Columbus, OH, viewed November 9, 2019; Aaron Baker, inter-view by author, November 8, 2019.

260 **Ohio State Buckeyes**: "Buckeye Chicken," Slow Food Foundation for Biodiversity, https://www.fondazioneslowfood.com/en/ark-of-taste-slow-food/buckeye-chicken/.

261 **He bought birds from a breeder**: Christopher McCary, Facebook message to author, January 6, 2019.

262 **"Nettie" Williams**: Nettie Metcalf, "History of the Buckeyes," http://www.shumakerfarmbuckeyechickens.com/nettie-metcalf.html. Accessed January 9, 2022; "Net-tie Metcofee in the 1940 United States Federal Census," https://www.ancestry.com/sharing/27015003?h=ece548&utm_campaign=bandido-webparts&utm_source=post-share-modal&utm_medium=copy-url; "Annette "Nettie" Williams," https://www.ancestry.com/family-tree/person/tree/83336627/person/44482459080/facts; "Cyrus Turner Metcalf," https://www.ancestry.com/family-tree/person/tree/83336627/person/44482591290/facts; "Nettie Metcalf in the California, U.S., Death Index, 1940-1997," https://www.ancestry.com/sharing/27015501?h=4f5f30&utm_campaign=bandido-webparts&utm_source=post-share-modal&utm_medium=copy-url.

262 **"I kept chickens"**: Mrs. Frank Metcalf, "History of the Buckeyes by the originator," *Pacific Fancier* 7, no. 4 (April 1909): 9.

263 **Metcalf tried in vain**: Mrs. Frank Metcalf, "History of the Buckeyes, Part Two," *Poultry Success*, October 1917, 8, http://www.americanbuckeyepoultryclub.com/BuckeyeHistory2.html..

263 **She bred the next generation**: "The BB Red Old English Game Bantam," Townline Poultry Farm, https://townlinehatchery.com/breed-spotlight-the-bb-red-old-english-game-bantam/chickens/. Accessed January 9, 2022.

263 **"Frank scolded, of course, . . . a red breed of fowls"**: Metcalf, "History of the Buckeyes by the originator," 9–10.

264 **Metcalf's new breed**: Metcalf, "History of the Buckeyes by the originator," 9.

264 **The Metcalfs renamed their farm . . . annual meetings of the APA**: Metcalf, "History of the Buckeyes, Part Two."

264 **a daring car ride . . .** : Metcalf, "History of the Buckeyes by the originator," 10.

264 **"It is very brave"**: Metcalf, "History of the Buckeyes by the originator," 11.

265 **"The demand created"**: Metcalf, "History of the Buckeyes," 8.

265 **For a time, Metcalf remained president**: Metcalf, "History of the Buckeyes by the originator," 11.

265 **In 1907, the *Los Angeles Times***: "Poultry Show Opens with Big Entry List," *Los Angeles Herald*, December 7, 1907, 3.

265 **"I am content"**: Metcalf, "History of the Buckeyes by the originator," 11.

265 **Frank took up ranching**: "1920 United States Federal Census for Nettie Metcalf," https://www.ancestry.com/imageviewer/collections/6061/images/4293703 -00632?pId=237911; "Notes from the Meetings of the Board of Education," *Los Angeles School Journal* 2 (1918): 84.

265 **She also composed music**: "Catalog of Copyright Entries: Musical compositions, Part 3," Library of Congress Copyright Office, 1907, 957.

265 **less than 500 birds**: Christopher McCary, interview by author, November 8, 2019; Jeannette Beranger, interview by author, April 19, 2021.

266 **between 600 and 1,000 breeding-age Buckeyes**: Jeannette Beranger, email to author, January 6, 2022.

# INDEX

Recipes are listed in **bold**.

# ENDANGERED
EATING

## *Sarah Lohman*

# ENDANGERED EATING

## Sarah Lohman

### DISCUSSION QUESTIONS

1. In *Endangered Eating*, Sarah Lohman shares what she learned during her travels across the United States, and what she wants readers to know about American food histories, endangered foods, and food processes. Are there action(s) you think you might take to help preserve the Ark of Taste entries that Lohman pursues?

2. Throughout *Endangered Eating*, Lohman interacts with many individuals from indigenous communities. What did you learn about these communities as you read? How may their relationships to food and food practices relate to and/or inform your own culinary history and food practices?

3. Gender and familial structures play a large role in both indigenous and non-indigenous cultures. How do Queen Lili'uokalani of Hawaii, the Black women of Charleston with their groundnut cakes, and Diné women challenge or redefine their roles as women? How do their identities fit, or not, in the context of the cultures from which they come?

4. Many of the communities associated with the ingredients or processes discussed in the book undergo displacement. How are the ties between displacement and food significant to these culinary histories? Why is it important to explore these connections? How do you think your own (or your ancestors') migration, immigration, and/or displacement journeys influence your current culinary practices and preferences?

5. In chapter two, Lohman shares the legacy of Hawaiian sugarcane and explores the tensions between the preservation and com-

mercialization of endangered foods. When might foods and food processes be best served by staying within their indigenous communities, and when might commercialization be beneficial to preservation?

6. In several chapters, Lohman visits local restaurants, small growers and producers, and niche festivals that highlight the endangered food or food process. Can you think of a way in which some of these and similar food providers might assist in the preservation of the local foods or techniques without perpetuating micro-colonization?

7. Explore other Ark of Taste entries. Why do you think Lohman chose to focus on the ones shared in the book? What other entries in the Ark of Taste interest you and why?

8. Did *Endangered Eating* challenge any of your existing assumptions about American food histories? If so, how has your understanding changed?

9. What recipe(s) from the book will you try? Why?

# ENDANGERED EATING

## Sarah Lohman

*A conversation between the author and* **Tonya Hopkins**, *aka "The Food Griot," who served as a food and drink historian for Carla Hall's Soul Food, and has written and hosted shows for—and appeared on— radio and television. Hopkins is the lead culinary history advisor for the Old Stone House of Brooklyn's Food & Public History Program, and she cofounded the James Hemings Society (named for Thomas Jefferson's enslaved, French-trained chef), which looks to rediscover the origins and evolution of American cuisine in creative and inclusive ways.*

**TH:** To begin, I have to say kudos, Sarah! Of course I haven't read every food history book out there, but given what I have read, your book feels different, unique. You're serving up real history in this book. With food, culture, language, respect, geography, and science—there is so much packed in here, so much substance. You're like one of those moms who hides nutrients and vegetables in a child's food.

**SL:** The food is the trick in this case! Whereas for the mom it's the blueberry muffin with the spinach inside. A friend of mine called my first book 'a secret ode to immigration,' which it absolutely was, and this book is very much about indigenous nations. And as far as the research and details go, I felt like I owed it to the people who gave me access and let me into their lives to explain this history as best I could.

**TH:** You're right. If *Eight Flavors* was an ode to the immigrant nation of America, I feel like this book was the exact opposite, in that it speaks about the two groups that don't really fit that immigrant narrative: indigenous, Native American people, and enslaved Africans who were brought here, and that is not immigration. It's importation of Africans to the New World and transportation of Indigenous peoples—definitely not immigration.

Was that your intent? Did you stumble upon, or intentionally seek out the Ark of Taste, and was that the muse or impetus behind it?

**SL:** Yes, muse is a good word. The ideas for the chapters fell into place both regionally and in terms of the fact that they had deeper stories, but after building that initial list, I realized that half of these stories were going to be about Indigenous nations.

And I was really scared, Tonya. I'm not going to lie. I was really scared and intimidated, because at that moment I didn't even know anyone who was Indigenous, which is a genuine shame, but I'm also sure I had that in common with a lot of non-Native Americans.

Now I do feel blessed to have people I call my friends from Indigenous nations across the country. And I feel like I'm a better person after writing this book, because I went to these places, and made these connections, and spent time with these stories, and really thought about them and processed them. That's what they say about pushing yourself out of your comfort zone, right?

**TH:** Absolutely. And in addition to your sense of curiosity and adventure, there is a bravery. I know you're exploring the Ark of Taste, but it makes me think of the Ark of the Covenant, as if you're Indiana Jones, fighting against the powers of historical injustice and the industrial food system!

**SL:** I hope that people see it that way. In our larger conversations in the last decade between when I published *Eight Flavors* and *Endangered Eating*, we—as in, white American culture—started this idea that, as activists, we need to "give voice to the voiceless." But, quickly, everyone else was saying: "We've got our own voices! You don't have to talk for us."

**TH:** It can be tricky to represent or be an ally; you have to proceed with caution, because you don't want to speak for them. For us.

**SL:** Right, you have to be a good ally. So, when I sat down and had a talk with myself about how to do this, I thought about how I had access to resources, right? I had this book that was going to be published, and so I can use the access and the privilege that I have in order to create a platform for other people. So, as much as possible, I wanted it to be their words, not mine. I'm there to bring everyone along on the journey.

But I hope this book helps people. That's always the intention behind my work, even if it's indirect in terms of providing broader education. I wanted to reveal the connections between genocide, assimilation, and colonialism that the American government perpetuated against Indigenous peoples, and to show that food was one of the big turnscrews in all of it.

**TH:** For sure. Your work in general, and your approach, is in line with so much of the mission of my work in terms of shifting the focus from the patriarchy, the white lens, the Eurocentricity of it all, to say, "Wait a minute." There are two groups of people that you cannot ignore if you are going to talk about American food history. You cannot *not* start with the wisdom and cultivating genius of the Indigenous people who were here, and with the enslaved people who were brought over. They were not only the cooks of the nation from the beginning and for centuries—the origins of American fine dining can be traced to plantation kitchens and such—but they are also the source of American agriculture, growing so many crops, problem solving, and finding solutions that have informed the makings of many food and beverage industries.

**SL:** Researching this book is also when I first learned about the phrase "the braid" from Jessica Harris, which says that American food is this braid of Anglo-European, enslaved African, Indigenous, and, I like to add that fourth piece of hair in there, for the immigrant communities, because I do think they are in the blend, too. But I loved that idea that all these cultures and communities are separate, but together in the creation of American food.

**TH:** You mentioned that it took you five years to write this book. The time that it takes to find the resources and to figure out the travel logistics—did these things take more time than the writing of the book itself, or did the book write itself along the way? Would you like to talk about how your writing of the book worked with those extra steps of your process?

**SL:** The travel planning and connections with people happened in the first six months. I made those initial connections, and asked the initial question: If I want to come and experience this foodway, when do I need to be there? That was my most important question, so I could start building a schedule. I was on the road two weeks a month writing this book. When I returned from these trips, I organized the research. Not just backing things up and getting things transcribed but working on an outline. I would sit down, write the chapter title, and do an outline while it was fresh in my head, because at that point, even if I didn't know all the details, I had a pretty good idea of the scenes of the story, and where to take it.

I also tried—before I went to the place and talked to whomever I was going to talk to—to read everything available on the topic that was already out there. I read more than sixty books to write this book, on topics that were sometimes very niche. Because what's the point of me traveling across the country to talk to somebody and asking them questions they've been asked a million times before if I miss the questions that can only be asked of an expert in-person? The main body of writing took two and a half years.

**TH:** There are over 350 entries in the Ark of Taste from the United States. I take it you at least skimmed through all of them, and then only a few made the cut. Did you have criteria you were looking for? Was it connected to your original vision about focusing or zoning in Indigenous and African underpinnings of American food history?

**SL:** I created a longer list and whittled it down, but ten ended up in this book in one way or another. The stories of these ten surprised me.

We can take the first chapter as a good example: I didn't know we had a date industry in the United States, in Coachella Valley of all places. Certainly, all the things on the Ark of Taste are fascinating, even if it's just the adventure of planting a seed in a planter on your porch or your patio and seeing what this strawberry or tomato that isn't sold in the grocery store tastes like. That's an adventure, but I was drawn to things that had deeper cultural connections, impacts, broader stories, and surprising items, too.

**TH:** In addition to the fascinating topics, there are the people. There are so many different contemporary, real people who pop up in these chapters. Through them, you access a pathway or a portal to the topics and their historic and cultural significances.

**SL:** I feel like the more people of diverse communities that I have in my life, that I can check in with and learn from, that makes me a better human living in this world, a more considerate person.

We Americans can be very insular within our communities. We can have empathy for someone we know personally, but difficulty having empathy for someone we don't know, and that can end in tragedy.

**TH:** So true. You've mentioned before that readers often want to know about how climate change affects the foods you've chosen to explore. How many of these items will be—or have already been—impacted?

**SL:** Surprisingly, the answer is none of them. For the most part, these are extremely adaptable, highly resilient, traditional foods, that are not monocropped; some have been selectively bred, but have been bred for hardiness. These foods are survivors, and that's why they are still here, against all odds.

**TH:** Another thing I love about your book is that it is action oriented. You're not presenting a bunch of problems without solutions. Which is also a nice segue to another question that comes up for people—one you've kind of already touched on—about seeking out direct contact: the "where do I shop?" question.

**SL:** I get asked that at almost every in-person event I've done, and my answer is: shop wherever you want, shop where you like to, shop where you have the resources and access. If you have the resources and access to shop at a farmers market, that's a great thing to do! You're directly supporting local agriculture, and hopefully buying delicious food.

But I also remind people that just because something is in a grocery store doesn't mean it is inherently *bad*. You can go into a grocery store and make great choices. And many grocery store chains—especially if they are local non-national chains—will put local produce in their grocery stores. I always recommend CSAs (community supported agriculture) if you have access to them. These are institutions that are engaging directly with farmers, and money is going directly to them.

**TH:** I'm so glad you addressed that, because it's not about "don't shop here, don't shop there, only shop here!" That's just not it.

**SL:** I refuse to moralize food, and I refuse to moralize someone for their food choices. Someone is not a "good" or a "bad" person because they shop at their local grocery store instead of a big chain. Food shouldn't be about bestowing good morality on only those with money and access.

**TH:** It's an elitism that needs to be eradicated. I'm reminded of the sxwo'le reefnet process that you write about—some of these topics became vivid examples of how wisdom and tradition and knowledge transfer across generational exchange, and how food traditions are such a medium or vehicle for that. It's not just about the food item itself sometimes: it's also about that loss.

**SL:** Yes, of elders. And identity. Regarding the *manoomin* chapter: the idea is that if the wild rice is gone, then perhaps the Anishinaabe—the Ojibwe people—will also no longer exist. If you don't have *your* foods, how can you be yourself and your culture and community?

And one of the stories of loss that I touch on in the filé chapter, too, is how we have these elders in the community who were processing filé in a traditional way, and they are dying off with nobody picking up that tradition—that's a huge loss of traditional knowledge. If there are no younger people who want to invest in that traditional knowledge then it dies with those elder-keepers.

**TH:** There's something very poignant but semi-unsettling in the last sentence of that filé chapter, when you discuss how a food item can become history.

**SL:** If we keep food frozen in time and frozen in nostalgia, when those generations pass away, that food doesn't exist anymore. So, we have to continue to innovate. We have to let food grow and adapt.

**TH:** That's fascinating. Your book is very hopeful, but as you point out in the eighth chapter, 75 percent of vegetable varieties worldwide have been permanently lost, and 95 percent of America's historical produce has been permanently lost—I gasped at that. But every once in a while, something that was thought to be extinct comes out of nowhere, which is part of the optimism and the hope of the book. The Carolina African Runner Peanut is a great example.

**SL:** It was thought to be extinct and was rediscovered, and it's not the only food in the Ark of Taste that has that story arc either! The stories are truly incredible and surprising. But of course, that chapter was a real point of frustration for me in a book that was otherwise very hopeful. I wish there was a greater emphasis on making sure that these food items are rematriated to the groups in which they are extraordinarily culturally important. For instance, I spoke to a Black chef who was saying, "Yeah, I wanted to work with them, but I couldn't even find them." So, we've got this peanut that's part of traditional Black culture that's not going back to Black culture, and it makes me so frustrated and so angry, because it should be about making sure this traditional food is preserved among its traditional people.

We all seem to want to center ourselves in the story, in that "it's not worth saving a food unless *I* get to try it," and the truth is that I hope the readers of this book make the effort to try these foods, because that means they are engaging in local culture and spending money to support these communities—but it shouldn't be all about us. It shouldn't be all about *me*.

**TH:** Right—and this peanut story is the one that really exemplifies that. And as you well know, Sarah, I certainly expressed some of that same frustration too—as evidenced in the "choice words" I used where I'm quoted in that chapter!

I know you expressed some surprises you had along the way,

but in general, is this the book you set out to write? Are you happy with it?

**SL:** I'm really proud. After I'd read the book for about the fiftieth time, and by then you are so sick of your own work—but there was a bit of a break, because it was one of the last read throughs, so I had a little rest from my work. When I came back to it, I remember thinking, "You know what? I'm proud of this." As creatives, we're so self-critical with what we're doing and what we want to put out there. But I read the book and told myself that I worked hard and did the best I possibly could. I'd gone into the process knowing that there would be mistakes and things I would learn—that's just a part of living your life and coming back and doing it better.

**TH:** It absolutely sounds like the book that you set out to write. So what's next?

**SL:** The next book is about the history of ice cream! The story of ice cream is the story of Black Americans and women—and of course that's what I want to write about. You're the one who told me about Alfred Cralle, who invented the modern ice cream scoop, and Augustus Jackson, who created Philadelphia-style, eggless ice cream. I wanted to read their autobiographies, but then I found only two paragraphs written about both of them that get repeated endlessly.

**TH:** Indeed, you'll have to be a detective, in addition to a food history researcher and a writer, to get those answers. Because in many instances people of color, Black people in particular, were intentionally not documented or were written out and not credited to the entire extent of their contributions. A form of erasure. Lies of omission I find necessary to raise awareness to.

**SL:** And you've done as much research as there is out there right now, so now I'm going to try and see what I can dig up and how I can shout out the names of these people who were incredible entrepreneurs and affected our culinary history.

**TH:** Oh wow, that's very exciting to hear—good luck! I have much faith that you'll be able to dig deeper to unearth more details than the scant info that's generally available or accessible when researching Black lives—especially of the enslaved, *previously* enslaved, and/or those born during or before the nineteenth century. Thank you, Sarah. It's been wonderful talking with you —as always!

| | |
|---|---|
| Meghan Kenny | *The Driest Season* |
| Nicole Krauss | *The History of Love* |
| Don Lee | *The Collective* |
| Amy Liptrot | *The Outrun: A Memoir* |
| Donna M. Lucey | *Sargent's Women* |
| Bernard MacLaverty | *Midwinter Break* |
| Maaza Mengiste | *Beneath the Lion's Gaze* |
| Claire Messud | *The Burning Girl* |
| | *When the World Was Steady* |
| Liz Moore | *Heft* |
| | *The Unseen World* |
| Neel Mukherjee | *The Lives of Others* |
| | *A State of Freedom* |
| Janice P. Nimura | *Daughters of the Samurai* |
| Rachel Pearson | *No Apparent Distress* |
| Richard Powers | *Orfeo* |
| Kirstin Valdez Quade | *Night at the Fiestas* |
| Jean Rhys | *Wide Sargasso Sea* |
| Mary Roach | *Packing for Mars* |
| Somini Sengupta | *The End of Karma* |
| Akhil Sharma | *Family Life* |
| | *A Life of Adventure and Delight* |
| Joan Silber | *Fools* |
| Johanna Skibsrud | *Quartet for the End of Time* |
| Mark Slouka | *Brewster* |
| Kate Southwood | *Evensong* |
| Manil Suri | *The City of Devi* |
| | *The Age of Shiva* |
| Madeleine Thien | *Do Not Say We Have Nothing* |
| | *Dogs at the Perimeter* |
| Vu Tran | *Dragonfish* |
| Rose Tremain | *The American Lover* |
| | *The Gustav Sonata* |
| Brady Udall | *The Lonely Polygamist* |
| Brad Watson | *Miss Jane* |
| Constance Fenimore Woolson | *Miss Grief and Other Stories* |

Available only on the Norton website